THE
READING
LIST
CONTEMPORARY
FICTION

▲

A Critical Guide to the
Complete Works of 110 Authors

▼

EDITED BY DAVID RUBEL

AN OWL BOOK
HENRY HOLT AND COMPANY
NEW YORK

For Howard H. Schless (1924–1997), the most humane man I have known

An Agincourt Press Book

President: David Rubel
Art Director: Tilman Reitzle

Cover and Interior Design: Tilman Reitzle
Contributors: Russell Shorto, Sam Tanenhaus, Mark Hoff, Chris Tower,
    Julia Banks Rubel, Polly Morrice, Elizabeth Ward, James Martin,
    Richard Hardack, John Miller-Monzon, David Rubel
Copy Editor: Ron Boudreau
Proofreader: Laura Jorstad

Henry Holt and Company, Inc.
Publishers since 1866
115 West 18th Street
New York, New York 10011

Henry Holt® is a registered trademark of Henry Holt and Company, Inc.

Copyright © 1998 Agincourt Press
All rights reserved.
Published in Canada by Fitzhenry & Whiteside Ltd.,
195 Allstate Parkway, Markham, Ontario L3R 4T8.

For photo credits, see page 368.

Library of Congress Cataloging-in-Publication Data
The reading list. Contemporary fiction: a critical guide to the
complete works of 110 authors/David Rubel, editor.
p.   cm.
"An owl book."
1. Fiction—20th century—Bibliography.   2. Fiction—20th century—
Stories, plots, etc.   I. Rubel, David.
Z5916.R38   1998
[PN3353]
016.8083—dc21   98-12456
                       CIP
ISBN 0-8050-5527-4

Henry Holt books are available for special promotions and
premiums. For details contact: Director, Special Markets.

First Edition 1998

Printed in the United States of America
All first editions are printed on acid-free paper. ∞

10 9 8 7 6 5 4 3

CONTENTS

INTRODUCTION

R EFERENCE BOOKS ORGANIZE INFORMATION. The Yellow Pages, for example, lists phone numbers. It's a useful book, although it would be even more useful if it listed plumbers by skill level instead of alphabetically. Fortunately for you, this isn't a phone book. It's better, because we list the plumbers—or, in this case, the books—by merit.

What Is *The Reading List?* • This book is a guide to the works of 110 authors of contemporary literary fiction. Its single purpose is to help you find books that you might like to read. For each of the authors included, we present brief descriptions, with excerpts from major reviews, of every book of fiction that each author has written—the complete oeuvre, but not omnibus editions or collections of previously published work. If you've heard of T. Coraghessan Boyle but don't know much about him, this book will fill you in fast. You'll find out quickly that he has written eleven books, four of them short-story collections; that the novels *Water Music*, about explorer Mungo Park's search for the source of the Niger River, and *World's End*, a historical novel set in the Hudson Valley, are considered his best; that *New York Times* critic Lorrie Moore once described his work as "Don DeLillo crossed with Dr. Seuss"; that he changed his middle name from John to Coraghessan when he was seventeen; and even what he looks like.

Who's in *The Reading List?* • The books of the 110 authors profiled here are but a small eclectic sampling of the vast amount of fiction currently available from large and small presses. However, because we didn't want to sell you a book the size of the Yellow Pages, we had to pick and choose, so we developed a number of criteria to narrow the list: Each person had to be living and currently writing, the author of more than one book, and not associated primarily with a particular genre. This still left a long list, so we narrowed it further by taking into account the critical reception that each author had received, including prizes that the author had won. Finally, we added back a little diversity in the form of several promising younger authors.

We don't claim that these 110 authors are the best, or even the most widely read, novelists around, only that—according to the *New York Times*, the *Washington Post*, the *New York Review of Books*, *Time*, *Newsweek*, and other authorities—they are good and deserve their audiences, which might include you. Of course, not all of their books will appeal to you, but we've included enough information to help you figure that out as well. And authors that *you* don't like might well strike someone else's fancy.

What's in an Author Entry? • For each author, *The Reading List* presents his or her complete fictional works in chronological order. Each book description includes something about the plot, a suggestion of how the book fits into the larger body of the author's work, and an excerpt from one or more significant reviews that address what the book is like to read. For every book, there are always at least a few critics who love it and at least a few who hate it; the reviews excerpted, however, were chosen because they reflect, to the extent that one exists, the critical consensus.

Stars (*) are used to indicate an author's most important work(s). Each starred description is followed by a lengthy excerpt from a contemporary review. If you're interested in reading an author, and you want our advice, we suggest that in most cases you consider one of the starred works. With Doris Lessing, for example, *The Golden Notebook* is overwhelmingly considered her greatest work; however, science fiction fans will probably have more fun with *The Making of the Representative for Planet 8*. Similarly, many critics believe that *Sabbath's Theater* is one of Philip Roth's best books, yet we left it unstarred because it can be difficult to read for someone who hasn't read Roth before. So use your judgment.

The bibliographic information for each book includes the first edition, any revised editions, and—in the case of foreign authors—the first American edition. Each entry concludes with a brief biography of the author.

What is NEXT ON THE READING LIST? • This feature is intended to direct you from authors that you know you like to others whose writing is similar—for one reason or another. Often the similarities are quite straightforward: For instance, Ivan Doig and Larry McMurtry both write about ranch life in the West; Thomas McGuane and Cathie Pelletier are both known for their raucous humor. At other times, however, we've been a little creative: Peter Høeg and Jane Smiley have both written novels set in Greenland; also, Høeg and Paul Auster have both experimented successfully with the mystery genre.

Our only regret is that space considerations have prevented us from including more information and, especially, more authors. There are many writers that we wanted to include in this volume and hope to include in future ones, when we will also update entries to include works published between now and then. At that point, perhaps, we'll have to think about giving Joyce Carol Oates her own edition....

David Rubel
March 1998

Chinua Achebe

(b. November 16, 1930)

"Mr. Achebe is a novelist who makes you laugh—and then catch your breath in horror."
—*Nadine Gordimer*, New York Times

∗ Things Fall Apart (HEINEMANN, 1958; MCDOWELL, OBOLENSKY, 1959) • Achebe established his reputation as a world-class novelist with this first attempt. Set in an Ibo village during the 1880s, *Things Fall Apart* tells the story of Okonkwo, a chief who skillfully exploits his tribe's traditions until the coming of the British produces some terrible changes—among them a new religion (Christianity), some new forms of social organization, and an old idea (racism). Okonkwo's traditionalism makes his confrontation with the colonial government both inevitable and tragic. Critics praised Achebe's skillful handling of the story, especially the way he gracefully revealed his characters' minds and hearts.

> *"The great interest of this novel is that it genuinely succeeds in presenting tribal life from the inside. Patterns of feeling and attitudes of mind appear clothed in a distinctively African imagery, written neither up nor down."* (Times Literary Supplement)

No Longer at Ease (HEINEMANN, 1960; OBOLENSKY, 1961) • Achebe brings the Okonkwo family history forward into the 1950s, when Okonkwo's grandson, the university-educated Obi, returns from England to join Nigeria's colonial civil service. Obi falls in love with a British-trained nurse, Clara, and plans to marry her. But financial problems coupled with the adamant opposition of his family threaten the union, and Obi soon finds himself caught between his family's traditionalism and the practical difficulties of his modern professional life. With this highly regarded novel, Achebe introduced a theme that soon became the basis for an entire genre of post-colonial fiction: the character trapped between two cultures.

Arrow of God (HEINEMANN, 1964; DAY, 1967; REVISED, HEINEMANN, 1974; REVISED, ANCHOR, 1989) • Achebe's third novel is an account of Ibo social life set during the 1920s. Ezeulu, chief priest of the local god Ulu, must overcome factionalist infighting if he's to hold together a group of six villages divided and demoralized by European meddling. Although *Arrow of God* describes Ibo village life often and in great detail, Achebe explains almost none of it, which can make the book very hard going for non-African readers.

A Man of the People (DAY, 1966; REVISED, HEINEMANN, 1988; REVISED, ANCHOR, 1989) • Achebe's devastating critique of political corruption in 1960s Nigeria focuses on a young teacher, Odili Samalu, who runs an idealistic campaign against the corrupt M. N. Nanga. Achebe's depiction of modern Nigeria, sparing neither the powerful nor the poor, reveals both the determination of Nigeria's leaders to remain in power at any cost and the moral poverty of ordinary citizens who willingly participate in corruption despite its ruinous effect. The novel, which culminates in a military coup, was hailed by reviewers as remarkably prescient when the Nigerian army seized control of the country just months before its publication.

Girls at War and Other Stories (HEINEMANN, 1972; DOUBLEDAY, 1973) • This collection of short stories elaborates on many of the themes Achebe explored in his earlier work: the role of education in contemporary Africa, the disintegration of tribal life, the long-term effects of British colonialism, and internecine strife among African tribes. In the title story, an Ibo girl is demoralized by the Biafran war. According to *The New Yorker*, "These are worldly, intelligent, absorbing stories."

✶ Anthills of the Savannah (HEINEMANN, 1987; ANCHOR, 1988) • Achebe's eagerly awaited fifth novel, published two decades after *A Man of the People*, features three childhood friends who have since risen to high government office in the imaginary West African nation of Kangan. Sam, a military officer, has become president. Chris is his commissioner of information and Ikem the editor of the state-owned newspaper. When Sam's plans to become president for life are thwarted, he turns against his friends. State security police murder Ikem and force Chris underground. This experience opens Chris's eyes to the widespread suffering of his nation's ordinary people, especially its women. The story is tragic, but Achebe lightens the plot with pervasive humor and irony.

"Anthills of the Savannah *is a study of how power corrupts itself and by doing so begins to die. It is also about dissent and love. 'Writers don't give prescriptions,' one of [Achebe's] characters notes. 'Writers give headaches.' All those who have inundated Achebe with critical analysis, and who spoke of him as the grandfather of African literature before he was 36, have this novel to wrestle with for some time to come. Chinua Achebe has found new creative fire."*
(*Ben Okri,* The Observer)

BIOGRAPHY

CHINUA ACHEBE WAS BORN IN the Nigerian village of Ogidi. The son of Ibo missionaries, he attended a church-run elementary school and then studied at an elite Nigerian government school before moving on to Nigeria's Ibadan University. Although initially intending to become a doctor, he switched to English literature and soon made up his mind to become a writer.

Achebe taught for a year before joining the Nigerian Broadcasting Corporation in 1954. His career there was successful, and he became director of the Voice of Nigeria in 1961. In the meantime, however, Achebe taught himself much of the Nigerian cultural and social history that he incorporated into his first novel. Although (by his own admission) Achebe never had to endure the privations of a starving artist, the 1958 publication of *Things Fall Apart* launched his literary career with a bang. One reason was that it came at a propitious time: the end of colonial rule. Achebe's novel, with its exploration of African community, demonstrated to Nigerians that they could use their own native culture as a base upon which to build a new, independent nation.

Achebe's maturation as a writer thus coincided with Nigeria's own evolution as a nation. Citing the writer's responsibility to criticize and educate, he spoke out often against what he disliked in Nigeria, especially the foolish and corrupt behavior of its leaders. Achebe was widely praised for this frank analysis of Nigeria's social and cultural dilemmas, but some critics thought he paid too much attention to politics and not enough to the novelist's art. Achebe's invariable response was that he didn't pursue "art for art's sake"; rather, he believed in an art that always responds to social, religious, and philosophical concerns.

After 1966, Achebe's alternate careers (he worked both as a university professor and as a publisher) took their tolls on his literary output. However, with the publication of *Anthills of the Savannah* in 1987, Achebe reestablished his position as Nigeria's preeminent novelist. He is currently the Charles P. Stevenson Jr. Professor of Language and Literature at Bard College in Annandale, New York.

NEXT ON THE READING LIST: Nadine Gordimer, Naguib Mahfouz, Toni Morrison, V. S. Naipaul

Isabel Allende

(b. August 2, 1942)

*"While [Allende's] prose at times verges on soap opera, that
is also one of its charms. She can just as deftly depict loving
tenderness as convey the high fire of eroticism. And when
you've successfully mingled sex and politics with a noble
cause, how can you go wrong?"*
—Gene H. Bell-Villada, New York Times

* In the House of the Spirits (PLAZA & JANES, 1982; KNOPF, 1985) • Set in
an unnamed country recognizable as Chile, Allende's first novel tells the
seventy-five-year story of a family shaken by domestic and political conflict.
The book's patriarch, Esteban Trueba, serves as a metaphor for the
strengths and weaknesses of Latin American society. A worldwide best-seller,
In the House of the Spirits generated a great deal of critical attention, due in
part to its similarity to Gabriel García Márquez's *One Hundred Years of
Solitude* (the books share the form of a family chronicle, as well as the use
of magical realism and parallel characters). Yet despite her undeniable
debt to García Márquez, Allende presents a distinctive voice that's particularly noticeable in her straightforward journalistic treatment of events surrounding the Chilean military coup.

> *"Part of the [book's] power comes from the fact that real events form the back-
> ground for the fictional story. The unbridled fantasy of the protagonists and
> their enchanted spirits is played out against the story of the demented and tragic
> country once free, now possessed by the evil spirits of a military dictatorship."*
> (*Marjorie Agosin*, Christian Science Monitor)

Of Love and Shadows (PLAZA & JANES, 1984; KNOPF, 1987) • Set, like its celebrated predecessor, in a Chile of the imagination, *Of Love and Shadows*
concerns two lovers, a reporter and a photographer, who labor to expose
the fate of fifteen peasants "disappeared" by the secret police. Once again,
critics applauded Allende's ability to blend thinly disguised historical
events into the everyday lives of her fictional characters. Some reviewers,
however, pointed out that here the elements weren't quite as well blended
as they were in her previous novel.

Eva Luna (PLAZA & JANES, 1987; KNOPF, 1988) • Allende's third novel is a
modern, almost picaresque narrative about a young woman who learns to
spin tales. At first, these tales merely help her tolerate a life of abject
poverty, but eventually they lead her to fame and fortune as a television
writer. Finally, Eva Luna falls in love with an Austrian filmmaker, and
their own tale plays itself out against the backdrop of an anonymous

South American country's turbulent coming of age. Although lauded for its finely honed political and feminist sensibilities, *Eva Luna* was criticized for being overly sentimental and relying much too heavily on hunky left-wing males.

The Stories of Eva Luna (PLAZA & JANES, 1990; ATHENEUM, 1991) • Like *The Thousand and One Nights* of Arabian literature, these twenty-three tales, told by the fictional Eva Luna to her lover, combine fantasy, magic, biting social satire, and psychological insight. The various settings sample Latin America from the humid Caribbean to the chilly southern tip of Argentina, and the themes range even farther, from the extinction of native tribes in the Amazon to a modern theory that love can conquer cancer. In keeping with her brand of "magic feminism," Allende's protagonists abound in resilience and down-to-earth good sense; however, some critics faulted them for being superwomen, pointing out that Allende's heroines are most moving, credible, and exemplary when they fail.

The Infinite Plan (PLAZA & JANES, 1991; HARPERCOLLINS, 1993) • Allende's fourth novel (her first as a U.S. resident) features Gregory Reeves, the son of a tent preacher, who struggles to succeed, only to learn that everything once important to him has been lost along the way. While many critics noted that the "otherness" of Allende's American characters allowed them to provide useful insights from the margins of society, some complained that *The Infinite Plan* reminded them only sporadically of the rich language that they enjoyed in Allende's earlier novels.

BIOGRAPHY

ISABEL ALLENDE WAS BORN IN LIMA, Peru, where her Chilean diplomat father was then stationed. Although her contact with this aristocratic yet decadent man ceased after her parents' divorce, she remained close to his family—particularly to her uncle/godfather, Salvador Allende, who was elected president of Chile in 1970. After spending her adolescence in Bolivia, Europe, and the Middle East with her mother and stepfather (also a diplomat), Allende settled as an adult in Chile, where she became a journalist. She wrote a column for a radical feminist journal, edited a magazine for children, and hosted a weekly TV program.

Allende's life changed dramatically in 1973, when Gen. Augusto Pinochet Ugarte led a military coup that resulted in the overthrow of Salvador Allende's socialist government and the murder of Allende himself. Although she remained in Chile following the takeover, her efforts to undermine the Pinochet regime ultimately threatened her safety. In 1975, she escaped with her family to Venezuela. Allende's literary career commenced several years later, when she began writing a letter to her dying grandfather in Chile. She never sent the letter, but the memories it evoked became the basis for *In the House of the Spirits*.

Allende's protagonists are typically women whom she endows with the empowering gift of storytelling. Her heroines weave stories to preserve the past, gain control over their lives, and safeguard the future. It's not surprising that Allende defines the novel as a vehicle for bearing witness, overcoming silence, and asserting the human values of love, justice, and reconciliation. In 1995, she published the highly acclaimed memoir *Paula,* recounting both her own dramatic life story and her daughter's losing battle against porphyria, a hereditary metabolic disorder.

NEXT ON THE READING LIST: Laura Esquivel, Carlos Fuentes, Gabriel García Márquez, Toni Morrison, Mario Vargas Llosa, Alice Walker

---

Dorothy Allison
(b. April 11, 1949)

"Whether she's writing about family, lovers, or the violence of poverty, Allison's emotions come sailing through her work. That's not always easy for me as a reader. There were times her anger and disdain frightened me; times when her narrator's lost sense of self and all-consuming pain were too much like my own.... But [Allison's work], honest and gripping, is a challenge to readers and writers everywhere."
—Liz Galst, Women's Review of Books

Trash (FIREBRAND, 1988) • These fourteen interrelated stories—which Allison called "not biography, and yet not lies"—describe the struggle of an adult narrator to assimilate memories of her painful childhood. The woman—"the one who got away," according to Allison—grew up during the 1950s amid white southern violence and poverty. The first story, "River of Names," wrenchingly recounts specific episodes of domestic violence and sexual abuse. (Liz Galst wrote in the *Women's Review of Books* that this story "laid me out for a week.") Other stories concern the narrator's adult problems, particularly those related to her lesbian-feminist sexuality. "I sometimes found Allison's style clunky, but her stories cut to the core," Galst concluded. "I was deeply touched by nearly every story in *Trash.* "

* Bastard Out of Carolina (DUTTON, 1992) • The heroine of this highly autobiographical novel, a National Book Award nominee, is a young girl in a poor southern family. Illegitimate Ruth Anne Boatwright is called Bone by her large and eccentric extended family because when she was born prematurely, she was "no bigger than a knucklebone." Her mother, Anney, tries to create a more traditional home for her and her half sister by marrying Daddy Glen, the son of a wealthy local family, but he soon begins to beat and rape Bone regularly. The abuse continues for five years, until Anney sends Bone to live with her lesbian aunt, Raylene, a former carnie whom Bone very much admires.

"If Bastard Out of Carolina *is rooted in autobiography, it never takes on the obsessive tone of a confessional or the crusading fervor of an exposé. Allison has turned the rage she describes so brilliantly...into a compressed, exacting language that need never raise its voice to grab our attention. 'I made my life, the same way it looks like you're gonna make yours—out of pride and stubbornness and too much anger,' Aunt Raylene tells Bone. It's that volatile combination that saves Bone and gives* Bastard *an extraordinary pent-up power."* (*Vince Aletti,* Voice Literary Supplement)

BIOGRAPHY

DURING NUMEROUS INTERVIEWS, Dorothy Allison has frankly acknowledged the many similarities between herself and Bone, the protagonist of *Bastard Out of Carolina.* "A lot of the novel is based on real experience," she has said. "The characters are modeled on members of my family and on stories I heard when I was growing up." Born in Greenville, South Carolina, the illegitimate daughter of a waitress, Allison suffered as a child, as Bone does, the physical and sexual abuse of a violent stepfather. "It's true that I had a painful, difficult relationship with my stepfather, that he was physically violent, and that he raped me as a child," she continued. "But the book is not autobiography. Rather, it is telling my emotional truth."

Allison's childhood was also marked by extreme poverty. "I come from bigoted violent people; shotguns, beer, and pickup trucks," she has explained. "The word *poor* doesn't describe it enough. I feel like I came out of a world nobody knows about, that maybe doesn't exist anymore." In 1967, she left that world by winning a scholarship to Florida Presbyterian College, where she "met the people I had always read about: girls whose fathers loved them—innocently; boys who drove cars they hadn't stolen."

Allison originally came to the attention of the literary world as a poet when she published *The Women Who Hate Me* in 1983. This collection was well received, although some critics objected to its graphic descriptions of lesbian sex. A self-described "lesbian feminist," Allison has spoken out often about her "perverse" sexuality: "When I was in my twenties, I tried to renounce sex and be good, because it seemed to me that my sexuality was inherently sick and twisted, evil. The very things I needed to come were so horrifying to me, connected to the brutality of my childhood. Then one day I just decided this is fucked. I thought, *I am not getting what I want....* So I just threw up my hands and said, 'OK, I *am* that evil person.'"

Subsequently, while living in New York, Allison formed the Lesbian Sex Mafia, a support group for perverse women. "I was into anonymous sex," Allison remembered. "I did not want a lover. I didn't want all the lesbian buy-a-house shit. I just wanted to fuck around. I believed that the best way to get to know a woman was to go to bed with her. The second best way was to take her by the throat and see what she did. So pretty much everywhere I've lived I've had a real bad reputation. But it has gotten me a lot of interesting dates."

NEXT ON THE READING LIST: Russell Banks, Larry Brown, Pete Dexter, Kaye Gibbons, David Leavitt, Reynolds Price, Melanie Rae Thon

---

Julia Alvarez
(b. March 27, 1950)

"In the current wave of Latina novelists, [Alvarez] strikes me as among the least theatrical and vociferous, the one listening most closely to the subtleties of her own artistic call. She stands apart stylistically, a psychological novelist who uses language skillfully to depict complex inner lives for her fictional creations."
—*Ilan Stavans,* The Nation

* How the García Girls Lost Their Accents (ALGONQUIN, 1991) • Alvarez's debut novel recounts, through fifteen interrelated stories, the experiences of the four García sisters, both before and after their family's exile from the Dominican Republic (their father had participated in a botched coup against Dominican dictator Rafael Leonidas Trujillo). The book begins during the late 1960s with the siblings already Americanized—sex, drugs, and mental breakdowns are all the rage—then rolls back to the difficult period of assimilation and closes with the girls' childhood in the Dominican Republic. The novel was generally well received by critics, who found it bright, lively, engaging, and innovative without being difficult.

> *"[Alvarez] has... beautifully captured the threshold experiences of the new immigrant, where the past is not yet a memory and the future remains an anxious dream."* (*Donna Rifkind,* New York Times)

In the Time of the Butterflies (ALGONQUIN, 1994) • In her second novel, Alvarez recalls a grim incident in Dominican history: the untimely deaths of the three Mirabal sisters, all outspoken critics of Trujillo's oppressive regime. The book is divided into four sections, one for each martyred sister plus one for Dede, their surviving sibling. In metaphorically bringing these women back to life, Alvarez confirmed her skill as an architect of complex narrative structures. However, some critics complained that she lacked a compelling style, and others faulted her for not making her readers more aware of the story's broader political context.

Yo! (ALGONQUIN, 1997) • The title of Alvarez's disappointing third novel is a triple pun: *Yo* in Spanish means "I"; it's a yell for attention; and it's the nickname of Yolanda García, a Latina novelist famous for her highly auto-biographical prose (and the central character of Alvarez's first novel). Alvarez arranged this book into three parts, each divided into sections that offer a portrait of one of Yo's chagrined "characters": suitors, husbands, relatives, friends, and even hapless bystanders who become the object of her literary indulgence. Although praised by some for its playful inventiveness, *Yo!* was widely criticized for its skin-deep characterizations and failure to achieve either a rhythm or a narrative crescendo.

BIOGRAPHY

ALTHOUGH BORN IN NEW YORK CITY, Julia Alvarez was raised in the Dominican Republic, where her powerful extended family resided in a Kennedy-like compound of luxurious homes. However, when her cultured father (a man who could trace his Spanish ancestry back to the conquistadors) became involved in a failed coup much like that described in her first novel, Alvarez's family was forced into exile in the United States. She was ten years old at the time.

Alvarez grew up in the Bronx, where her sense of alienation "caused a radical change in me. It made me an introverted little girl." She immersed herself in books and eventually, encouraged by a teacher, began to write: "'Language is the only homeland,' the exiled Polish poet Czeslaw Milosz has said, and that was where I landed when we left the Dominican Republic, not in the United States but in the English language." Alvarez graduated summa cum laude from Middlebury College in 1971, then earned an M.F.A. from Syracuse University in 1975. She published her first book, a poetry collection called *Homecoming,* in 1984.

NEXT ON THE READING LIST: Sandra Cisneros, Edwidge Danticat, Laura Esquivel, Cristina Garcia, Oscar Hijuelos, Jamaica Kincaid

Jorge Amado

(b. August 10, 1912)

*"Mr. Amado has long been Brazil's best known and most
loved novelist. Like many of his Latin American counterparts, he concerns himself with the mixing of race, religion,
and custom, with the syncretism that underpins much
of magic realism."*
—*Allen Josephs,* New York Times

Jubiabá (OLYMPIO, 1935; AVON, 1984) • The first of Amado's novels to
achieve some commercial success, *Jubiabá* is both the picturesque chronicle of a rogue and a powerful protest against the miserable living conditions endured by Brazil's poor. However, although suffused with the
sights and smells of Amado's native Bahia, this novel isn't great literature. "Character, plot, and literary form are consistently neglected," one
critic observed.

Sea of Death (OLYMPIO, 1936; AVON, 1984) • Perhaps the most elegant of
Amado's novels, *Sea of Death* tells the story of Guma, an impoverished sailor
who lives on a boat with his devoted Livia. Set during a time of deep economic depression in Brazil, *Sea of Death* relates the hardships suffered by
Guma and Livia as Amado simultaneously describes in great emotional
detail the beauty and the terror of the sea. Kristiana Gregory, writing in the
Los Angeles Times, praised the translator's success in retaining Amado's "lyrical, almost mystical style."

Captains of the Sands (OLYMPIO, 1937; AVON, 1988) • Resuming the social
realism that had become his signature style, Amado describes the harsh
lives led by a group of homeless children living in an empty warehouse in
Bahia. Forced to survive on their wits alone, often as criminals, Amado's
fierce and wily children struggle to find their place in a world that has
abandoned them. In criticizing the novel, most reviewers complained that
Amado had excessively sentimentalized a serious social problem. "Lack of
restraint is a defect in his novels," noted one.

✱ The Violent Land (MARTINS, 1942; KNOPF, 1945; REVISED, KNOPF, 1965) •
Considered the most accomplished of Amado's early novels, this sprawling
narrative describes the opening of the Brazilian frontier to ambitious cacao
farmers. Its plot concerns the bloody rivalry between two powerful families,
each of which wants badly to acquire the last remaining tract of virgin land
between their two estates. Many reviewers, citing the book's great historical
breadth and suspenseful narration, remarked that *The Violent Land* seemed
quite accessible to American readers despite its exotic setting.

"To the raw violence and action of one of our gold-rush, claim-jumping, frontier tales, this novel adds an exuberant, tropical lyricism." (*Bertram D. Wolfe,* New York Herald Tribune)

St. George of Ilheus (MARTINS, 1944; PUBLISHED IN THE U.S. AS *THE GOLDEN HARVEST,* AVON, 1992) • This novel portrays Amado's native town of Ilheus as it experiences a cycle of boom and bust in its production of cacao, the region's principal cash crop. The major action involves a land grab by a group of exporters well versed in the art of forging deeds and titles. Reviewers praised Amado's skillful handling of a complicated plot, as well as his descriptions of cacao cultivation, political intrigue, and the machinations by which ambitious, unscrupulous planters have amassed their wealth.

* Gabriela, Clove and Cinnamon (MARTINS, 1958; KNOPF, 1962) • The first of Amado's comic novels to achieve runaway popular success, *Gabriela, Clove and Cinnamon* describes the on-again, off-again relationship between Nacib, the Syrian-born owner of the popular Vesuvius Bar, and Gabriela, the dirt-poor mulatto woman he hires as a cook. Gabriela's substantial culinary talents create a booming business at the bar, while her romantic ones seduce Nacib into marrying her. However, the carefree Gabriela soon regrets choosing the dull, joyless life of a lawful wife who can no longer serve drinks, walk barefoot, or join in street dances. Amado's charming solution to this problem, typically Brazilian in its frank acceptance of sensuality, perhaps accounts for the novel's international success.

> *"It is in* Gabriela, Clove and Cinnamon *that [Amado] really finds himself. One hardly knows what to admire most: the dexterity with which Amado can keep half a dozen plots spinning; the gossamer texture of the writing; or his humor, tenderness, and humanity."* (*Harriet de Onis,* Saturday Review)

Home Is the Sailor (MARTINS, 1961; KNOPF, 1964) • The life of sea captain Vasco Moscoso de Aragão is recounted from two opposite perspectives in this tale narrated by a young historian from Bahia. Although Vasco regales the historian with exciting tales of his long service in the merchant marine, other informants insist that Vasco's memories are pure fantasy. Amid this confusion, the captain of a passenger ship dies suddenly, obliging Vasco to take command. Writing in the *New York Times,* Virgilia Peterson declared that "*Home Is the Sailor* makes a wondrously amusing and thought-provoking tale."

The Two Deaths of Quincas Wateryell (SOCIEDADE DOS CEM BIBLIOFILOS DO BRASIL, 1962; KNOPF, 1965) • In this Brazilian version of an American tall tale, Quincas, a respectable middle-class functionary, abandons his family to run wild in the streets, whoring and drinking. He dies shortly thereafter—to the great relief of his scandalized family—but not before he attracts the attention of several tabloid journalists. The fun begins when his riffraff pals decide to kidnap his body from the funeral home and bury it at sea. According to one reviewer, this "rollicking" satire ably skewered Brazilian bourgeois hypocrisy.

Shepherds of the Night (MARTINS, 1964; KNOPF, 1967) • Amado again draws on the picturesque life of Brazil's lower classes in this story of ne'er-do-wells from the shantytowns of Bahia. Written in the form of a pastoral, this novel revealed in particular a wealth of detail about Afro-Brazilian religious cults. Many reviewers admired Amado's colorful depictions of the book's roguish characters but objected to what they saw as his shallow treatment of the wealthy and powerful. For example, John Wain in the *New York Review of Books* called *Shepherds of the Night* "a strange, rich, unsatisfactory book."

* Dona Flor and Her Two Husbands (MARTINS, 1966; KNOPF, 1969)• This comic masterpiece, often compared to *Gabriela, Clove and Cinnamon,* describes the problem faced by Dona Flor after her womanizing husband, Vadinho, dies during Carnival as a result of overindulgence and she marries the hardworking pharmacist Dr. Teodoro, a man in every way the opposite of Vadinho. Her troubles begin when Vadinho reappears, invisible and mute to everyone but his widow, determined to share her bed. Most reviewers interpreted Amado's clever juxtaposition of these two social archetypes, Vadinho and Teodoro, as a sly comic allegory on both the Brazilian class structure and the national psyche.

> "Dona Flor *is rich and leisurely, as much verbal aphrodisiac as novel… One reason for [Amado's] expansive mood is that he is really writing a love letter to Bahia… [Amado] romanticizes his Bahians into virile lovers, darkly sensual* morenas, *whores and neighbors, all larger than life. According to rumor, Dona Flor's friends are not the Bahian poor, but Amado's own circle of artists and intellectuals, whom he has costumed as peasants for a literary romp à clef."* (Time)

Tent of Miracles (MARTINS, 1969; KNOPF, 1971)• This novel focuses on a Bahian mulatto named Pedro Archanjo, who discovers that his racist bête noire is actually a distant cousin. The serious reviews were mixed, but as L. J. Davis pointed out in the *Washington Post,* "One doesn't read a novel like this because it is good but because it is fun."

Tereza Batista: Home from the Wars (MARTINS, 1972; KNOPF, 1975) • The prostitute Tereza is another of Amado's sensuous, long-suffering heroines. During the course of this novel, she undergoes a series of humiliations, including enslavement by a sadistic thug. Later, she leads her fellow prostitutes out on strike. Alas, most critics weren't impressed. According to Stephen Brook in the *Times Literary Supplement,* "Amado is too sentimental, too self-indulgent, too lush, too sprawling; but, like his heroine's, his heart is in the right place."

Tieta, the Goat Girl (EDITORA RECORD, 1977; KNOPF, 1979) • Tieta, once the goat girl of a small town, has slept her way to the top, earning a fortune in the process. She wants to share her good fortune, but her return home upsets the conservative social order of the town and triggers a political confrontation. While some reviewers praised Amado's zany plot, others objected to the book's wordiness and shallow characterizations. "There are tender, even moving, passages and moments of ironic comedy," one critic observed, "but everything is repeated over and over."

Pen, Sword, Camisole (EDITORA RECORD, 1979; D. R. GODINE, 1985) • This novel tells the story of a 1940 campaign to prevent two military officers—one a Nazi sympathizer, the other a despised authoritarian—from gaining seats in the Brazilian Academy of Letters. Amado's humane vision of a world in which freedom always triumphs over political oppression appealed to some reviewers, but most panned the book for its heavy-handed sermonizing. According to Nancy Ramsey in the *New York Times,* "Mr. Amado's didactic style is unfortunate, because his intent is an honorable one."

Showdown (EDITORA RECORD, 1984; BANTAM, 1988) • Like *The Violent Land, Showdown* chronicles in epic style the life of a small town, Tocaia Grande (literally, "big ambush"), over the course of several generations. "This might be the story of Brazil itself, seen through a dark glass lovingly, honed into a compact metaphor implying a whole nation's tumultuous vigor," Paul West wrote in the *New York Times.*

The War of the Saints (EDITORA RECORD, 1988; BANTAM, 1992)• In this book, which contains the full complement of colorful characters one expects to find in an Amado novel, the lovely young Manela falls in love with a taxi driver. Although their romance is soon thwarted by Manela's coldhearted puritanical aunt, circumstances change when a statue of a local saint miraculously comes to life. "*The War of the Saints* is unabashedly triumphant," Allen Josephs declared in the *New York Times.* "Its long parade of Bahian saints and sinners will snake through your mind like a Carnival procession."

BIOGRAPHY

BORN ON HIS FAMILY'S CACAO FARM in southern Bahia, Brazil, Jorge Amado knew hardship from an early age. By the time he had turned ten, Amado had survived a smallpox epidemic, floods, the death of a younger brother, and the attempted murder of his father. In boarding schools, the young Amado discovered the works of such nineteenth-century novelists as Dickens, Balzac, and Sir Walter Scott. As a young adult, he joined a group of bohemian writers in Bahia, working as a reporter for a local newspaper and writing his first novel, *O país do carnaval* (1932), about the slums of Salvador, the Bahian capital. In 1933, he married his first wife and moved to Rio de Janeiro, where he planned to enter law school. By 1935, however, Amado had established himself among a new generation of Brazilian writers who championed social causes and preached leftist solutions to Brazil's crushing poverty.

Soon Amado's books began to generate a great deal of controversy, as much for their frank depictions of sex as for their heavy-handed political messages. The dictatorship then in power in Brazil jailed him twice and publicly burned his books. In later years, he was exiled several times, usually moving his family to Paris during these periods. In the meantime, Amado grew less enchanted with social realism and its incessant sermonizing. By 1958, when he published *Gabriela, Clove and Cinnamon,* he had expanded his style to include humor, irony, and caricature. *Gabriela*'s mixing of social themes with broad comedy—not to mention its sensual descriptions of sexual pleasure—shocked Brazil's leftist orthodoxy as well as its conservative readership. Needless to say, the novel became a runaway best-seller, gaining for Amado his first broad popular following.

The 1966 publication of *Dona Flor and Her Two Husbands,* Amado's most famous work, extended his celebrity beyond Brazil to the world at large. Because he now finds it impossible to write in Brazil (his home in Bahia has become a tourist attraction), Amado and his second wife, the writer Zélia Gattai, divide their time between Bahia and Paris.

NEXT ON THE READING LIST: Isabel Allende, T. Coraghessan Boyle, Louis de Bernières, Gabriel García Márquez, Naguib Mahfouz, Philip Roth

Martin Amis
(b. August 25, 1949)

"There is, quite simply, no one else like him…. While most of his counterparts in Britain content themselves with painting cozy pictures on small canvases, and those in the United States gaze rapturously at the undulations of their own navels, Amis plunges like Dickens reincarnate into the life of the city, wallowing in its messiness and nastiness and desperation."
—*Jonathan Yardley,* Washington Post

The Rachel Papers (JONATHAN CAPE, 1973; KNOPF, 1974) • At the age of twenty-four, Martin Amis burst like a ripe pimple onto the British literary scene, and his first novel turned out to presage two of the characteristics that have marked his writing since: a manic verbal inventiveness and loathsome characters whom the narrator delights in detailing right down to their dandruff.

Charles Highway—a madly precocious twenty-year-old child of privilege—expends all his available energy pursuing and bedding the eponymous Rachel. And that's it: Sex is the thing—gorgeous, ugly sex in 1970s Britain.

Dead Babies (JONATHAN CAPE, 1975; KNOPF, 1976) • Amis puts the weekend-in-the-country theme through a meat grinder in a second novel that, as the *New York Times* said, "aims to shock and disgust, and it certainly succeeds." Pointless friends with ugly lives ingest drugs and alcohol with abandon, hallucinate that their teeth are falling out, and vomit a great deal. Reviewers found it by turns "savage," "brilliant," and "uniformly unpleasant."

Success (JONATHAN CAPE, 1978; CROWN, 1987) • Far more readable than its predecessor, Amis's third novel is equally satiric. Gregory and Terry are foster brothers who live together in a London flat. Gregory, the aristo, has all the charm, wit, luck, and money; Terry is a cockney have-not who knows full well what he hasn't got...and yet fortunes turn. This novel has been accurately called "a parable about the decline of the old order in England and the new raj of the yobs."

Other People: A Mystery Story (JONATHAN CAPE, 1981; VIKING, 1981) • Mary Lamb can't remember who she is, or what she is, or what anything is. As a total amnesiac, she wanders the world, attempting to discover herself, and in the process discovers that life is pretty ugly. *Other People* is a departure for Amis—a fable—and he has a hard time managing the format: Rapists and drug addicts, for instance, don't fit well into Mary Lamb's nursery rhyme. "It remains," as one reviewer wrote, "more of a 'Mystery Story' than, one suspects, was intended."

* Money: A Suicide Note (JONATHAN CAPE, 1984; VIKING, 1985) • Amis's masterpiece (according to many) reprises all the dirt and drugs and sheer revulsion of his earlier works, yet it does so to greater effect. Filmmaker John Self arrives in New York flush with the opportunity of directing a feature. He's fat and ugly and is a glutton for alcohol, fast food, and cheap sex; it is Self's repeated plunging into squalid excess, rather than the plot of his trying to make a film, that carries this book.

> "Money *really needs to be read twice (at least): the first time for the sheer pleasure of encountering the grotesque and lovable John Self.... The second time round (when, as Self would say, you are all laughed out) you can begin to relish the book's marvellously intricate design."* (*Ian Hamilton,* London Review of Books)

Einstein's Monsters (HARMONY, 1987) • In a true shift of theme and style, Amis reveals an obsession that has real depth to it: nuclear war. The long introduction to this collection of five sci-fi stories tells of Amis's continual, nagging fear and his endless puzzling over the problem of what to do with nuclear bombs. These tales of apocalypse all broil with his customary word-play and promise *A Clockwork Orange*–like freshness, but the seriousness of their theme drags Amis into an unaccustomed preachiness.

✳ London Fields (HARMONY, 1989) • It's millennium time, and the dark clouds of ecological ruin and nuclear holocaust are coming on fast. Nicola Six, an evil beauty who represents the dark side of love (anal sex is the only type that she sanctions) controls the fates of a loathsome yob called Keith Talent, a loathsome richie called Guy Clinch, and American writer Samson Young. Her ingenious master plan is to have herself murdered: Which unwitting male will do the deed?

> *"In my judgment* [London Fields] *borders on but never quite achieves brilliance, largely because of Amis's insistence on mounting the pulpit, but its shortcomings are more than outweighed by its heartbreaking ambition and the huge risks it takes."* (*Jonathan Yardley,* Washington Post)

Time's Arrow (HARMONY, 1991) • Time reverses direction in this slim allegory that begins at a man's deathbed in contemporary Middle America and retraces his steps backward through various identities and careers until the reader learns that the man was a Nazi death camp doctor. It's a smart conceit: a topsy-turvy look at upside-down Nazi morality. (As the book rewinds, Jews at Auschwitz have their gold fillings restored, corpses spring to life, and so on.) *Time's Arrow* is Amis's most overtly moral book, yet it doesn't quite come off; the conceit simply can't stand up to a full-length treatment.

The Information (HARMONY, 1995) • A hilariously unsuccessful literary novelist (people who attempt to read his latest book succumb to various nervous disorders before page ten) watches his supposed best friend become a staggeringly successful writer of trashy novels. Richard Tull plots to bring about Gwyn Barry's destruction, and for a time we delight in observing an unsavory outsider's attempt to foil an unsavory insider. But soon enough Amis gets sidetracked by his own postmodernist tics, the plot wanders off, and we're left wallowing in *The Information,* which turns out to be nothing more than the random stuff of life.

Night Train (JONATHAN CAPE, 1997; HARMONY, 1998) • This small book, less than two hundred pages, conceals its purpose beneath the patina of an American detective novel. Homicide cop Mike Houlihan, a forty-four-year-old broad-shouldered broad, used to be an alcoholic before Col. Tom Rockwell took her in and dried her out. Now the colonel's golden-girl daughter, Jennifer, is dead, apparently a suicide—except that an autopsy has revealed three bullets in her head. The colonel asks Mike to investigate, but the more Mike learns about Jennifer, a hot theoretical physicist, the less she seems to know. "The true criminal is the Amis language, the virtuoso performer who won't yield the spotlight," Jonathan Levi wrote in the *Los Angeles Times*. "His language, his perfect generic mixture of high culture and low, dime-store Dostoevsky and pulp Wittgenstein, is such a massive performer that it sucks up all character, light, and matter, leaving us feeling black-holed."

BIOGRAPHY

MARTIN AMIS IS THE SON of famed English novelist Kingsley Amis, whose *Lucky Jim* distinguished him as one of the smart, bratty chroniclers of Britain's postwar fall from empire. With a dad of scathing literary reputation, it would have been safe for Amis to choose a career in politics or international finance. But after his graduation from Oxford, he instead made a beeline for the editorial staff of the *Times Literary Supplement*. Amis's first novel, published in 1973, won a Somerset Maugham Award, given to writers under age thirty-five.

Amis's next three novels marked him as a ruthless recorder of his generation's follies; by the time *Money* was published in 1984, he was generally considered to have surpassed his father in literary standing. In 1995, he achieved even greater heights of fame with the publication of *The Information*, a tale of London literary society that became prophetic when Amis's fat advance and infamous agent switching caused enough of an uproar to warrant tabloid coverage.

Still, there remains much similarity between father and son: As Richard Eder pointed out in the *Los Angeles Times*, both "write of intellectual phonies and pretenders, assorted degenerates and a rotted-out youth in an England of depraved popular culture and not the slightest social or moral structure." However, Martin Amis spent several of his early years in America and Spain, and this experience has given his books a broader scope and the sense of a wider world out there. He has become the most gorgeous chronicler of everyday ugliness in the last half of the twentieth century, but he also appears trapped in the eddies of postmodernism. For example, it's almost de rigueur now for Martin Amis to appear as a character in each Martin Amis novel.

NEXT ON THE READING LIST: Madison Smartt Bell, Harry Crews, Don DeLillo, Umberto Eco, Thomas McGuane, Philip Roth, Thomas Pynchon

Margaret Atwood

(b. November 18, 1939)

"Margaret Atwood has always possessed a tribal bent: she has described and transcribed the ceremonies and experience of being a woman…. That women are individuals, difficult to corral, a motley and uneasy sisterhood: that in the war between the sexes there are collaborators as well as enemies, spies, refugees, spectators and conscientious objectors—all this has been brilliantly dramatized in Ms. Atwood's work."

—Lorrie Moore, New York Times

The Edible Woman (MCCLELLAND & STEWART, 1969; ATLANTIC MONTHLY, 1970) • Marian McAlpin, a "proper" young Toronto woman, becomes engaged and immediately begins to notice her appetite slipping away. At the same time, she feels as though she is herself being eaten, consumed like food. Most critics found Atwood's first novel to be irredeemably flawed, and even those who believed it was partly successful pointed out its clumsy mechanics. One of the latter described *The Edible Woman* as "a work of feminist black humor [employing] comic distortion [that] veers at times into surreal meaningfulness."

✴ Surfacing (MCCLELLAND & STEWART, 1972; SIMON & SCHUSTER, 1973) • Dubbed a "psychological ghost story" by one reviewer, *Surfacing* tells the story of a young artist on vacation at a secluded cabin in northern Quebec. Searching for her missing father, she learns how closely violence and death lurk beneath the surface of everyday life. Although *Surfacing* has often been compared to Sylvia Plath's *Bell Jar* because of its depiction of a descent into madness, the unnamed narrator in *Surfacing* isn't mentally deranged. Rather, she is, according to one critic, "coming to terms with the haunting, separated parts of [her] being." This book was Atwood's breakthrough, earning her a flood of excellent reviews and praise for its terrifying story of self-discovery.

> *"Atwood has…outsoared her previous status as a widely respected younger poet…. She has become the literary standard-bearer of a resurgence of nativism and nationalism in Canada, eclipsing established Canadian writers."* (*Paul Delany*, New York Times)

Lady Oracle (MCCLELLAND & STEWART, 1976; SIMON & SCHUSTER, 1976) • One day, Joan Foster is a bored wife, poet, and pseudonymous author of passionate romance novels. The next, her feminist opus, vaults her into superstardom. However, when her fame brings painful love affairs, criminally inclined fans, blackmail, and other menaces, Joan decides to fake her death in order to start life over again. Coming as it did so soon after

Atwood's success with *Surfacing, Lady Oracle* encouraged many reviewers to comment on the parallels between Atwood and her narrator. Some concluded that *Lady Oracle* was thinner than Atwood's previous novels, but her many admirers thought the book a successful parody that exquisitely critiqued contemporary society.

Dancing Girls and Other Stories (McCLELLAND & STEWART, 1977; SIMON & SCHUSTER, 1982) • In the fourteen stories that make up this volume, Atwood uses a combination of humor and vivid detail to continue her exploration of the gap between the private and the public self. One of many reviewers to praise the collection, Anne Tyler in the *New York Times* called it "stunning." Atwood, she continued, maintains "superb control and selectivity with an almost rambunctious vitality."

Life Before Man (McCLELLAND & STEWART, 1979; SIMON & SCHUSTER, 1980) • Atwood's fourth novel conducts three principal characters through midlife crises. Specifically, Elizabeth is losing her husband, Nate, to boredom and the alluring Lesje, a woman who prefers dinosaurs to men and has just lost her lover to suicide. Using paleontology as a metaphor for the extinction of monogamy, feeling, and just plain polite conversation, Atwood makes her characters' lives minefields of failed childhoods, failed marriages, failed affairs, and failed sex. Critics were divided: Some felt that Atwood's parody had degenerated into little more than stereotyping, that her story was as "tight as a poem in which nothing much happens," though others hailed *Life Before Man* as among Atwood's finest works, an "anatomy of melancholy."

Bodily Harm (McCLELLAND & STEWART, 1981; SIMON & SCHUSTER, 1982) • Having survived a bout of life-threatening cancer, Rennie Wilford decides to recuperate in the Caribbean. Much to her surprise, she becomes involved in weapons smuggling and political assassination. Most reviewers loved this suspense-filled spy thriller, lauding Atwood as a "female Graham Greene" and commenting repeatedly on her versatility. According to Anatole Broyard in the *New York Times,* "It knocked me out. Margaret Atwood seems to be able to do just about everything: people, places, problems, a perfect ear, an exactly right voice."

Bluebeard's Egg and Other Stories (McCLELLAND & STEWART, 1983; HOUGHTON MIFFLIN, 1986) • In her second collection of stories, Atwood investigates bonding, bondage, and women's own complicity in their victimization. She also explores the clichés of femininity and the ways in which different women cope with these limitations. As one critic noted in the *London Review of Books,* "The endings of Margaret Atwood's fiction tend to leave things slightly up in the air." Another compared Atwood to an academic at a conference asking, Are there any questions? "Many of the stories in *Bluebeard's Egg* implicitly ask the same thing."

* The Handmaid's Tale (MCCLELLAND & STEWART, 1985; HOUGHTON MIFFLIN, 1986) • A certified best-seller that was later made into a feature film, *The Handmaid's Tale* is certainly Atwood's most important work to date. It's also her only work of science—or, more accurately, speculative—fiction. Often compared to such dystopian classics as Orwell's *1984* and Huxley's *Brave New World, The Handmaid's Tale* uses current social trends to postulate a frightening world in which women are subjugated by a religiously fundamentalist male-dominated state. In this literally barren world, women may be only wives, servants, nunlike teachers, or handmaids (a euphemism for childbearers). Though a fair number of reviewers thought *The Handmaid's Tale* unbelievable and insufficiently imagined, just as many considered Atwood's bleak, unnerving work to be visionary.

> *"Atwood concentrates on what happens to women, especially to one woman...in a fascist country controlled by a group strikingly similar to the Moral Majority.... The depth and complexity of Atwood's critique of contemporary society are stunning.* The Handmaid's Tale *is a stark, even gruesome book, but it does not yield to despair."* (*Cathy Davidson*, Ms.)

Cat's Eye (DOUBLEDAY, 1989) • A coming-of-age novel infused with autobiographical overtones, *Cat's Eye* surveys the landscape of childhood—its secrecies, betrayals, brutalities, and struggles. Elaine Risley returns to her hometown, Toronto, for an exhibition of her artwork. Soon after, memories of her childhood friend Cordelia begin to haunt her, and Elaine begins to untangle the knot that her life has become, Cordelia being the central tangle. Measuring *Cat's Eye* against *The Handmaid's Tale,* most reviewers found it much less worthy, but some still discerned merit. The *Women's Review of Books* compared *Cat's Eye* to "a single breaking ocean wave.... Fizzling, it disperses its brilliant waters ineffectually, allowing them to be sucked into the general stream."

Wilderness Tips and Other Stories (DOUBLEDAY, 1991) • Atwood's third story collection earned her praise from the majority of those who reviewed the book. Its ten stories once again explore her familiar territory of regret, disillusionment, and loneliness with scathing wit and moments of poignancy. Told in a voice that's detached and often monotonous, the stories are bleak and pessimistic. Atwood's limited vision, as one critic wrote, is like "a black-and-white television continuously tuned to the nightly bad news."

Good Bones (COACH HOUSE, 1992; PUBLISHED IN THE U.S. AS *GOOD BONES AND SIMPLE MURDERS,* DOUBLEDAY, 1994) • This explicitly feminist collection of miniatures and musings consists of monologues, fables, parodies, and postmodern fairy tales, adding a few new stories to those originally published as *Murder in the Dark* (1983). One reviewer described this volume's short works as occupying "that vague, peculiar country between poetry and prose." With her characteristically wry wit, Atwood ruminates on women's novels, women's bodies, bread, poppies, and bats. One reviewer described the stories as born of an outrage at a society that "builds bombs and destroys forests" but praised Atwood for her "sense of humor about it all, and [her] recognition that, despite the pain, life is still mysterious and praiseworthy."

The Robber Bride (DOUBLEDAY, 1993) • Loosely based on "The Robber Bridegroom," a Brothers Grimm fairy tale, *The Robber Bride* focuses on women and their relationships with one another. Tony, Roz, and Charis, friends since college and now middle aged, have all had men stolen by the manipulative Zenia. The three friends believe Zenia to be dead until the book's start, when she walks into a restaurant where they're having lunch. In Zenia, Atwood creates a predatory, diabolical female of the sort that most feminists prefer to ignore, yet Zenia raises important issues of solidarity. According to one impressed reviewer, "*The Robber Bride* is as smart as anything Atwood has written and she is always smart.... [It's her] funniest and most companionable book in years."

Alias Grace (DOUBLEDAY, 1996) • After two years of exhaustive research, Atwood brought to life a story that had haunted her for decades—the tale of Grace Marks, Canada's Lizzie Borden. Grace has no memory of the celebrated murders for which she has been imprisoned until an American doctor coaxes out her story. In the interstices of this work, *Alias Grace* provides an authentic view of the daily lives of lower-class Victorian women down to the most minute domestic detail. Francine Prose, writing in the *New York Times,* criticized Atwood for being excessively pedagogical and thereby distancing the reader from her subject. However, Prose nevertheless praised *Alias Grace* for being both "beautifully written and convincingly imagined."

BIOGRAPHY

MOST OF MARGARET ATWOOD'S NOVELS have been set in or near Toronto for the obvious reason that she lives there. Although born in Ottawa, Atwood moved to Toronto as a child and has lived there most of her adult life. Because of her father's work as a forest entomologist, her family owned a cottage in the remote bush country of northern Quebec, where the Atwoods spent many summers. These months of isolation turned Atwood into an avid reader; she even read her father's scientific journals, and she has kept on reading them, as many of the scientific themes in her work demonstrate. Her familiarity with science has also helped her develop a keen analytical eye.

Atwood began writing poetry and stories in high school and continued her efforts as an undergraduate at the University of Toronto and later as a graduate student at Harvard. She published her first book of poetry, *Double Persephone,* in 1961, the year that she graduated from Toronto. During the late 1960s, Atwood taught at a number of Canadian universities; meanwhile, her poetry began to attract considerable attention. In 1968, she received a Governor General's Award, Canada's top literary honor, for a collection of poems entitled *The Circle Game*. Atwood won a Governor General's Award again, twenty years later, for *The Handmaid's Tale*.

Canada's most eminent writer, Atwood has led a somewhat tumultuous public life. Having been castigated by critics, who accused her of being a contentious misandryst, she has grown cautious of interviews and became a reluctant public figure. One critic has written that Atwood's characters are "so prone to suffering, you wonder how their creator can get up in the morning." Yet Atwood describes her life as mundane and happily domestic. In her typically terse, understated fashion, she boasts about having "managed togetherness" since the 1970s with fellow novelist Graeme Gibson. "We have, altogether, three children...and a cat." Her life, she says, "is pretty close to the leaves-in-the-backyard model I [once] thought would have been out of bounds forever.... I find that doing the laundry with the aid of my washing machine is one of the more relaxing parts of my week." Yet Atwood doesn't wholly lead the life of a recluse. She has remained politically active, particularly in support of persecuted writers and environmental causes. "I should never have been a Brownie in childhood," Atwood says. "I was told to go out and sell those cookies. It was a good cause, but it ruined me for life."

NEXT ON THE READING LIST: Ann Beattie, Anita Brookner, A. S. Byatt, Gail Godwin, Joyce Carol Oates, Carol Shields, John Updike

---

Paul Auster
(b. February 3, 1947)

"[The plots of Auster's mysteries] draw one in like those of any other page-turner. But once the door bangs shut, the clue-sniffing reader finds himself on a swift elevator to a loftier plane. Soon he is deposited, still sniffing, on the heady heights of metafiction, where 'Who done it?' has been transformed into 'Who's asking?'"
—*Stephen Schiff*, New York Times

City of Glass (SUN & MOON, 1985) • Although Auster's first novel exploits the conventions of the mystery genre (and was even nominated for an Edgar Award), critics immediately recognized that there was much more going on. As the book opens, detective novelist Daniel Quinn receives a phone call intended for a real detective (named Paul Auster). Posing as Auster,

Quinn agrees to shadow a recently released mental patient named Stillman, who was put away for keeping his son locked in a room for nine years. (A brilliant linguist, Stillman had hoped that this experiment in isolation would uncover the original language spoken by Adam and Eve.) As the first volume of Auster's New York Trilogy progresses, however, its detective story morphs into an existential search for identity. Although some reviewers noted that Auster loses his way toward the end, Geoffrey O'Brien of the *Village Voice* praised *City of Glass* as a "dance of doppelgängers, [which] suggests that in the apparent dead ends of genre conventions, infinite fresh possibilities can still be found."

Ghosts (SUN & MOON, 1986) • This is the second volume in Auster's New York Trilogy. Its plot line is simple: White hires Blue, a detective, to keep an eye on Black "for as long as necessary." As Blue prepares to go undercover, he warns his fiancée that he won't be able to contact her for the duration of the case—and then the case goes on for years. According to Dennis Drabelle of the *Washington Post,* "All [Blue] can do is stare at Black, eternally writing a book in the rented room across the street, and draw a weekly paycheck…. Blue is trapped…into doing nothing." And like Quinn in *City of Glass,* he's nearly destroyed by his need to learn "the answer." "We get the answer to the questions within the story; we find out who White and Black are and what they have been up to," Rebecca Goldstein wrote in the *New York Times.* "But we don't get the answer to the metamystery. What, in fact, did it all mean? Perhaps nothing at all."

* The Locked Room (SUN & MOON, 1986) • The last, and best, novel of Auster's New York Trilogy is both less abstract and more accessible than its predecessors. The nameless narrator, a biographer, has been summoned by the wife of a childhood friend, the gifted writer Fanshawe, who has disappeared and is presumed dead. Fanshawe has left behind some unpublished manuscripts along with publication instructions for his friend. As time passes, the narrator eases into Fanshawe's life, marrying his wife and becoming the subject of rumors that he and Fanshawe are the same person. Then, suddenly, the narrator receives from Fanshawe a message that plunges him into danger. *New York Times* reviewer Stephen Schiff particularly applauded Auster's shift from third-person to first-person narrative: "Mr. Auster's philosophical asides now sound heartfelt instead of stentorian and his descents into semiological *Angst* feel genuinely anguished and near."

> *"When Auster finally allows himself the luxury of character, what a delicious treat he serves up for the reader!"* (*Carolyn See,* Los Angeles Times)

In the Country of Last Things (VIKING, 1987) • For this novel set in an apocalyptic future, Auster apparently abandoned the mystery genre for science fiction. However, as Katharine Washburn pointed out in the *Review of*

Contemporary Fiction, the story is really about "a hellish present" whose "citizens are no more inhabitants of the future than Swift's Houyhnhnms are native to some unmapped mid-Atlantic island." The heroine of this epistolary novel is Anna Blume, who has journeyed to an urban wilderness that once was New York (or perhaps Boston) in search of her missing journalist brother. In the crumbling city, where neither law nor order obtains, garbage is the principal natural resource and human bodies are burned for fuel. Writing in the *New York Times,* Padgett Powell called the book "daring" and complimented Auster for not subjecting readers to "a didactic, finger-pointing account of how we ruined ourselves."

Moon Palace (VIKING, 1989) • With this novel, Auster began to outgrow his reputation as an eccentric genre writer. *Moon Palace* chronicles the ups and downs experienced by Marco Stanley Fogg, an orphan raised in New York City by his Uncle Victor, an itinerant clarinet player. After Victor's death, Marco, now a destitute young man, lives for a time in a Central Park cave until a rich old man hires him to record that man's life story, important scenes of which take place in the desert Southwest. This moonlike landscape eventually becomes the setting for the final act of Marco's own picaresque saga. "The plot of the novel is so unbelievable, its narrator often has trouble being convinced by it himself," Joyce Reiser Kornblatt wrote in the *New York Times.* "Yet the story is, finally, so good-hearted and hopeful, so verbally exuberant, that [its familiar motifs], its obvious architecture, its shameless borrowings, may be forgivable."

The Music of Chance (VIKING, 1990) • First Jim Nashe's wife takes off, then his estranged father dies. However, his father leaves him some money. So, parking his daughter with some relatives, Jim takes to the road in search of himself. He drives his Saab around the country until, with little money left, he meets a poker player named Jack Pozzi and agrees to back him in a game against two eccentric lottery winners. When Jim and Pozzi lose, they become trapped on the lottery winners' estate, paying off their substantial debt by building a stone wall of Egyptian dimension. "If *The Music of Chance* is not Paul Auster's best novel," *New York Times* reviewer Madison Smartt Bell wrote of this PEN/Faulkner Award nominee, "it is still a very good one."

Leviathan (VIKING, 1992) • "Only a courageous and confident novelist takes the kind of chance Paul Auster takes in *Leviathan,*" Mark Childress wrote in the *Los Angeles Times.* "On the very first page, he unveils the climax of his story. The rest of the book is spent explaining how we got to that shattering beginning." On that first page, writer turned radical activist Benjamin Sachs dies when one of his bombs explodes prematurely. His friend Peter Aaron investigates his death, uncovering the sort of secret identities and previously unknown connections that one expects to find in an Auster novel. However, most reviewers complained that the pace slackens as Auster treats his characters to overlong monologues. "Although he re-deploys his clutch of themes as captivatingly as ever," Julia O'Faolain declared in the *Times Literary Supplement,* "their significance has shrunk."

Mr. Vertigo (VIKING, 1994) • The time is the 1920s. On a remote Kansas farm, a mystical showman named Master Yehudi teaches a nine-year-old orphan, the foulmouthed Walter Rawley, how to fly. Walt the Wonder Boy subsequently barnstorms the country, becoming increasingly famous. Then, on the verge of stardom, Walt enters puberty and loses his power. Although Phil Edwards of *New Statesman & Society* grumbled that "the book's symbolism seems labored and arbitrary," Jonathan Yardley of the *Washington Post* called *Mr. Vertigo* "a winning, accessible book that establishes its author not merely as a gifted literary stylist but also as a completely ingratiating entertainer."

BIOGRAPHY

PAUL AUSTER GREW UP in the suburbs of Newark, New Jersey. His father was a landlord, but his uncle, Allen Mandelbaum, was a skilled translator. As a boy, Auster read many of the books that his uncle kept in storage at his parents' house. Later, Mandelbaum encouraged his nephew's first attempts at writing poetry. In 1965, Auster entered Columbia College and spent the first semester of his junior year in Paris. After receiving a bachelor's degree from Columbia in 1969 and a master's in Renaissance literature the following year, he worked for six months as a merchant seaman aboard the oil tanker *Esso Florence.* Then, in February 1971, he returned to Paris.

To support himself, he worked as a switchboard operator for the Paris bureau of the *New York Times* and also began translating some French literary works. In late 1973, he moved with his college girlfriend, Lydia Davis, to Provence, where they became caretakers of a farmhouse. They returned to New York City in July 1974 and were married three months later. Their son, Daniel, was born in 1977.

During the first five years of his marriage, Auster published two volumes of poetry, *Unearth* (1974) and *Wall Writing* (1976), and translated works by Jean-Paul Sartre and Stéphane Mallarmé, among others. However, he was nearly always suffering from money problems. By 1979, the year of his divorce, his need for cash became so pressing that he nearly gave up writing. As chance would have it, his father died, leaving Auster an inheritance that provided some breathing room. "A bad family event took place—my father died before his time—but, because of that, I was able to continue," Auster has said. "I thank him every day of my life, just for having thought about me and taken care of me in that way."

Auster's career as a writer began to improve markedly when he switched from writing poetry to writing novels. Although rejected by seventeen publishers, his New York Trilogy became a literary sensation, particularly in Europe. In these three books, Auster turned instances of confused and mistaken identity, familiar to mystery fans, into postmodern metaphors for contemporary urban life. Mixing hard-boiled prose and film noir detailing with intellectual allusions and epistemological theorizing, he created a singular style that Dennis Drabelle of the *Washington Post* called "postexistentialist private eye."

In addition to *The Invention of Solitude* (1982), a memoir of his relationship with his father, and *Hand to Mouth* (1997), an account of his early failures, Auster has written the screenplays for two Wayne Wang films, *Smoke* (1995) and *Blue in the Face* (1995). He currently lives with his second wife, Siri Hustvedt, whom he married in 1981, and their daughter, Sophie.

NEXT ON THE READING LIST: Don DeLillo, Stephen Dixon, Mark Helprin, Peter Høeg, Steven Millhauser, Richard Powers, Thomas Pynchon

Beryl Bainbridge
(b. November 21, 1933)

"She has opened a thrift shop in English literature, a home for frayed, faded, out-of-fashion and inexpensive people.... Ms. Bainbridge's people have all missed the train, or boat, the main chance. They are stranded in themselves."
—Anatole Broyard, New York Times

A Weekend with Claud (HUTCHINSON, 1967; DUCKWORTH, 1981; BRAZILLER, 1982) • This is a difficult, too determinedly literary book, in which crisscrossing streams of consciousness cloud (rather than elucidate) the story of a young woman and the men in her life. Bainbridge herself has said of it, "It just goes on and on."

Another Part of the Wood (HUTCHINSON, 1968; DUCKWORTH, 1979; BRAZILLER, 1980) • A mean-spirited man leads a misbegotten group of family and friends on a holiday retreat. The *Washington Post* thought it a "harrowing study of manners in the British middle and working classes, of the effects of dependency on a variety of weak people and of the lies we all tell ourselves to make life bearable."

Harriet Said (DUCKWORTH, 1972; BRAZILLER, 1973) • Actually the first novel Bainbridge wrote as an adult (see *Filthy Lucre*), *Harriet Said* was deemed by one publisher in 1959 "too indecent and unpleasant even for these lax days," and apparently his colleagues agreed. *Harriet Said* is a dark and spare little tale—a horror story, almost—about two girls who, out of boredom, seduce a middle-aged man, with tragic consequences.

* The Dressmaker (DUCKWORTH, 1973; PUBLISHED IN THE U.S. AS *THE SECRET GLASS*, BRAZILLER, 1974) • In this small novel, written in eight weeks, Bainbridge comes into her own. A seventeen-year-old girl living with two maiden aunts in wartime poverty (she sleeps between them for warmth) hopes for escape with an American GI, but his interests are baser.

> *"So intense, pure and unsentimental is the feeling Miss Bainbridge draws from these lives of proud desperation...that a great stillness comes over the reader."* (*Pearl K. Bell*, The New Leader)

The Bottle Factory Outing (DUCKWORTH, 1974; BRAZILLER, 1975) • Workers at a wine-bottling plant (where Bainbridge was herself once employed) attempt to take a holiday together. Bainbridge tells the story so crisply that its humor and eventual horror are inextricably connected. As Guy Davenport wrote in the *New York Times*, "Amenities perfected by the Late Stone Age, such as eating, defecation, conversation, and sex, are all insurmountable problems in this novel."

Sweet William (DUCKWORTH, 1975; BRAZILLER, 1976) • This novel is even lighter than Bainbridge's previous ones, but just as nasty. The eponymous William, a playwright and bounder, seduces Ann, our deluded heroine, in the most charming way. He virtually broadcasts his duplicity (his play is called *The Truth Is a Lie*), but Ann gets sucked into his lair anyway because she enjoys the deceit.

A Quiet Life (DUCKWORTH, 1976; BRAZILLER, 1977) • A mother's death sets off a reminiscence about a "quiet" family of four. Or is it? The between-the-lines picture Bainbridge paints is of spouses living in mutual hatred, an adulterous mother, and a narrator-son who blocks out events too painful to bear. The result is an exquisite psychological study of people who aren't the sort to wind up on a therapist's couch.

Injury Time (DUCKWORTH, 1977; BRAZILLER, 1978) • Middle-aged mother-of-three Binny wants a bit of culture. She forces her lover, Edward, to invite friends to a dinner party, yet the disasters that occur during the planning stages are nothing compared to the event itself, which is ultimately hijacked by a gang of fugitive bank robbers. The *Times Literary Supplement* rated *Injury Time* a "first-class minor novel."

* Young Adolf (DUCKWORTH, 1978; BRAZILLER, 1979) • This truly daring work is built around an odd historical footnote. Learning that Hitler had a half brother who lived for a time in Liverpool, Bainbridge's hometown, and that Adolf may have visited him there as a young man, the author weaves a very dry comedy around an imagined visit. The title character himself comes off not as a monster but rather as a misfit, a boob. It should be noted that one must read the book keeping the history that followed in mind for *Young Adolf*'s irony to have effect.

> *"The idea is disconcerting.... It is the measure of this highly original, immensely skillful novel that such literary risks are successfully taken."* (Neal Ascherson, New York Review of Books)

Winter Garden (DUCKWORTH, 1980; BRAZILLER 1981) • Ashburner, a self-described "ordinary and boring" man, leaves his wife behind and goes off on a Russian holiday with another woman. The story then takes an appropriately Soviet-era turn when the other woman disappears and Ashburner is mistaken for someone else. The *Times Literary Supplement* called it "high comedy."

Watson's Apology (DUCKWORTH, 1984; MCGRAW-HILL, 1985) • Again taking her cue from history, Bainbridge tells a pleasantly dark little tale. Using documents from a legendary Victorian-era murder trial—most notably, letters written by the participants during their courtship—she constructs a story of two tawdry lives and the eventual tragedy that enveloped them.

Mum and Mr. Armitage (DUCKWORTH, 1985; MCGRAW-HILL, 1987) • Bainbridge's first collection of short stories is less elegant and pleasing than her longer fiction. It seems that the dingy lives she tends to examine require more space to come alive. Michiko Kakutani wrote in the *New York Times* that, when tackling the shorter format, Bainbridge's muse settles for "implausible and overly tricked-up plots."

Filthy Lucre (DUCKWORTH, 1986) • This novel, written when Bainbridge was thirteen, shows amazing control of a (consciously) Dickensian plot. "The book bursts with dramatic touches and with the recklessly abundant vocabulary of early adolescence," according to the *Times Literary Supplement.*

An Awfully Big Adventure (DUCKWORTH, 1989; HARPERCOLLINS, 1991) • Bainbridge goes back to her teenage years as an actress in a Liverpool rep company for the plot of this novel. Its sixteen-year-old heroine is world weary, yet her youthful misunderstanding of much of the intrigue going on around her gives this story its charm.

The Birthday Boys (DUCKWORTH, 1991; CARROLL & GRAF, 1994) • The real-life occasion for Bainbridge's fourteenth novel is Robert Falcon Scott's celebrated turn-of-the-century race to the South Pole with Norwegian explorer Roald Amundsen. Once again exploiting historical material to advantage, Bainbridge tells a complex story that's not quite about heroism and not quite about failure (Scott's team lost by a month), but about, as the *New York Times* said, "a microcosmic society of flawed individuals."

Every Man for Himself (CARROLL & GRAF, 1996) • Bainbridge uses a handful of imagined passengers aboard the *Titanic* to study the vanished society of pre–World War I England in this Whitbread Award winner. What turns out to be most absorbing is the way she portrays the disbelief with which the passengers view the impending disaster. According to the *New York Times* reviewer, it's "difficult to imagine a more engrossing account of the famous shipwreck than this one."

BIOGRAPHY

"EVERYTHING ELSE YOU GROW out of, but you never recover from childhood," Beryl Bainbridge has said. She was born in Liverpool and spent her childhood in a lower-middle-class family, variously attracted to and repelled by her failed salesman of a father, who "paid the bills from a little tin box kept on the side table" and gave Bainbridge her love for storytelling and the past. Although she sided with her mother in the many fights her parents had, to the point of attempting to wrestle her father to the ground, she also felt suffocated by her mother's unreflective middle-class striving for respectability.

Bainbridge broke free of all this at fifteen, when she ran off to join a repertory theater company. She worked on and off as an actress for more than twenty years, during which time a failed marriage left Bainbridge with three children and plenty more material for her work. She has since developed a strict method for constructing her novels, and this helps to explain her steady and considerable output. Her lean prose and black-comic approach to life have made her broadly popular in England, although she remains mostly a cult figure in the United States.

NEXT ON THE READING LIST: Pat Barker, Roddy Doyle, Barbara Kingsolver, Penelope Lively, David Lodge, Alison Lurie, Fay Weldon

---

Russell Banks
(b. March 28, 1940)

"[Banks] writes about people a notch or two down: blue-collar workers looking for something better, the young underprivileged trying to make it, migrants and emigrants; in short, all those who seek to acquire the kind of bed in which you can dream the American dream. The search is active and forlorn; and because it means muscling in on what is already taken, it can be deadly."
—*Richard Eder,* Los Angeles Times

Family Life (AVON, 1975; REVISED, SUN & MOON, 1988) • Banks's first novel is a heavy-handed, painfully literary fable, blending satire and fantasy and set in an imaginary kingdom. The subject is the contemporary dysfunctional family, with a king, a queen, and a prince serving as stand-ins for the conventional trinity of father, mother, and son. "The jokes are lame indeed," one critic wrote about this book, whose overriding sexual theme is rather strained in the presentation.

Searching for Survivors (FICTION COLLECTIVE, 1975) • The stories in this well-received collection deal with the confusions of young people wandering through the landscape of modern America during the 1960s and 1970s. In some instances, Banks ironically links their experiences with celebrated or heroic events in American history, such as the explorations of Henry Hudson and the Wright brothers' triumph at Kitty Hawk. Ordinary modern Americans, Banks suggests, are no less adventurous than the great explorers and inventors of yesteryear, even as their efforts to master life end in defeat or disappointment.

The New World (UNIVERSITY OF ILLINOIS, 1978) • In his second short-story collection, Banks again combines fancy with fact, literary invention with historical truth. The stories fall under two headings: The first, "Renunciation," features tales that are more or less conventional—such as "The Conversion," a coming-of-age story marked by Banks's penetrating sympathy for ordinary people. The second grouping, "Transformation," relates the imaginary adventures of such real-life figures as Simón Bolívar. Critics noted the influence of Gabriel García Márquez and Jorge Luis Borges but pointed out that Banks lacked their imagination and precision.

Hamilton Stark (HOUGHTON MIFFLIN, 1978) • The first of Banks's works to attract wide attention, this kaleidoscopic novel deals with the multiplicities of perception. The unnamed narrator is writing a novel about his mysterious and many-sided friend Hamilton Stark. Is Stark a hero, as the narrator maintains, or is he "self-centered, immature, violent, cruel, and possibly insane"? This latter judgment is put forward by Stark's daughter, who's also writing a novel about him. Parodying a formal literary work, Banks's book—at times "hilarious," said the *New York Times*—features an introduction, footnotes, and philosophical digressions. Some of the devices work better than others, yet together they capture the many contradictions of the eponymous hero, though he never actually appears in the book.

The Book of Jamaica (HOUGHTON MIFFLIN, 1980) • More straightforwardly realistic than Banks's earlier fiction, this novel is set in contemporary Jamaica, an island overwhelmed by rapid change. Its unnamed narrator, a vacationing thirty-five-year-old white college teacher, becomes obsessed with the plight of members of a religious sect called the Maroons. Befriended by a Maroon, the narrator receives an education in the long history of preyed-on local blacks dating back to the era of slavery. "What makes Banks so good," wrote the *Chicago Sun-Times,* "is that he doesn't exploit his readers."

* Trailerpark (HOUGHTON MIFFLIN, 1981) • These interrelated stories established Banks as an acutely fine and sympathetic chronicler of poor and uneducated Americans, the "trailer trash" often absent from contemporary fiction. Banks's small but diverse cast of outsiders and losers all inhabit the same trailer park. Each story focuses on a different member of this ad-hoc community and the mistreatment he or she receives at the hands of the others.

> *"They are bleak stories set in a bleak place, yet there is a wicked comic edge to them. Banks has a terrific eye, mordant yet affectionate for the bric-a-brac and the pathos of the American dream." (Jonathan Yardley,* Washington Post)

The Relation of My Imprisonment (SUN & MOON, 1983) • This experimental novel "came as a gift," Banks has said. "The voice appeared in my ears and almost dictated it." *Relation* is the term seventeenth-century Puritans gave to highly detailed and personal confessions written by clerics imprisoned for violating religious orthodoxy. Often the account included a vivid description of the author's sinful act. Banks uses this form—"a strong and radical departure," according to the *Boston Review*—to create a parable about a coffin builder jailed after his vocation is deemed heretical. Writing from his cell, the carpenter tells the story of his transgression in language that embraces remorse, lust, and a kind of visionary fantasy.

* Continental Drift (HARPER & ROW, 1985) • An epic tale of have-nots adrift in the 1980s, this novel made Banks famous. Bob Dubois, a furnace repairman in a failing New Hampshire town, travels with his wife to Florida, to stake his claim on the frontier of "Disney World and land deals and fast-moving high-interest bank loans." Getting nowhere, with his wife pregnant, he falls in with a dangerous crowd of misfits and predators, all of them betting on a big payday. Banks contrasts—and then connects—Bob's story with the parallel tale of a young Haitian woman's determined efforts to reach America. Critics hailed the power and sympathy of Banks's narrative and his feel for the suffering at the heart of so many American lives.

> "Continental Drift *is the most convincing portrait I know of contemporary America: its greed, its uprootedness, its indifference to the past.... It show how ordinary, decent men can find themselves enmeshed in events of unspeakable enormity, and be destroyed by them." (James Atlas,* Atlantic Monthly)

Success Stories (HARPER & ROW, 1986) • Many of the twelve stories in this collection—set in economically depressed small New England towns—reveal the dashed hopes and growing disillusionment of the working-class characters Banks understands so well. There's a strong autobiographical element in five of these stories, linked episodes in the life of Earl Painter, who pursues, without much direction, a vision of ordinary middle-class "success." John Domini, writing in the *Boston Review,* thought *Success Stories* was "an idiosyncratic triumph," but Fred Pfeil wrote in *The Nation* that the book has merely "the precise force of a steady, measured outrage."

* Affliction (HARPER & ROW, 1989) • This bleak novel explores the author's most familiar theme: the rage, hopelessness, and despair that have overtaken a blue-collar America left behind by an increasingly impersonal, technological society. Banks focuses on the misfortunes of a single family doomed by the closing of a local mill in a dying town. The story, narrated by Rolfe Whitehouse, describes the final two weeks in the life of Rolfe's brother Wade, a hard drinker and holder of odd jobs whose chief vocation in life is trying to cope with all that has gone sour.

> *"The reader is made to care for an unlikable man and to believe that others have loved him. Banks's dour vision is realized intensely and impressively in this novel, and it should strengthen the reputation he earned with* Continental Drift.*" (Robert Towers,* New York Review of Books)

The Sweet Hereafter (HARPERCOLLINS, 1991) • Based on an actual incident, this novel dramatizes the ways in which a small town is shaken when a school bus skids off a road in winter, killing fourteen children. The story is told by four narrators, who relate their own experiences and those of their neighbors, providing a group portrait of a community stricken by calamity. "I wanted to write a novel in which the community was the hero, rather than a single individual," Banks said of this work, called "much more than the sum of its excellent parts" by Richard Eder in the *Los Angeles Times.*

Rule of the Bone (HARPERCOLLINS, 1995) • Chappie Dorset, the wised-up yet innocent fourteen-year-old who narrates this picaresque, is a literary descendant of Huckleberry Finn. A pot-smoking mall rat with a nose ring, a Mohawk, and a taste for shoplifting and vandalism, Chappie flees from an abusive parent and embarks on a series of misadventures that involve him with a dubious cast of raffish characters. Critics admired the ingenuity Banks brought to this 1990s version of Twain's American classic, praised the cadences of Chappie's first-person voice, and found Banks's portraits of lost Americans as accurate as ever.

BIOGRAPHY

LIKE SO MANY OF HIS CHARACTERS, Russell Banks grew up in New Hampshire in a working-class family that fell on hard times. The eldest of four children, he retains vivid memories of his family's hardships, including his parents' divorce and their periods of near-poverty. In 1958, he enrolled at

Colgate but left after two months, feeling misplaced as "a poor kid" among "the sons of the captains of American industry." He ended up in a Florida trailer park, working as he could and writing his first fiction. After traveling in Mexico and Jamaica, he received a degree in English from the University of North Carolina. He teaches today at Princeton and has been married four times.

Banks began publishing regularly during the 1970s, writing novels and stories that blended fantasy with realistic detail. Though his early work gained some attention, he found his metier with *Trailerpark,* published in 1981. Thereafter, his reputation grew as a troubadour of the lives of forgotten Americans—the drifters, the working poor, the marginalized. He achieved another breakthrough in 1985 with *Continental Drift,* a novel that captured better than any other the dislocations occurring beneath the surface of the economic boom of the 1980s.

Banks has received a number of honors, including an award from the American Academy of Arts and Letters and a Guggenheim Fellowship, but he still sees himself, he has said, as an outsider. There's also an element of protest in much of his work, as befits one who was involved in the civil rights movement of the 1960s and in anti–Vietnam War protests. "I'm sensitized," Banks has said, "to people who are in pain because of political or social reasons, oppression of one form or another, power; they're at the bottom, the weak side of a power relationship.... I have faith in humanity that if we only open our eyes and see, then we will alter how we treat people."

NEXT ON THE READING LIST: Dorothy Allison, Larry Brown, Harry Crews, Pete Dexter, Richard Ford, Cormac McCarthy

---

Pat Barker
(b. May 8, 1943)

"Barker has an original voice, blunt but tactful, deft but plainspoken, and...her books offer reads no less provocative for being fast. Her feminism and her class concerns—that's to say, her interest in those women who are in the wrong class to be feminist—stay connected down to the core of her vision."
—*Carola Dibbell,* Voice Literary Supplement

Union Street (VIRAGO, 1982; PUTNAM, 1983) • What Edna O'Brien did for the women of rural Ireland—giving them a strong voice in fiction—Pat Barker does here for the working women of industrial England. *Union Street*

encompasses seven interconnected tales—hard, slummy, grim, and strong—woven together using a technique that the author calls "the compound-eye approach." Writing in *The New Statesman,* Eileen Fairweather called the book a "working-class masterpiece."

Blow Your House Down (PUTNAM, 1984) • In her second novel, Barker upped the ante, giving us not merely working women in straitened circumstances but prostitutes. Although Barker also added a serial killer into the mix, she nevertheless kept her focus on the women and their work, making this an original and engaging story. According to Katha Pollitt in the *New York Times,* "*Blow Your House Down* is swift, spare, and utterly absorbing—you'll probably read it, as I did, in one tense sitting."

The Century's Daughter (PUTNAM, 1986) • The eponymous heroine of this book is a working-class woman in her eighties who has lived in the same neighborhood all her life. However, times have changed, and her neighborhood is slated for demolition. When a gay social worker appears to help her move out, she tells him the story of her life—lots of hardship, a son who died in World War II—and we get a history of privation in the twentieth century. "What's made Barker's unromantic vision of working-class life so attractive is her refusal to abandon hope," Robert Christgau wrote in the *Voice Literary Supplement.*

The Man Who Wasn't There (VIRAGO, 1989; BALLANTINE, 1990) • *The Man Who Wasn't There* presented Barker's first venture into the male mind. The space next to "Father" on Colin's birth certificate is blank. Ignoring his mother's lie—that his father was shot down in the war—Colin creates an elaborate mythology to stand in for his real dad. Kathleen Jamie, writing in the *Times Literary Supplement,* observed that "in Colin [Barker] perfectly creates the mind of a 1950s twelve-year-old, a latch-key kid."

* Regeneration (VIKING, 1991; DUTTON, 1992) • This novel began Barker's World War I trilogy, in which the central character is Dr. William H. R. Rivers, the real-life specialist who made *shell shock* a household term. *Regeneration* focuses on the soldiers committed to a psychiatric hospital under Rivers's care, and its story is propelled by the doctor's moral dilemma: If his treatment succeeds, the soldiers will be sent back to the front.

> *"Although* Regeneration *is essentially a moral drama, it is never static, never weighty. Barker is an energetic writer who achieves much of her purpose through swift and easy dialogue and the bold etching of personality."* (*Claudia Roth Pierpont,* The New Yorker)

The Eye in the Door (VIKING, 1993; DUTTON, 1994) • The second novel in Barker's World War I trilogy tells the story of Dr. Rivers and a young homosexual patient whose war experience has left him an amnesiac. As in all three works, the brilliance of her conceit allows her to dwell, à la Oliver Sacks, on the many fascinating manifestations of traumatic stress disorder, all within a rich historical setting. Writing in the *Times Literary Supplement,* Julia O'Faolain remarked that the book had "greater buoyancy" than its predecessor and "an equally impressive ability to anchor major issues in the experiences of her real and invented characters."

The Ghost Road (DUTTON, 1995) • The complex psychological interplay between Dr. Rivers and gay working-class soldier Billy Prior continues here, yet the story widens, taking us back into both men's childhoods to show that they have much in common. The book, which was universally acclaimed, won Britain's Booker Prize. "This subtle novel provides a worthy conclusion to a gripping series, which combines fact and fiction in an unusually satisfying manner," Tony Gould wrote in *New Statesman & Society.*

BIOGRAPHY

PAT BARKER WAS BORN INTO a working-class family in the industrial town of Thornaby-on-Tees in northern England. After her graduation from the London School of Economics and while she was working as a teacher, she tried her hand at writing. The initial output—several unpublished novels of English gentility—seemed empty to her. However, at a writer's conference she happened to meet the English short-story writer Angela Carter, who encouraged her to use her own experiences in her work. Barker then began to contemplate the hard and unattractive lives led by the women of her mother's and grandmother's generations. The resulting novel, *Union Street,* published in 1982, inspired critics to name Barker one of Britain's twenty best young writers.

For her subsequent works, Barker has received uncommonly uniform praise. In 1989, *Union Street* appeared as the feature film *Stanley & Iris,* starring Robert De Niro and Jane Fonda. However, the highlight of Barker's career thus far has clearly been the 1995 Booker Prize that she won for *The Ghost Road.* She currently lives in Durham, just south of Newcastle and not very far from Thornaby, with her husband, zoology professor David Barker, and their two children.

NEXT ON THE READING LIST: Beryl Bainbridge, Louis de Bernières, Richard Ford, Jane Hamilton, Edna O'Brien, Michael Ondaatje

Andrea Barrett

(b. July 17, 1954)

"Ms. Barrett's narrative laboratory is stocked with a handsome array of equipment.... Seen against a larger fictional landscape overpopulated with the sensational and affectless, her work stands out for its sheer intelligence, its painstaking attempt to discern and describe the world's configuration. The overall effect is quietly dazzling, like looking at handmade paper under a microscope."
—*Thomas Mallon,* New York Times

Lucid Stars (DELTA, 1988) • This story of contemporary family life begins on a Vermont mountaintop in 1955, when nineteen-year-old Penny, an astronomy buff, falls for Ben, a ski bum. She quickly finds herself married, pregnant, and miserable because Ben chases other women. After eleven years, they divorce and Ben marries a younger woman, Diane. Later, he divorces Diane and marries an even younger woman. Barrett's underlying metaphor for this extended family is that its various members resemble heavenly bodies moving in space, "elements joining and separating and recombining into changing patterns." According to Margaret Bradham, writing in the *Times Literary Supplement,* "Where many have written novels thick with detail and thin on character development, Barrett, much to her credit, has reversed the emphases."

Secret Harmonies (DELACORTE, 1989) • The unifying theme in Barrett's disappointing second novel is music. The heroine is Reba Dwyer, a rebellious musical talent with a pure singing voice and an ear that can hear the radiator groan in E. She grows up on a run-down chicken farm in Massachusetts, leaves home to attend a conservatory, but returns after her father abandons the family. She marries Luke, her best friend from childhood, but cheats on him because she's selfish and miserable. Most critics agreed with *Kirkus Reviews* that "there's some fine writing here—Barrett really does know about the secret harmonies that hum below the surface of family life—but the novel, while never really flat, doesn't hit many high notes."

The Middle Kingdom (POCKET, 1991) • Like Reba in *Secret Harmonies,* Grace Hoffmeier must overcome her unhappiness in order to gain some control of her life. In 1986, she accompanies her second husband, biologist Walter Hoffmeier, on a trip to China, where she becomes seriously ill. While Walter continues to tour China with his new lover, Grace recalls her childhood, her college years, and her first marriage. Then, recovered, she takes a Chinese lover and decides to stay on in Beijing. "Barrett does not, perhaps, cross new thresholds into the soul of women or the heart of China,"

Katherine A. Powers wrote in the *Washington Post,* "but her novel is engaging. She writes with felicity, intelligence, and humor."

The Forms of Water (POCKET, 1993) • Sensing that he's near death, Brendan Auberon, a crippled former monk, persuades his down-and-out nephew, Henry, to break him out of his nursing home and drive him to land that he owns near a Massachusetts reservoir. Henry's sister, Wiloma, a New Age convert, chases after them so that she can help Brendan find the Light before the end. Not far behind are Wiloma's and Henry's worried children. En route to Massachusetts, these characters recount the events that led to the demise of their appealingly wretched family. "The sense of family dislocation is well caught, Brendan is believable and touching, and there are original characterizations of other lonely, unloved, and luckless people who deserve better than they get," Molly Giles wrote in the *San Jose Mercury News.* "Despite all this, *The Forms of Water* bogs down in the middle and never develops the strong ideas suggested at the start. The plot collapses into a farce, with one family member after another surfacing at the reservoir."

✳ Ship Fever and Other Stories (NORTON, 1996) • Barrett's National Book Award winner contains stories of science and passion in various combinations, especially women passionate about science and scientists passionate about one another. In the title novella, a Canadian doctor works obsessively to cure Irish immigrants during an 1847 typhus epidemic. In "The Littoral Zone," a botanist and a zoologist fall in love. In particular, Barrett focuses on the often humorous naiveté of otherwise great nineteenth-century science, such as Carl Linnaeus's contention that swallows hibernate under water. "Barrett's prose tends to be colorless, even melancholy," David Holmstrom wrote in the *Christian Science Monitor.* "But the brilliance of the monochrome shades is dazzling."

> *"Barrett builds her fictions like stones thrown in prose ponds: Science is the stone, while human dramas, personal and social, are the concentric rings that radiate beautifully outward."* (*Nomi Eve,* Newsday)

BIOGRAPHY

ANDREA BARRETT GREW UP ON CAPE COD, where she has said that she developed a love for the ocean and became fascinated by the natural world. As an undergraduate at Union College in Schenectady, New York, she studied biology and even applied to graduate schools so that she could make a career for herself in the field. However, things didn't work out for Barrett as she had intended.

"Not until a very brief stay in a graduate zoology program did I understand that I wasn't cut out to be a scientist," Barrett has written. "What I'd really wanted to be was a version of Darwin or Wallace; I wanted to see and describe and appreciate and name, not to analyze. Slowly I learned that those were the traits of a naturalist—a nineteenth-century profession. After I abandoned science, a brief but intense bout of studying history weaned me from the academic life for good; once more it was the stories of the field that captured me. I'm a slow learner, but at that point I finally turned to writing fiction."

Barrett's first four novels received a good deal of praise, yet none of it compared with the accolades she won for *Ship Fever*—along with a National Book Award. As she told *USA Today*, Barrett celebrated that prize by taking a four-day hike in the Adirondacks with her husband, a biologist. She currently lives in Rochester, New York.

NEXT ON THE READING LIST: T. Coraghessan Boyle, A. S. Byatt, Barbara Kingsolver, Mona Simpson

---

Ann Beattie
(b. September 8, 1947)

"Miss Beattie's power and influence...arise from her seemingly resistless immersion in the stoic bewilderment of a generation without a cause.... In the now swollen chorus of minimalist fiction, it was she who first found the tone for the post-Vietnam, post-engagé mood, much as Hemingway found the tone for his own generation's disenchantment."
—*John Updike,* The New Yorker

* Chilly Scenes of Winter (DOUBLEDAY, 1976) • Most of the characters in Ann Beattie's first novel, written just after the 1960s had flamed out, are waiting for their lives to happen—none more so than Charles, Beattie's lonesome protagonist, who can't get his former girlfriend Laura out of his mind. Laura has reconciled with her nondescript husband (they had been separated), yet Charles can't give up the idea of winning her back. Typical of the novel's droll despondency, Beattie sets her story during the 1974 Christmas season, apparently to accentuate the unhappiness of her characters.

> "Chilly Scenes of Winter *is...the funniest novel of unhappy yearning that one could imagine. Funnier. It is continually, inventively, and perceptively humorous, both in what it reports and in the quietly elegant shape of its reporting."*
> (*J. D. O'Hara,* New York Times)

Distortions (DOUBLEDAY, 1976) • In comparing this collection of Beattie's early *New Yorker* pieces to *Chilly Scenes of Winter,* which was published simultaneously, many reviewers called it disappointing. "The stylistic excellence of her writing is undeniable, but Beattie is unable to make us feel any empathy for most of the characters," Kristin Hunter wrote in the *Washington Post*. According to Susan Horowitz in the *Saturday Review*, "The characters...are fleshed out (or, rather, painted by number) in a collection of disjointed details, so that, although they are sometimes intriguingly eccentric, they lack an emotional core. Childhood histories, kinship patterns, recipes, and tastes in pop music do not necessarily add up to anyone we care about or remember."

Secrets and Surprises (RANDOM HOUSE, 1978) • Each of these stories features a couple—sometimes married, sometimes not—in a relationship that generally doesn't work. As Terence Winch pointed out in the *Washington Post*, all the characters have "survived the social turbulence of the '60s only to find themselves confused by the emotional turbulence of the '70s." Most reviewers, citing Beattie's highly developed observational skills, noted that the stories worked better as social history than they did as fiction. However, a few critics found something more: "Some of these stories are disappointing," Winch wrote, "but the five or six solid successes are works of vivid honesty and insight that confirm Beattie's reputation as one of our best young writers."

Falling in Place (RANDOM HOUSE, 1980) • Like her other work, Beattie's second novel uses an accumulation of detail to locate its mood and develop its characters. *Falling in Place* also elaborates on Beattie's familiar themes of anger and self-pity. "Yet," Richard Locke declared in the *New York Times*, "nothing Ann Beattie has written quite prepares us for her new novel. It's like going from gray television to full-color movies." For the first time, Beattie employs multiple narratives—in fact, she presents no fewer than five points of view. Among the central characters in the novel are forty-year-old advertising executive John Knapp, whose suburban family is disintegrating; his twenty-five-year-old mistress, Nina; her former lover, Peter; and Peter's current girlfriend, Cynthia, who is John's daughter's summer school teacher. "The details are small," Margaret Atwood remarked in the *Washington Post*, "but the picture of our lives and times built up from them is devastating."

The Burning House (RANDOM HOUSE, 1982) • In these stories, Beattie presents another listless batch of brooding baby boomers, their lives steeped in emotional loss and regret. While most reviewers saw simply more of the same from Beattie, *New York Times* critic Anatole Broyard noted some significant differences: "Miss Beattie seems to be changing—in my opinion, for the better. Most of her characters now have recognizable desires, color in their cheeks, energy in their movements.... There's pathos in these stories, in the characters themselves, rather than in the sadness of what's missing in their makeup."

Love Always (RANDOM HOUSE, 1985) • Fourteen-year-old Nicole, star of the soap opera *Passionate Intensity,* visits her sultry aunt Lucy in Vermont, where Lucy works as a lonely-hearts columnist for an urbanely countercultural magazine called *Country Daze.* In addition to these stars, Beattie's third novel features more than a dozen principal players who fail at love both sexual and familial. Their stories, however, read more like Keystone Kops scripts than a novel. Pointing out that Beattie should never have attempted satire, most reviewers advised her not to try again. "*Love Always* is relentlessly jokey, without being funny," Frank Rich complained in *The New Republic.* "Beattie is beginning to sound like a broken record. And the needle is stuck in a narrow groove that emits only the muffled sounds of the wealthy, Waspy, childless, and most narcissistic baby boomers."

Where You'll Find Me (SIMON & SCHUSTER, 1986) • Although not autobiographical, Ann Beattie's characters have always shared her own personal time frame. When she was in her twenties, so were they. When she was part of the Me Generation, so were they. And now that, coincident with the publication of this collection, she's experiencing the onset of middle age, so are they. Yet the hollowness of their lives doesn't seem to change: In the widely praised "Janus," for example, a real estate agent becomes obsessed with a beautiful bowl given to her by a former lover. Yet the bowl, like her life, is always empty. On the other hand, Beattie's writing has grown more personal and more poetic with time. "In her earlier bleakness," Mark Silk wrote in the *Boston Review,* "Beattie had a way of twisting a knife in the guts of her stories; a grim finality was almost always achieved. But putting across a happier or more open-ended message is trickier business, and she still seems to be struggling to figure out how to manage it."

* Picturing Will (RANDOM HOUSE, 1989) • Acknowledging that it contained more of her own personal view of the world than any of her previous works, Beattie called *Picturing Will* "the single hardest thing I've ever worked on." Her fourth novel tells the story of five-year-old Will, whose father, Wayne, deserted him when he was just an infant. Will's mother, Jody, becomes a wedding photographer but aspires to something more—a career as an art photographer in New York City. She eventually gets her wish with the help of her lover, Mel, and his connections. The second half of the novel describes Will's disturbing journey to visit Wayne in Florida.

> *"No plot summary can do justice to the disquieting reverberations that* Picturing Will *sets going in the reader's mind. The adjective* haunting—*though normally used by reviewers to describe melodramatic fiction that is anything but—comes to mind as the only one that applies to Ann Beattie's work at its best." (Gene Lyons,* Vogue)

What Was Mine (RANDOM HOUSE, 1991) • Beattie's fifth collection of short stories has left the 1960s far behind. Its characters, now well into their forties, have good jobs and second homes. Yet, as Ron Hansen remarked in the *New York Times,* they're "too haunted by their fully reasonable fears and forebodings to do more than hang on or hide out." Continuing her evolution in style, Beattie delves deeper than ever before into her characters, producing stories that Hansen praised as some of her best yet: "Ms. Beattie has forsaken irony for honest introspection, and her famous detachment has given way to greater sympathy and tenderness."

Another You (KNOPF, 1995) • Initially, *Another You* reads like many other novels of campus adultery. Its protagonist, Marshall Lockard, is an English professor at a small New Hampshire college. His real estate agent wife, Sonja, plays sex games with her boss in houses that they list, and his colleague Jack McCallum has become sexually involved with a student. Marshall himself considers a similar dalliance—yet Beattie isn't really interested in these petty affairs. Instead, what she's up to has more to do with the mysterious, undated letters that end nearly every chapter, in which an unidentified man writes to a woman about the care of his children. Only at the end do we learn how these two narratives are related. Among the mixed reviews that *Another You* received, *Los Angeles Times* critic Alan Cheuse called it "a novel of some distinction," while Martha Duffy wrote in *Time* that it was "enough to make you wince." "*Another You* works its magic slowly," Dan Cryer wrote in *Newsday.* "Patience is required, but the rewards are substantial, even munificent."

My Life, Starring Dara Falcon (KNOPF, 1997) • The needy heroine of this novel, Jean, dropped out of college to marry Bob and move with him to a small New Hampshire town, where she types other people's manuscripts and socializes with her in-laws. One day in 1976, a selfish, mendacious would-be actress named Dara Falcon blows into town and mesmerizes sweet, naive Jean. Realizing that she's unfulfilled (yet—incredibly—not realizing what everyone else knows: that Dara is a predator), Jean leaves her husband and goes back to school. In fact, Jean's naiveté seems to be invincible—hence the irony of the title, a story of one woman's liberation, starring someone else. Most reviewers found Jean unbelievable and Dara even worse—uninteresting. According to Michiko Kakutani in the *New York Times,* "*My Life, Starring Dara Falcon* must surely mark a low point in this gifted writer's career."

BIOGRAPHY

ANN BEATTIE HAS NEVER LIKED being called a spokesperson for her generation, yet critics have found that label difficult to resist. Beattie herself is partly to blame, because she has consistently and skillfully written about people her own age, who dress as she does and listen to the same sort of music. In fact, most of her fiction has chronicled the milieu and angst of the Woodstock Generation as it moved from counterculture to narcissism and later into middle age.

Beattie was born in Washington, D.C., where her father worked as a government bureaucrat. She attended American University, graduating in 1969 with a bachelor's degree in English. Next, she attended graduate school, earning a master's degree from the University of Connecticut in 1970 before dropping out of its Ph.D. program two years later. That year, 1972, she married her first husband, David Gates. (Gates and Beattie were divorced in 1980, and Beattie subsequently married painter Lincoln Perry.)

Beattie has said that she began writing because she felt frustrated at the way literature was being taught in her graduate courses. "I never had a burning ambition to become a writer," she explained. "I started writing because I was bored with graduate school—in some kind of attempt to care about literature again.... [Choosing writing as a career] was just sort of a process of elimination. I don't have tremendous skills in a tremendous number of areas. I never really set out to be a writer. I just sort of backed into it."

While a graduate student at Connecticut, she placed a few stories in minor journals—and received twenty rejections from *The New Yorker* until "A Platonic Relationship" was accepted for publication in 1974. Thereafter, Beattie became a frequent contributor, whose work was often compared with that of fellow *New Yorker* regulars John Cheever and John Updike.

Beattie has explained that she tends to write in brief bursts of energy. She wrote her novel *Falling in Place* in seven weeks, burning out two typewriters in the process. During these bursts, she sometimes writes eighteen hours a day, then allows herself long intervals between books to recuperate. "What I do most is *not* write," she has said.

NEXT ON THE READING LIST: Margaret Atwood, Amy Bloom, Richard Ford, Mary Gaitskill, Ellen Gilchrist, Lorrie Moore, John Updike

Madison Smartt Bell
(b. August 1, 1957)

"Madison Smartt Bell renders the marginal, the underground, the twisted or seedy with quirky attentiveness. His array of lost souls gets onto the page without the least preemptive hint of authorial sympathy, yet he captures the poignant in the freakish."
—Elizabeth Tallent, New York Times

The Washington Square Ensemble (VIKING, 1983) • Set in New York City, Bell's ambitious first novel, like so many of his later works, deals with the underside of contemporary America—a demimonde of junkies, petty criminals, and street hustlers. The protagonist is a drug dealer with the rock-'n'-roll name of Johnny B. Goode. The book's hard-edged depiction of Johnny's dangerous world impressed reviewers, who praised Bell's evocative prose yet also found fault with his plotting and pacing.

Waiting for the End of the World (TICKNOR & FIELDS, 1985) • A hybrid of apocalyptic thriller and nightmare tour of New York's mean streets, this novel veers toward the fanciful in its depiction of contemporary urban terrorism. The evil genius Simon Rohnstock gathers around him a crew of terrorists—Vietnam vets, drug addicts, and ex-1960s rebels—who plot the destruction of New York City with a homemade atomic weapon. The story stretches credulity, but its vision of urban life is compelling, and the psychotic characters emerge with admirable clarity and authenticity.

Straight Cut (TICKNOR & FIELDS, 1986) • The central character of Bell's third novel is Tracy Bateman, a film editor turned drunken wastrel who lives the marginal drifter's existence so typical of Bell's protagonists. He and his estranged wife, Lauren, become trapped in an international drug deal that involves Tracy in hair-raising escapades in Europe and New York. One reviewer suggested that Bell's uncharacteristically lean, clipped, and understated prose might have been patterned after that of Raymond Chandler. However, another remarked, "The voice is so dry and the eye so unremarkable that most of the novel reads like a screenplay—impersonal, objective, and...monotonous."

Zero db and Other Stories (TICKNOR & FIELDS, 1987) • Critics hailed Bell's first collection of stories for its remarkably varied distillation of his nightmare world. The seven highly distinctive stories, most told in utterly different narrative voices, cover a wide range of human experiences and render them with an exactitude of detail that's almost pointillist. "Considered separately, the stories...are astonishing," Anne Bernays wrote in the *New York Times*. "Considered together, they are even more astonishing."

The Year of Silence (TICKNOR & FIELDS, 1987) • This taut novel, among the most carefully structured of Bell's works, centers on a young woman's suicide. Bell begins and ends with this event, then moves backward and forward in time, approaching the story from different angles. The effect is prismatic, as the heroine, Marian, is perceived through the eyes of a vivid cast, who again inhabit the chaotic and violent New York underworld that remains the center of Bell's bleak universe—one becoming rather too familiar, said some critics at the time.

* Soldier's Joy (TICKNOR & FIELDS, 1989) • In his fifth novel, Bell shifts locale to his native region, the South, and gives his story a rural setting along with some biblical overtones. Thomas Laidlaw, wounded in Vietnam, returns to the hill country of Tennessee to find his father dead and the family homestead in ruins. Seeking spiritual recovery by playing the banjo, he soon enters a social world circumscribed by his friendship with two black men and the menacing overtures of the local Klansmen.

> *"What Mr. Bell does far better than almost all contemporary writers is to capture nuances.... His genius—and it's a word one must use—is for old-fashioned rendering of lush but significant details that here create a rich religious and political symbolism infused with a compelling, rewarding sense of place."* (*David Bradley*, New York Times)

Barking Man and Other Stories (TICKNOR & FIELDS, 1990) • Bell's second short-fiction collection includes ten stories linked by the theme of survival in a hard, unsparing world. As in his first collection, the author exhibits an unusual variety and daring in his choice of topics and his range of narrative styles. The hero of "Holding Together" is a white mouse who has memorized the entire *I Ching*. In another story, a tobacco farmer who has endured Job-like suffering turns his home into a shelter for juvenile delinquents. Critics praised the conviction with which Bell evoked these disparate worlds.

Doctor Sleep (HARCOURT BRACE JOVANOVICH, 1991) • Set in London, Bell's sixth novel—another thriller—features the recovered heroin addict Adrian Strother, who's also a hypnotherapist. His freakish clientele include an agoraphobe who exhibits multiple personalities and a drug addict who wants to kick his habit. Meanwhile, Adrian is being followed by a pair of shadowy punks. Some reviewers suggested that the novel's mix of reality and fantasy felt forced in places, though Bell's prose "generally moves at an effective narrative clip," Elizabeth Tallent wrote in the *New York Times*.

Save Me, Joe Louis (HARCOURT BRACE, 1993) • In this dark but engrossing buddy story, a pair of grifters—Charlie, an ex-con, and Macrae, an AWOL marine—stumble along the margins of society, exerting themselves just enough to pay for another day's drink and dope. When they finally become enmeshed in more serious wrongdoing, Charlie and Mac head for the road, although they both know there's no real escape. This book, clear eyed yet sympathetic, "is a remarkable read," opined Harry Crews in the *New York Times*. "I encourage people everywhere to go out and put their money down and take this book home."

* All Souls' Rising (PANTHEON, 1995) • In this monumental historical epic, nominated for a National Book Award, Bell re-creates an actual eighteenth-century Haitian slave rebellion. The large cast of characters, black and white, make up a virtual catalog of Haitian society and its competing factions. The protagonist, French doctor Antoine Hebert, serves as the reader's guide through the carnage of the uprising, during which thousands were murdered and 180 sugar plantations burned. Bell's enormous descriptive powers make the action graphically vivid, even as he places the story accurately within its historical context and shows its relevance to our own period.

> *"Bell's style can be as evocative and eerie as a cathedral full of candles, or as luminous as a rainbow. And he has a way with a Gothic image that would make Faulkner (or Poe) proud."* (*Diane Roberts,* Atlanta Journal and Constitution)

Ten Indians (PANTHEON, 1996) • Mike Devlin, a forty-six-year-old child psychologist, has all the external paraphernalia of middle-class success: a career, a family, a house. But what he doesn't have is purpose, so he opens a tae kwon do school for young gang members in inner-city Baltimore. Bell's fast-paced novel includes both a traditional narrative of Mike's transformation and the first-person accounts of "witnesses"—the kids themselves—written in the singsong patois of the 'hood. The *Philadelphia Inquirer* called the book "an altogether absorbing tale of a man trying to bring about small, human changes," but Charles Johnson, writing in the *New York Times,* thought *Ten Indians* "does a disservice to both inner-city black youth and the world of the martial arts."

BIOGRAPHY

MADISON SMARTT BELL WAS BORN and raised in Nashville, Tennessee. His father was a lawyer and his mother a farmer. Bell attended Princeton, where he won an array of writing prizes and graduated summa cum laude. He also earned an M.A. in the writing program at Hollins College.

Bell then moved to New York City, where he supported himself in a succession of jobs, some with publishing houses, until he established himself as a writer during the early 1980s. His novels, with their searing portrayal of New York City's lower depths, gained him attention immediately, in part because his character-rich stories and lushly detailed prose set his work apart from the muted "minimalist" writing then in vogue. Bell, in fact, has been a vocal critic of such writing, which he considers self-absorbed. He instead advocates fiction that's attentive to social, political, and sociological themes, especially the very American subject of violence.

Bell has spread this message farther by teaching fiction workshops, a vocation in which he takes considerable pride. "I have come to believe," he has said, "that the apprentice writers who succeed are the most stubborn, the most intransigent, the ones who won't believe what anybody else tells them unless they discover it on their own."

The prolific Bell is much admired by his fellow novelists. Critics, however, while respectful, have been more reserved, pointing out his work's structural weaknesses, trendy subjects, and occasional lapses in tone. Even so, Bell remains one of his generation's more accomplished novelists.

NEXT ON THE READING LIST: Martin Amis, T. Coraghessan Boyle, Robert Olen Butler, Harry Crews, Tim O'Brien, Robert Stone

Amy Bloom

(b. June 18, 1953)

"Although her stories may be full of tragic implications, Ms. Bloom's characters possess extraordinary dignity that lifts them beyond pity. Those whom circumstances might otherwise define as victims or villains reveal heroic potential in the author's skillful, empathic hands."
—*Barbara Kaplan Lane,* New York Times

* Come to Me (HARPERCOLLINS, 1993) • Many of the twelve stories in Bloom's debut collection, a finalist for a National Book Award, read like Freudian case studies (the good ones). Getting better as the volume goes along, they focus on the often troubled emotional states of characters, ranging from a schizophrenic in "Silver Water" to an adulterous pianist in "The Sight of You" to a newly widowed mother in "Sleepwalking." Although Bloom is herself a practicing psychotherapist, she has repeatedly insisted that none of her characters resembles any of her patients.

> "Come to Me *is so rich, moving, and gracefully written, it's hard to believe [Bloom] hasn't been doing this all her life."* (*Elizabeth Benedict,* Los Angeles Times)

Love Invents Us (RANDOM HOUSE, 1997) • Bloom's first novel begins with a nearly verbatim reprinting of the story "Light Breaks Where No Sun Shines" from *Come to Me.* The heroine is Elizabeth Taube, a chubby Long Island girl who privately models sables (in her underwear) for an elderly furrier. Either ignored or teased by her classmates, Elizabeth just wants to be loved, and *Love Invents Us* is the tale of her troubled and unconventional romantic life, from the back room of Furs by Klein to middle-aged single motherhood. Although reviewers uniformly agreed that Bloom's writing remained excellent and that Elizabeth was "splendidly realized," according to Dan Cryer in *Newsday,* they disagreed about how well Bloom had made the transition from short story to novel: "*Love Invents Us* is defined by a curiously episodic quality, as though each chapter were a self-contained short story," Cryer wrote. "Yet something is lost in this almost staccato narrative form—a certain thickness, the density of daily life, that would make Bloom's secondary characters fully real."

BIOGRAPHY

AMY BLOOM WAS RAISED on Long Island by her father, a journalist, and her mother, a group therapist and also a writer. As a child, she spent much of her time in the local library, reading nineteenth-century English novels. Among her favorites were *The Scarlet Pimpernel* and *A Tale of Two Cities.* "I spent a lot of time as a misfit," she has said. "I remember in the playground, while in fourth grade, someone said, 'You might have friends if you didn't sound like you swallowed a dictionary.'" Later, however, her oddness became acceptable. "Sometime in mid-adolescence, it became very cool to be very odd," Bloom remembered. "The world became a much bigger and more manageable place. My weirdness was now highly appreciated."

She attended college at Wesleyan, where she double-majored in theater and government, graduating in 1975. Two years later, she married Donald Moon, a professor of government at Wesleyan. In 1978, she received a master's degree in social work from Smith, and since 1981 she has practiced psychotherapy in Middletown, Connecticut, where Wesleyan is located. "I became a therapist because I am not judgmental," Bloom told one interviewer. "People have always liked to tell me their stories. Even when I was seventeen, taking the Long Island Rail Road to a summer job, the conductor sat down to tell me his life story."

She began writing about 1990, and she currently divides her time between writing and therapy. According to Bloom, "[There were] two things I learned at home. One was that there was no reason not to be your own boss, and two was if you wrote, you got paid for it. It never occurred to me that I would write and put it in my desk drawer. Even if it was crap, you still sent it out and hoped that someone would publish it."

She currently lives in Durham, Connecticut, with her husband and two daughters. "My editor calls me an optimist with a twisted mind," Bloom admitted. "I am fascinated by people's struggle to be loved, to make compromises and to live with their compromises."

NEXT ON THE READING LIST: Margaret Atwood, Ann Beattie, Ellen Gilchrist, Alice Hoffman, David Leavitt, Melanie Rae Thon, John Updike

---

T. Coraghessan Boyle
(b. December 2, 1948)

"It is hard to think of writers to compare him with. In his sheer energy and mercilessness, his exuberantly jaundiced view, he resembles perhaps a middlebrow Donald Barthelme, or Don DeLillo crossed with Dr. Seuss, or Flannery O'Connor with a television and no church."
—*Lorrie Moore,* New York Times

Descent of Man (ATLANTIC MONTHLY, 1979) • The best that the Iowa Writers' Workshop had to offer was exhibited in Boyle's debut, short stories packed with mad verbal and situational gusto. In "Dada" (Idi Amin as a work of art at a Dadaist art festival), "The Big Garage" (taking a car in for repairs becomes a pointedly Kafkaesque experience), and "We Are Norsemen" (narrated by a bard who accompanies pillagers as "they sack the Irish coast…and pitch the ancient priceless Irish manuscripts into the sea. Then I sing about it"), Boyle attempted to pitch previous generations of short-story masters—the Clean, Well-Lighted Place folks—into the sea of history.

* Water Music (ATLANTIC MONTHLY, 1981) • Boyle's first novel, based loosely on eighteenth-century explorer Mungo Park's search for the source of the Niger River, runs amok in the historical genre. Some reviewers were put off by the book's self-aware anachronisms and antic wordplay, but others expressed their awe, as if before a symphony. It's one of the most gorgeous novels this reviewer has ever read.

> "Water Music *is a historical novel unlike any other, for the language is simultaneously that of its period (circa 1800) and that of street-wise America (circa 1980).… After all this meticulous research cum high jinks, Boyle surprisingly allows us to care about Mungo Park's end, as the seductive music of the Niger rushes him toward death. An astonishing performance.*" (George Kearns, Hudson Review)

Budding Prospects: A Pastoral (VIKING, 1984) • The daydream of every 1970s dude—quitting the rat race to grow a secluded patch of marijuana—is the theme of Boyle's second novel. The irony is that, through this illegal and childish venture, the loser-hero becomes businesslike, diligent, and thoughtful—in short, an adult. *Budding Prospects* was less well received than *Water Music* because it's less ferociously inventive and lacks the soul that Boyle's first novel hid under its many layers.

Greasy Lake and Other Stories (VIKING, 1985) • Once again, Boyle kicks in with a clutch of stories featuring almost psychotically imaginative settings: Eisenhower falls in love with Khrushchev's wife; a ballplayer is trapped in a baseball game that never ends; a candidate wins the presidency promising to replace the moon with a new uncratered version. In the *Detroit News*, Peter Ross pointed out that Boyle was now being welcomed into "the select cadre of great American humorists."

* World's End (VIKING, 1987) • The novel that brought Boyle respectability is a multigenerational tale set in New York's Hudson Valley. It's a morality play about power, real estate, and class that shifts back and forth between the seventeenth century, when the wealthy Van Wart clan obtains its land from the Indians, and the late twentieth century, when a bizarre motorcycle accident forces a sort of moral reckoning. Highbrow critics gave Boyle their seal of approval for finally wedding his literary frat-boy style to a serious theme, but some long-term admirers felt that Boyle's best side—his manic creativity—was stifled in the process.

> *"For all the sweep and clatter of the tale, for all the Grand Guignol exuberance which undercuts its doctrinal base, a grave compassionate calm resides in the telling of* World's End, *the sense of a creator finally at home in his work."*
> (*John Clute,* Times Literary Supplement)

If the River Was Whiskey (VIKING, 1990) • Boyle's third collection of stories, especially coming after a lauded novel, seemed a letdown to many reviewers, reprising Boyle's can-you-top-this inventiveness without as much soul. The title story, however, is happily the reverse: Heartfully told with very little mannerism, "If the River Was Whiskey" is the portrait of a boy who desperately fans a few sparks of fatherly attention into something he can call love.

East Is East (VIKING, 1991) • A Japanese sailor jumps ship off the coast of Georgia and swims ashore, only to find himself trapped in that oddest of self-contained worlds: the writer's colony. Boyle gives a very knowing and often hilarious account of life in this place (individual cottages are reverently named after artists who have committed suicide), though he's far less at home with his Japanese protagonist. Critics thought the story funny and refreshingly straightforward, but Hiro (get it?) Tanaka turns out to be a hollow and awkwardly conceived vehicle for a novel.

The Road to Wellville (VIKING, 1993) • What better way to parody the current health mania than by skewering an earlier one? John Harvey Kellogg, the man who brought cornflakes into the world, was a bit of a flake himself, and his Battle Creek Sanitarium for turn-of-the-century health faddists (five enemas a day) provides the perfect setting for this surprisingly light, fat-free romp.

Without a Hero (VIKING, 1994) • "Filthy with Things" should have been the title story of this collection because it sums up the genius of Boyle's satirical vision. A couple hires a "professional organizer," straight out of infomercial hell, to cure them of their addiction to "things." The man suffers from terrible withdrawal, for without his collections of bookends and antique rocking chairs "there's nothing there…. Nothing at all." Writing in the *New York Times*, Lorrie Moore called these stories "artifacts of psychic aberrance" that fill the reader with "the giddy nausea of our cultural and theological confusions."

The Tortilla Curtain (VIKING, 1995) • A sort of *Bonfire of the Vanities* transplanted to Los Angeles, *The Tortilla Curtain* brings about a literal (automotive) collision between white suburban culture and that of illegal Latino immigrants. The two couples involved watch as their lives intertwine and their fates vault toward cataclysm in this fairly straight, gimlet-eyed telling. The book's flaw, however, according to Scott Spencer in the *New York Times*, is that Boyle fails to make sense of the very real dilemma of money and class that he has set up: "Where the socially engaged novel once offered critique, Mr. Boyle provides contempt."

Riven Rock (VIKING, 1998) • Once again drawing his characters from history, Boyle gives us Stanley McCormick, wealthy son of the reaper king, and Katherine Dexter McCormick, his equally wealthy suffragette wife. The novel's title refers to the Santa Barbara estate in which Stanley has spent most of his adult life secluded and mad. He's been driven to that state by a sexual confusion that has left him terribly mixed up: He thinks that his only sexual partner, a Parisian whore, was a virgin and that his wife, the true virgin, is actually a whore. "This is Boyle in shivery pessimistic mode, more kin to the somber introspection of his *World's End* and *The Tortilla Curtain* than to the deliciously over-the-top satire of *The Road to Wellville* and *East Is East*," Dan Cryer observed in *Newsday*.

BIOGRAPHY

T. CORAGHESSAN BOYLE REPRESENTS A BREAK from American writers of the past in two distinct ways: He's the product of a creative writing program, a feature of the literary landscape only since the 1970s, and he's the owner of a carefully crafted *nuevo* literary image. He was born Thomas John Boyle (he added the Coraghessan when he was seventeen) in Peekskill, New York, a town whose landscape he richly conveys in *World's End*. As a youth, Boyle did a lot of drug consuming and hanging out, working hard only to avoid serving in Vietnam. He says that he had no particular ambition in life until one of his short stories was published in *North American Review*. On the strength of this clipping, he was accepted into the Iowa Writers' Workshop, where he found his ambition.

In Iowa, Boyle also found a persona: the protopunk writer, the guy who veered at the last minute from the heroin needle into the literary pantheon. To keep up appearances, he began sporting a goatee, spiked hair, and primary-color clothing, but these appurtenances belie the reality of a man who has been married to the same woman since 1974 and is a father of three and a UCLA professor.

In any case, the image fits the fiction: eternally childlike, reality drunk, playful, delighting in both absurdity and moral comeuppance (bad guys—usually—get their due). In Boyle, moreover, we have the marriage of literary seriousness to American entrepreneurship. As he once told an interviewer, speaking of his publishers, "I'm going to make them forget the name of Stephen King forever, I'm going to sell so many copies. I would like to be a guy like Vonnegut for my generation, who could wake up people a little bit and show them that literature is fun and entertaining, and also serious at the same time."

NEXT ON THE READING LIST: Paul Auster, Madison Smartt Bell, Louis de Bernières, Don DeLillo, E. L. Doctorow, Mark Helprin, Thomas Pynchon

Anita Brookner
(b. July 16, 1928)

"[Brookner] has written about genteel Englishmen or women who have lived circumscribed lives, seeking but never finding the kind of romantic love glorified in literature. They are often dutiful sons or daughters to self-absorbed mothers who do not deserve such loyalty.... We find them at a moment when they hope to change their lives, when they are on the verge of doing something outrageous, but they never do. Instead, they retreat, resigned and regretful."
—*Linda Simon*, New York Times

A Start in Life (JONATHAN CAPE, 1981; PUBLISHED IN THE U.S. AS *THE DEBUT*, LINDEN, 1981) • In its review of this first novel, the *Los Angeles Times* noted that Brookner, "who studied portraiture and landscapes, also knows the terrain of the heart." Despite its title, *A Start in Life* is a story of resignation and slow suffocation: Inspired by Balzac, forty-something literary scholar Ruth Weiss pursues a romantic affair (her sense of love is one of her many attitudes "warped" by literature). When the affair goes sour, Ruth resigns herself to a lonely life caring for her ailing parents.

Providence (JONATHAN CAPE, 1982; PANTHEON, 1984) • Featuring another protagonist drawn from academia, *Providence* introduces Kitty Maule, a demure professor of Romantic literature at a small British college. The daughter of French and Russian immigrants, Kitty feels alien and outcast in British society even before her relationship with a staunchly Catholic colleague fails. The reviews of *Providence* were quite favorable, with one critic generously praising Brookner's attention to detail and her "graceful economical way with words."

Look at Me (PANTHEON, 1983) • As a medical librarian, Frances Hinton spends her days archiving pictures of different, often lethal, diseases. A solitary young woman, she spends her evenings writing in a journal about the events of her day. However, when she becomes friendly with coworker Nick Fraser and his wife, she discovers an entirely new social side to her personality. Julia Epstein in the *Washington Post* called *Look at Me* "a nearly impossible achievement...simultaneously a tragedy of solitude and loss and a triumph of the sharp-tongued controlling self."

* Hotel du Lac (PANTHEON, 1984) • Winner of a Booker Prize, England's most prestigious literary award, Brookner's fourth novel describes the lonely life of a discriminating educated woman who dreams of love and happiness ever after. She's Edith Hope, a thirty-nine-year-old romance novelist living in London who leaves her fiancé at the altar. Fleeing to a hotel in Switzerland, she intrudes herself into the lives of the other guests and begins work on her next novel. Although Brookner used similar characters and themes, reviewers distinguished this novel from her previous work because, in the words of *New York Times* reviewer Anne Tyler, Edith is "more philosophical from the outset, more self-reliant, [and] more conscious that a solitary life is not, after all, an unmitigated tragedy."

> "[Brookner] is one of the finest novelists of her generation....[Hotel du Lac is] a novel about romance, and reality, and the gap between them and the way the need for romance persists in the full knowledge of that gap." (*John Gross,* New York Times)

Family and Friends (PANTHEON, 1985) • After four novels about solitary women yearning for romance, Brookner produced this one about the Dorn family, which relocates to London after World War I. During the course of the novel, the Dorn parents attempt to hold on to their Jewish traditions, while the wayward and progressive Dorn children step into the modern age. In the end, *Family and Friends* is a heartwarming tale about the loyalties that keep families together. According to Michiko Kakutani in the *New York Times*, Brookner's subject "is not one waif-like woman, but an entire family; her focus, not simply the consequences of romantic love, but also the effects of the enduring, changing bonds between parents and their children."

The Misalliance (PANTHEON, 1986) • Jilted by her husband, Blanche Vernon visits museums and otherwise lives the solitary existence typical of a Brookner heroine. On these museum visits, she contemplates the women in the paintings and wonders whether she resembles the nymphs or the saints. Because she's not honest with men or clever about them, neither category seems to fit. "In writing about these lonely women," Jonathan Yardley gushed in the *Washington Post,* Brookner "has universal business in mind: the peculiarities and uncertainties of love, the relationship between fate and will, the connections—and disconnection—between art and reality."

A Friend from England (PANTHEON, 1987) • Emotionally disfigured by the deaths of her parents and a humiliating affair with a married man, Rachel merely survives, working at a London bookstore and living in a spartan flat. Then, suddenly, her luck changes when her accountant wins a football pool and generously shares with her his family's new extravagant lifestyle. However, as the novel progresses, Rachel becomes detached from her emotions, aloof and calculating, and ever more diabolical. Reviewers found her as repulsive as she was compelling. However, Michael Gorra in the *Washington Post* pointed out that the opening passages of *A Friend from England* are as "classically elegant as anything Anita Brookner has written."

Latecomers (PANTHEON, 1988) • In *Latecomers*, for the first time in her writing career Brookner takes on males as her protagonists: Thomas Fibich and Thomas Hartmann are orphans who escaped Nazi Germany as boys and soon became lifelong friends. Now they're partners in a London-based greeting card company. Fibich, who suffers from stress, worries about coming to terms with his past, while Hartmann lives in the present, apparently carefree. One critic, who praised Brookner's handling of these male characters, observed that "such developments indicate a new generosity of spirit on Miss Brookner's part, and they make for a more capacious fictional world."

Lewis Percy (PANTHEON, 1989) • Brookner followed *Latecomers* with another book about men—in this case, one man's quest for serenity. Shattered after his mother's death, the title character marries library coworker Tissy, whose life is just as desolate as his own (and those of Brookner's other repressed heroines). When Tissy suspects that Lewis is having an affair with a coworker (he's not), Lewis's attempts to act honorably get him in trouble. In true Brookner fashion, noted one reviewer, "both characters find living a trickier business than reading about it." Another pointed out that *Lewis Percy* "glowed with a new serenity and reality."

* Brief Lives (JONATHAN CAPE, 1990; RANDOM HOUSE, 1991) • This time around, Brookner trades in the timorous librarians of *Lewis Percy* for Fay Langdon, a confident and successful businesswoman entering her later years. Though generally a sensitive and restrained person, Fay is having an affair with her best friend's husband.

> *"It is a testimony to Ms. Brookner's gift for portraying the depth beneath the calm that we remain engaged by Fay's chronicle, despite the character's self-effacement and her repressed spirit. Like Barbara Pym and Kazuo Ishiguro, two writers who are equally skilled at conveying the passions their British protagonists are capable of containing, Anita Brookner locates her narrative close to the edge of her character's lifelong denial."* (*Joyce Reiser Kornblatt,* New York Times)

A Closed Eye (JONATHAN CAPE, 1991; RANDOM HOUSE, 1992) • Harriet Blakemore's parents all but force her to marry twice-her-age Freddie, with whom she has a daughter who's later killed in a car accident. One reviewer

described Harriet as a "classic" Brookner heroine: "innocent, fearful, obe-
dient, unable to bear guilt, to seize life, to face reality." Another found *A
Closed Eye* to be "bleak but elegantly constructed."

Fraud (JONATHAN CAPE, 1992; RANDOM HOUSE, 1993) • Unlike Brookner's other
novels, this one begins with a mystery: the disappearance of a middle-aged
single woman named Anna Durrant. Yet *Fraud* is more than a whodunit, as
Brookner recounts Anna's life from childhood to the present, charting the
terrible effects of her mother's "hellish and absorbing love." According to
Ursula Hegi, writing in the *New York Times*, "*Fraud* is an immensely satisfying
novel with unsettling insights into what can happen when the boundaries
between aging parents and their children dissolve."

A Family Romance (JONATHAN CAPE, 1993; PUBLISHED IN THE U.S. AS *DOLLY*, RANDOM
HOUSE, 1994) • Brookner's thirteenth novel concerns Jane Manning—"a
creature resigned to a muted half-life," wrote one reviewer—and her relationship with her free-spirited aunt by marriage, Dolly, whom she "inherits"
when her parents die. According to Merle Rubin in the *Christian Science
Monitor*, "Only a writer of great passion, conviction, and artistry could transform Dolly's petulance, Jane's priggishness, and the emotional parsimony of
their lives into a spellbinding portrait of the dreams and frustrations of the
human heart."

A Private View (RANDOM HOUSE, 1994) • George Bland, a retired personnel
manager with a fitting surname, has just lost his best friend (he died) and
the only woman he ever loved (she left him for another man). Soon, however, his solitary, listless existence is disturbed by Katy Gibb, a New Age
neighbor half his age. Does this sound like many other Brookner plots?
Many reviewers thought so. In the words of Linda Simon in the *New York
Times*, "her plot, her characters, and especially Ms. Brookner's bleak view of
reality have become tiresome."

Incidents in the Rue Laugier (RANDOM HOUSE, 1995) • This novel "begins
warily," one reviewer wrote, "as if the business of storytelling might be an
infringement of good manners. A history is to be reconstructed, a history
of a life that has left few good traces." Its protagonist is Maffy, daughter of
Maud, who finds long-lost journals belonging to her dead mother, a
woman too aloof and reserved for her daughter to know very well. "One of
the many great strengths of this novel is the way its characters settle into
their places on the continuum between will and fate, motivated by constel-
lations way beyond them," Salter Reynolds wrote in the *Los Angeles Times*.

Altered States (RANDOM HOUSE, 1996) • During the course of this novel,
middle-aged London solicitor Alan Sherwood reflects on a one-night stand
that he had fifteen years ago with the granddaughter of his father's first wife.
As Brookner reveals him, Alan is at first crazed with love and later desperate

to reestablish order in his life. In the *New York Times,* Deborah Mason called Alan the "most engrossing" character of Brookner's recent work and "a person whose muffled existence summons up the magisterial sterility of T. S. Eliot's 'hollow men.'"

Visitors (JONATHAN CAPE, 1997; RANDOM HOUSE, 1998) • Relying even less on plot than in her previous works, Brookner gives us Dorothea May, a reclusive self-sufficient widow entering her seventies. She's a familiar Brookner heroine: sensitive, profoundly private, lonely, and alienated. Her only social contacts are with her late husband's sisters. Early in the novel, one of them announces that her American granddaughter is coming to London to be married. Mrs. May is soon pressed into service, putting up the gay best man. "In her excellent new novel," Jacqueline Carey wrote in the *New York Times,* "[Brookner] has thrown off all extraneous accumulations in character and story, giving us the starkest delineation yet of her particular pessimism, still in that same beguiling, finely shaded prose."

BIOGRAPHY

ANITA BROOKNER WAS BORN in London to two Polish Jewish parents, whom she loved "painfully" and cared for until their deaths. Describing them as "bizarre and eccentric," she has explained in interviews that she was a disappointment to them because she failed to marry young and produce grandchildren. "They never should have had children," Brookner has said of her parents. "They didn't understand them and couldn't be bothered." However, they did bother themselves with their daughter's education. Beginning when Anita turned seven, her father insisted that she read the complete works of Dickens. Meanwhile, her formal education began at James Allen's Girls' School. It continued at King's College, London, where she studied history, and later at the Courtauld Institute of Art, where she earned a Ph.D. in art history.

Brookner then began an academic career, teaching at the University of Reading from 1959 until 1964, when she accepted a job at her doctoral alma mater. She remained at the Courtauld Institute until 1977, and then she became a reader in the history of art at Cambridge. During those years, Brookner made a reputation for herself as a brilliant instructor and also published a number of definitive academic studies in her field, French art of the eighteenth and nineteenth centuries.

Brookner began writing fiction in 1980. "It was most undramatic," she has said of the transition. "I had a long summer vacation in which nothing seemed to be happening, and I could have got very sorry for myself and miserable, but it seemed such a waste of time to do that, and I'd always got a lot of nourishment from fiction. I wondered—it just occurred to me to see whether I could do it." The critical success of her first novel, *A Start in Life,* encouraged her to write more novels during the summer vacations that followed. When her fourth novel, *Hotel du Lac,* won a Booker Prize in

1984, her "avocation" finally eclipsed her academic career. She relinquished her teaching job in 1987 and has kept to her pace of a novel a year ever since.

NEXT ON THE READING LIST: Margaret Atwood, A. S. Byatt, Kaye Gibbons, Gail Godwin, Penelope Lively, Joyce Carol Oates, Muriel Spark

---

Larry Brown
(b. July 9, 1951)

"Brown—a fireman-turned-writer from Oxford, Mississippi—has developed a literary voice perfectly suited to his stories of working people, tales of often frightening pathologies fostered by a lifetime of hard use at work and at home."
—*Neil Gordon,* Boston Review

Facing the Music (ALGONQUIN, 1988) • Suicide, alcoholism, and spouses falling out of love: That's the stuff of Brown's first short-fiction collection. It's grim, but there's a lot of talent in it. The stories are set in the rural South, "yet for all the ramshackle bars, convenience stores, sick cows, and tacky ladies' house slippers that litter his prose," Barry Walters wrote in the *Village Voice*, "Brown's worldview isn't so different from that of flashy young city slickers, and neither is his writing. He's as miserable and cruel as Bret Easton Ellis."

Dirty Work (ALGONQUIN, 1989) • Two former GIs, one white and one black, sit in a VA hospital, hashing over the Vietnam War and comparing the disasters that their lives have become. It's a brashly straightforward conceit for a novelist to choose, but Brown pulls it off. Among the many reviewers who gave it high praise, Herbert Mitgang in the *New York Times* called *Dirty Work* "powerful and original." According to William Becker in *Theology Today*, "The spirituality of these…vets is mature, self-critical, tempered by continuing struggle, [and] purified by tears of compassion."

Big Bad Love (ALGONQUIN, 1990) • The down-at-the-heels southerners in Brown's stories aren't stuck in a Dixie time warp so much as in a Lynyrd Skynyrd/Grand Funk Railroad zone: They stopped moving ahead only a few decades ago. "For all the drinking and sex…and violence of one kind or another," Harry Crews wrote in the *Los Angeles Times*, "these are stories of affirmation." As for the prose in this collection, there's "nothing tricky about it," Crews remarked, "just good straightforward writing."

* Joe (ALGONQUIN, 1991) • In this stark fablelike novel, Joe is the head of a "poisoning crew" that kills and then removes diseased trees from lumber company groves. He hires Gary, a dirt-poor teenager right out of Faulkner country, and teaches him the ropes. Both characters grow in the relationship, but not neatly and not prettily.

> *"By the end of the novel, Joe has passed on to Gary his virtues and his vices and though in some ways he has freed the boy and made him stronger, in others he has poisoned him, much as he would an unwanted tree."* (Daniel Woodrell, Washington Post)

Father and Son (ALGONQUIN, 1996) • In Brown's third novel, set in small-town Mississippi during the 1960s, a man who has just been released from prison slinks back home like a snake, seething with venom and hot with the anger that he has nurtured during his imprisonment. Most of this anger he directs at his father, whose alcoholism made his childhood a hell. Although well told, the story seems more pat than Brown's previous inventions. Writing in the *New York Times*, Anthony Quinn called *Father and Son* "engrossing" but also "overschematized."

BIOGRAPHY

THE PUBLICITY THAT ACCOMPANIED Larry Brown's emergence as a writer made him seem like a character in one of his own fictions. No creative-writing program stamp here: Born and raised in Oxford, Mississippi, Brown is the son of a farmer and the local postmistress. For financial reasons, college wasn't an option for him; instead, he went to work as a firefighter. Meanwhile, he decided to teach himself how to write because "it seemed like it would be something anybody could learn if he applied himself to it."

Doggedly, Brown went about dissecting the novels and short stories of his favorite writers, including Flannery O'Connor, Stephen King, and Raymond Carver. "I tried the New York publishers over and over for years without any success," he said. Then Algonquin Books, a small literary house in Chapel Hill, North Carolina, gave him a chance. He was immediately rewarded when his first work of fiction, *Facing the Music*, published in 1988, won an award from the Mississippi Institute of Arts and Letters. In 1990, after sixteen years of service, he quit the fire department to write full time.

Brown still lives in Oxford, where he continues to be questioned about what it's like to live and work in the shadow of William Faulkner. According to Brown, "I just say that I don't pay a lot of attention to it." Brown is married to Mary Annie Coleman, with whom he has three children.

NEXT ON THE READING LIST: Dorothy Allison, Russell Banks, Robert Olen Butler, Pete Dexter, Cormac McCarthy, Reynolds Price

Robert Olen Butler

(b. January 20, 1945)

"He writes of soldiers and citizens, prostitutes and grandfathers, sons and fathers and mothers and daughters, and of children left behind. The reader is left overwhelmed by the compassion in his voice."
—*Larry Brown,* Washington Post

The Alleys of Eden (HORIZON, 1981) • The alleys are in Saigon, but this novel is not so much a Vietnam memoir as a culture-clashing love story that uses the war as a backdrop. Cliff, an American GI, hooks up with Lanh, a Vietnamese woman forced into prostitution, and the narrative follows their relationship from South Vietnam to Middle America. In the *New York Times,* Anatole Broyard called *The Alleys of Eden* a "remarkable first novel" and compared Butler with Ford Madox Ford and Chekhov.

Sun Dogs (HORIZON, 1982) • In this book, which develops a minor plotline from Butler's first novel, Vietnam veteran Wilson Hand returns home and struggles to reintegrate himself into American society. The biggest obstacle that he encounters, however, isn't his Vietnam experience but his wife's suicide. Reviewers criticized Butler for using as a plot device an oil company that turns out to be evil—an obvious contrivance, many wrote—but this was a small complaint. Most critics agreed with Ronald Reed, writing in the *Fort Worth Star-Telegram,* that "Butler is showing himself to be a master stylist."

Countrymen of Bones (HORIZON, 1983) • Moving away from Vietnam and into the 1940s, Butler spins this complex, idea-heavy tale about a physicist working in New Mexico on the atom bomb project, an archaeologist excavating a nearby Aztec burial site, and a woman who knows them both. "Though *Countrymen of Bones* is a brilliant novel of ideas, it is never pretentious or didactic," Anatole Broyard wrote in the *New York Times.*

On Distant Ground (KNOPF, 1985) • This book completes Butler's Vietnam trilogy as another minor character from *The Alleys of Eden* becomes the center of a cross-cultural morality play. Capt. David Fleming, himself a former

POW, is being court-martialed for inexplicably aiding a Vietcong prisoner. His reason has to do with the phrase "Hygiene is healthful," which was written on the wall of his own prison. According to Joe Klein in the *New York Times*, "It is a tribute to Mr. Butler's skill as a writer that his story's pyramiding absurdities seem not merely plausible but inevitable."

Wabash (KNOPF, 1987) • This book, generally considered Butler's weakest, recounts the effects of the Great Depression on a family in Wabash, Illinois. Jeremy, who works in a blast furnace, agonizes over the death of his daughter three years earlier. The plot becomes particularly tortured when Jeremy cooks up a plan (thwarted by his wife) to murder his evil boss. Even so, Tom Nolan in the *New York Times* called *Wabash* "eventually engaging.... The period itself comes vividly to life in marches and rallies with police on horseback and company thugs and spies."

The Deuce (SIMON & SCHUSTER, 1989) • The protagonist of this novel is the child of an American soldier and a Vietnamese prostitute. He has two names and identities—one Vietnamese, the other American—and the split in his personality is tearing him apart. He seeks relief by running away from his father's New Jersey home to New York City, where he creates for himself a third identity as a street punk called "The Deuce." Writing in the *New York Times*, Scott Spencer complained that the story moves at times "rather close to the edge of melodrama," but he also called the book "haunting."

* A Good Scent from a Strange Mountain (HOLT, 1992) • For this Pulitzer Prize–winning collection of short stories, Butler uses the narrative milieu of the Vietnam War. However, his interest is less in the epicenter of the event than in the shock waves that ripple out from it. The narrators of these stories, for example, are all Vietnamese immigrants to a small Louisiana town, and Butler won high praise for creating so many convincing voices.

> *"This book offers a rare and privileged glimpse of what the Vietnamese in the U.S. think of each other and also of what they think of the rest of us.... Any reader of this book will feel a strange and perhaps salutary sense of exposure."* (*Madison Smartt Bell*, Chicago Tribune)

They Whisper (HOLT, 1994) • Butler tells this story of a married couple principally by using the husband's sexual memories. The stumbling blocks to Ira and Fiona's happiness are the Vietnam War, which separates them physically, and the Catholic church, which divides them emotionally. Writing in the *New York Times*, Jane Smiley was "horrified" by Butler's frank expression of male sexual fantasies, yet she nevertheless described the book as "complex and intriguing."

Tabloid Dreams (HOLT, 1996) • In his second collection of short stories, Butler uses tabloid journalism as a path into the lurid heart of America.

The titles of these stories tell it all: for example, "*Titanic* Victim Speaks through Waterbed," and "Boy Born with Tattoo of Elvis." According to the *Atlanta Journal and Constitution*, "The stories wittily evoke the grotesque extremes of American life in the 1990s."

The Deep Green Sea (HOLT, 1998) • In this erotic fablelike novel that raises such Big Issues as the difference between knowledge and truth and the price of each, Butler again explores the emotional and psychological aftermath of the Vietnam War. He alternates between two points of view, those of 'Nam veteran Benjamin Cole and his lover, Le Thi Tien, the daughter of a prostitute and an American GI. Because the couple's sexual encounters in Ho Chi Minh City take up much of this book, reviewers seemed reluctant to give it a thumbs-up: In the *Los Angeles Times*, Susie Linfield called the book "Butler Lite," while Dwight Garner wrote in the *New York Times* that *The Deep Green Sea* "finds its center of gravity at crotch level."

BIOGRAPHY

ROBERT OLEN BUTLER'S CAREER as a writer has been shaped by the year that he spent in Vietnam, where his experience wasn't that of a typical GI. Following basic training, the army gave Butler a year of language instruction so that he could work in counterintelligence and as an interpreter. This ability to speak the language gave Butler a deeper understanding of the Vietnamese people and culture than the average soldier had. As a result, on his return to the United States, he suffered painful withdrawal symptoms. "After I came back," he has said, "there were a hundred flashes of memories, prompted by a smell of overripe fruit, a certain perfume, a glimpse of a woman's ankle. And I was filled with the same sense of nostalgia, loss, and even aspiration that the Vietnamese in my stories feel."

Before his army service, Butler—who was born in Granite City, Illinois, and grew up around the Midwest—had trained as an actor and a playwright. However, after the war he devoted himself to journalism, spending 1975 to 1985 as editor in chief of an energy industry trade journal. In 1979 he enrolled in a creative writing course being taught by *New York Times Book Review* editor Anatole Broyard. Two years later, Butler published his first novel. With the exception of *Wabash*, all his books have been well received, yet sales remained modest until, unexpectedly, *A Good Scent from a Strange Mountain* won a Pulitzer Prize in 1992. Butler currently teaches creative writing at McNeese State University in Louisiana. He has been married four times and has one son.

NEXT ON THE READING LIST: Madison Smartt Bell, Larry Brown, Pete Dexter, Tim O'Brien, Robert Stone, John Edgar Wideman

A. S. Byatt

(b. August 24, 1936)

"Anyone who has read Antonia Byatt's...previous novels or her critical study of Iris Murdoch knows that this English writer has an acute, supple mind not always primarily interested in the narrative mode as such. She excels at finely attuned brooding and an emphatic introspection, which reveal so much of how it feels to be a certain character that we don't always care what the character does next."
—Paul West, New York Times

The Shadow of the Sun (HARCOURT, BRACE & WORLD, 1964) • Byatt conceived this novel when she was just seventeen, then dabbled with it for several years. The result traces the adolescence and early adulthood of Anna Severall, an insecure young woman determined to separate herself from the paralyzing influence of her father, a self-absorbed novelist who "looked like a cross between God, Alfred Lord Tennyson, and Blake's Job." Faulted for its earnest sensitivity, Byatt's first novel was also criticized for the sort of excessive exposition and ornamental rhetoric that a more experienced writer would have pruned.

The Game (CHATTO & WINDUS, 1967; SCRIBNER'S, 1968) • Written in what critics felt was a more polished, controlled, and confident voice than that evident in her first novel, *The Game* established Byatt's reputation as an important contemporary novelist. It features two sisters, Julia and Cassandra Corbett, who shared an extraordinarily close childhood bond but now are vying for the attention of renowned herpetologist Simon Moffitt. With epigraphs from Charlotte Brontë and Samuel Taylor Coleridge, *The Game* poses as its central theme the power of the imagination. Yet for Cassandra, a medievalist at Oxford, and Julia, a writer of popular fiction, this shared fantasy life assumes ominous and ultimately fatal proportions.

The Virgin in the Garden (CHATTO & WINDUS, 1978; KNOPF, 1979) • Conceived as the first volume in a tetralogy, *The Virgin in the Garden* introduces the adolescent Frederica Potter, who is attracted to artists and passionately desires to be an actress. Among the secondary characters are Frederica's visionary brother, Marcus, and the biology teacher who communicates telepathically with him. Byatt's interest in early Romantic poets is reflected in her convincing portrayal of characters who occasionally achieve transcendent states reminiscent of Wordsworth's "celestial light." Although much denser than her previous novels, *The Virgin in the Garden* achieves a style that suits Byatt, making use of her acquisitive intellect while simultaneously satisfying her compulsion to tell imaginative stories.

Still Life (SCRIBNER'S, 1985) • In this second installment of Byatt's tetralogy, Frederica Potter floats away to Cambridge to study literature while her sister, Stephanie, rejects a professional career in favor of traditional motherhood. The central question posed in this autobiographical novel is one confronted by all writers of realistic fiction: How accurately can language be made to represent actual phenomena? To exemplify this problem, Byatt chooses the medium of painting, representing Vincent van Gogh through his letters (which are extensively quoted) and his paintings (which various characters discuss in detail). Critics, however, thought that Byatt was too reticent in exploring the psychology of her characters and wished that she had played to her literary strengths: her intellectual curiosity and meticulous attention to emotional detail.

Sugar and Other Stories (SCRIBNER'S, 1987) • Byatt's major theme in this collection of short stories is a quintessentially British one: the struggle between passion and manners, between need and propriety. Its most forceful illustration, "The Dried Witch," is set in a primitive village where an aging widow, her desires thwarted by the rigors of custom, studies witchcraft to gain a measure of power. A few perceptive critics noted that the tone of this book suggests a late-Victorian intellect trapped by twentieth-century social and personal dilemmas—a peculiar literary stance that results in a great deal of strain and tightness.

* Possession: A Romance (RANDOM HOUSE, 1990) • Hailed as a spectacularly erudite novel of ideas and intrigue, this winner of a Booker Prize tells the story of Roland Mitchell and Maud Bailey—the former, an expert on nineteenth-century poet Randolph Henry Ash; the latter, an authority on Christabel LaMotte, an obscure writer of fairy tales who has only lately been rediscovered by feminists. Together, Roland and Maud uncover evidence that the married Ash and the supposedly lesbian LaMotte were having an affair, and their joint investigation leads to an affair of their own. The clandestine relationship between LaMotte and Ash is presented through letters, journal extracts, and—in Byatt's most daring touch—entire poems written by the protagonists as part of their courtship.

> "Possession *is...generous, teeming with more ideas than a year's worth of ordinary novels.... The novel is capacious, ambitious, occasionally overwrought: it is marvelous.*" (*Anita Brookner,* The Spectator)

* Angels & Insects (RANDOM HOUSE, 1992) • Byatt's exquisitely executed, intelligent, and diverting sequel to *Possession* contains two novellas also set in the Victorian era. The first, "Morpho Eugenia," concerns a naturalist of humble birth who marries into an aristocratic family, only to discover its ugly secret. Among the séance enthusiasts in the second novella, "The Conjugal Angel," is Emily Tennyson Jesse, the poet's sister. Emily had been engaged to marry Arthur Henry Hallman, the very same man whose death at age twenty-two inspired Tennyson to express the faith and doubts of his era in "In Memoriam A.H.H."

> *"Byatt's characters—fictional and historical—ponder the nature of love—temporal and eternal—in images and concepts that are authentically Victorian, yet not that far removed from the hopes and fears still felt by their descendants a century later."* (*Merle Rubin,* Christian Science Monitor)

The Matisse Stories (CHATTO & WINDUS, 1993; RANDOM HOUSE, 1995) • In this second collection of Byatt short stories, each one makes some reference to impressionist painter Henri Matisse. With its publication, critics felt that Byatt had entered a new phase in her career, one that embraced a more concrete style that still advanced her technique and range.

The Djinn in the Nightingale's Eye (CHATTO & WINDUS, 1994; RANDOM HOUSE, 1997) • This clever collection of modernized fairy tales—tradition with a twist, you might call them—explores the evolution of storytelling and its role in our collective psyche. The volume contains two stories familiar to readers of *Possession*, "The Glass Coffin" and "Gode's Story," but its more significant fare are the three new works. Writing in the *New York Times*, Nancy Willard noted that "when Byatt superimposes the fairy-tale style on contemporary material, events in the stories do not hark back to an earlier time. Instead, the magic of the earlier time is brought into our own." Other reviewers agreed with Willard that the collection's title story, about a middle-aged academic who finds a genie in a bottle, was its best.

Babel Tower (RANDOM HOUSE, 1996) • Frederica Potter, the precociously bookish schoolgirl in *The Virgin in the Garden* and the zealous Cambridge literata in *Still Life*, emerges here as a tireless literary freelancer in London during the mid-1960s. Like the two earlier novels in Byatt's tetralogy, *Babel Tower* aspires to speak for an age. This time, however, the story is faster paced and the unhappily married heroine has new depth, making (critics agreed) for a bolder novel. Reviewers also pointed out that Byatt seemed less preoccupied with what books couldn't say and more intent on squeezing as much discordant life as possible into them.

BIOGRAPHY

A. S. BYATT WAS BORN Antonia Susan Drabble in Sheffield, England. The daughter of a judge, she graduated with first-class honors from Newnham College, Cambridge, in 1957. Her lengthy curriculum vitae includes teaching posts at several London universities during the 1960s and 1970s.

From the beginning of her writing career, Byatt's métier has been the traditional realistic novel. To compose effectively within this framework, she has made use of her own experiences and those of her friends and family members. Her novels tend to feature characters who, like Byatt and her acquaintances, are primarily academicians and artists. Byatt's talent for writing is shared by her younger sister, Margaret Drabble, whose 1963 novel *A Summer Bird-Cage* (along with Byatt's *The Game*) caused many reviewers to speculate about their personal relationship. Although Byatt's books certainly contain some autobiographical information, she remains understandably reluctant to discuss this aspect of her work and prefers to avoid the subject of her personal life entirely.

As a novelist, a critic, an editor, and a lecturer, Byatt makes remarkable use of her astounding competence in a great variety of areas: She's at ease explaining a Wallace Stevens poem, a Willa Cather novel, a van Gogh painting, or the Renaissance itself. She often writes for the *Times of London* and even broadcasts for the BBC. According to Byatt, "Perhaps the most important thing to say about my books is that they try to be about the life of the mind as well as of society and relations between people. I admire— am excited by—intellectual curiosity of any kind and also by literature as a complicated, huge, interrelating pattern."

NEXT ON THE READING LIST: Andrea Barrett, Mark Helprin, Alice Hoffman, Kazuo Ishiguro, Iris Murdoch, Michael Ondaatje, Susan Sontag

<hr />

Bebe Moore Campbell

(b. 1950)

"By showing lives lived, and not explaining ideas, Ms. Campbell does what good storytellers do—she puts in by leaving out. Consequently, her characters dominate her story, unlike the flat characters of less skillfully written novels."
—*Clyde Edgerton,* New York Times

* Your Blues Ain't Like Mine (PUTNAM, 1992) • Campbell based her first novel on the story of Emmett Till, a black teenager from Chicago who was killed in Mississippi in 1955 for whistling at a white woman. Similarly, pool hall owner Floyd Cox kills teenager Armstrong Todd for speaking French to Lily, Floyd's wife. However, most of this novel, which spans thirty years in just 332 pages, takes place after Floyd's acquittal. Campbell describes the effects of the murder on Armstrong's relatives in the Delta, on his mother in Chicago, and on Floyd and his family as well, making the point that racism destroys its perpetrators as well as its victims. "I really wanted to show the boomerang of racial hatred," Campbell has said.

"Much of the power of this novel results from Ms. Campbell's subtle and seamless shifting of point of view. She wears the skin and holds in her chest the heart of each of her characters, one after another, regardless of the character's race or sex,...or need for pity, grace, punishment, or peace." (*Clyde Edgerton*, New York Times)

Brothers and Sisters (PUTNAM, 1994) • Campbell sets her second novel in a Los Angeles just recovering from the 1992 riots. Her heroine is Esther Jackson, a regional operations manager for Angel City National Bank. Esther grew up on Chicago's South Side and doesn't like whites, but she hides her antagonism beneath Ellen Tracy jackets and Jones New York silk blouses. Her ambition is to become a loan officer like white, suburban Mallory Post. And among others, *Brothers and Sisters* tells the story of how Esther and Mallory overcome their racial baggage to become friends. Although some reviewers, particularly those writing for black-oriented publications, praised the novel extravagantly, most thought that Campbell's pulpier, more caricatured writing style didn't match the excellence of *Your Blues Ain't Like Mine*. According to Erin J. Aubry, writing in the *Los Angeles Times*, "[*Brothers and Sisters*] aspires to dizzying heights, trying in a 476-page fell swoop to...resolve the burning question of whether or not we can all get along. But Campbell is simply not up to the literary task she sets for herself here."

BIOGRAPHY

BEBE MOORE CAMPBELL FIRST attracted literary attention in 1989, when she published *Sweet Summer: Growing Up with and without My Dad*, a memoir of her childhood. After her parents' divorce, she lived with her mother in Philadelphia during the school year but spent her summers in North Carolina with her wheelchair-bound father (who had been injured in a car accident). In *Sweet Summer*, Campbell sharply contrasts these two worlds— one dominated by women, in which she was encouraged to speak well, behave properly, and study hard; and the other freer and rougher, the world of her father's family. Campbell also describes her feelings after she learned that her father's car accident had been caused by his own speeding, as had another accident in which a boy had died. That Campbell managed to overcome her disillusionment and maintain a positive, loving relationship with her father struck a nerve in the black community. Commentators such as *Washington Post* reviewer Nikki Giovanni hailed *Sweet Summer* as "a corrective to some of the destructive images of black men that are prevalent in our society."

At the University of Pittsburgh, Campbell studied education and graduated summa cum laude. She also found out that she wanted to write. After her graduation, she sent Toni Morrison, then an editor at Random House, some of her work. "She rejected my stories for publication," Campbell recalled, "but she said she wished me well in what she knew would be a brilliant career. She took the time to be personal." Later, at the suggestion of an *Essence* editor, Campbell began soliciting freelance work. Beginning about 1978, she supported herself with assignments from *Ebony*, *Ms.*, the *New York Times*, the *Washington Post*, *Working Mother*, and other publications. In fact, her first book, *Successful Women, Angry Men: Backlash in the Two-Career Marriage* (1986), developed out of a cover story that she wrote for *Savvy*.

Although details of her first marriage and subsequent divorce are sketchy, the union did produce a daughter, the actress Maia Campbell, who has appeared in the films *Poetic Justice* and *South Central*. During the mid-1980s, Campbell married her second husband, banker Ellis Gordon Jr., and moved to Los Angeles. She still lives there, writing fiction, serving as a contributing editor to *Essence*, and offering regular commentaries on National Public Radio.

NEXT ON THE READING LIST: Ellen Gilchrist, Charles Johnson, Terry McMillan, Toni Morrison, Gloria Naylor, Alice Walker

Sandra Cisneros
(b. December 20, 1954)

"Noisily, wittily, always compassionately, Cisneros surveys woman's condition—a condition that is both precisely Latina and general to women everywhere.... The girls who tell their brief stories are so alert they seem almost to quiver; the mature women, in their longer stories, relish the control they have painfully acquired."
—*Peter S. Prescott and Karen Springen, Time*

The House on Mango Street (ARTE PUBLICO, 1983) • The focus of this volume of forty-four vignettes is Esperanza Cordero, a poor but intelligent Hispanic girl. Esperanza longs for a room of her own and a house of which she can be proud, ponders the disadvantages of choosing marriage over education, and experiences the sense of confusion associated with growing up. Written in what Penelope Mesic in *Booklist* called "a loose and deliberately simple style, halfway between a prose poem and the awkwardness of semiliteracy," *The House on Mango Street* won praise for its powerful narratives as well as its vivid language. "I wanted stories like poems, compact and lyrical and ending with reverberation," Cisneros has said.

✳ Woman Hollering Creek (RANDOM HOUSE, 1991) • The twenty-two narratives in this collection describe the lives of Mexican Americans living near

San Antonio, Texas. Ranging in length from a few paragraphs to several pages, they present the interior monologues of Hispanics who have become assimilated into American culture despite their affinity for Mexico. Cisneros's range of characters is broad and lively—from drag queen Rudy Cantu, in whose ears the crowd's applause sizzles as when "my ma added the rice to the hot oil," to a young Hispanic woman who feels guilty because she can't speak Spanish. Cisneros's prose, *Kirkus Reviews* noted, "brings to vibrant being the sights, smells, joys, and heartaches of growing up female in a culture where women are both strong and victimized, men are unfaithful, and poverty is mitigated only by family, community, and religious ties."

> "My prediction is that Sandra Cisneros will stride right into the spotlight— though an aura already surrounds her. These stories about how and why we mythologize love are revelations about the constant, small sadnesses that erode our facades, as well as those unpredictably epiphanic moments that lift our hearts from despair." (*Ann Beattie*)

BIOGRAPHY

SANDRA CISNEROS GREW UP, mostly on Chicago's working-class South Side, as the only daughter in a family of seven children. Concerning her childhood, Cisneros has said that because her brothers expected her to assume a traditional female role, she often felt as though she had "seven fathers." Her mother, however, never forced her to do housework or learn to cook. Because the family frequently moved back and forth between Mexico and the United States (her father had chronic homesickness), Cisneros has said that she often felt homeless and displaced: "Because we moved so much, and always into neighborhoods that appeared like France after World War II—empty lots and burned-out buildings—I retreated inside myself."

After graduating in 1976 with a B.A. in English from Loyola University, Cisneros attended the prestigious University of Iowa Writers' Workshop, where she began to focus her work on conflicts directly related to her upbringing, including her divided cultural loyalties, her feelings of alienation, and the degradation of poverty. As a result, her distinctly Hispanic characters are often isolated from the American mainstream, especially in the way they talk and think. "If I were asked what it is I write about, I would have to say I write about those ghosts inside that haunt me, that will not let me sleep, of that which even memory does not like to mention," Cisneros has explained. "Perhaps later there will be a time to write by inspiration. In the meantime, in my writing as well as in that of other Chicanas and other women, there is the necessary phase of dealing with those ghosts and voices most urgently haunting us, day by day."

Cisneros has also published a number of volumes of poetry, including *The Rodrigo Poems* (1985), *My Wicked, Wicked Ways* (1987), and *Loose Woman* (1994). In addition, she's the author of the bilingual children's book *Hairs: Pelitos* (1994).

NEXT ON THE READING LIST: Julia Alvarez, Laura Esquivel, Mary Gaitskill, Cristina Garcia, Oscar Hijuelos, John Nichols

Pat Conroy
(b. October 26, 1945)

"Conroy's main asset is his emotional range. He's a warm and decent man who expresses love and nostalgia without embarrassment; he also can portray hate and meanness in convincing detail and make us understand, perhaps more than we want to, how mean and hateful people came to be that way."
—*Michael Harris,* Los Angeles Times

The Great Santini (HOUGHTON MIFFLIN, 1976) • This highly autobiographical novel describes a southern family ruled by an autocratic ex-marine of a father. Conroy locates the book's greatest emotional tension in the relationship between Bull Meecham and his eighteen-year-old son, Ben. The *Virginia Quarterly* called Conroy's descriptive writing "somewhat juvenile" but admired his firm realism.

The Lords of Discipline (HOUGHTON MIFFLIN, 1980) • This coming-of-age story was inspired by Conroy's experiences as a cadet at the Citadel. Given the job of looking after the first black cadet at the military school, Will runs up against a shadowy Klan-like group called the Ten. According to the *Washington Post*, some sections of this book read like a Hardy Boys adventure. Writing in the *New York Times*, Harry Crews agreed that "after a very auspicious start, Pat Conroy's creative energies are sidetracked."

* The Prince of Tides (HOUGHTON MIFFLIN, 1986) • This hugely popular novel tells the story of Savannah Wingo, a suicidal southern poet who lives in New York City, and her unemployed football coach brother, Tom, who comes up from coastal South Carolina to help his sister recover from a nervous breakdown. In conversations with Savannah's psychiatrist, Tom relates their bizarre and tragic family history. Gail Godwin in the *New York Times* echoed many critics who disliked "the implausible, the sentimental, and the florid" in the novel, but less exacting reviewers considered the book an enjoyable read.

"Sometimes he stumbles and strays off course.... The terrain is rough in Conroy country and the climate stormy, but the views are often spectacular. The Prince

of Tides, *his largest and darkest novel, will unquestionably establish Pat Conroy as a popular novelist of depth and distinction.* " (*Brigitte Weeks*, Washington Post)

Beach Music (DOUBLEDAY, 1995) • Jack McCall lives in Rome, where he's trying to figure out why his wife killed herself. In search of an answer, he begins a sprawling journey across continents and back through his own family history. Along the way, Conroy introduces a numbing quantity of characters and subplots. According to the *New York Times*, the "historical scene setting is pretty thin stuff" and the book "heaves with self-conscious sincerity." Meanwhile, the *Atlanta Journal and Constitution* complained about the "irritatingly obvious setup lines" used in *Beach Music* and its descriptions that "go to purple."

BIOGRAPHY

PAT CONROY WAS BORN into a family apparently dominated (as in *The Great Santini*) by an abusive marine. "My father's violence is the central fact of my art and my life," Conroy has said. However, he has also said that he realized much later that it was his mother, with her "Byzantine and remarkable powers of intrigue," who really ran things. After attending high school in Beaufort, South Carolina, Conroy entered the Citadel, a military college in Charleston that also became a focal point of his writing. One of the most dominant themes in Conroy's fiction, many critics have noted, is his ambiguous portrayal of military discipline: His characters both respect it and rebel against it.

Conroy's first book, *The Boo* (1970), presented a journalistic account of his years at the Citadel. Another memoir, *The Water Is Wide* (1972), recounted his experiences as a schoolteacher on an isolated island off the coast of South Carolina. *The Water Is Wide*, the title of which referred to the physical and cultural gulf that separated the poor black students from the rest of American society, became the basis for the poignant film *Conrack* (1974), starring Jon Voight. *The Great Santini*, *The Lords of Discipline*, and *The Prince of Tides* have also become feature films.

Many literary critics have dismissed Conroy's work because of its mawkishness and his sometimes shameless use of plot gimmicks. However, according to Steven Harvey in the *Atlanta Journal and Constitution*, "[Conroy] has learned how to animate best-seller conventions with the force of his childhood myth, a power so incandescent in him that it transforms any subject that comes his way."

NEXT ON THE READING LIST: Ivan Doig, Kaye Gibbons, Jane Hamilton, William Kennedy, Larry McMurtry, Anne Tyler

Harry Crews
(b. June 6, 1935)

"Crews's fictional landscape—'macabre and slapstick, howlingly funny and sad as a zoo,' in the words of Jean Stafford—has always mirrored his bent for perversity. His novels are populated with freaks.... Like Crews himself, his novels are not for the faint of heart."
—Michelle Green, People

The Gospel Singer (MORROW, 1968) • In Crews's debut novel, a popular southern evangelist returns to his hometown. Trailing him, feeding off his success, is a traveling freak show. When the preacher's old girlfriend is found murdered, things turn bizarre, then lurid. Martin Levin observed in the *New York Times* that *The Gospel Singer* had "a nice wild flavor and a dash of Grand Guignol strong enough to meet the severe standards of southern decadence."

Naked in Garden Hills (MORROW, 1969) • Fat Man owns a phosphate mine in a small Florida town. When the phosphate runs out, Fat Man and his extremely slender attendant, Jester, become entertainers, starring in a townwide carnival of freaks. "It is Southern Gothic at its best," Jean Stafford declared in the *New York Times*, "a Hieronymus Bosch landscape in Dixie inhabited by monstrous, darling pets."

This Thing Don't Lead to Heaven (MORROW, 1970) • Reviewers generally agreed that Crews went flat in this novel, which recounts the events at an old folks' home in Georgia after a voodoo-crazed Cuban shows up. The book's problems stem from the author's uncharacteristic reserve and his distance from the characters, which together make the whole business seem cold. According to Guy Davenport, writing in the *National Review,* "The impact of [Crews's first two novels] has either dulled our response, or Mr. Crews is writing too fast."

Karate Is a Thing of the Spirit (MORROW, 1971) • The plot of Crews's fourth novel gives him yet another chance to assemble a collection of oddities in a damned southern landscape. Munroe, a midget karate master, serves as spiritual leader to a group whose deadly skills make them unfit for the usual martial arts competitions. When Kaimon enters their circle, he must endure strange rituals of pain and abuse to become initiated. John Deck in the *New York Times* wrote that "the novel takes off, in the manner of a firestorm, rushing at amazing speed, eating up oxygen, scorching everything it touches."

Car (MORROW, 1972) • In this thoroughly bizarre and sometimes hilarious novel, Crews gives us a hero, Herman Mack, who has decided to eat his car, piece by piece. Soon Herman's daily ceremonies of consuming and defecating pieces of metal become media events, even religious occasions. *Newsweek* called Crews's fifth novel, which amounts to an extreme parody of car worship, "his best yet."

The Hawk Is Dying (KNOPF, 1973) • Awash in depression, overwhelmed by the conviction that life is meaningless, a man concentrates on the training of a hawk as a means to truth. However, as Crews describes it, this process quickly becomes a course in grim macho discipline. Phoebe-Lou Adams in the *Atlantic Monthly* called *The Hawk Is Dying* "immensely convincing" because it reveals "the underlying patterns of desperation over wasted time and neglected abilities."

The Gypsy's Curse (KNOPF, 1974) • Marvin, the most anguished and horrific of all Crews's freak protagonists, is deaf, dumb, and legless. He earns his living performing bizarre acrobatic stunts and spends his free time lusting after a woman named Hester. However, Hester's beauty belies a moral ugliness that causes Marvin to commit several savage acts. In the *Washington Post,* Jonathan Yardley wrote that with *The Gypsy's Curse,* "Crews seems at last to be rounding his formidable talents into shape."

* A Feast of Snakes (ATHENEUM, 1976) • Mystic, Georgia, holds an annual rattlesnake roundup that lures a number of former residents back to town. The festival gives Joe Lon Mackey, once a high school football star and now a local loser, the chance to compare himself to those who've left town, especially his former girlfriend. He doesn't like what he sees—not at all.

> *"Few writers could pull off the sort of finale that has mad-eyed rednecks rushing in sudden bursts across a snake-scattered, bonfire-bright field, their loins enflamed by the local beauty contestants, their blood racing with whisky, their hearts ready for violence. Crews does."* (*Paul Zimmerman,* Newsweek)

All We Need of Hell (HARPER & ROW, 1987) • Crews's macho obsessions are focused here on Duffy Deeter—lawyer, handball zealot, and fanatical competitor. Crews sets Duffy up as a parody of the driven male and then knocks him over by introducing an even manlier man, a pro-football player who (as the story turns out) teaches Duffy a thing or two about stopping to smell the roses. Writing in the *New York Times,* Russell Banks called this an "excellent, edgy novel" but pointed out that "plotting is not this book's strong suit."

The Knockout Artist (HARPER & ROW, 1988) • Eugene Biggs is both a hilarious and a pathetic hero: A boxer forced into retirement, he develops an act in which he knocks himself out for the amusement of spectators. This exhibition of self-loathing becomes even more pointed when a beautiful psychology student decides to write her dissertation about him. Overall, *The Knockout Artist* received mixed reviews: Some critics complained that the book's message was about as subtle as Eugene's fist, while others praised that same lack of complexity as a strength.

Body (POSEIDON, 1990) • Generally, the freaks who populate Crews's novels have been born that way. However, in *Body,* which describes the phenomenon of body building, their freakishness is self-created. Shereel Dupont, née Dorothy Turnipseed, is determined to win the Ms. Cosmo competition, and Crews describes her pursuit of that goal in great detail as Shereel willingly starves herself and endures incredible physical punishment. Fay Weldon was fascinated by this study of a world in which, as she wrote in the *New York Times,* "sex is for losing weight, food is for fuel, other people for rivalry, love for exploitation, family for leaving; you yourself are for changing into something else."

Scar Lover (POSEIDON, 1992) • Pete and George stack cellophane for a living. George, a Rastafarian, has scars on his back, one burn for each year of his marriage. Pete doesn't have any outward scars, but inside he's branded by the memory of an incident from his childhood when he hit his younger brother with a hammer, causing brain damage. Reviewers generally respected this painful, difficult book for its honesty, but they didn't fall in love with it. According to George Stade in the *New York Times,* "*Scar Lover* aims to please, which it does, and to instruct, to teach us how to live with our scars—a more difficult enterprise."

The Mulching of America (SIMON & SCHUSTER, 1995) • Crews's thirteenth novel lampoons a once popular but now obscure character: the door-to-door salesman. Hickum Looney sells soap for "the Boss." Although a slow-witted loser, Hickum somehow manages to break the Boss's legendary sales record, which infuriates his ferociously competitive superior. Hickum, however, has some hidden assets, including his own weirdo support group. Dick Roraback in the *Los Angeles Times* called *The Mulching of America* "hilariously crass."

Celebration (SIMON & SCHUSTER, 1998) • A drop-dead-gorgeous eighteen-year-old named Too Much (who could pass for fourteen "if she had not had...well, too much") shows up, from either heaven or outer space, at a moribund South Florida trailer park called Forever and Forever. It's a last way station for tattered retirees on their journey to the Great Beyond, and an occasional visit from the ambulance is about all that happens there. But Too Much has a special power in which she rejoices (in addition to her *Playboy* centerfold looks): "to bring life where there had only been death, to bring joy and celebration where there had only been resignation and despair." Although *New York Times* reviewer Karen Karbo described Too

Much's rejuvenation of the trailer park as "ludicrous, and never particularly believable," she did note that *Celebration* contains "shards of brilliance and of the gonzo wit that has made Crews's reputation as a dead-on satirist."

BIOGRAPHY

As RECOUNTED IN HIS highly regarded memoir, *A Childhood: The Biography of a Place* (1978), Harry Crews's early life in Bacon County, Georgia, rivals the plots of many of his novels for its oddity and pathos. After his father's death when he was two years old, Crews was raised by his mother and his father's brother, a violent man whom his mother married for a time. A bout of polio that left him temporarily paralyzed and a hideous accident in which he fell into a bath of scalding water physically traumatized the young Crews. On top of that, his family was so poor that he had to eat clay in order to make up for the mineral deficiencies in his diet.

The Sears Roebuck mail-order catalog became the unlikely device by which Crews and his friends escaped into fantasy. Crews in particular made up stories about the impossibly clean and healthy models pictured alongside the merchandise. "I had decided that all the people in the catalog were related, not necessarily blood kin but knew one another," Crews wrote. "And it was out of this knowledge that I first began to make up stories."

After serving in the marines, Crews began work on *The Gospel Singer,* developing the straight-ahead prose style and twisted characterizations that would mark all his fiction. Every year or so, another novel appeared until 1976, when the cumulative effects of alcoholism made it too difficult for Crews to write fiction. Aided by a former student (Crews has long taught creative writing at the University of Florida), he reemerged in 1987 with *All We Need of Hell.* Critical response to the novels that have appeared since suggests that Crews's second life as a writer will be at least as freakish and fruitful as his first.

NEXT ON THE READING LIST: Martin Amis, Russell Banks, Madison Smartt Bell, Jim Harrison, John Irving, Thomas McGuane

Edwidge Danticat

(b. January 19, 1969)

"Danticat seems to be overflowing with the strength and insight of generations of Haitian women. In the past under Papa Doc, in New York now, and on the leaky rafts in between, she speaks through the dead and through the living and the walking wounded alike, her tone changing without apparent effort to be as various as the need."
—*Joanne Omang,* Washington Post

Breath, Eyes, Memory (SOHO, 1994) • Danticat's debut novel, originally composed as a master's thesis, explores the darkness and grace of the Haitian experience as lived by immigrants from that troubled Caribbean island. Twelve-year-old Sophie Caco leaves Haiti and the beloved aunt who has raised her to join a mother she knows only from a photograph. Their reunion in Brooklyn ignites tortured memories for Sophie's mother, Martine, who subjects her daughter to an abusive ritual in order to confirm her virginity. Reviewers praised Danticat's self-assurance, noting that she rendered her difficult material, both sexual and political, with clarity and power.

* Krik? Krak! (SOHO, 1995) • A finalist for a National Book Award, this collection of nine stories (with an epilogue) solidified Danticat's reputation as a literary spokeswoman for Haitian-Americans. The title refers to a call-and-response tradition in Creole storytelling: "Krik?" asks the storyteller; "Krak!" responds his or her eager audience. The stories in *Krik? Krak!* include loosely linked variations on two signature Danticat subjects: the experiences of Haitians acculturating to life in the United States and the oppression faced by those who have remained at home. Some reviewers criticized the collection for being uneven, but even these few found several pieces to be extraordinarily effective—particularly "Children of the Sea," an account of Haitian refugees making a doomed voyage to Miami.

> *"The best of [the stories in* Krik? Krak!*], using the island tradition of a semi-magical folktale or the witty, between-two-worlds voices of modern urban immigrants, are pure beguiling transformation."* (*Richard Eder,* Los Angeles Times)

BIOGRAPHY

EDWIDGE DANTICAT SPENT HER FIRST twelve years in a poor neighborhood in Port-au-Prince, Haiti. Both of her parents had emigrated to Brooklyn before she was five, leaving her and a younger brother in the care of an aunt and her husband, a Baptist preacher who brought the family to "every funeral he presided over," Danticat remembered. Theses services reinforced Danticat's perception that "in Haiti, death was always around us."

In 1981, she was finally reunited with her parents. Although on her arrival she spoke only French and Creole, Danticat soon mastered English and gained admission to one of New York City's elite public high schools. Her parents hoped that she'd pursue a medical career, but Danticat's desire to write was too intense. She earned her undergraduate degree in French literature from Barnard College in 1990, and three years later, she completed work on her master's degree at Brown.

As she was finishing up at Brown, Danticat sent a copy of her master's thesis to a book editor at Soho Press. "And then, like a week later, we were having a really expensive lunch....[and] I realized...it was a Cinderella story," she said of the subsequent publication of *Breath, Eyes, Memory*, her well-received first novel. That same year, the *New York Times Magazine* named Danticat one of thirty young artists "among those most likely to change the culture." A year later, *Krik? Krak!* appeared. Although one critic judged a few of the book's stories to be "out of place in a collection presumed to represent polished, mature work," his overall assessment, echoed by many others, was enthusiastic.

NEXT ON THE READING LIST: Julia Alvarez, Sandra Cisneros, Cristina Garcia, Jamaica Kincaid, Amy Tan

---

Louis de Bernières
(b. December 8, 1954)

"Miracles and magic...and other [Latin American] clichés abound, mocked only very gently, in the novels of de Bernières. These are unabashedly 'light' comic works which, while making no claims to either gritty realism or penetrating satire, do, none the less, manage to fashion a vividly mythic setting from...worn stereotypes."
—Michael Kerrigan, Times Literary Supplement

The War of Don Emmanuel's Nether Parts (MORROW, 1990) • De Bernières sets this novel in an imaginary Latin American country that resembles the Spain of Cervantes as much as it does late-twentieth-century Colombia. Of its inhabitants, he writes, "It is as though they have never heard that the days of Tirant lo Blanc and Don Quixote are long dead." The plot begins with the efforts of Doña Constanza Evans, wife of a wealthy white landowner, to divert the Mula River so that she can fill her private swimming pool. Soon a farcical war breaks out between the villagers and the army—fought with Spanish muskets, M-16s, spells, and a bulldozer. Meanwhile, de Bernières litters the novel—it's really a romance—with magical subplots that recall García Márquez but, according to *New York Times* reviewer Susan Lowell, are much "funnier...and more hopeful." Lowell called *The War of Don Emmanuel's Nether Parts* a "racy, brilliantly mischievous first novel."

Señor Vivo and the Coca Lord (MORROW, 1991) • Philosophy professor Dionisio Vivo begins writing regular letters to *La Prensa* denouncing the out-of-control cocaine trade. His letters attract the attention of both President Veracruz, who considers giving Dionisio a knighthood, and cocaine kingpin Pablo Ecobandodo, who wants Dionisio silenced. Ecobandodo's men make several assassination attempts, but each fails, persuading the superstitious coca lord that the professor's life may be charmed. Meanwhile, as Vivomania spreads among a public yearning for law and order, de Bernières brings back some of the best characters from his first novel to liven things up. "The cadences of his prose swell and flow as if they had been rendered with lavish affection and exactitude from a Spanish serenade," Margaria Fichtner wrote in the *Miami Herald*. "*Señor Vivo and the Coca Lord*...is brave, ironic, and wise."

The Troublesome Offspring of Cardinal Guzman (SECKER & WARBURG, 1992; MORROW, 1994) • Cardinal Guzman, corrupted by power and troubled by inner demons, launches a moral crusade to enforce religious orthodoxy. He then turns over the crusade's leadership to a monsignor who believes that the best way to save a soul is to extract a confession from it and then kill it before it has a chance to change its mind. This doesn't bode well for Cochadebajo de los Gatos, the magical village featured in de Bernières first two novels, where most of the residents believe in "salvation through good times and fornication." As Phoebe-Lou Adams wrote in the *Atlantic Monthly*, "One can foresee approximately what will happen to the Cardinal's...crusade when it reaches the town, but the details of the action are wildly fanciful, comically grotesque, mercilessly savage, and altogether unpredictable."

* Corelli's Mandolin (PANTHEON, 1994) • For his fourth novel, de Bernières leaves Latin America (and magical realism) far behind, moving his setting to a small Greek island in the Ionian Sea. The novel opens just before World War II, and soon enough the island is overrun by Italian and German soldiers. The principal characters are Corelli, commander of the island's Italian garrison; Dr. Iannis, in whose house Corelli is billeted; and the doctor's beautiful daughter, Pelagia. Corelli is a handsome, cultured man who plays the mandolin exceedingly well and falls in love with Pelagia. Thus love transcends the barbarism of war. Yet, more than love, de Bernières seems fascinated by history—what is it, who makes it—and he builds this novel from various bits and pieces of "fact": letters, memoirs, speeches, books, dialogues, and even a propaganda pamphlet. History, de Bernières writes in a concluding author's note, is "hearsay tempered with myth and hazy memory."

"War...floats Corelli's Mandolin *off its whimsical dry dock. It provides rigors and tragedies that give the author scope to exercise his powers for horror, irony, and sweet human comedy without seeming forced."* (*Richard Eder,* Los Angeles Times)

BIOGRAPHY

ALTHOUGH HIS FRENCH-SOUNDING name confuses some people, Louis de Bernières is thoroughly British: His ancestors arrived with the rest of the Normans about a thousand years ago. He was born in Jordan but raised in Surrey. When he was nineteen, he spent a few months as a cadet at Sandhurst, the British military academy, before realizing that he didn't like giving or taking orders. He then traveled to Colombia, where he spent a year teaching in the morning and working as a cowboy in the afternoon. Returning to Britain, de Bernières received a bachelor's degree in philosophy (with honors) from Manchester University in 1977. His postgraduate education included a teaching certificate from Leicester Polytechnic, earned in 1981, and a master's degree in English from the University of London, granted in 1985.

In 1981, de Bernières began a teaching career in London that supported him as he developed his writing. "I have always known I was going to be a writer," he told one interviewer. "I like to read and write books on a grand scale. I am interested in situations where ordinary people are caught up in abuses of power or historical crises."

De Bernières set his first three novels in an unnamed South American country that obviously made use of his experiences in Colombia. Now he lives, as he has most of his adult life, in an apartment above a junk shop in South London. He keeps a workshop there well stocked with the tools necessary to repair stringed musical instruments—such as guitars, zithers, and, of course, mandolins. "I have only women friends. I don't like or understand most men," de Bernières admitted. "I [also] hate waste and try to do everything myself."

His novels—especially his breakthrough book, *Corelli's Mandolin*—have been praised for the way in which they wrestle with major issues while still maintaining a sense of humor and a graceful utopianism.

NEXT ON THE READING LIST: Jorge Amado, T. Coraghessan Boyle, Laura Esquivel, Gabriel García Márquez, Salman Rushdie, Mario Vargas Llosa

Don DeLillo

(b. November 20, 1936)

"Don DeLillo knows our secrets—American anxieties, obsessions and dreads, our silent spaces and the noise of entertainment and explanation we use to fill them. No wonder that...DeLillo has to be 'discovered' with each new book. This Samuel Beckett of Americana we'd just as soon forget."
—*Tom LeClair, USA Today*

Americana (HOUGHTON MIFFLIN, 1971) • DeLillo announced his career's theme in the title and subject of this first novel. The sprawling story literally roams the continent, following a television executive who hopes to remove the junk-culture patina from his own and his nation's image. According to Michael Levin in the *New York Times*, "There is no real identity to be found in this heaping mass of word-salad. There are thickets of hallucinatory whimsy, an infatuation with rhetoric, but hardly a trace of a man."

End Zone (HOUGHTON MIFFLIN, 1972) • The angle on America in DeLillo's second novel is football, but the characters are no ordinary grunts. Gary Harkness, the hero, views the game as a symbol of modern warfare, in which violence is gussied up with rules. Another player, Anatole Bloomberg, objects to "the Europeaness of my name. Its Europicity." This is America not as it is but as DeLillo processes it: an acquired taste. It was evidently a taste yet not acquired by the *Times Literary Supplement*, which concluded that DeLillo's attempt to mythologize football read "like an academic's apologia for leaving the library."

Great Jones Street (HOUGHTON MIFFLIN, 1973) • From football, DeLillo jumped to popular music as a possible key to his country's brainlock. Having had his fill of glamour, rock star Bucky Wunderlick tries to regain his obscurity in an apartment off the Bowery in New York City—only to find that dropping out makes him an even bigger star. The story gets weird when a new drug enters the picture, one that renders speech incomprehensible (Bucky's next album is titled *Pee-Pee-Maw-Maw*). Reviewers were pretty much of a mind: "flat," "unsuccessful," "dull."

Ratner's Star (KNOPF, 1976) • In his fourth novel, DeLillo exploits both science and science fiction. Billy, a fourteen-year-old mathematics genius, is asked to interpret pulsations emanating from a distant star. Apparently they have meaning, but that meaning is so abstruse as to be incommunicable. Can there be such a thing as untransmittable meaning? George Stade, writing in the *New York Times,* said that with this novel, "DeLillo has arrived." However, *Newsweek* found the book "virtually unbearable."

Players (KNOPF, 1977) • Lyle and Pammy are successful, bored New Yorkers. A murder at the New York Stock Exchange, where Lyle works, brings spice to their lives. Pammy ends up leaving Lyle, who gets involved with the terrorists responsible for the murder. William Kennedy called *Players* a "remarkable new novel of menace and mystery." He also suggested that its success owed much to the fact that it was half the length of DeLillo's earlier, meandering works.

Running Dog (KNOPF, 1978) • Pornography and political intrigue provide the landscape for a novel that Anthony Burgess criticized for having "no humanity at all." The book does, however, have an enormous amount of verve. While investigating the porn business, a left-wing journalist joins a hunt for the ultimate aphrodisiac: an erotic film supposedly made in Hitler's bunker. Many reviewers noted that DeLillo's deliberate starkness of language deprived the book of his greatest gift.

The Names (KNOPF, 1982) • An atmosphere of WASP expatriate ennui runs against this novel's thriller undercurrent. The lives of American profession-als scattered across three countries coalesce in the search for a mysterious Greek cult that calls itself The Names and may have been responsible for a murder. *Los Angeles Times* reviewer Charles Champlin thought *The Names* was "exotic, atmospheric, curiously suspenseful," but this reviewer found DeLillo's writing heavy with self-indulgence.

* White Noise (VIKING, 1985) • A terrific novel that won DeLillo an American Book Award, *White Noise* is about a professor of "Hitler studies" (a notion rife with black-comic possibilities) who has a neurotic fear of death and a wife with an even greater fear of death. The "white noise" is the back-ground of media static in which we swim and which distracts us from the big questions—but it's also death itself, and the sound death makes.

> "White Noise *is a stunning performance from one of our finest and most intel-ligent novelists. DeLillo's reach is broad and deep, combining acute observation of the textures of American life and analytic rigor.... Because he is so deadly serious, it is not said often enough that DeLillo is tremendously funny." (Jay McInerney, The New Republic)*

* Libra (VIKING, 1988) • DeLillo has many times expressed his view that the Kennedy assassination was the defining moment in the psyche of his gener-ation. In this novel about the life of Lee Harvey Oswald, DeLillo takes on the assassination directly. *Libra* is daring storytelling that imagines Oswald as a man longing to be swept up in (and annihilated by) the orgasmic rush of history.

"DeLillo's novel is like a stop-motion frame of the crossfire, a still picture of an awful moment, in which the deadly trajectories have a seductive clarity.... It's his best novel, because it goes right to the source—to Dallas in November, 1963, the primal scene of American paranoia." (*Terrence Rafferty,* The New Yorker)

Mao II (VIKING, 1991) • In DeLillo's tenth novel, he finally got around to using a writer as his protagonist. Bill Gray is a famous, reclusive novelist who has lost his fictive touch, in part because he senses that nobody listens to writers and artists anymore. Meanwhile, another character takes us into the world of the Moonies, and terrorists and media culture also reemerge as themes. "Like [DeLillo's] previous sorties against the dismay of our times," Richard Eder wrote in the *Los Angeles Times,* "*Mao II* is winged and agile, flying us to odd and seemingly unreachable vantage points."

Underworld (SCRIBNER'S, 1997) • This large, sweeping secret history of the Cold War begins at the Polo Grounds on October 3, 1951, just before Giants slugger Bobby Thomson hits his famous "shot heard 'round the world," when an aide whispers to J. Edgar Hoover that the Soviets have exploded another atomic bomb. From that point, DeLillo sways back and forth in time, disgorging an impressive amount of tightly controlled plot. The central characters are Nick Shay, who grows up to lead a worldwide waste disposal empire, and conceptual artist Klara Sax, who disposes of waste in her own unusual way, turning decommissioned B-52s into sculpture. As you might guess, the novel's principal theme is excreta, but its unifying symbol is Thomson's home-run ball, the arc of which DeLillo traces across enormous expanses of political and cultural history (as well as time and space). "*Underworld* may or may not be a great novel," Martin Amis concluded in the *New York Times,* "but there is no doubt that it renders DeLillo a great novelist."

BIOGRAPHY

DON DELILLO IS A WRITER so intent on portraying American fads, fashions, and junk obsessions that it seems incongruous when he points to his Catholic upbringing as a major force in his work. Born into an Italian-American family in New York City, DeLillo attended Catholic primary and secondary schools before enrolling at the Jesuit Fordham University. He has traced the underlying "sense of last things" in his writing to his Catholic childhood and especially to the Catholic focus on death and eternity.

School, however, was definitely not an important influence on DeLillo—or, perhaps, it was a negative one. He despised the classroom and found his real education in the museums and jazz clubs of New York. He has said that, more than any particular authors, it was bebop and abstract expressionism that led him to become a writer. Thus, at age twenty-eight, he left the advertising agency where he had been working and devoted himself full time to writing, taking magazine assignments while completing his first novel. When *Americana* was published in 1971, it got enough attention to convince DeLillo to pursue fiction exclusively. By the time *Ratner's Star* came out five years later, critics were beginning to rank DeLillo among the important American novelists. *White Noise* put him into the first tier.

Famously reclusive, DeLillo refuses to make publicity appearances and has granted only a handful of interviews. "It's my nature to keep quiet about most things," he has said.

NEXT ON THE READING LIST: Martin Amis, Paul Auster, T. Coraghessan Boyle, E. L. Doctorow, Mark Helprin, Steven Millhauser, Thomas Pynchon

Pete Dexter
(b. 1943)

"Pete Dexter's men are emotionally walled off, utterly contained within their skins. They are also incapable of identifying what they feel, unless what they feel is sexual frenzy or the urge to tear someone's head off. Hemingway opened this territory, but Dexter is rapidly claiming it as his own. His novels represent a kind of archeology of the American male psyche—particularly that part of men that is most feral and unreachable by means of love."
—Brent Staples, New York Times

God's Pocket (RANDOM HOUSE, 1984) • Drug-addicted bricklayer Leon Hubbard prompts his own demise when he threatens a black coworker with a straight razor. Glad to be rid of him, the other workers and the foreman tell the police that Hubbard's death was accidental. But Leon's mother and her devoted second husband, Mickey, believe otherwise. While some reviewers criticized this picaresque romp for being too ambitious, most commended Dexter for his masterful control of the book's comic situations, as well as its fluent prose and idiomatic dialogue.

Deadwood (RANDOM HOUSE, 1986) • Dexter's second novel is a wily yarn about the eponymous Dakota town known, if at all, for the fateful day in August 1876 when Jack McCall shot Wild Bill Hickok in the Number 10 Saloon. No longer the crack shot he once was, the former Kansas marshal turned Wild West show performer drinks to ease his pain until one day McCall puts a bullet in his head. Unfortunately, most critics bemoaned the lack of an overriding plot and felt that Dexter never overcomes the crippling effect of losing his most interesting character much earlier in the novel than readers expect.

∗ Paris Trout (RANDOM HOUSE, 1988) • Written in colloquial prose that blends Dexter's trademark violence and tension with subtle wit, *Paris Trout* tells the story of a ruthless murder and the effect that it has on a small southern town. The antihero of this National Book Award winner is a white grocer and loan shark who, unable to collect a debt, kills a fourteen-year-old black girl. Trout, Dexter writes, "was principled in the truest way. His right and wrong were completely private." Some critics faulted Dexter for making his plot too predictable, but others lauded his solid characterizations.

> *"Rather than pinning his characters down, [Dexter] treats them as curiosities that might at any moment reveal hidden depths or unsuspected strengths. And they do—he gives complex portraits not just of Paris Trout, but also of his lawyer and of Hanna, his abused wife, who comes to understand her husband better than anyone else."* (*Maureen Freely*, The Observer)

Brotherly Love (RANDOM HOUSE, 1991) • The tragic fate of eight-year-old Peter Flood becomes apparent when, in the opening pages of this novel, he watches a neighbor's car skid on a patch of ice and slam into his three-year-old sister. He then spends the rest of his life searching for an inner peace that's impossible to come by in South Philadelphia's white working-class ghetto. Intelligent and acutely sensitive yet self-destructive in his unremitting guilt, Peter grows to manhood amid a blighted world. Dexter's "lean and swift" prose and "probing pen" reveal that, in the end, Peter can help neither others nor himself.

The Paperboy (RANDOM HOUSE, 1995) • Dexter's fifth novel is set in rural northern Florida, where a fearsome backwoodsman named Hillary van Wetter is sentenced to death for murdering the racist sheriff of Moat County. While on death row, Hillary becomes engaged to a sexually allur-ing postal worker who, convinced of his innocence, contacts a Miami news-paper. The "paperboy" of the title is reporter Ward James, who succumbs to what Dexter believes is contemporary journalism's mortal sin: not the need to know, but the need to tell. While some critics felt that Dexter's story meandered, others thought that the slow pace forced readers to linger among the novel's eerie emotions.

BIOGRAPHY

PETE DEXTER'S CAREER PATH has been anything but straight. Born in Pontiac, Michigan, but raised in Georgia and South Dakota, he spent "about eight" undergraduate years studying English at the University of South Dakota before he finally graduated in 1970 and took a job in Florida as a reporter for the *West Palm Beach Post*. After two years, he left that job ("I wasn't the best writer there"), worked with another former *Post* reporter at a gas station ("I wasn't even the best writer in the gas station"), and also toiled as a truck driver, mail sorter, construction worker, and salesman.

Dexter was finally rescued from career limbo in 1972 by a phone call from the *Philadelphia Daily News*. A decade later, he was badly beaten in a barroom with baseball bats and tire irons by residents of a Philadelphia neighborhood angry at a column he'd written about a drug-related murder. They broke Dexter's back and hip, but he survived, albeit with a literally new sense of taste (caused by the blows to his head). He had to give up drinking, which had been his favorite pastime, because he says that beer now tastes like battery acid. Instead, he began devoting his spare time to writing.

Dexter's novels are famous for their well-rounded, eccentric characters and for the resourceful way that they blend violence with humor. Reviewers have also praised Dexter for his realistic dialogue and the sharp eye that he displays when it comes to describing local color. The author now lives on an island in the Puget Sound, from which he writes a regular column for the *Sacramento Bee*.

NEXT ON THE READING LIST: Dorothy Allison, Russell Banks, Larry Brown, Robert Olen Butler, Richard Ford, Jim Harrison, Cormac McCarthy

---

Joan Didion
(b. December 5, 1934)

"[Didion] writes with a razor, carving her characters out of her perceptions with strokes so swift and economical that each scene ends almost before the reader is aware of it; and yet the characters go on bleeding afterward. A pool of blood forms in the mind. Meditating on it, you are both frightened and astonished. When was the wound inflicted? How long have we to live?"
—John Leonard, New York Times

Run River (OBOLENSKY, 1963) • Didion's first novel begins and ends on a luridly melodramatic note—with the firing of a gun—but the intervening pages subtly evoke a haunting world of pain and loss. Lily Knight marries Everett McClellan, who like herself grew up on a prosperous ranch in the Sacramento Valley. Initially so promising, the pairing turns disastrous, issuing in adultery, abortion, and finally murder. As in so much of Didion's later fiction, the California landscape, superbly captured, becomes a metaphor for her characters' interior emptiness. Reviewers applauded the book's formal perfection and finely wrought prose, though some agreed with *National Review* critic Guy Davenport that Didion seemed too detached, too ironic, and had "polished her prose too well for her own good."

* **Play It as It Lays** (FARRAR, STRAUS & GIROUX, 1970) • Short-listed for a National Book Award, this stark parable, set on the fringes of fast-lane Hollywood, catapulted Didion to fame. Technically, the novel owes much to the rhythm of contemporary filmmaking, with its quick cross-cuts, rapid dissolves, and lightning transitions. The benumbed narrator, Maria Wyeth, a model turned actress, sleepwalks through an eerie half-lit world peopled by predatory hustlers. The novel opens with Maria in a mental institution, separated from her cruel husband and brain-damaged daughter. Her enigmatic first words—"What makes Iago evil? some people ask. I never ask"—are among the most celebrated and debated in modern fiction. Is the affectless Maria a tragic symbol of the age or a shallow example of trendy nihilism?

> "Play It as It Lays *is a Hollywood novel in the same peripheral sense that* The Day of the Locust *is, attacking the subject with the indirection of art rather than the directness of commerce. Like Nathanael West's classic it is also brief, grotesque, allusive, and chilling. Perhaps too much so.*" (*Richard Shickel,* Harper's)

* **A Book of Common Prayer** (SIMON & SCHUSTER, 1977) • Charlotte Douglas is a Californian, but unlike earlier Didion heroines she's drawn, however passively, into the larger world around her—specifically into the violent political extremism of the late 1960s and early 1970s. Charlotte's second husband, a leading San Francisco lawyer, defends radical clients, while her teenage daughter by a previous marriage becomes a terrorist and disappears underground. In the hope of finding her, Charlotte travels to Boca Grande, an imaginary Central American country also awash in political violence.

> "More technically elaborate and thematically richer than Didion's other works, A Book of Common Prayer *is distinguished by uncommonly vivid social details, voices and landscapes and the clenched intensity of its prose.*" (*Richard Locke,* New York Times)

Democracy (SIMON & SCHUSTER, 1984) • In this challenging work, set in 1975, Didion resumes her examination of politicohistorical questions and their impact on troubled families. Inez Christian Victor, wife of a U.S. senator, loves dashing CIA operative Jack Lovett. Meanwhile, Lovett's daughter, Jessie, travels to Saigon at the moment of its fall. Didion presents the plot, which unfolds cryptically, as a postmodernist puzzle in which the novelist herself appears as a character. Many critics admired Didion's vision of a culture dominated by the political values of secrecy and power, though others found the book overly mannered and portentous.

The Last Thing He Wanted (KNOPF, 1996) • Published twelve years after her previous novel, this fable, like its predecessor, explores the impact of violent politics on the private lives of characters in turmoil. Set in 1984 and grounded unmistakably in Nicaragua's civil strife, the story unfolds like a thriller, although narrated in the author's usual fragmentary style. The heroine, Elena McMahon—married, a mother, and a sometime reporter for the *Washington Post*—flies to Latin America, where she meets Treat Morrison, an American diplomat and self-described "crisis junkie," who involves her in an illegal transfer of arms to a rebel group. The book, briefly a best-seller, was widely praised for its blend of intrigue and high seriousness and, in the words of *New York Times* reviewer Michael Wood, for its "marvelous notation of disaffection and despair."

BIOGRAPHY

JOAN DIDION IS A SIXTH-GENERATION native of California. Raised in Sacramento, she was rejected for admission to Stanford and so enrolled at the University of California at Berkeley, where she wrote her first fiction. She graduated in 1956 and won, that same year, *Vogue*'s Prix de Paris Award. She went to New York City to join the magazine's staff and remained an editor there until 1963, the year her first novel, *Run River*, established Didion, not yet thirty, as a major new voice in fiction. She has said that the discipline of writing captions for *Vogue* initiated her into the mysteries of writing economical prose. During this time Didion also contributed articles and essays to *Mademoiselle* and *National Review*. More remarkably, she overcame her extreme shyness and appeared three nights running on a TV quiz show, *Crosswits*.

But Didion's true milieu, as she knew, was California. In 1964, after she married *Time* writer John Gregory Dunne, the couple moved to Los Angeles to pursue careers as independent writers. Their combined earnings for that first year totaled seven thousand dollars. But soon they found their footing and became a successful screenwriting team whose credits include *The Panic in Needle Park* (1971) and *True Confessions* (1981).

During the 1960s and 1970s, Didion further emerged as one of the era's most brilliant journalists. Some of her pieces were collected in two classic volumes, *Slouching towards Bethlehem* (1968) and *The White Album* (1979). Whatever her medium, Didion's home topic has been California, its outer and inner landscapes and the eerie conjunction of the two. "The typical Joan Didion picture," Alfred Kazin has observed, is of "Hell as Sunny California...the hills on fire in Malibu and the surfers joyfully sporting below." It was a surprise, much remarked on, when Didion and Dunne left Los Angeles during the mid-1990s and settled in Manhattan, where they now live on the Upper East Side.

NEXT ON THE READING LIST: Francisco Goldman, Peter Høeg, William Kennedy, E. Annie Proulx, Susan Sontag, John Edgar Wideman

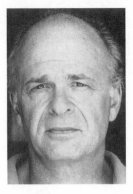

Stephen Dixon
(b. June 6, 1936)

"One doesn't exactly read a story by Stephen Dixon; one submits to it. An unstoppable prose expands the arteries while an edgy, casual nervousness overpowers the will."
—Alan H. Friedman, New York Times

No Relief (STREET FICTION, 1976) • Dixon's first book-length collection of short fiction depicts young men and women learning about love, friendship, and the intractable problems of communication between the sexes. The opening story, "Mac in Love," presents a narrator who, through devious and ultimately absurd devices, attempts to delay his lover's rejection of him. Among the reviewers gratified by *No Relief* was Frederick Guidry, who in the *Christian Science Monitor* summarized Dixon's technique as "fashioning a pleasant, questing hero and generating sympathy for his hesitant approach to life."

Work (STREET FICTION, 1977) • Dixon's first published novel is the 189-page story of unemployed actor Claude Martez, who gets a job as a bartender and then loses it. In the meantime, we eavesdrop on the minutiae of Claude's life, including his telephone conversations with his girlfriend, Oona, and his attempts to find work. Writing in the *South Carolina Review*, Thomas Stumpf complained that *Work* lacked theme and plot development, but he pointed out that this "lack of intensity is part of Dixon's truth."

Too Late (HARPER & ROW, 1978) • Dixon's second novel—which resembles, in style and theme, his short stories—describes the various complications that ensue when a couple attend a movie and the woman walks out because she objects to the picture's violence. The man, who's also the narrator, returns home to an empty house and spends the rest of the novel searching desperately for his missing lover, despite police indifference and the obstacles thrown up by assorted oddball characters. According to Jerome Klinkowitz in the *North American Review*, "*Too Late* is a tangled web of disruptions and distractions, the very stuff of Steve Dixon's fiction."

Quite Contrary: The Mary and Newt Story (HARPER & ROW, 1979) • The eleven stories in this collection portray various aspects of an on-again/off-again relationship between two young lovers. Dixon's main point is that the couple rely on their repeated breakups to stimulate intimacy. Although reviewers noted that Dixon's fragmented prose style suits his subject well, only a few liked the book, and some even found its stories boring. "Though usually witty," Mary A. Pradt wrote in *Library Journal*, "Dixon does go on."

14 Stories (Johns Hopkins University, 1980) • The title story of this collection, which contains thirteen stories, charts the effects of a man's death after he jumps from the fourteenth story of a shabby hotel. Another story, "Streets," explores the problems that develop when certain urban codes of behavior are ignored. Allen Wier in the *Washington Post* described these tales, drawn from Dixon's early work, as "shaggy-dog stories." He also noted that "Dixon is aware of the possibilities of language; his prose is flat, clean, wry."

* Movies (North Point, 1983) • This collection displays Dixon's talent for black humor. The title story presents the predicament of a man who attends a surrealistic film with his wife and then finds the surreality infecting his life when she announces her intention to leave him for the woman she sat next to in the movie theater. "Layaways," winner of the 1982 O. Henry Prize, features a young man whose decision to fight back during a store robbery results in the death of his mother. *Movies* helped to establish Dixon as a contemporary master of the short-story form. "At his absolute best, and he's there surprisingly often, Dixon is both gut-wrenching and funny," Mike Moyle wrote in the *South Carolina Review*.

> "Dixon's narratives run and jump through hoops of possibilities, taking on, as always, lives of their own. Ringing true to the rhythms of life—the spoken word, the unspoken thought—these tales are 'documentaries.' They are also farce; Dixon makes us laugh, cry, and feel the world of the little man or woman, inescapably the one we're in." (*Peter Bricklebank*, Carolina Quarterly)

Time to Go (Johns Hopkins University, 1984) • Although this collection presents themes and characters similar to those in *Movies*, most critics judged it less successful. The title story features one of Dixon's favorite characters, writer and professor Will Taub, who carries on an extended conversation with his dead father. Other stories depict the day-to-day lives of characters in excruciating detail. For example, the closing story, "Reversal," monitors the thoughts of a man as he changes his child's diaper. Dixon "ends up compounding a lack of imagination with a near absence of passion," John Domini wrote in the *New York Times*. "His characters' theorizing all starts to sound the same after a while, and his endings, deprived of even the least bubble of poetic effect, suffocate."

Fall and Rise (North Point, 1985) • Dixon's third novel traces in fragmented experimental prose the thoughts and movements of Daniel Krin, a translator of Japanese poetry, as he pursues Helene, a beautiful woman whom he meets at a party. According to one reviewer, "This is a dense and rambling novel: Reading it is like driving ninety miles per hour over an endless gravel road full of potholes." Most critics agreed that the novel's prose style, though innovative, was tiring.

Garbage (Cane Hill, 1988) • Things begin to go wrong for bar owner Shaney Fleet after he decides to resist a local garbage hauler's attempt to extort him. First, his apartment house burns down. Then he's arrested and beaten so badly that he winds up in the hospital. Although Shaney even loses his bar in the end, he still retains his fighting spirit. Echoing the book's many positive reviews, Albert E. Wilhelm in *Library Journal* called *Garbage* "a well-wrought parable of modern urban life." Michael Heaton in the *Cleveland Plain Dealer* was even more effusive: "Put simply, *Garbage* is glorious."

The Play and Other Stories (Coffee House, 1989) • In this collection, Dixon writes primarily of disaffected men suffering from the accumulated effects of frustration and failure. In "The Rescuer," one such man sees a young child fall to his death from an apartment window. His failure to catch the child induces a hallucinatory depression. "This author's world will not be everyone's cup of tea," Jenifer Levin observed in the *New York Times*. "It is not always mine. But one is nevertheless moved to admire his work. At its best, it is understated poetry: witty, heartbreaking, eye-opening."

Love and Will (British American, 1989) • The characters in this collection talk a lot but rarely communicate. Only in the final story, "Takes," is the pessimism relieved by Dixon's redemptive vision of a woman praying in a church for the safety of another woman abused the previous night. "By reaching for humor, however dark, and a jazzy staccato prose style that entertains even as it embodies anxiety, Mr. Dixon manages to avoid the gloom his vision inspires," Joyce Reiser Kornblatt wrote in the *New York Times*.

All Gone (Johns Hopkins University, 1990) • Dixon's eighth volume of short stories offers a potpourri of incidents that dramatize, in an exaggerated fashion, life's persistent lack of fairness. In one story, a husband fails to persuade the authorities that his wife is beating him. In another, a gunman forces a cab driver to drive recklessly, then tells the police who "rescue" him that the cab driver had hijacked him. Although praised for its absurd humor, *All Gone* was criticized for Dixon's unfortunate habit of recycling plot devices. As a result, "*All Gone* risks becoming tedious," Steve Erickson warned in the *New York Times*.

Friends: More Will & Magna Stories (Asylum Arts, 1990) • This collection resurrects the two central characters of *Time to Go* and *Love and Will:* writer Will Taub and his wife, Magna. As before, Dixon torments these people with the problem of sustaining a relationship despite their independent professional lives. Although not in the most positive terms, one critic admired Dixon's industry in uncovering the psychological richness of this couple's married life: "As always, there is Dixon's habitual questioning and reconsiderations."

* Frog (BRITISH AMERICAN, 1991) • This lengthy novel reads more like a collection of short stories because its characters disappear and reappear throughout a disjointed narrative. The result is a crazy-quilt portrait of writer Howard Tetch, complete with extended stream-of-consciousness passages and vivid depictions of Tetch's self-absorbed, often paranoid imaginings. In the book's key sequence, Tetch goes for a swim, leaving his young daughter in the care of a woman he has met on the beach. When he returns, his daughter is gone and the woman denies ever having seen her. Thereafter, a grief-stricken Tetch devotes his life to finding her. Although Dixon's anxious, edgy prose earned him PEN/Faulkner and National Book Award nominations, *Frog* isn't an easy read. However, its ready wit will reward the persistent.

> *"In exhibiting his extraordinary ordinariness for 769 pages, Mr. Dixon has handed us yet another great-grandchild of Leopold Bloom. Mr. Dixon's Frog, like John Updike's Rabbit, acquires a cumulative density that can't possibly rival Bloom's fecundity, but makes one think of Joyce anyway. It is exasperating that the book called* Frog—*which I take to be an agglomeration of short stories; which displays neither Joyce's wizardry nor Updike's range; which relies on the crude honesty of tom-tom prose in a freewheeling structure— should nevertheless be a work of undeniable resonance."* (Alan H. Friedman, New York Times)

Long Made Short (JOHNS HOPKINS UNIVERSITY, 1993) • This collection presents some typical Dixon characters, writers and academics, confronting their sense of loss and regret through memory. In "Battered Head," a father attempts to strengthen his relationship with his daughter despite the interference of his selfish ex-wife. In "The Rare Muscovite," a man contemplates with regret the sudden death of a Russian tour guide he had known. "For all their playfulness with time and perception, these stories are grounded in the simplest emotions of anger, fear, and abiding family love," Linda Barrett Osborne wrote in the *New York Times*.

* Interstate (HOLT, 1995) • According to Dixon, this novel begins with "the worst possible thing that could ever happen": Nathan Frey is driving with his two daughters along the interstate between New York and Baltimore when two men in a van fire shots into his car, fatally wounding one of the girls. The rest of the novel explores Nathan's inability to cope with his loss. According to Allen Barra in the *Los Angeles Times*, Nathan becomes a "suburban Mad Max," searching America's interstates for his daughter's killers. Reviewers praised some of Dixon's experimental techniques but warned that his extensive use of interior monologues and insistence on recounting even Nathan's pettiest thoughts make *Interstate* difficult to read.

> *"Italo Calvino and Alain Robbe-Grillet have also written novels that begin again and again, revising themselves, but the subjects of these novels are only*

themselves. Neither of them has brought off anything like the broken eloquence of Nathan's voice, which is as distinct and original and American as Mark Twain's, if otherwise very different." (George Stade, New York Times)

Gould: A Novel in Two Novels (HOLT, 1997) • This rambling stream-of-consciousness tale describes the machinations of a smart, self-absorbed, highly sexed womanizer named Gould Bookbinder. Gould's early goal in life is to bed as many women as he can, yet during the course of the novel he grows into an almost likable professor, literary critic, and family man. "While the book may not have an altogether reader-friendly style," Anthony Quinn wrote in the *New York Times*, "its chronicle of one man's life and loves is never less than absorbing." On the other hand, *Los Angeles Times* critic Richard Eder was less forgiving: "There are 277 pages and only one paragraph. Paragraphs, we realize, are like windows. The air in *Gould* becomes thick and heavy."

BIOGRAPHY

STEPHEN DIXON WAS BORN Stephen Ditchik in Brooklyn, New York. When he was six years old, his Jewish parents changed his last name to Dixon (but not their own). Dixon was educated in New York City, graduating from the City College of New York in 1958 with a bachelor's degree in international relations. For a time he worked as a journalist, first in Washington, D.C., and later with CBS News in New York.

Having decided at a relatively early age that he wanted to become a writer, Dixon studied creative writing at Stanford University during the mid-1960s. He was productive yet didn't begin publishing his work with small presses until the 1970s, when he was nearly forty. In the meantime, he supported himself with a variety of jobs: schoolteacher, school bus driver, tour leader, department store sales clerk, artist's model, bartender, waiter, reporter, and magazine editor. These jobs, most of them part time, provided Dixon with the hours that he needed to develop his fiction. In 1979, he returned to teaching, taking a job with New York University's School of Continuing Education. A year later, he moved to the writing department at Johns Hopkins University, where he has taught ever since, becoming a full professor in 1989.

In 1983, Dixon married Anne Frydman, a translator and teacher of Russian literature, with whom he has fathered two daughters, Sophia and Antonia. The Dixons currently live in Baltimore and New York City and spend their summers on the coast of Maine. Dixon's hobbies include listening to "serious" music. In addition to his books, he has published more than four hundred works of short fiction in magazines ranging from *Playboy* to the *Paris Review*.

NEXT ON THE READING LIST: Paul Auster, Umberto Eco, Milan Kundera, Steven Millhauser, Kenzaburo Oe, Michael Ondaatje, Salman Rushdie

E. L. Doctorow
(b. January 6, 1931)

"The imaginative universe of E. L. Doctorow is as unbounded in time as it is spatially restricted by his love and hatred of New York. He travels through history by means of inference, from old buildings. His characters are like genies conjured up by the mental stroking of New York City landmarks—the Morgan Library in Ragtime, *Bathgate Avenue in* Billy Bathgate, *the fairgrounds in* World's Fair, *P.S. 70 in* The Book of Daniel."
—*Jonathan Franzen*, Los Angeles Times

Welcome to Hard Times (SIMON & SCHUSTER, 1960) • Although Doctorow's first novel, set in the nineteenth century, received very little attention on publication, it has since won many admirers because of its taut narrative and lean prose. *Welcome to Hard Times*, a Western, plays against the stereotypes of that genre to tell a story about good and evil. The narrator, Blue, the mayor of Hard Times, a frontier town in the Dakota Territory, leads an effort to rebuild the community even as its existence is threatened by Turner, "the Bad Man from Bodie."

Big as Life (SIMON & SCHUSTER, 1966) • Doctorow's second novel, and the least read of his books, also draws on a familiar genre: science fiction. In the near future, two naked humanlike colossi from outer space cause a panic when they suddenly appear in New York Harbor. Authorities blockade the city, but this only adds to the crisis atmosphere. Doctorow describes the impact of these doomsday events on the lives of ordinary citizens who choose to remain on Manhattan and meet their fate. One reviewer called the tale George Orwell "in a minor key."

✻ The Book of Daniel (RANDOM HOUSE, 1971) • Doctorow's first major work, hailed as one of the best political novels of recent memory, deftly evokes the complex anxieties of Cold War America. A fictional retelling of the Rosenberg spy case, this National Book Award nominee shuttles back and forth in time from the 1950s, when Paul and Roselle Isaacson are convicted and electrocuted, to the late 1960s, when their troubled son, Daniel, a graduate student at Columbia, must deal with the consequences of his unusual birthright.

> "The Book of Daniel *is a book about children of trials, trials that mostly do not take place in palaces of justice. It is a book about crisis and because of that, it is a book of infinite detail and tender attention to the edges of life as well as to its dead center."* (*Jane Richmond*, Partisan Review)

* Ragtime (RANDOM HOUSE, 1975) • This novel—winner of a National Book Critics Circle Award and one of the most acclaimed works of the 1970s—is also Doctorow's most popular publication. A kaleidoscopic historical epic, *Ragtime* reimagines the United States of 1902 to 1917 by means of a plot that ingeniously brings together real-life figures—such as Henry Ford, J. P. Morgan, Harry Houdini, and Emma Goldman—with Doctorow's array of invented characters, among them an immigrant street artist and a black ragtime pianist. The result—set forth in lyrical, musical prose—exquisitely distills the jazzed-up energies that flourished at the outset of the "American century."

> *"The grace and surface vivacity of* Ragtime *make it enormous fun to read. But beneath its peppy, bracing rhythms sound the neat, sad waltz of* Gatsby *and the tunes of betrayed or disfigured promise that the best American novels play in one key or another. History resonates with special clarity here."* (Walter Clemons, Newsweek)

Loon Lake (RANDOM HOUSE, 1980) • Again Doctorow returns to the past, this time to the 1930s, in an ambitiously constructed novel that features several narrators. The principal characters are Warren Penfield, a failed poet, and Joe Kozeniowski, a workingman whose wanderings capture the panorama of depression America. While many critics admired Doctorow's finely honed prose, others found that the book's disparate pieces didn't quite add up to a coherent whole.

Lives of the Poets (RANDOM HOUSE, 1984) •This novella and six stories marked Doctorow's return to more conventional narratives. Although he again makes use of the past, here it's his own past that the author explores. The protagonist of the title novella, Jonathan, a Greenwich Village writer who has just turned fifty, reflects on his art and life, its triumphs and failures. Critics were divided over the book: Some found it rich in its honest self-exploration; others accused Doctorow of vanity and self-indulgence.

* World's Fair (RANDOM HOUSE, 1985) • Winner of an American Book Award, this tender memory piece hybridizes the genres of novel and memoir. Doctorow's purpose, he has said, was to "break down the distinction between formal fiction and the actual, palpable sense of life at it is lived." The book revisits the 1930s, the decade of Doctorow's own childhood, to describe a boy's experience growing up in New York City during the Great Depression. Although the story is circumscribed by the boy's family and its interrelationships, Doctorow's deeply textured prose imbues these mundane matters with emotional and psychological richness.

> *"You get lost in* World's Fair *as if it were an exotic adventure. You devour it with the avidity usually provoked by a suspense thriller.... [The 1930s] are savored in retrospect by a mature intelligence whose memory of childhood is so*

uncannily vivid, yet who keeps his unsentimental distance with the mock solemn prose that has become Mr. Doctorow's inimitable music." (*Christopher Lehmann-Haupt,* New York Times)

∗ Billy Bathgate (RANDOM HOUSE, 1989) • Narrator Billy Bathgate, at age fifteen, is a cross between a Horatio Alger hero and Huck Finn. When Billy becomes a gofer for the notorious mobster Dutch Schultz—the novel's setting is once again New York City in the 1930s—he exuberantly plunges into, in his own words, a "thrilling state of three-dimensional danger." Critics praised Doctorow's vivid evocation of the gangster milieu and his subtle blending of diverse literary motifs, drawing on both high literature and such popular art forms as the dime novel and the low-budget movie.

"Billy Bathgate is the kind of book you find yourself finishing at three in the morning after promising yourself at midnight that you'll stop after one more page.... It boasts a plot that's almost perfectly constructed...and it abounds in character as well." (*Anne Tyler,* New York Times)

The Waterworks (RANDOM HOUSE, 1994) • Doctorow turns the clock back to the late nineteenth century in this modern version of a Gothic tale rooted in the fiction of Edgar Allan Poe and set in the New York City of Boss Tweed and Tammany Hall. The narrator, McIlvaine, a newspaper editor, guides us through the lawlessness of the era, with its greedy tycoons, corrupt police, "street rats," and numerous other "species of dead-and-alive souls," as one critic put it. At the center of the novel is the city's massive waterworks, an example of the ways in civilization harnesses the forces of nature for its own murky ends. Writing in the *New York Times,* Simon Schama praised the book's "devilish cunning" and called it "the most intellectually designed of all of Mr. Doctorow's books."

BIOGRAPHY

NAMED FOR EDGAR ALLAN POE, Edgar Laurence Doctorow was born in New York City, where most of his fiction is set. His father, David, owned a music store but lost it during the depression and then supported the family by working as a salesman. These hardships, coupled with the radical political views once espoused by his parents, deeply inform Doctorow's fiction. Critics have often remarked that his work contains a long-running indictment of capitalism and of American politics in the twentieth century.

Doctorow attended the Bronx High School of Science and then Kenyon College, where he majored in philosophy and was active in theater. After earning his B.A. in 1952, he became a graduate student at Columbia University and then served in the U.S. Army, which stationed him in Germany. In 1954, he married Helen Setzer. They have three children.

For several years, Doctorow worked as a script reader for film and production companies in New York, an experience that introduced him to the visual techniques he employs so effectively in his novels. During the early 1960s, while publishing his first novels, Doctorow flourished as a book editor; in 1969, he became editor in chief at Dial. In later years, he has taught writing and literature at a number of colleges, including Sarah Lawrence, Princeton, and New York University, where he holds an endowed chair.

With *The Book of Daniel*, Doctorow emerged, at age forty, as an important American novelist with a strongly political bent. "It seems to me certainly a message of the twentieth century that people have a great deal to fear from their own governments," he told an interviewer at the time. "It's the nature of the governing mind to treat as adversary the people being governed." The publication of *Ragtime* four years later then propelled Doctorow to the top rung of literary celebrity.

His work, however, has had its detractors. Some reviewers have found his serious musings more facile than deep, and others have complained that the political messages in his novels tend to be heavy handed and formulaic. Yet few critics question the seductive beauties of Doctorow's prose, his narrative talent, his feel for atmospherics, or his ability to tap the historical past in a way makes it at once mysterious and familiar. His body of work is among the most substantial of any American writing fiction today.

NEXT ON THE READING LIST: T. Coraghessan Boyle, Don DeLillo, Mark Helprin, William Kennedy, Joyce Carol Oates, Philip Roth, Jane Smiley

---

Ivan Doig
(b. June 27, 1939)

"Unlike most Scots, Ivan Doig wears his heart on his sleeve. He is a man more than half in love with history, his own included.... In matters of work and grief, of place and kinship, he can make you remember with him and sometimes weep—unless, of course, you have a heart of stone and come from the effete East."
—Timothy Foote, New York Times

The Sea Runners (ATHENEUM, 1982) • Doig's first novel pits man against the elements in its re-creation of a stupendously arduous nineteenth-century canoe expedition from Alaska to the Washington coast. Building on just the bare facts of the event, Doig creates a blunt, driving adventure story. The book, wrote Mary Lee Settle in the *New York Times*, "goes beyond being 'about' survival and becomes, mile by terrible mile, the experience itself."

* **English Creek** (ATHENEUM, 1984) • The first book in Doig's wistful Montana Trilogy opens in 1939, with fourteen-year-old Jick McCaskill about to learn one of life's great lessons, thanks in part to his older brother's decision to reject college for a life in the saddle. Writing in the *Christian Science Monitor*, James Kaufmann called *English Creek* "old-fashioned in the best sense of the word."

> *"Two things make this nostalgic western novel especially delightful: old Jick's idiosyncratic theories…about everything from in-laws to General Custer; and young Jick's reluctance to come of age, coupled with his precocious understanding that that's exactly what he's doing."* (*Janice Eidus,* New York Times)

Dancing at the Rascal Fair (ATHENEUM, 1987) • In this prequel, Doig describes the arrival in America of Angus Alexander McCaskill and Robert Burns Barclay, the Scottish forebears of the McCaskills of *English Creek*. Their story is as big as the Montana sky and filled with good honest hardship (as well as lots of bears and coyotes). Even so, it's fairly stale stuff. According to Lee K. Abbott in the *New York Times*, the plot is "achingly familiar," suffused with "the usual melodrama of suffering and triumph."

Ride with Me, Mariah Montana (ATHENEUM, 1990) • The finale of Doig's Montana Trilogy presents Jick McCaskill as a depressed old man who has lost both his wife and the family ranch. The absence of a blue-sky future gives Doig's prose more bite than in his previous novels, which adds to the poignancy of Jick's departure in a Winnebago in search of new things in which to believe. According to the *New York Times*, "The characters are feisty and the plot entertaining, but what sets this book apart is the view from the Winnebago's window, a view that is fast disappearing."

Bucking the Sun (SIMON & SCHUSTER, 1996) • Doig returns to Montana for the setting of his fifth novel. The time is the Great Depression, and the Duffs, an extended family of hard-bitten Scottish immigrants, are all engaged in the construction of a WPA-funded dam on the Missouri River. Doig's focus is on the contest between nature and "progress," but he occasionally indulges in some historical fun and games, such as the sequence in which FDR comes to visit the dam site. The prose is timeless—it could have been written forty years ago—and perhaps for that reason Brad Knickerbocker praised the book's "grit and warmth" in the *Christian Science Monitor*.

BIOGRAPHY

IVAN DOIG HAS SAID THAT a writer should write what he knows. Doig knows that he was born in White Sulphur Springs, Montana, and that his father was a ranch hand. These two simple facts have informed nearly all his literary output. In addition to his novels, Doig has written several successful works of nonfiction that also tell and retell the stories of cowboy country. *This House of Sky: Landscapes of a Western Mind*, which describes how Doig's Scottish ancestors came to settle in Montana, was nominated for a National Book Award in 1978.

After earning a master's degree in journalism from Northwestern University in 1962, Doig worked for several years as a newspaperman in Illinois before returning to school, this time for a Ph.D. in history, which he obtained from the University of Washington in 1969. Soon afterward, he began to write books. Although Montana figures prominently in most of them, it hasn't been his exclusive region of interest. One of Doig's early nonfiction books, *Winter Brothers: A Season at the Edge of America* (1980), describes a nineteenth-century survey of the Pacific Northwest, and his first novel, *The Sea Runners*, is likewise set there. "I am Montana-born and now live within half a mile of Puget Sound," Doig has said. "Inevitably, or so it seems to me, my books are the result of those popular pulls of the Rocky Mountains and the Pacific."

NEXT ON THE READING LIST: Pat Conroy, David Guterson, Thomas McGuane, Larry McMurtry, Cathie Pelletier, Melanie Rae Thon

---

Roddy Doyle
(b. 1958)

"Roddy Doyle has perfect pitch from the get-go. He can write pages of lifelike, impeccably profane dialogue without a false note or a dull fill, economically evoking every lark and emotional plunge in the life of an entire Irish family."
—*Tim Appelo*, Los Angeles Times

The Commitments (KING FAROUK, 1987; VINTAGE, 1989) • Inspired by the rhythm-and-blues music of James Brown and Marvin Gaye, Jimmy Rabbitte Jr. places a musicians-wanted ad in the local newspaper: "Have you got soul? If yes, the world's hardest working soul band is looking for you." This deliciously profane comedy about the formation and breakup of a working-class Irish band—committed, in the words of its hustling manager, to "bringing the music of the people to the people"—was the first installment in Roddy Doyle's Barrytown Trilogy. It remains his best-known work, thanks to the popular 1991 film version. As *Rolling Stone* enthused, Doyle "possesses a rare gift for capturing the metaphysical life of live music."

The Snapper (Secker & Warburg, 1990; Penguin, 1992) • Like its predecessor, Doyle's second novel is written in hilariously foulmouthed Irish vernacular with little descriptive intrusion. Unmarried and pregnant, twenty-year-old Sharon Rabbitte steadfastly refuses to reveal the paternity of her "snapper," provoking turmoil within her own family and prompting much amused speculation among the neighbors. Critics were duly impressed with Doyle's talent for turning the humdrum into high comedy.

The Van (Secker & Warburg, 1991; Viking, 1992) • Short-listed for a Booker Prize, Doyle's third Barrytown novel centers on fun-loving Jimmy Sr., the ribald patriarch of the Rabbitte clan. Jimmy and his equally unemployed best friend open Bimbo's Burgers, a portable fast-food restaurant housed in a greasy van (it's a health inspector's nightmare). These two middle-aged ex-bakers start off as equal partners, but when business booms during the 1990 World Cup, their relationship becomes complex and troublesome. Critics responded enthusiastically to *The Van*, with Doyle receiving special praise for his ability to balance humor with an increasingly dark portrayal of midlife crisis.

* Paddy Clarke Ha Ha Ha (Secker & Warburg, 1993; Viking, 1994) • The first of Doyle's books to glance back at the past, *Paddy Clarke Ha Ha Ha* addresses such recurrent Doyle themes as friendship, religion, and familial relationships. Set in 1968 in a working-class neighborhood in northern Dublin, this somewhat autobiographical novel is told from the point of view of Paddy Clarke, a high-spirited ten-year-old whose humorous escapades become more violent and disturbing as the story progresses. While some reviewers criticized this winner of a Booker Prize for its lack of introspection and reliance on anecdotes, most applauded its realism, effective use of dialect, and engaging descriptions of childhood in proletarian Ireland.

> *"With remarkable sensitivity, Mr. Doyle...shows how trouble at home propels Paddy from the warm, familiar comforts of childhood into a cold, indifferent world where the laughter of the novel's title finally echoes hollowly."* (*Christopher Lehmann-Haupt,* New York Times)

The Woman Who Walked into Doors (Viking, 1996) • Thirty-nine-year-old Paula Spencer, among the most complex and memorable female characters in recent fiction, could have been Paddy Clarke's mother. When a policeman informs Mrs. Spencer that her abusive husband has been killed in a botched robbery attempt, it's the resolution of a life that had included beatings, unrelieved poverty, and drink. Paula's deeper tragedy, however, is that she wasn't always tragic. Previously admired for his comic ability, Doyle proved with this novel that he could indeed be a "serious" writer. One reviewer called Paula Spencer "Molly Bloom's sadder and wiser younger sister."

BIOGRAPHY

RODDY DOYLE'S FIRST THREE NOVELS, known as the Barrytown Trilogy, were all international successes. Each of these fresh, witty books focuses on a particular member of the Rabbitte family, residents of the Barrytown neighborhood of Dublin. Typical of the Irish working class, the Rabbittes are a lively, resilient household with a boisterous sense of humor that doesn't disguise any of the affection they feel for one another. Despite the unemployment, poverty, alcohol abuse, and limited social mobility that bedevil them, they thrive by virtue of their own brand of family values.

In his native land, however, Doyle's unvarnished portrayal of working-class Ireland has evoked as much censure as praise. "I've been criticized for the bad language in my books—that I've given a bad image of the country," Doyle says. "There's always a subtle pressure to present a good image, and it's always somebody else's definition of what is good." The author, born in Dublin, currently resides there with his wife and two sons in the same neighborhood in which he grew up. From 1968 until 1992, he taught at a local high school but gave up his teaching job after the publication of *The Van* to write novels full time.

NEXT ON THE READING LIST: Beryl Bainbridge, T. Coraghessan Boyle, Edna O'Brien, Cathie Pelletier, William Trevor

---

Umberto Eco
(b. January 5, 1932)

"Since Mr. Eco is a semiotician—one who interprets the meaning of signs and symbols—he shouldn't mind too much if I call him an academic conjurer more than a novelist.... Once the reader gets on the Eco carousel—going around in circles but never quite catching the brass ring because the author is too honest or too clever to have a cheap reward waiting at the end of the ride—it's hard to get off."
—Herbert Mitgang, New York Times

* The Name of the Rose (BOMPIANI, 1980; HARCOURT BRACE JOVANOVICH, 1983) • "The early history of comedy is obscure," Aristotle wrote in his *Poetics*, "because it was not taken seriously." Whether or not the Greek sage meant to make a joke, this first novel written by Italy's premier intellectual expands on his theme. *The Name of the Rose* is a deep, brilliant, and remarkably engaging detective story about a series of deaths at a monastery in fourteenth-century Italy. Moreover, behind the murders lurks the "true" story of the missing second volume of the *Poetics*, in which Aristotle delves into the divine nature of comedy.

"In its range, The Name of the Rose *suggests an imaginative summa, an alchemical marriage of murder mystery and Christian mystery. It conveys remarkably the desperation of a dying culture, while at the same time touching on perennial issues of love, religion, scholarship, and politics."* (*Michael Dirda,* Washington Post)

Foucault's Pendulum (BOMPIANI, 1988; HARCOURT BRACE JOVANOVICH, 1989) • Eco's dizzying intellectual inventiveness here yields a historic maze that's almost as fascinating as it is bloodless. Three editors at an Italian publishing house become enamored of a weird manuscript about the Knights Templar and other secret societies; half jokingly, they make up a secret society of their own...and find out that it may already exist. Writing in *The Observer,* Salman Rushdie was clear enough in his feelings: "It is humourless, devoid of character, entirely free of anything resembling a credible spoken word, and mind-numbingly full of gobbledygook of all sorts. Reader: I hated it." This reviewer, while also finding the book too dense to cuddle, was nevertheless swept up in the mad puzzle making.

The Island of the Day Before (BOMPIANI, 1994; HARCOURT BRACE, 1995) • Eco can't tell a straight story: That's both his strength and his weakness as a novelist. Here a seventeenth-century shipwreck maroons a sailor just across from an island. Between the deserted ship and the island lies the International Date Line. Because the sailor can't swim or reach the island in any other way, he's always staring at yesterday. The plot, which mostly comes in flashbacks, revolves around a truly bizarre mystical powder that, when placed on the sword that has inflicted a wound, causes the wound to heal. Like *Foucault's Pendulum,* this novel is intellectually dazzling, filled with rich wordplay, and utterly lacking in soul.

BIOGRAPHY

THE TOWN OF ALESSANDRIA, where Umberto Eco was born, lies in the Piedmont, a district of Italy whose residents are traditionally more caustic and reserved than other Italians. Recognizing these tendencies in himself, Eco has said, "Certain elements remain as the basis for my world vision: a skepticism and an aversion to rhetoric. Never to exaggerate, never to make bombastic assertions."

His father, an accountant, pushed him to study law, but he gravitated to medieval history instead, receiving a doctorate in 1954. He then went on to teach aesthetics, architecture, and semiotics, mostly at the University of Bologna. His idea-hungry essays have covered everything from Thomas Aquinas to wax museums to James Joyce.

Eco was already highly regarded as one of Europe's towering intellectuals when his first novel, *The Name of the Rose*, became a surprise best-seller. Reviewers expressed bewilderment that this thick compendium of medievaliana (numerous pages, for example, devoted to the figures carved into a single church doorway) could wow them in Peoria. But the simple fact was that Eco's novel had a grip: It spun an old-fashioned yarn about good and evil, as well as murder, love, and madness. It also painted an amazingly thorough picture of a distinct place and time, transporting the reader back across the centuries and providing one of the basic pleasures of fiction: escape. Eco's next two novels didn't match the critical success of the first, but both have also sold hugely.

Eco and his wife, Renate, have two children and live in Milan. He still teaches at the University of Bologna, writes a weekly column for *L'Espresso*, smokes a great deal, and plays the recorder.

NEXT ON THE READING LIST: Martin Amis, Louis de Bernières, Don DeLillo, Stephen Dixon, Steven Millhauser, Richard Powers, Susan Sontag

---

Louise Erdrich
(b. July 6, 1954)

"Louise Erdrich can do it in spades, for not only are each of her novels cannily and precisely plotted, but, as their several strands interconnect, there are further 'Oh-hos' and 'Eurekas' for the attentive reader.... Erdrich is like one of those rumored drugs that are instantly and forever addictive. Fortunately, in her case, you can just say yes."
—*Thomas Disch*, Chicago Tribune

✳ Love Medicine (HOLT, 1984; REVISED, HOLT, 1993) • This National Book Critics Circle Award winner, the first of an ongoing series, chronicles the lives of several Chippewa families as they struggle to maintain their tribal bonds through several twentieth-century generations. Set in North Dakota, *Love Medicine* relates fourteen interconnected tales told by seven narrators from two Chippewa families, the Kashpaws and the Lamartines. The novel's use of multiple perspectives and nonlinear plotting led a number of reviewers to term Erdrich's writing style "poetic," especially given her obvious ability to transform complicated emotions into concrete images. "At its best, the writing is admirably graphic, full of unexpected and arresting images and brilliantly dramatized small scenes," praised Robert Towers in the *New York Review of Books*. Erdrich later expanded

Love Medicine, adding four new chapters in anticipation of *The Bingo Palace*, the fourth novel in the series.

> *"With this impressive debut, Louise Erdrich enters the company of America's better novelists, and I'm certain readers will want to see more from this imaginative and accomplished young writer."* (*Marco Portales*, New York Times)

The Beet Queen (HOLT, 1986) • *The Beet Queen* continues Erdrich's narration of the lives of the Chippewa residents of fictional Argus, North Dakota. This time, however, Erdrich expands the domain of her work to include whites and half-breeds, focusing on the tensions that develop when the white world and the Indian intersect. The main action in *The Beet Queen* involves three female characters: Mary Adare, who is abandoned (along with two brothers) when her mother runs off with a stunt pilot; her cousin Sita; and their friend Celestine. In the difficult lives of Erdrich's characters, *New Republic* reviewer Dorothy Wickenden observed, "sexual love is furtive and disappointing, family love fierce and destructive, and friendship stolen and betrayed." Josh Rubins, writing in the *New York Review of Books*, lauded *The Beet Queen* as "a rare second novel, one that makes it seem as if the first, impressive as it was, promised too little, not too much."

* Tracks (HOLT, 1988) • Erdrich's third novel opens in 1912 in the aftermath of two epidemics that have decimated the Chippewa. Its initial scenes of Indian desolation and death announce a dramatic shift in Erdrich's tone. Much more overtly political than her two previous works, *Tracks* confronts and condemns the ploys used by whites to appropriate Chippewa land, the tribe's identity, and its ethos. Politically sympathetic reviewers loved the novel, but as Robert Towers argued in the *New York Review of Books*, Erdrich's portrayal of Indian privation aroused "the suspicion that the author herself was determined to exploit its exotic and bizarre aspects for all they are worth."

> *"Ever since her first novel,...Erdrich has been populating a specific place...with characters as strong and original, as funny and tough, as furious and vivid as any who have recently graced the American literary landscape."* (*Jean Strouse*, New York Times)

The Crown of Columbus (HARPERCOLLINS, 1991) • This novel—written jointly with her late husband, Michael Dorris—leaves Argus behind for the world of academe. The novel's two narrators are professors at Dartmouth College, where Erdrich and Dorris met. Roger, at work on a long narrative poem about Christopher Columbus, falls in love with Vivian, an anthropologist working on the discovery of America from a Native American point of view. On the whole, reviewers didn't like the book. "In the end," Robert Houston declared in the *New York Times*, "*The Crown of Columbus* never really finds itself."

The Bingo Palace (HARPERCOLLINS, 1994) • Although Erdrich's previous Chippewa novels all spanned at least a decade, *The Bingo Palace* concentrates on events that take place within a single recent year. Another break from precedent is Erdrich's use of a single central character, Lipsha Morrissey, who seeks to find a true "vision" of himself that can make sense of his Indian ancestry as well as the encroaching world of commerce represented by the reservation's new gambling hall. Using the vision quest as a literary device gives Erdrich the opportunity to make the invisible visible and the magical real. Soon enough, Lipsha meets his dead mother in the tribal bingo parlor, where he exchanges his car for a fistful of tickets guaranteed to pay off. Writing in the *New York Times*, Lawrence Thornton observed that *The Bingo Palace* "shows us a place where love, fate, and chance are woven together like a braid, a world where daily life is enriched by a powerful spiritual presence."

Tales of Burning Love (HARPERCOLLINS, 1996) • In the fifth of her Argus novels, Erdrich explores the lives of four women trapped in a Ford Explorer during a blizzard. To keep themselves awake and alive, the women tell stories about their ex-husbands. After *Love Medicine* provided a long, establishing shot, each of the subsequent Argus books has moved in tighter and tighter. In this sense, *Tales of Burning Love* is a close-up shot made with a telephoto lens. On the other hand, Erdrich's treatment of her characters' inner lives has broadened as she explores questions that deeply concern her: whether God exists, what love is, and whether faith can be sustained. According to Mark Childress in the *New York Times*, "Miracles and possibilities come together here to produce a kind of earthy magic that is more potent than magic realism."

BIOGRAPHY

SOME CRITICS HAVE OBSERVED that Louise Erdrich, the daughter of a Chippewa mother and a German-American father, seems almost genetically predisposed to move between two worlds, one Indian and the other white. However, her path as a writer wasn't always clear. After graduating Dartmouth, where she met future husband Michael Dorris, Erdrich worked as a beet weeder, a waitress, and a lifeguard before turning to fiction full time (and making subsequent use of those experiences).

One of the most striking aspects of her work is its use of multiple viewpoints. Erdrich's books teems with a variety of voices and inflections that cohere for a greater purpose, as individual tiles form a mosaic. In interviews, Erdrich has emphasized the collaborative nature of her writing: that her books are a product of not only her mind but also the ideas of others, most notably those of her husband and fellow author, Michael Dorris. According to Erdrich, the two passed drafts back and forth, reworking one another's prose until both were satisfied. The collaboration ended when Dorris committed suicide in 1997.

In assessing the breadth and scope of Erdrich's five Argus novels, critics have likened her achievement to that of Faulkner in his creation of Yoknapatawpha County. Also like Faulkner, Erdrich has made ample and astute use of the tools of modern fiction, especially multiple voices and nonlinear time lines. Yet her unreserved sympathy for tribal traditions comes out in her passionate, almost nineteenth-century use of imagery, such as when she describes a woman discovered after a blizzard as having "her hair loaded with melting stars."

NEXT ON THE READING LIST: Cristina Garcia, William Kennedy, John Nichols, Cathie Pelletier, E. Annie Proulx, Leslie Marmon Silko

Laura Esquivel
(b. 1950)

"Sex and food are the two most important forces in Esquivel's world, and both are controlled by women.... Politics and principles, companionship and trust pale beside a longing for food and sex."
—*Laurie Muchnick*, Village Voice

✳ Like Water for Chocolate (EDITORIAL PLANETA MEXICANA, 1989; DOUBLEDAY, 1992) • Subtitled *A Novel in Monthly Installments, with Recipes, Romances, and Home Remedies*, Esquivel's celebrated first novel parodies nineteenth-century women's serial fiction, which was often published in Mexico alongside recipes, home cures, dress patterns, moral exhortations, and calendars of church events. Written in the genre of magic realism popularized by García Márquez, *Like Water for Chocolate* tells the story of Tita, who loves Pedro but must (as the youngest daughter) remain unmarried so that she can care for her tyrannical mother. Pedro marries Tita's sister Rosaura, though Tita's powers in the kitchen are such that she's able to bake her profound sorrow into their wedding cake. "The Mexican revolution is raging, and soldiers from both sides float benignly in and out of the story," Laurie Muchnick observed in the *Village Voice*, "but it is in the kitchen and the bedroom that the true conflicts seem to take place."

> *"In Esquivel's reality, the beating of a human heart is as significant as the thumping of any revolutionary drum. Cooking...is a constant reminder of the alchemy between perceived and unseen forces."* (*Molly O'Neill*, New York Times)

The Law of Love (GRIJALBO, 1995; CROWN, 1996) • The heroine of this "multimedia novel" (it comes with a CD and a comic strip) is Azucena, an "astroanalyst" whose job in twenty-third-century Mexico City is to help people cope with their past lives. Meanwhile, she searches her own previous incarnations—she has fourteen thousand of them—for Rodrigo, her "twin soul" and true love. Complicating matters is the evil Isabel, a candidate for planetary president, who has claimed to be a reincarnation of Mother Teresa and must eliminate anyone—including Azucena—who can prove otherwise. While the *Los Angeles Times* praised Esquivel's "romantic ambition and imaginative vision," Judith Dunford of *Newsday* dismissed the novel as nearly incoherent: "*The Law of Love* reminds me of a bedtime story told by an outlandishly voluble babysitter. Lots of top-of-the-head improvisations. An occasional giggly patch. But the results are the same—you fall asleep before the end."

BIOGRAPHY

THE THIRD OF FOUR CHILDREN born to a telegraph operator and his wife, Laura Esquivel was raised in Mexico City, where she attended the national teachers' college. After teaching kindergarten for eight years, she became involved with a children's theater workshop and, learning that little suitable material existed, began writing her own plays. This soon developed into a career writing for children's public television. Her husband, director and actor Alfonso Arau, later encouraged her to segue into the film industry.

Esquivel's literary career began in earnest after she wrote the script for Arau's 1985 film *Chido One*, the story of a soccer player transformed by fame. The film's success encouraged the couple to continue their professional collaboration, and Arau later directed *Like Water for Chocolate* when it was adapted for the screen after becoming a number one Mexican best-seller. The resulting 1993 Spanish-language film, for which Esquivel received an Ariel Award (the Mexican Oscar) for best screenplay, attracted such a large audience in the United States that it propelled the English translation of *Like Water for Chocolate* onto the *New York Times* best-seller list.

Many publishers have credited *Like Water for Chocolate* with sparking interest in Latin American authors among mainstream American readers. In the wake of her sudden fame, however, Esquivel's twelve-year marriage to Arau ended, and she has since met and married dentist Javier Valdez.

NEXT ON THE READING LIST: Jorge Amado, Isabel Allende, Julia Alvarez, Louis de Bernières, Carlos Fuentes, Gabriel García Márquez

Richard Ford

(b. February 16, 1944)

"Richard Ford is among the most traditional of contemporary American writers and also among the most original.... Ford's sinewy and distinctively American voice contains the echoing tones of...an allegiance to the Hemingway legacy.... His fascination with a world of male rituals [has] led him to write about duck hunting and car theft and fishing and football."
—Michael Gorra, New York Times

A Piece of My Heart (HARPER & ROW, 1976) • Set in Ford's native Mississippi, this first novel narrates the demise of an itinerant construction worker named Robard Hewes, who leaves his wife for a married cousin. Reviewers pointed out that Ford's Mississippi Delta settings were more cliché than reality—a little *too* reminiscent of Faulkner—but many also praised his vivid characters and their true-to-the-ear dialogue.

The Ultimate Good Luck (HOUGHTON MIFFLIN, 1981) • Ford's hard-boiled second novel tells the story of Harry Quinn, a Vietnam vet who unwisely agrees to help a former lover free her drug-dealing brother from a Mexican prison. In the *Hudson Review*, Gilberto Perez compared the book to "a cheap action picture in which hastily collaborating hacks didn't quite manage to put a story together." On the other hand, Walter Clemons in *Newsweek* wrote that *The Ultimate Good Luck* was a "tighter, more efficient" novel than *A Piece of My Heart* "and a good one."

* The Sportswriter (VINTAGE, 1986) • Although Frank Bascombe has a talent for writing fiction, he writes about sports because he finds athletes uncomplicated and "happy to let their actions speak for them...never likely to feel the least bit divided. Or alienated." However, after his son dies and his marriage disintegrates, Frank finally begins writing about himself, recounting his fantasies, his "dreaminess," and his unpromising affairs. Ford received nearly universal praise for this "remarkably gentle and meditative book," a PEN/Faulkner Award winner.

> *"The Sportswriter is not a 'big' novel.... Like its protagonist...[it] charms us with the freshness of its vision and touches us with the perplexities of a 'lost' narrator who for once is neither a drunkard nor a nihilist but a wistful, hopeful man adrift in his own humanity."* (*Robert Towers*, New York Review of Books)

Rock Springs (ATLANTIC MONTHLY, 1987) • Ford sets most of these stories in Montana—although "it could be New Jersey," complained one reviewer, because the prose lacks a "peculiarly Western twang." Ford's characters are all white men between the ages of twenty-five and forty who consider success in sports, sex, violence, and crime the ultimate proof of manliness. Curiously, women keep showing up unexpectedly in their sacred places—fishing holes, hunting grounds—such as the two women in "Going to the Dogs," who bag a deer. One wants to snuggle with the male narrator, while the other steals a train ticket from his wallet. According to *Time*, *The Sportswriter* "established [Ford's] glittering reputation. The stories in *Rock Springs* confirm it."

Wildlife (ATLANTIC MONTHLY, 1990) • When Jerry Brinson loses his job after being falsely accused of theft, he's forced to take another as a firefighter. While he's away in the Montana mountains digging trenches, his wife, Jeanette, begins an affair with a wealthy bachelor. Meanwhile, their high-school-aged son, Joe, simply watches. "For all the drama—fires, betrayals, and confusions—the events in *Wildlife* are curiously undramatic," Sheila Ballantyne wrote in the *New York Times*.

* Independence Day (KNOPF, 1995) • Winner of both a Pulitzer Prize and a PEN/Faulkner Award, this novel picks up the story of Frank Bascombe six years after the action in *The Sportswriter*. Now a real estate salesman, Frank seems less alienated, yet the death of his son Ralph still haunts Ralph's fifteen-year-old brother, Paul, who occasionally barks like a dog and faces charges for shoplifting and assault. Meanwhile, Frank's new girlfriend complains that he doesn't love her enough. Many reviewers, now approving of Ford's deliberate pace, compared Frank Bascombe with Arthur Miller's Willy Loman and John Updike's Harry Angstrom as great American mythic characters.

> *"Anybody who can keep the reader going through 451 pages about a holiday weekend [of] pit stops at the Baseball Hall of Fame [and] the Vince Lombardi Rest Stop on the New Jersey Turnpike...may be the greatest writer of all time...because for dead-on dialogue and a perfect rendering of small-town and suburban distractedness, writing doesn't get much better than this."* (*Barbara Ehrenreich*, The New Republic)

Women with Men: Three Long Stories (KNOPF, 1997) • Each of the long stories in this collection focuses on its protagonist's angst regarding a broken or dissolving marriage. In "The Womanizer," Martin Austin, supposedly devoted to his wife, becomes obsessed with a Frenchwoman. In "Jealous," the most praised of these tales, seventeen-year-old narrator Larry and his schnapps-guzzling aunt Doris visit Larry's mother in Seattle, where she has moved after separating from Larry's father. The last story, "Occidentals," tells of a midwestern professor's affair in Paris, which ends in a fatal twist. According to *Booklist*, "There is no question that [Ford] is a gifted story-teller, albeit a morose and relentlessly precise one."

BIOGRAPHY

RICHARD FORD HAS SAID that he's a habitual mover. In fact, he has boasted of living in twenty houses in as many years and fourteen states in his life thus far. His wanderlust began when he was eight, shortly after his father—a Jackson, Mississippi, starch salesman—suffered a nearly fatal heart attack (the fatal one came eight years later). As a result of his father's condition, Ford shuttled back and forth between Jackson and Little Rock, where his maternal grandfather, a former prizefighter, owned a hotel. "Nothing ever got stale," Ford has said. "I remember one night in 1961, I had a date with a flight attendant—somewhat older than I was at the age of seventeen— and what we did on our date was drive from Little Rock to Jackson and back again, all in a few hours. I have a pleasant memory of that."

Intending to become a hotel manager, Ford enrolled at Michigan State, which had the best hotel science school in the country. Once there, however, Ford decided to study literature instead. He graduated with a bachelor's degree in 1966 and, while struggling to find a job, married his college sweetheart, Kristina Hensley. A series of brief careers followed— including teaching, basketball coaching, and working for the CIA—before Ford left law school to pursue an M.F.A. in fiction at the University of California, Irvine. After receiving his degree in 1970, he taught at the University of Michigan, Princeton, and Williams College while working on his first two novels. "Writing is the only thing I've done with persistence, except for being married," Ford told one interviewer. "It's such an inessential thing. Nobody cares if you do it, and nobody cares if you don't." After the 1981 publication of his second novel, *The Ultimate Good Luck*, Ford took a job as a writer for *Inside Sports*. Although the magazine soon folded, Ford's experience there inspired him to write his break-through novel, *The Sportswriter*.

Ford currently lives with his wife in New Orleans, where she directs the city planning commission. He owns both a plantation along the Mississippi and a cabin in Chinook, Montana, where he spends some of his time. Although Ford admits that the life of a writer can be "solitary and obsessive," he has said that he loves it: "No one makes me [write]. If it was too hard, I'd quit."

NEXT ON THE READING LIST: Russell Banks, Pat Barker, Ann Beattie, Pete Dexter, Jim Harrison, William Kennedy, Robert Stone, John Updike

Carlos Fuentes
(b. November 11, 1928)

"Fuentes is a novelist who builds structures in one's imagination. We feel that even at his most fantastic there is nothing trivial in his work, or merely sensational, or merely decorative. On the contrary, he writes with the authority of a great poet who, like his master Buñuel, needs [realism] as a medium for getting at the dark interior of the past."
—Guy Davenport, New York Times

Where the Air Is Clear (FONDO DE CULTURA ECONOMICA, 1958; OBOLENSKY, 1960) • Inspired by John Dos Passos's *U.S.A.* Trilogy, Fuentes's first novel tries to embody the entire history of postrevolutionary Mexico. Although he makes use of a large palette of characters, the book's unifying consciousness belongs to Ixca Cienfuegos. The enigmatic Ixca is many things—an adviser, a go-between, a gigolo—but, most important, he's an incarnation of the Aztec sun god Huitzilopochtli and is determined to avenge himself on the modern descendants of the sixteenth-century Spanish conquistadors. Although many Mexican critics objected to Fuentes's controversial socialist critique of his country's indigenous poverty, American reviewers simply hailed the book as a dazzling fusion of anthropology, sociology, music, painting, and—because of its use of montagelike sequences—film. "With the bravery of a young man," Anthony West observed in *The New Yorker*, "Fuentes has cleared all ideas of what a novel ought to be from his mind and has decided, quite simply, to put what it is to be Mexican, and all of Mexico, into his book."

The Good Conscience (FONDO DE CULTURA ECONOMICA, 1959; OBOLENSKY, 1961) • In temporary rebellion against his bourgeois family, young Jaime Ceballos shelters a fugitive union organizer, befriends an Indian scholarship student who dreams of class warfare, flagellates himself in the desert, and masturbates in church. Later, he changes his mind and embraces the moneymaking career for which his parents have prepared him. Writing in *Commentary*, Fernanda Eberstadt called the novel "gripping and colorful" despite its "glib cynicism" and "its crude lashings of self-pity."

* The Death of Artemio Cruz (FONDO DE CULTURA ECONOMICA, 1962; FARRAR, STRAUS & GIROUX, 1964; NEW TRANSLATION, FARRAR, STRAUS & GIROUX, 1991) • The remarkable Artemio Cruz, born an illegitimate mulatto, has risen during his profitable lifetime to become one of Mexico's leading financiers. Now on his deathbed, he recalls through a series of flashbacks his progress to the top, during which he and his bourgeois peers betrayed the ideals of the Mexican Revolution. Using three distinct narrative voices, all belonging in some way to Cruz, Fuentes masterfully weaves together chaotic interior monologues, subconscious observations, and terse omniscient description.

"Since Fuentes is a sophisticated writer...the gradual hardening and corruption of his hero is done with a good deal of subtlety and intelligence. He is never allowed to become a monster since the process he represents, though monstrous enough, is also natural." (A. Alvarez, New York Review of Books)

Aura (ERA, 1962; FARRAR, STRAUS & GIROUX, 1965) • This somewhat incomprehensible novella, written in the style of magic realism, marked a shift in Fuentes's work away from naturalistic social criticism toward the mythic and the bizarre. Narrator Felipe Montero, stalled in his doctoral dissertation and bored with his job as a secondary-school teacher, yearns to pry the reclusive Aura away from her elderly harridan aunt. What follows is open to interpretation: Is Fuentes writing about dreams or the supernatural? Is it a literal or figurative ghost that invades Felipe's body and soul? At least one thing is certain: Aura and her aunt are both more and less than they appear. "I would not like to be asked to say what precisely happens in *Aura*," Denis Donoghue admitted in the *New York Times*.

A Change of Skin (MORTIZ, 1967; FARRAR, STRAUS & GIROUX, 1968) • Four principal characters—Elizabeth, Javier, Frank, and Isabel—travel together through Mexico, stopping by the holy city of Cholula, where Cortes slaughtered thousands of Aztec priests in 1519. Along the way, using a disordered chronology, Fuentes retrieves moments from their pasts. Although Mexican by birth, Javier's wife, Elizabeth, has been cursed by her New York Jewish upbringing with both increased intellectual awareness and greater anxiety. Javier's lover, Isabel, by comparison, is less conflicted and inhibited but also largely unformed. One critic called *A Change of Skin* "Fuentes's most ambitiously designed work," yet many others considered it problematic at best and largely unsuccessful.

Terra Nostra (MORTIZ, 1975; FARRAR, STRAUS & GIROUX, 1976) • This novel, both ambitious *and* successful, reflects Fuentes's abiding interest in the Aztec religion and its suppression by the Spanish. The book is divided into three sections: "The Old World," set in Spain during the reign of Philip II; "The New World," about the Spanish conquest of Mexico; and "The Next World," which opens in 1999 as the millennial apocalypse draws near. Although Robert Coover, writing in the *New York Times*, noted that "the book seems largely to have been a labor more of duty than of love," he added that "if *Terra Nostra* is a failure, it is a magnificent failure." In the *Washington Post*, Larry Rohter called the book "at once savage and erudite, as complex and contradictory as Latin America itself."

The Hydra Head (FARRAR, STRAUS & GIROUX, 1978) • Fuentes dedicated this spy novel to the memories of actors Conrad Veidt, Sidney Greenstreet,

Peter Lorre, and Claude Rains—all of whom appeared in *Casablanca*. Set during the Arab oil embargo of the early 1970s, the plot concerns Mexican attempts to protect recently discovered petroleum reserves from greedy gringo oil interests. Fuentes's hero, secret service agent Felix Maldonado, battles an array of credible, menacing villains as he jets from Mexico City to Houston to Galveston and back. According to *New Republic* reviewer Alan Cheuse, "*The Hydra Head* is a tour de force, but unlike, say, Borges's detective fiction, beneath its impeccable surface lurks serious social content that adds incomparably to its intensity."

Burnt Water (FARRAR, STRAUS & GIROUX, 1980) • This anthology includes short stories from three collections previously published in Mexico: *Los dias enmascarados* (1954), *Cantar de ciegos* (1964), and *Chac Mool y otros cuentos* (1973). Reviewers found Fuentes in full command of both form and language, slipping effortlessly from realism to fantasy and the casual to the profound. Tales such as "Chac-Mool" emphasize a frequent theme: the violent eruption of a pre-Columbian past into twentieth-century Mexican bourgeois life. Yet reviewers were much more impressed with Fuentes's more heartfelt stories: "At his deepest, or most tragic, he abandons the ambulatory stone idols and ghostly old ladies in order to describe what truly touches him: the belt of misery around Mexico City, where men hunt rabbits and toads to eat, a temporary job as a flute player with a little band seems like a miraculous stroke of luck, and a woman's most valuable possession is an old photograph in which her husband—who was a stable hand—may be seen standing not far from President Calles," Evan S. Connell wrote in the *New York Times*.

Distant Relations (ERA, 1980; FARRAR, STRAUS & GIROUX, 1981) • In this fanciful ghost story about the extended Heredia family of Mexico, France, Haiti, and Spain, Fuentes explores the complex and powerful interaction between the Old World and the New. In his *Washington Post* review, William Kennedy described the plot and then acknowledged, "I don't expect anyone to really understand the preceding paragraph. You barely understand the book as you read it.... But you read on, held by the strangeness of it all." Or, as Guy Davenport noted in the *New York Times*, "we become deliciously confused."

* The Old Gringo (FARRAR, STRAUS & GIROUX, 1985) • Fuentes's best-known and most straightforward novel examines the longstanding cultural differences between Mexico and its northern neighbor. The "old gringo" of the title is the acerbic Ambrose Bierce, who left the United States for Mexico in 1913, presumably to join Pancho Villa's army, and never returned. The novel describes the rest of Bierce's life, as Fuentes imagines it, narrated by Harriet Winslow, a teacher who naively clings to her missionary faith amid Mexico's chaotic revolution. A notable exception to the chorus of praise for this novel was John Updike's review in *The New Yorker*, which faulted *The Old Gringo* for being "a very stilted effort, static and wordy."

"[Fuentes] has succeeded in welding history and fiction, the personal and the collective, into a dazzling novel that possesses the weight and resonance of myth." (*Michiko Kakutani,* New York Times)

* Christopher Unborn (FONDO DE CULTURA ECONOMICA, 1987; FARRAR, STRAUS & GIROUX, 1989) • Set during 1992 (the quincentennial of Columbus's first voyage) in a Mexico City beset by dramatic social and ecological problems, this novel is narrated by the omniscient fetus Christopher Palomar, whose initial joy at being conceived is undermined by his mother's subsequent rape and abandonment. Although Fuentes includes a great deal of farce, slapstick, and clever wordplay to leaven the novel's violence, he neverthe- less uses its many traumas to probe the Mexican capacity to endure and survive both natural and human-made adversity.

> *"In* Christopher Unborn, *Carlos Fuentes has imagined the worst for his coun- try's near future, but he's done it with so much humor, verve, invention, erudi- tion, and baroque whirligig plotting that the result is a vital, hopeful book, a great salvage operation in the trash heaps of Western culture, Spanish literature, and Mexican history."* (*Suzanne Ruta,* New York Times)

Holy Place and Birthday (FARRAR, STRAUS & GIROUX, 1988) • This volume contains two novellas previously published in Mexico: In *Holy Place* (1967), Fuentes evokes yet another Aztec deity—Tlazoltéotl, the goddess of filth and carnal desire—as he "expertly fuses Aztec, classical Greek, and Egyptian myths," according to one critic. On a more mundane level, the plot concerns aging film star Claudia Nervo and her possessive (perhaps incestuous?) attachment to her son. In *Birthday* (1969), Fuentes's first major fiction set outside Mexico, he returns to the magic realism of *Aura*—but makes the story even less realistic. Its central figure is an insane thirteenth-century theologian turned supernatural entity, who requires human offerings to prolong his "life." For now, he wants George, a com- fortable London architect.

Constancia and Other Stories for Virgins (MONDADORI, 1989; FARRAR, STRAUS & GIROUX, 1990) • Fuentes lingers over each of these five long stories to the point at which, as Denis Donoghue commented approvingly in the *New York Times,* "if he were to stay with it a moment longer, he would have to explain everything, and ruin it. Nothing is explained. We may inter- pret each story as we choose, but we cannot call on the teller to endorse our choice." And there's a lot to interpret in these bizarre tales: In "Viva Mi Fama," Goya and John Dillinger become contemporaries. In "La Desdichada," two students steal a wooden mannequin from a department store window and bring her to life. "By the time one of the students comes to 'kill' the wooden mannequin," Donoghue remarked, "he has moved beyond any of his normal relations to anything." So, one might infer, has the reader.

The Campaign (MONDADORI, 1990; FARRAR, STRAUS & GIROUX, 1991) • This historical saga, which the *New York Times* called "Fuentes's best novel so far," recounts the Latin American struggle for independence during the early nineteenth century. Although Fuentes focuses on three young Argentine idealists, the action covers a vast territory that reaches as far north as Mexico. The protagonists dream of actualizing the ideas of Voltaire, Diderot, and Rousseau, though Fuentes makes clear the futility of imposing European ideologies on Latin America. "Mr. Fuentes exploits skillfully the dramatic and even comic results of this faulty fit," *Times* reviewer Roberto Gonzalez Echevarria concluded. "In contrast to other Latin American historical novels, which can be ponderous and complicated, *The Campaign* is a very entertaining book, with a finely wrought plot and memorable characters and scenes."

The Orange Tree (ALFAGUARA, 1993; FARRAR, STRAUS & GIROUX, 1994) • Each of the five long stories in this collection depicts a moment when Mexico's two cultures—the Spanish and the Indian—meet, sometimes embracing, more often clashing. Although the settings range from the historical to the modern to the fantastic, Fuentes uses a number of leitmotivs to unite them, including the titular "tree of life," which flourishes in the New World as it never had in the Old. "What a wonderful mixture Fuentes brews here with all of the strangeness of the fated past reinvigorated and all of the immediacy of his country's present agonies laid bare," opined National Public Radio critic Alan Cheuse.

Diana: The Goddess Who Hunts Alone (ALFAGUARA, 1994; FARRAR, STRAUS & GIROUX, 1995) • This roman à clef recounts a brief early 1970s affair between a cosmopolitan leftist novelist named Carlos and Diana Soren, a beautiful young actress reminiscent of Jean Seberg. (Seberg committed suicide after being harassed by the FBI because of her sympathy for the Black Panthers and other radical groups.) Most reviewers, aware of Fuentes's fascination with the interplay between myth and reality, were prepared to tolerate his elevation of the Seberg character to tragic-heroic status. However, they didn't understand why Fuentes inserted himself into this tale. "Even if parts of *Diana* are beautiful, it's more of an idea—a probing, evocative essay—than a fully realized story," Dan Cryer wrote in *Newsday*. "Next time, please, more Diana and less Carlos."

The Crystal Frontier: A Novel in Nine Stories (ALFAGUARA, 1995; FARRAR, STRAUS & GIROUX, 1997) • Calling this a novel doesn't make it one. Each of the nine stories referred to in the subtitle features a character with some connection to Leonardo Barroso, a powerful, ruthless, somewhat shady Mexican businessman. Yet the stories exist more in isolation than they do as a coherent whole. Their common thread, if one exists, is the recurrent theme of miscommunication between Mexicans and Americans. The stories that stand up best are those in which Fuentes's political message serves, rather than undermines, his fictional aim. "While the long narrative of *The Crystal Frontier* is cleverly structured, the stories vary in quality," Valerie Miner wrote in the *Los Angeles Times*. "Fuentes sometimes scrawls prosaically, forfeiting fresh, distilled language to flat, cerebral statements."

BIOGRAPHY

BORN IN PANAMA CITY to a career Mexican diplomat, Carlos Fuentes spent most of his childhood living in the capital cities of North and South America, including Washington, Buenos Aires, Santiago, and Rio de Janeiro. While in Rio, where his father served as secretary to Mexican ambassador Alfonso Reyes, Fuentes developed a relationship with Reyes, a distinguished poet and essayist who later became Fuentes's literary mentor. After World War II, Fuentes attended the Colegio de México, later undertaking graduate work at the Institut des Hautes Études in Geneva before returning to Mexico for law school. During the early 1950s, he worked as press secretary for the United Nations Information Center in Mexico City, publishing his first book, the short-story collection *Los dias enmascarados*, in 1954.

While his literary career developed, Fuentes followed his father into the diplomatic corps, serving from 1957 to 1959 as director of international cultural relations for the Mexican Ministry of Foreign Affairs. Two decades later, well after his literary reputation had been established, he served for two years as Mexico's ambassador to France. Since then, he has adopted the role of "ambassador without portfolio," seeking to define more clearly the proper relationship between the United States and Latin America as well as to promote international understanding.

A novelist, a playwright, a short-story writer, a screenwriter, an essayist, and a critic, Fuentes has created a prolific amount of prose noted for its innovative language and narrative technique. Regarded by many as Mexico's foremost novelist, he has searched in all his work for a viable yet affirming Mexican national identity. More often than not, he looks into the past, to myth and legend and religion, for his answers. In a *Paris Review* interview, Fuentes said that "every Latin American writer goes around dragging a heavy body, the body of his people, of his past, of his national history. We have to assimilate the enormous weight of our past so that we will not forget what gives us life. If you forget your past, you die." Speaking of his tendency toward the bizarre and the inscrutable, Fuentes has said, "I'm looking for readers I would like to make...to win them...to create readers rather than to give something that readers are expecting. That would bore me to death."

NEXT ON THE READING LIST: Isabel Allende, Stephen Dixon, John Nichols, Salman Rushdie, Mario Vargas Llosa

Mary Gaitskill

(b. November 11, 1954)

"Sentence by sentence, Mary Gaitskill charts the twists and turns of emotion and desire, in fanatically analytical prose that zips along in a fever of self-consciousness that would seem loony if her observations weren't so sane.... She has an icy eye, but there's forgiveness in her heart."
—Craig Seligman, New York Times

* Bad Behavior (POSEIDON, 1988) • Everybody behaves badly in these finely crafted stories that positively reek of New York in the 1980s. All the characters live in closet-sized apartments; they all deal or buy drugs; and prostitutes are as ubiquitous as cockroaches. The men in Gaitskill's stories are vile, motivated by sex and cheesy greed; the women, as often as not, give themselves knowing full well they'll be abused.

> *"The desperate search for love, for fundamental human connection, is the central theme of all the nine stories in this collection.... These are accomplished, satisfying stories in which even the worst behavior is redeemed by small, harmonious affirmations of life."* (*Regina Weinreich,* American Book Review)

Two Girls, Fat and Thin (POSEIDON, 1991) • Loosed from the structured elegance of the short story, Gaitskill wanders. While there's much of the same fine analysis at work in this novel (in which two women look back on their childhoods), it seems that Gaitskill thought that writing a novel was simply a matter of using more words in each sentence. As a result, this book has none of the tautness of her stories. Yet Meg Wolitzer wrote in the *Washington Post* that "*Two Girls, Fat and Thin* is a deliberately overblown and demanding novel, imperfect in its excesses, but admirable in its weight."

Because They Wanted To (SIMON & SCHUSTER, 1997) • Gaitskill's long-awaited second collection of stories is broader in its characterizations and settings and more mature than *Bad Behavior,* though just as daring and cutting. The most elegant piece is "The Dentist," in which a woman falls absurdly in love with the brute maleness of her dentist as he attempts to extract one of her teeth. Writing in the *Los Angeles Times*, Richard Eder remarked that Gaitskill's prose "seems deliberately to combine mastery and jagged roughness."

BIOGRAPHY

MARY GAITSKILL WAS BORN IN Lexington, Kentucky, where her father was a teacher and her mother a social worker. She ran away from home at age sixteen and lived, by her own account, a very rough life on the road. She spent two years in Toronto working as a stripper and admits to at least one stint as a prostitute. She also spent some time in a mental hospital. Somehow she eventually earned a B.A. from the University of Michigan.

All these events have, of course, contributed to her writing. As she once explained, "My experience of life as essentially unhappy and uncontrollable taught me to examine the way people, including myself, create survival systems and psychologically 'safe' places for themselves in unorthodox and sometimes apparently self-defeating ways."

New York City turned out to be the perfect place for Gaitskill to settle down and create such an unorthodox "safe" place for herself. Of late she has divided her time among Greenwich Village, San Francisco, and Marin County.

NEXT ON THE READING LIST: Ann Beattie, Sandra Cisneros, David Leavitt, Melanie Rae Thon

Cristina Garcia
(b. July 4, 1958)

"Garcia is an enthralling storyteller. But what makes her storytelling especially seductive is the subtle synergy between intellect and emotion. Her characters earn their insights by dint of passionate experience, and Garcia frames the action within the clarifying context of twentieth-century Cuban history."
—*Dan Cryer,* Newsday

* Dreaming in Cuban (KNOPF, 1992) • Garcia's first novel, a National Book Award finalist, surveys three generations of a Cuban family divided by Castro's 1959 revolution. The saga begins during the 1930s, when Celia falls for a married Spaniard. After the Spaniard returns to his wife, Celia marries unhappily and has two daughters, Lourdes and Felicia. When the revolution comes, Celia backs Castro wholeheartedly, but Lourdes, who has been raped by a revolutionary, immigrates to New York City and becomes a successful capitalist. The last phase of the novel, which takes places during the late 1970s and early 1980s, describes the efforts of Lourdes's daughter, Pilar, to visit her grandmother and thereby regain her Cuban heritage.

"Fierce, visionary, and at the same time oddly beguiling and funny, Dreaming in Cuban *is a completely original novel. It announces the debut of a writer,*

blessed with a poet's ear for language, a historian's fascination with the past, and a musician's intuitive understanding of the ebb and flow of emotion." (*Michiko Kakutani,* New York Times)

The Aguero Sisters (KNOPF, 1997) • Once again Garcia chronicles three generations of a Cuban family divided by the 1959 revolution, and once again she produces excellent results. Reina Aguero and Constancia Aguero Cruz are the children of famous Cuban naturalists. By the early 1990s, when the main action of the novel takes place, Reina, a master electrician, is living in one room of a Havana apartment; Constancia has become a successful capitalist in the United States. After a lightning strike forces Reina to reevaluate her life, she flees Cuba and, in tandem with her estranged sister, begins to probe her mother's mysterious 1948 death. Garcia tells the story from three points of view: those of Constancia, Reina, and their late father, Ignacio, using his journals. Compared with *Dreaming in Cuban,* Dan Cryer wrote in *Newsday, The Aguero Sisters* "is even better, a deeper, more profound plunge into the mysteries of loyalty, love, and identity."

BIOGRAPHY

CRISTINA GARCIA WAS BORN IN Havana just six months before Fidel Castro came to power. A year after that, her parents immigrated to New York City, where Garcia grew up mostly in the borough of Queens. Although she now lives in Southern California, she has said that "I really consider myself a New Yorker, if I consider myself anything."

She attended Barnard College, graduating in 1979. Two years later, she earned a master's degree from Johns Hopkins University. In 1983, she went to work for *Time* as a researcher. She was promoted to correspondent in 1985, and during the late 1980s she served as *Time*'s bureau chief in Miami. In 1988, she moved from Miami to Los Angeles and two years later married Scott Brown and left the magazine. Garcia and Brown have since divorced, but Garcia continues to live in the Westwood section of Los Angeles so that she and her former husband can share custody of their daughter, Pilar, who was born in late 1992.

"I grew up with a very bifurcated sense of myself," Garcia told one interviewer. "I worked to develop an American side, with my Cuban side being more private." Then, at some point during her early thirties, she "became incorrigibly Cuban. It sort of hit me retroactively, this identity thing." Her transformation from journalist to novelist also came as a surprise, sparked when she first began to read poetry seriously about the age of thirty. "After that," she recalled, "there was no turning back. It was just this explosion of language and possibility that I hadn't known existed." According to Garcia, "[Writing *Dreaming in Cuban*] was a haphazard thing. It began as a poem, then I thought it was a short story, then a novella. I had no clue for at least a year what it was I was working on."

NEXT ON THE READING LIST: Julia Alvarez, Sandra Cisneros, Edwidge Danticat, Louise Erdrich, Oscar Hijuelos, Jamaica Kincaid, Amy Tan

Gabriel García Márquez

(b. March 6, 1928)

"García Márquez tells his stories with a strange omniscience. He is as capable of seeing the dignity in homeliness and poverty as the hidden jokes and rituals of opulence, as comfortable with science, magic, voodoo, ghosts, as with the riddles of Catholicism."

—*Mona Simpson*, London Review of Books

In Evil Hour (GRAFICAS "LUIS PEREZ," 1962; HARPER & ROW, 1979) • This novel portrays a small Latin American town beset by political violence and pervasive corruption. It's no doubt flavored by García Márquez's own experience of La Violencia, the period of civil strife that plagued Colombia during the 1950s. Writing in the *New York Times*, Robert Coover praised *In Evil Hour* for its "wit, perception, imaginative richness, and easy accessibility."

No One Writes to the Colonel and Other Stories (HARPER & ROW, 1968) • This collection of short fiction gathers together several García Márquez works previously published in Spanish, including a number of his best-known tales. In the title novella, which first appeared in 1955, the colonel of the title waits endlessly for a pension, his perpetual anxiety mirroring the life in his small Latin American town. Another story, "Big Mama's Funeral," introduces several characters who later appear in *One Hundred Years of Solitude*.

* One Hundred Years of Solitude (EDITORIAL SUDAMERICANA, 1967; HARPER & ROW, 1970) • This acclaimed novel introduced the genre of Latin American magical realism to a worldwide audience. A tragicomic epic, it chronicles the lives of six generations of the Buendía family, from the founding of their sleepy town of Macondo until its apocalyptic end. What fascinated and excited readers most about García Márquez's work was its fantastical plotting, not to mention its vivid symbolism: rains that continue without relief for years; the ascent of a girl into heaven, together with her bedsheets; a levitating priest; a cascade of yellow flowers that falls from the sky when a Buendía patriarch dies. Voracious readers bought up printing after printing.

"When García Márquez's utterly original One Hundred Years of Solitude *came out here in 1970, I read it—I experienced it—with the same recognition of a New World epic that one feels about* Moby Dick.*"* (*Alfred Kazin,* New York Times)

Leaf Storm and Other Stories (HARPER & ROW, 1972) • This collection includes some of García Márquez's earliest writing—such as the title story, which he began when he was just nineteen—as well as other short pieces written during the late 1960s. In "The Handsomest Drowned Man in the World," a corpse washes ashore near a small village, where all the women fall in love with it. Another story tells of a talented embalmer who preserves deceased viceroys so well that they continue governing after their deaths. "García Márquez manages to make a story out of each of these— not too ambitious, but just graceful enough to be itself," Alfred Kazin wrote in the *New York Times.*

The Autumn of the Patriarch (PLAZA & JANES, 1975; HARPER & ROW, 1976) • Although written in the same richly descriptive prose as *One Hundred Years of Solitude,* this novel carries a more overtly political message. The patriarch of the title, a dictator, has ruled as long as anyone can remember. Recognizing the allegory, John Sturrock of the *Times Literary Supplement* called *The Autumn of the Patriarch* "a novelist's revenge for the political abjection of his native country." The prose itself, however, isn't so clear: In the *National Review,* Ronald de Feo called the novel "a difficult book to stay with…not because of the sentences that run on for pages or the absence of paragraphs, but because of an overabundance of riches." Walter Clemons in *Newsweek* also found the book disappointing, calling it "both oversumptuous and underpopulated."

Innocent Eréndira and Other Stories (HARPER & ROW, 1978) • The five short stories collected here, as well as the title novella, were all previously published in Spanish. These works present more themes and characters typical of García Márquez's work. There's the larger-than-life grandmother who exploits Eréndira, prostituting her because she supposedly burned down their house. There are also many satirical swipes at government, religion, and capitalism, all made with García Márquez's trademark surrealistic brush. As one reviewer noted of the characters, "Fantasy is the rule, the dominant and organizing force of their lives."

Chronicle of a Death Foretold (OVEJA NEGRA, 1981; HARPER & ROW, 1980) • Based on an actual incident, this novel dramatizes the story of a young bride whose husband returns her after their wedding night because she's not a virgin. Subsequently her brothers set out to murder the man whom she names as the "perpetrator." A former resident who has returned to reconstruct these event narrates the story, which is as much about the townspeople as about the main characters. Bill Buford in the *Times Literary Supplement* called *Chronicle of a Death Foretold* "a mesmerizing work that clearly establishes Márquez as one of the most accomplished and the most 'magical' of political novelists writing today."

Love in the Time of Cholera (OVEJA NEGRA, 1985; KNOPF, 1988) • This novel about love, marriage, and mortality is a boy-meets-girl story with a twist. When Dr. Juvenal Urbino dies attempting to rescue a parrot from a tree, his departure clears the way for Florentino Ariza to resume his courtship of the doctor's widow, which had ended fifty years earlier. Thomas Pynchon, writing in the *New York Times*, called *Love in the Time of Cholera* a "shining and heartbreaking novel." However, according to Michael Dorris's review in the *Chicago Tribune*, "While a Harlequin romance might balk at stretching this plot for more than a year or two of fictional time, García Márquez nurses it over five decades."

The General in His Labyrinth (OVEJA NEGRA, 1989; KNOPF, 1990) • García Márquez's historical interests find expression in this account of the last months in the life of Simón Bolívar. The Bolívar of this novel is a melancholy, prophetic figure who has seen his dream of a united South America dissipate into partisan squabbling. By calling into question the saintly image of Bolívar, while also disapproving of Bolívar's rivals, García Márquez "managed to offend all sides," according to John Butt in the *Times Literary Supplement*.

Strange Pilgrims (OVEJA NEGRA, 1992; KNOPF, 1993) • García Márquez returns here to the form of the short story. The unifying theme of this collection, as implied by its title, is that of exile—specifically, Latin Americans exiled in Europe. In one story, a Colombian man struggles for decades to persuade the Vatican to canonize his late daughter. In another, a Mexican woman enters a Spanish insane asylum looking for a telephone, only to be mistaken for a patient. The critical response was respectful but not effusive. Michael Dirda in the *Washington Post* made clear his opinion that these stories lacked "the soul-stirring magic of García Márquez's earlier short fiction," yet he admitted that "one could hardly wish for more readable entertainments, or more wonderful detailing."

Of Love and Other Demons (NORMA, 1994; KNOPF, 1995) • Twelve-year-old Sierva Maria is bitten by a rabid dog. The local bishop, suspecting that she has been possessed by demons, sends her to a young priest to be exorcised. The priest, however, falls in love with her. *Los Angeles Times* critic Richard Eder's reaction was typical: The novel was "a good one, though not quite among [García Márquez's] best." Eder also wrote that "some of the magical ironies are as fresh as ever; others display more magician than magic."

BIOGRAPHY

GABRIEL GARCÍA MÁRQUEZ WAS BORN IN the village of Aracataca, Colombia. Because his parents were very poor and had twelve children, he was raised by his maternal grandparents. García Márquez's grandfather, whom he once called "the most important figure of my life," was a retired colonel and veteran of two civil wars. His tales of Aracataca during the banana boom of the early twentieth century presented García Márquez with a lifetime's worth of material. In fact, many of the locations and characters that García Márquez has used in his novels—the lavish houses, banana plantations, eccentric colonels, and gringo entrepreneurs—come directly from his grandfather's memory.

When he was eight, García Márquez was sent to Zipaquirá, near the Colombian capital of Bogotá, to be schooled. Later, he studied law at the University of Bogotá but disliked it so much that he never completed his degree. Instead, in 1950, he moved to the coastal town of Baranquilla, where he wrote a column for the local newspaper and began his literary career, studying the works of Faulkner, Hemingway, Woolf, Kafka, and Joyce. In 1958, he married his childhood sweetheart, Mercedes Barcha.

After the 1959 Cuban revolution, García Márquez, always a committed leftist, helped found the Bogotá office of Prensa Latina, Fidel Castro's official press agency. García Márquez subsequently worked for Prensa Latina in Bogotá and Havana before becoming an assistant bureau chief in New York City. However, he soon left New York for Mexico City, where he worked as an advertising copywriter.

This was a difficult time for García Márquez, who in his fictional work was suffering from writer's block. His mind finally cleared during a drive from Mexico City to Acapulco in 1965, when the inspiration came to him for *One Hundred Years of Solitude*—suddenly, and in great detail. For the next year and a half, he went into seclusion, writing furiously for eight to ten hours a day. "I didn't know what my wife was doing," he told William Kennedy in an *Atlantic Monthly* interview, "and I didn't ask any questions.... We always lived as if we had money. But when I was finished writing, my wife said, 'Did you really finish it? We owe twelve thousand dollars.'"

The new novel, published in 1967, was a watershed in García Márquez's artistic career: In place of the clipped journalistic prose of his earlier fiction, a lush, wordy, digressive style emerged to describe a fictional world full of potent symbols, eccentric characters, and surrealistic events. Although García Márquez didn't invent the genre of magical realism, his novels were certainly the most influential in promoting it. In recognition of this achievement, he was awarded the 1982 Nobel Prize in literature. As he once told Peruvian novelist Mario Vargas Llosa, "The writer is not here to make declarations, but to tell about things."

NEXT ON THE READING LIST: Isabel Allende, Jorge Amado, Louis de Bernières, Kenzaburo Oe, Salman Rushdie, Leslie Marmon Silko

Kaye Gibbons
(b. 1960)

"If southern novelists were painters, most would work in oils and lay them on the canvas darkly and thickly: brilliant hues, violent chiaroscuro. Kaye Gibbons, in contrast, is a water-colorist, deepening her meanings gradually by strokes of a fine, pale wash."
—*Michael Harris*, Los Angeles Times

Ellen Foster (ALGONQUIN, 1987) • Old Ellen, as the narrator of this spare and moving first novel calls herself, is eleven years old. After her mother commits suicide and her father tries to rape her, she winds up in the care of a moody, unloving grandmother. "The voice of this resourceful child is mesmerizing because we are right inside her head," gushed Pearl K. Bell in *The New Republic.* "The words are always flawlessly right."

A Virtuous Woman (ALGONQUIN, 1989) • A gentle, poignant love story, this novel is told from two alternating (and temporally disconnected) points of view: those of a husband whose wife has died of cancer and the wife who, in her final days, looks back on their life together. As in Gibbons's first novel, the book's setting is the Deep South and its pervasive theme is death. Roz Kavaney, writing in the *Times Literary Supplement,* observed that *A Virtuous Woman* "has the simplicity of a good country-and-western song."

* A Cure for Dreams (ALGONQUIN, 1991) • In this third novel, Gibbons expands her focus to encompass three generations of women in a southern family. Lottie, whose death sets the story in motion, was a dreamer born of Irish stock but raised in the hill country of Kentucky. Her daughter, Betty, recounts Lottie's life of hard times and determination and then continues on to chronicle her own, ending the story with the birth of her own daughter.

> *"[An] absolutely darling novel.... Gibbons's colorful, matter-of-fact style ('This uncle had purely by accident crawled in the fireplace as a baby, and thus nobody enjoyed looking at him') at times recalls that of Damon Runyon—who was, after all, a country boy."* (*Rhoda Koenig,* New York)

Charms for the Easy Life (PUTNAM, 1993) • Once again, Gibbons presents the story of three females in an extended southern family. Again, the women are strong, tough, and complex and the men, as one critic put it, "largely ineffectual." The central figure this time is Charlie, matriarch and faith healer. Stephen McCauley in the *New York Times* found her "so infallible, indefatigable, resolute, and resilient that by the end of the book she comes dangerously close to caricature."

Sights Unseen (Putnam, 1995) • As in her first novel, Gibbons here filters reality through the mind of an adolescent girl. Twelve-year-old Hattie Barnes lives, along with her father and brother, under the oppressive spell of a manic-depressive mother. Bernardine Connelly, writing in *Newsday*, complained that the story, told in an extremely spare style, "lies unexplored and inaccessible to the reader in the gaps between the beautifully rendered episodes and vignettes."

BIOGRAPHY

Kaye Gibbons was born and raised in Nash County, North Carolina, where she grew up believing that she'd become a schoolteacher. However, the sudden success of her first novel, published when she was twenty-seven, altered her career plans. *Ellen Foster* won the Sue Kaufman Prize for First Fiction given by the American Academy and Institute of Arts and Letters, as well as praise from the *New York Times*, *The New Republic*, and other respected journals. She has since settled into the groove of the career novelist, producing a new novel about every other year.

Gibbons's fiction draws substantially from her own life, her native geography, and the lives of her ancestors. The suicide or death of a mother, as portrayed in several of Gibbons's novels, mirrors the suicide of her own mother when she was ten. At first, when questioned by interviewers, Gibbons lied about her mother's suicide, later saying, "I didn't want the publicity hook to be my miserable childhood." However, she has since admitted the degree to which her own experience has helped her depict parental death as a black hole that draws into it all her characters' energies. Gibbons, who has been married once, lives in Raleigh, North Carolina, with attorney Frank Ward and her three daughters.

NEXT ON THE READING LIST: Dorothy Allison, Amy Bloom, Anita Brookner, Pat Conroy, Ursula Hegi, Reynolds Price, Mona Simpson

Ellen Gilchrist

(b. February 20, 1935)

"Ellen Gilchrist has consistently created heroines who are smart, impulsive and vulnerable. Usually hailing from locales with definable social codes—the garden district of New Orleans, the Mississippi Delta—Ms. Gilchrist's women, in contrast to their communities, are unconventional, nervy, outspoken. As grown-ups they are passionate to the point of recklessness, romantic in the midst of despair. "
—Roy Hofman, New York Times

* In the Land of Dreamy Dreams (UNIVERSITY OF ARKANSAS, 1981)
Gilchrist's first volume of short stories, set mostly in New Orleans, explores the shady and shabby remnants of southern aristocracy, featuring people whose lives are about a take a turn for the Gothic. There's the down-and-out teenage girl who holds up a bar full of macho blowhards; the perfectly respectable couple with a homicidal child; the young bride who persuades her father to arrange an abortion; the eight-year-old girl who befriends a war widow. "Gilchrist's stories are elegant little tragedies, memorable and cruel," wrote one critic about this highly popular collection.

> *"It's difficult to review a first book as good as this without resorting to every known superlative cliché—there are, after all, just so many ways to say 'auspicious debut.'"* (Susan Wood, Washington Post)

The Annunciation (LITTLE, BROWN, 1983) • Amanda McCamey Ashe is a prototypical Gilchrist heroine: a bored New Orleans housewife haunted by the memory of the baby that she gave up for adoption when she was fourteen, her childless marriage, and her abdication of an intellectual life for a drunken one. Miraculously, the forty-something Amanda turns her life around, replacing her stupor with a career in literary translation. Although some reviewers praised *The Annunciation* as "'women's fiction' par excellence," many complained that Amanda the wastrel was much more interesting than Amanda the self-realized artist.

* Victory Over Japan (LITTLE, BROWN, 1984) • This collection of short stories, called a "humdinger" by Jonathan Yardley in the *Washington Post*, won an American Book Award. "Those who loved *In the Land of Dreamy Dreams* will not be disappointed," reported Beverly Lowry in the *New York Times*. Although Gilchrist returned many of the same characters from her first collection, she also introduced several new ones who themselves became regulars. Of the mostly female characters, opined *Kirkus Reviews*, "They're all Zelda Fitzgerald—irrepressible, profligate, a little bigoted, more than a little stamp-a-foot demanding."

"You feel as though you are reading a novel; at the end, you have that satisfied, contented feeling only a good novel can give." (Jonathan Yardley, Washington Post)

Drunk with Love (LITTLE, BROWN, 1986) • In this mishmash of a collection, Gilchrist threw everything into the pot: two victims of domestic violence, a middle-aged woman who orders a young man from the L. L. Bean catalog, a woman on a starvation diet, a man who reviews church services for the *New York Times*, twin fetuses who gossip about their mother, and more. As is Gilchrist's habit, many of these stories revisit events and characters from previous volumes. "Well worth reading," Meg Wolitzer wrote in the *Los Angeles Times*. "There is little cohesion among the stories, but most of them contain small gems of prose, and even an epiphany here and there."

The Anna Papers (LITTLE, BROWN, 1988) • In this book's prelude, the writer Anna Hand learns that she has cancer. Her response is to drown herself before her successful, sexy, and stylish life gets ugly. The rest of the book, according to the *Times Literary Supplement*, recounts the ways in which Anna's death "brings far-flung relatives and lovers together and enriches their lives." Many critics found this premise difficult to take, calling the suicide gutless and Anna's canonization irksome: "We can only see Anna through a haze of adoration," Maggie Paley noted in the *New York Times*. "She's hardly more believable than the heroine of a Harlequin romance—though she certainly spends more time worrying about the meaning of life."

Light Can Be Both Wave and Particle (LITTLE, BROWN, 1989) • In this collection, Gilchrist indulges her interest in physics, yet she avoids loftiness by carefully grounding each of her stories in down-to-earth language. "The stories read like the conversation of a speedy, cologned southern lady with a hilariously irreverent taste for the anecdotal," Valerie Miner observed in the *Women's Review of Books*. Although reviewers generally disagreed on their picks and pans among the tales, most applauded Gilchrist's experiment.

I Cannot Get You Close Enough (LITTLE, BROWN, 1990) • Described as "three poignant, comic, and pitch-perfect novellas" and "stories rich with acrimony, wisdom, courage, and joy," this collection of short fiction, Gilchrist's fifth, focuses on the brilliant writer Anna Hand (of *The Anna Papers*) and her family. In the first two novellas, Anna travels to Turkey and then to Oklahoma, where she meddles in the relationships among her brother and his daughters. In the third novella, which takes place after her death, Anna still manages to interfere in the lives of her family. The result is "something more beguiling than yet another series of chapters in a family saga," Susan Spano Wells noted in the *New York Times*. "It's an invention that's pure Gilchrist, a screwball fugue on the theme of love."

Net of Jewels (LITTLE, BROWN, 1992) • Here Gilchrist gives a novel's worth of attention to spoiled nineteen-year-old southern belle Rhoda Manning, who spends the summer of 1955 reading novels, popping diet pills, and looking for trouble. Her energy all gone wrong, Rhoda destroys everything that might help her realize her potential. "As the book goes on, we both like her more and think less of her," Carol Anshaw wrote in the *Chicago Tribune*. In the *New York Times*, Eils Lotozo grumbled, "If only *Net of Jewels* delivered what it promises, we might have had a good novel instead of one that resembles its heroine: something with a lot of dazzle but little depth."

Starcarbon: A Meditation on Love (LITTLE, BROWN, 1994) • Gilchrist appropriately introduced this novel with a genealogy of the Hand family. Readers will need it to keep track of all the characters as they pursue love during the summer of 1991. (A "hormonal maelstrom," one critic called the ensuing turmoil.) The star character in this installment of the Hand family saga is Olivia de Havilland Hand, who rejects the Hand clan in favor of her maternal relatives, Cherokee living in Oklahoma. "*Starcarbon* is soap at its most elegant," ventured one reviewer. "Sex as life force comes through at every turn. Yet the novel's lyricism and Gilchrist's distinctive, flowing voice keeps one engaged throughout."

Anabasis: A Journey to the Interior (UNIVERSITY OF MISSISSIPPI, 1994) • This work of historical fiction, according to Gilchrist's introduction, "is an attempt to tell a story I made up when I was a child." Judging by their response, reviewers seemed to think that the story, set in ancient Greece, would have been better left untold. The heroine is Auria, an educated slave girl who escapes captivity, joins a community opposed to slavery, and teaches children how to read. (Like most Gilchrist heroines, the beautiful Auria also swears, writes poetry, falls in love, has good sex, marries, and suffers from family/work conflicts.) "This bland tale of a goody-good slave girl set in Greece in 431 B.C. lacks even a touch of irony," one reviewer complained. "The novel has the tone of a young-adult biography, sort of a *Little House on the Prairie* in tunics."

The Age of Miracles (LITTLE, BROWN, 1995) • The circumstances described in these stories are, wrote Susan Salter Reynolds in the *Los Angeles Times*, "stranger than truth and perfect for fiction." Among them: Adult children kidnap their mother to thwart her plans for a face-lift. A young girl complains that the suicide of her parents' friend is interfering with her social life. A fifty-eight-year-old woman reluctantly squeezes herself into a Laura Ashley dress so that she can get laid. A young woman and an older man find love on Exercycles. "Equanimity and humor," Reynolds concluded, "that's what the characters in these stories have in common."

* Rhoda: A Life in Stories (LITTLE, BROWN, 1995) • This collection includes twenty-two previously published stories (and two new ones) about Rhoda

Manning, one of Gilchrist's favorite characters and (she has admitted) her alter ego. A southern Becky Sharp, Rhoda is "passion, energy, light," Gilchrist wrote in her introduction; "smart, outrageous, oversexed" is how Heller McAlpin described the character in her *Newsday* review. *Rhoda: A Life in Stories* was widely admired, although the *Miami Herald* suggested that Rhoda's "charm starts to wear thin" and that "the older Rhoda may be wiser and more content, but she was more interesting when she was a rebellious seeker, all 'bravado and disdain.'"

> *"In one omnibus volume, we're taken from a life of privilege on a plantation to first loves and diet pills, to alcohol and free love, to Xanax and fearful flings in the age of AIDS. Throughout, Gilchrist's plucky heroine—from raising kids to having an abortion, to school and travels far and wide, and finally to a successful career as a writer—remains indomitable."* (Kirkus Reviews)

The Courts of Love (LITTLE, BROWN, 1996) • The first nine stories in *The Courts of Love* feature Nora Jane Whittington, the girl who gamely held up a bar in Gilchrist's first collection of short fiction, *In the Land of Dreamy Dreams*. By this time, Nora has become a wealthy matriarch who enjoys watching the gently lapping Pacific Ocean from the spacious windows of her new beachfront mansion. "Throughout the book, Ms. Gilchrist is unusually contemplative, her vivid visual descriptions often giving way to reverie," remarked Emily Barton in the *New York Times*.

Sarah Conley (LITTLE, BROWN, 1997) • Even more than most Gilchrist heroines, Sarah Conley has a lot of pluck, all of which she uses to get through her difficult life of emotional turmoil. She and her best friend both fall for Jack; the best friend marries him, while Sarah gets Jack's brother. Although the brother isn't much of a consolation prize, things get worse when she loses custody of her son in the subsequent divorce. Much later, after Sarah has diverted her romantic energies into work, the best friend dies. So now, at age fifty-two, Sarah's got a choice: a second chance at love with Jack or the golden career opportunity for which she's long been waiting. "It is here that Sarah may begin to grate on readers: She is just too smart, good-looking, sexy, and successful, and even her dilemma lacks the drama to make her completely appealing," *Publishers Weekly* warned.

BIOGRAPHY

ELLEN GILCHRIST'S PRIVILEGED CHILDHOOD included an abundance of both money and doting relatives. "My mother never said a cross word to me," Gilchrist remembered. "She thought it was funny as all get-out that I was wild and crazy." Born in 1935, Gilchrist spent much of her early life at Hopedale, her family's cotton plantation in Grace, Mississippi. When she was eighteen, she left the Delta for Vanderbilt University in Nashville. A year later, however, she ran away to get married. Thereafter, Gilchrist and her husband settled in Atlanta, where she quickly gave birth to three sons. "I was having babies all the time," she told one interviewer.

In 1981, after four marriages (two of them to the same man), the forty-six-year-old Gilchrist published her first work of fiction, the short-story collection *In the Land of Dreamy Dreams*, which established both her reputation and her popularity. Three years later, her second collection, *Victory Over Japan*, won an American Book Award. "I wanted to earn the name of writer for myself, and I went to work and did it," she recalled. "I am often awestruck at that fortunate occurrence."

Gilchrist is noted for the compelling quirkiness of her characters—many of them, she freely admits, plucked and polished from branches of her own family tree. According to Pat Ellis Taylor in the *Los Angeles Times*, "Ellen Gilchrist has created some of the most remarkable spoiled-brat-but-beautiful characters who have ever been unleashed on southern literature." And once she creates them, she doesn't like to let them go: Gilchrist's work abounds with prequels and sequels. "It's gotten to the point where it's impossible for me to create characters because the old ones keep grabbing up all the roles," she has said.

NEXT ON THE READING LIST: Ann Beattie, Amy Bloom, Kaye Gibbons, Alice Hoffman, Reynolds Price, Carol Shields, Mona Simpson, Anne Tyler

---

Gail Godwin
(b. June 18, 1937)

"More than any other contemporary writer, Gail Godwin reminds me of nineteenth-century pleasures—civilized, passionate about ideas, ironic about passions."
—*Carol Sternhell*, Village Voice

The Perfectionists (HARPER & ROW, 1970) • Godwin's first novel presents a gaggle of misfits on vacation in Majorca: an American woman, her British psychiatrist husband, his aloof son, and one of his patients. Also on hand are Karl, a painter who routinely has affairs with his models, and Karl's wife, Polly, who's quite aware of her husband's philanderings. The novel examines the tension between romantic ideals of marriage and the often unhappy reality of it. Godwin won praise from many critics, including Joyce Carol Oates, who called *The Perfectionists* "a most intelligent and engrossing novel," and Kurt Vonnegut Jr., who described it as a "darkly beautiful book."

Glass People (KNOPF, 1972) • This novel tells the story of another apparently perfect couple, the Bolts: Cameron is a district attorney and Francesca, his beautiful trophy wife. Although Cameron's image of Francesca is a sterile one, he works assiduously to maintain it. Meanwhile, stifled and isolated, Francesca becomes depressed and decides to visit her mother. The visit doesn't go well, but on her return she has an affair with a man in New York City who encourages her to become more independent. *Glass People* received generally good reviews, but many critics were disappointed with it because of the promise Godwin's first novel had shown. "The author, in not allowing Francesca even a glimmer of life beyond her victimhood, doesn't give us much to care about," Sara Blackburn wrote in the *New York Times*.

* The Odd Woman (KNOPF, 1974) • In this highly praised novel, Jane Clifford, who teaches English literature at a midwestern university, has an affair with a married colleague, Gabriel Weeks. When Jane's grandmother dies, she returns home to North Carolina, a trip that inspires much soul searching. Jane and Gabriel later meet in New York City, where their relationship reaches a crisis point.

> "The Odd Woman *is Gail Godwin's best and most ambitious book. It is not only twice as long as her previous novels, but far more complex, spanning several generations and a remarkable range of female characters, all successfully realized."* (*Lore Dickstein*, New York Times)

Dream Children (KNOPF, 1976) • This collection of short stories, Godwin's first, pursues her interest in the human capacity for romance. "The Woman Who Kept Her Poet" describes the meeting, courtship, and marriage of a young girl and an older poet. "Notes for a Story" examines the various facets of a close friendship between two women. Reviewers weren't impressed: "The stories, I'm afraid, expose further deficiencies that aren't evident in the longer and denser novels," Thomas Edwards observed in the *New York Times*.

Violet Clay (KNOPF, 1978) • Godwin's fourth novel explores the relationship between an artist and her work. Painter Violet Clay, who earns her living illustrating Gothic romances, experiences a sudden series of personal and professional crises: Her lover abandons her, her employer fires her, and her favorite uncle, a writer, commits suicide. Traveling to the Adirondacks to settle his estate, Violet ends up staying on there as she struggles to resolve her artistic and personal problems. Writing in *The New Statesman*, Zahir Jamal called *Violet Clay* a "pleasingly deft novel...managed by a crisp prose that never lets the dialogue down." However, *New Republic* reviewer Edith Milton called the book "simply half-baked, half-created."

* A Mother and Two Daughters (VIKING, 1982) • When Nell Strickland's husband dies, she and her two daughters, Cate and Lydia, are left to cope with their loss as they move on with their lives. Reviewers praised Godwin's expansive vision of an America in flux, her skillful management of the book's large cast of characters, and her realistic portrayal of men (not a strength in Godwin's previous fiction). Jonathan Yardley in the *Washington Post* called *A Mother and Two Daughters* "a work of complete maturity and artistic control, one that I am fully confident will find a permanent and substantial place in our national literature."

> "A Mother and Two Daughters *demonstrates, once again, Gail Godwin's uncommon generosity as a storyteller.... The most insignificant character travels on a stream of absorbing histories, past love affairs, coincidences, recurring themes."* (*Anne Tyler*, The New Republic)

Mr. Bedford and the Muses (VIKING, 1983) • This collection of six stories investigates the theme of creativity and its demands. The title story introduces aspiring writer Carrie Ames, who learns that authors must be merciless in exploiting their life experiences as raw material for their work. Although reviewers liked the book better than they did *Dream Children*, they once again concluded that Godwin's work was better suited to the novel form. In the *New York Times,* Judith Gies objected to the "problematic tone, chatty and oddly schoolmarmish, that runs through the entire book."

The Finishing School (VIKING, 1985) • The narrator of this novel, written in the first person, is successful middle-aged actress Justin Stokes. She recalls that when she was fourteen, her father and grandparents died in quick succession and she was sent with her mother and brother to live in upstate New York. A local bohemian actress takes Justin under her wing and regales her with tales of past glory, at the same time encouraging Justin's own theatrical ambitions. The novel's respectful reviews included Frances Taliaferro's assessment in the *New York Times* that *The Finishing School* was "a finely nuanced, compassionate psychological novel."

A Southern Family (MORROW, 1987) • Godwin's seventh novel resurrects Mountain City, the setting of *A Mother and Two Daughters,* and examines the reactions of various members of the Quick family to a murder-suicide committed by one of its own members—twenty-eight-year-old Theo, who's found dead after apparently killing his girlfriend. "Not merely is [the novel] psychologically acute," Jonathan Yardley wrote in the *Washington Post,* "it is dense with closely observed social and physical detail that in every instance is exactly right."

Father Melancholy's Daughter (MORROW, 1991) • In this novel, which received mixed reviews, Margaret Gower and her father, an Episcopalian priest, cope with the loss of Margaret's mother, who left the family when Margaret was six and died in an automobile accident a year later. Using different time perspectives, Godwin alternates between Margaret as a child and Margaret as a twenty-two-year-old. Richard Bausch in the *New York Times* didn't like Godwin's characterization of Margaret, but Nancy Wigston in the *Toronto Globe and Mail* called the novel "penetrating."

The Good Husband (BALLANTINE, 1994) • The ravages of cancer have brought contentious, opinionated Magda Danvers to her deathbed, where her family and friends gather to pay their respects. In addition to Magda, who has written a controversial academic study called *The Book of Hell*, we meet Francis, the "good husband" of the title; Hugo, an irascible southern novelist suffering from writer's block; and Hugo's wife, Alice, a reserved woman whose child was recently stillborn. According to Polly Paddock in the *Charlotte Observer*, "*The Good Husband* is further evidence that [Godwin] is one of the finest novelists writing in America today." On the other hand, *New York Times* critic Sara Maitland called the novel "overambitious" and "too full of unnecessarily 'meaningful' symbolism."

BIOGRAPHY

GAIL GODWIN WAS BORN IN Birmingham, Alabama, but grew up in Asheville, North Carolina. Following her parents' divorce when she was very young, she was raised by her mother and grandmother—both extremely influential figures in her life. Her mother taught writing to support the family and at night read to her daughter, sometimes making up stories that she "read" from a small blank address book. The first time that Godwin remembers meeting her father was at her high school graduation—she recalls throwing herself into his arms. He surprised her with an invitation to come live with him, which she accepted, but a short time later he killed himself.

Godwin attended Peace Junior College in Raleigh, North Carolina, before receiving her bachelor's degree from the University of North Carolina in 1959. She worked briefly as a reporter for the *Miami Herald*, and in 1960 married her first husband, newspaper photographer Douglas Kennedy. After her divorce from Kennedy a year later, she worked for the U.S. Travel Service at the American embassy in London from 1962 until 1965, when she embarked on another yearlong marriage, this time to British psychotherapist Ian Marshall. Her first novel, *The Perfectionists*, was based on this relationship.

Soon after the end of her second marriage, Godwin returned to the United States, enrolling at the University of Iowa Writers' Workshop, where she received a master's degree in 1968 and a Ph.D. three years later. She taught at the Writers' Workshop during the 1972–73 academic year before obtaining in 1974 a grant from the National Endowment for the Arts. The next year, she won a Guggenheim Fellowship. At the same time, she experienced a critical breakthrough with her novel *The Odd Woman*. Substantial commercial success followed eight years later with the publication of *A Mother and Two Daughters*. Godwin currently lives and writes in Woodstock, New York.

NEXT ON THE READING LIST: Margaret Atwood, Anita Brookner, A. S. Byatt, Joyce Carol Oates, Muriel Spark

Francisco Goldman
(b. 1955)

"Mr. Goldman is a writer who understands that not every novel is obliged to travel a straight line, as long as the novelist is skillful enough to keep the scenery interesting. He is indeed skillful enough to do that—and more.... Sharp satire, warm humor, and tenderness are all comfortably within Mr. Goldman's ken."
—Robert Houston, New York Times

* The Long Night of White Chickens (ATLANTIC MONTHLY, 1992) • This novel, a finalist for a PEN/Faulkner Award, was inspired by Goldman's experiences as a journalist in Central America during the 1980s, as well as by his own Guatemalan heritage. The book's somewhat autobiographical narrator, Roger Graetz, is, like the author, the son of a Guatemalan Catholic mother and an American Jewish father. The story opens with the murder of Flor de Mayo Puac, formerly the Graetz family maid and recently the head of a Guatemala City orphanage. Flor's death motivates Roger to return to Guatemala to find her killer and resolve his own identity problems. Some reviewers were confused by Goldman's unannounced time shifts among the past, the present, and the future, but most applauded his deft use of dark humor to offset the terrors of life under Guatemala's brutal dictatorship.

> "The Long Night of White Chickens...*takes you over, leaves you feeling like occupied territory, full of new memories of people and events that you obviously had forgotten somehow before you opened the book.... It reads [like] journal entries stitched together, with an anecdote here, a digression there. Some of it turns out to be crucial, other bits are irrelevant, much of it is funny, and all of it is by turns jarring and floating, like memory itself."* (Joanne Omang, Washington Post)

The Ordinary Seaman (ATLANTIC MONTHLY, 1997) • Small-time scammer Elias Tureen recruits fifteen Central Americans to crew the *Urus*, a freighter docked in Brooklyn. When the crew members arrive in New York, however, they discover that the *Urus* is nothing but "a broken eggshell," without power and unable to sail. Even so, without money or legal immigration papers, the sailors have no choice but to restore the ship for no pay and little food. Only after many months does the central character, nineteen-year-old Sandinista army veteran Esteban Gaitan, begin to leave the ship at night, discovering and falling in love with an immigrant Mexican manicurist named Joaquina. "The crew's ordeal almost fades in the bright light of Esteban's discovery of America," Edwin Frank wrote in the *New York Review of Books*. "This development suits Goldman's own generous spirit, manifest in the headlong energy of his writing as well as in his evident fondness for his characters." Goldman based this story, bleaker and less lush than his first novel, on a similar ordeal involving Central American sailors that he read about in the *New York Daily News*.

BIOGRAPHY

FRANCISCO GOLDMAN HAS ALWAYS remained close to his mother's Guatemalan roots. As a child, for example, even though he grew up for the most part in Needham, Massachusetts, he remained somewhat isolated from his father's American culture. "There was nobody around to tell me how to be an American kid, because I was raised essentially by Guatemalan maids," Goldman told one interviewer. "I mean, I spent all my time with Guatemalan teenage girls who were all out of convent orphanages and things. So I knew nothing—I was extremely naive."

A poor student throughout his school years, Goldman got into college largely because of his exceptional track-and-field abilities. After college, he pursued a writing career: "I remember being thirteen years old, and I had just read in *Life* magazine—I was always looking for omens—and in *Life* magazine Hemingway had said something like, 'Every writer knows he's going to be a writer by the time he's thirteen.' And I was thirteen, and I knew I wanted to be a writer.

"I'd never thought of being a journalist," Goldman continued. "But *Esquire* said they would send me any place I wanted, so I said I wanted to go back to Guatemala. Well, what happened then was that Reagan became president and declared war on Central America basically. So I just kept on going back there. Added all together, I lived in Guatemala City for a total of five years during the 1980s, although I did most of my journalism in other parts of Central America.... I loved the plain adventure of it all...in an almost boyish way. I was thrilled to have the chance to go running around in the war zones and out on patrols with the Sandinista army in Nicaragua and be shot at and all that."

Goldman began writing fiction seriously during the mid-1980s. He was working as a contributing editor to *Harper's* when his first novel, *The Long Night of White Chickens*, was published in 1992. He currently divides his time between New York City and Mexico City.

NEXT ON THE READING LIST: Louis de Bernières, Joan Didion, Milan Kundera, Tim O'Brien, Amos Oz, Graham Swift, Mario Vargas Llosa

Nadine Gordimer

(b. November 20, 1923)

"Ms. Gordimer can be a merciless judge and jury. Her portraits obtain a Vermeer-like precision, accurate and remorseless, with no room for hope, for self-delusion, no room even for the small vanities of ego and self-regard that allow us to proceed sometimes as if at least our intentions are honorable."
—John Edgar Wideman, New York Times

The Soft Voice of the Serpent (SIMON & SCHUSTER, 1952) • Gordimer's first major collection contains a number of stories that originally appeared in *Face to Face*, published in Johannesburg in 1949. In "The Catch," a young white couple give a lift to an Indian fisherman they have befriended. The reactions of the other passengers in the car, however, indirectly convey as much about the color bar in South Africa "as any editorial," one reviewer noted. Also singled out was "A Watcher of the Dead," an account of death as experienced by a Jewish family. While one reviewer complained that Gordimer's use of selective detail kept "everything at arm's length," more often than not she was praised for making her points delicately and obliquely. Writing in the *Saturday Review*, John Barkham called the collection "an unusually impressive debut."

The Lying Days (SIMON & SCHUSTER, 1953) • Gordimer's somewhat autobiographical first novel is a coming-of-age tale about a sheltered young Afrikaner named Helen Shaw. Having enjoyed a conventional middle-class upbringing, Helen goes off to university, where she has an affair with a social worker. Through this relationship, she becomes aware of the human toll of apartheid and begins to develop a political consciousness. Even given the positive response to *The Soft Voice of the Serpent, The Lying Days* generated an unexpected amount of praise, especially for Gordimer's "spontaneous honesty" and vivid evocation of place. Comparing the novel to Alan Paton's classic *Cry, the Beloved Country*, James Stern of the *New York Times* called Gordimer's work "the longer, the richer, and intellectually the more exciting."

Six Feet of the Country (SIMON & SCHUSTER, 1956) • The best stories in this collection describe small incidents that, when amplified, make a social or moral point. The protagonists are predominantly young white liberal women, and most of the stories are told from their point of view. Although reviewers noted Gordimer's limited gender range, they pointed out that her powers of observation had become keener since *The Soft Voice of the Serpent*. "Miss Gordimer is a writer of great gifts," Walter Allen noted in *The*

New Statesman. "She can illuminate life, and not merely South African life; yet it is when her material is specifically South African that she has the most to offer."

A World of Strangers (SIMON & SCHUSTER, 1958) • Banned by the South African government, this novel relates the efforts of a British writer to bring together his white intellectual friends and their black African counterparts. Gordimer's plot allows her to contrast the superficiality of the white liberal intelligentsia to the warmth and honesty of the black community in Johannesburg. The result, however, is fairly predictable. Considered a lesser work, *A World of Strangers* was criticized for being too didactic, and more than one reviewer suggested that Gordimer appeared to have difficulty expanding her ideas to fill an entire novel. "It is a conclusion in no way to Miss Gordimer's discredit to say that her novel would have made an excellent collection of short stories," the *Times Literary Supplement* observed.

Friday's Footprint (VIKING, 1960) • Each of the stories in this collection, Mary Ellen Chase wrote in the *New York Herald Tribune*, "probes mercilessly into human motives and human weaknesses, into guilt, fear, disillusionment, ambition, despair. Each reveals the universal human condition, whether in a Boer community or in Chicago, Paris, Hollywood, or the most isolated village anywhere at all." Reviewers repeatedly praised "The Bridegroom," in which the young overseer of a road gang prepares his dusty Kalahari campsite for the arrival of his bride. This story, according to Edward Weeks in the *Atlantic Monthly*, "speaks volumes about the delicate tissue of relations between white and black."

Occasion for Loving (VIKING, 1963) • Gordimer's third novel describes an affair between a black man and a white woman at a time when miscegenation was still illegal in South Africa. Complicating matters is the strained relationship between the woman and her inept teenage son. Reviewers weren't terribly impressed: Noting that *Occasion for Loving* failed to rise above "the atmosphere of daily melodrama which makes South African writing its own category," *Commonweal* concluded that "the book is only as good as it honestly can be."

Not for Publication and Other Stories (VIKING, 1965) • These stories, most written for American magazines, depict ordinary people defying apartheid in their daily lives. In the *Saturday Review*, Edward Hickman Brown noted that many of Gordimer's previous stories had suffered from a sense of detachment. He called *Not for Publication* "a giant step forward" because Gordimer had apparently overcome this problem. "There is no living writer of short stories more interesting, varied, and fertile than Miss Gordimer at her best," Honor Tracy agreed in *The New Republic*. Yet, Tracy continued, "in this new collection [Gordimer] does not always come up to her standard."

The Late Bourgeois World (VIKING, 1966) • Gordimer's fourth novel, which was also banned in South Africa, reconstructs the events leading up to the suicide of Max, a white political revolutionary who has betrayed his comrades in exchange for clemency. Although Gordimer places her political story more than ever within the broader social context of South African life, most reviewers felt her point—that apartheid victimizes whites as well as blacks—was made a bit too stiffly. The novel's protagonist, Max's thirty-something wife, Elizabeth, was cited as a particularly embarrassing failure: "How she could have supposedly lived through the events of her life and remained the tiresome adolescent that she is, boggles the mind," one critic nastily observed.

* A Guest of Honour (VIKING, 1970) • Gordimer's first novel set outside South Africa chronicles the return of Col. James Bray to his newly independent African homeland. (A white liberal, Bray had been expelled for supporting black revolutionaries.) Bray's triumphant homecoming is marred, however, by the discovery that the leaders of the new black-majority government are as corrupt and self-interested as those of the ousted white regime. Some reviewers complained that Gordimer too frequently commandeered Bray's train of thought to relate her own summary of the historical and political situation in South Africa, but most agreed that this was her finest work yet.

> *"Now at last, with* A Guest of Honour, *Miss Gordimer has consolidated all her achievements in a long, weighty, and magnificent novel, which not only reflects the mature political awareness that has always been implicit, but which also shows her special gift of patient and painstaking honesty as a writer to its fullest advantage."* (Times Literary Supplement)

Livingstone's Companions (VIKING, 1971) • The stories in this collection focus "almost claustrophobically," according to Elaine Feinstein in *London Magazine*, on the lives of those trapped, willingly or not, within South Africa's racist social system. Yet, the *Times Literary Supplement* observed, "even when she is making use of politics in a story, [Gordimer] is never guilty of pushing her characters to the sideline in order to make an overt political point." This, in turn, "enables her to demonstrate South Africa's political oddities more exactly; the country lives through the characters' experience of it." For example, in "Is There Nowhere Else We Can Meet?" the bruised but compassionate white victim of a black purse snatcher forgives him because they're both human and both sinners.

* The Conservationist (JONATHAN CAPE, 1974; VIKING, 1975) • In this winner of Britain's distinguished Booker Prize, a wealthy white industrialist who has long supported apartheid finds himself struggling to overcome his latent guilt when a group of poor black squatters settles on a portion of his cherished estate. This experience teaches him that he can no longer exert absolute dominion over blacks any more than he can control his cold and impulsive libido.

"Gordimer has the range and concerns of a mature and brilliant artist. Her writing has the tough precision of poetry and the closely observed naturalness of everyday life. It has all the power of romantic writing about nature but none of the defects, of overwriting and metaphysical pretentiousness, that sometimes mar this mode." (*Diane Johnson,* Washington Post)

Burger's Daughter (VIKING, 1979) • Although banned only briefly by the South African government, this ambitious novel examines white ambivalence toward apartheid just as frankly as Gordimer's previous books. The title character is Rosa Burger, daughter of the leader of South Africa's Communist party. Unable to sustain her father's antiapartheid crusade following his death, Rosa abandons both politics and South Africa, yet she can't escape the awareness that her martyred father has bequeathed to her. *"Burger's Daughter* is a remarkable book at the same time that it is difficult, repetitive, dense, and occasionally overwritten,"* Doris Grumbach wrote in the *Chronicle of Higher Education.* "We have in [this novel] perhaps the most serious study of South African white supremacy...ever transposed from jails and courtrooms into the realm of fiction." Reviewers unanimously praised Gordimer's treatment of the history of the Communist party in South Africa, but some pointed out that her thoroughness detracted from the novel's intensity.

A Soldier's Embrace (VIKING, 1980) • This collection offers an ironic overview of South African society from a historical point of view. As Frank Tuohy observed in the *Times Literary Supplement,* "A hard-won humanism is characteristic of these stories of an inhumane society." The story "Town and Country Lovers," about two illegal interracial couples, was described by Vivian Gornick in the *Village Voice* as "penetrating in its ability to bring home the Nazi Germany quality of everyday life in South Africa." "These are marvelous pieces," Edith Milton wrote in *New York,* "and Gordimer's dark insights go so deep that it is impossible in her description of her world not to recognize our own."

July's People (VIKING, 1981) • Gordimer set this novel in the immediate aftermath of a violent revolution that, at the time *July's People* was written, seemed inevitable. In this world turned upside down, a liberal white family now depends on the generosity of its former black servant, July. Unable to leave the country because rioting blacks have bombed the airports, Bam and Maureen Smales flee with their three children to July's isolated village, where they gather food and cook in the sort of clay vessels that Maureen once collected as ornaments. *"July's People* demonstrates with breathtaking clarity the tension and complex interdependencies between whites and blacks in South Africa," Anne Tyler wrote in the *New York*

Times. "It is so flawlessly written that every one of its events seems chillingly, ominously possible."

Something Out There (VIKING, 1984) • Returning to the present and its quickening black violence, this collection contains nine short works and a longer one. In the title novella, a baboon trespasses on the tidy lawns of white Johannesburg. Gordimer uses this episode to contrast the community's response to the baboon to its reaction to the first sporadic guerrilla actions. Few characters, white or black, escape her unsentimental yet humanizing gaze. As Leon Wieseltier pointed out in *Salmagundi,* "Her people may be divided into those that are aware of their corruption and those that are not, but all are corrupted." Gordimer admirers, notably Paul Marx in *The New Leader,* ranked three stories in particular—"A City of the Dead, A City of the Living," "Sins of the Third Age," and "Blinder"—among the best of the century.

A Sport of Nature (KNOPF, 1987) • The title of Gordimer's ninth novel refers to a botanical phenomenon: a plant that mutates spontaneously from its parent stock. The "mutated" offspring here is Hillela Capran, the beautiful, troublesome daughter of a middle-class Jewish family. A teenager with a penchant for wearing out her welcome, she flees South Africa with her boyfriend, an antigovernment journalist, when his cottage is ransacked by police. He dumps her in Dar es Salaam, where she uses her good looks to solicit new protectors from among the political expatriates there. She eventually marries an important black leader who becomes president of his liberated country. "Feminists may not be happy with a character whose identity and importance depend so thoroughly on the men she sleeps with," Paul Gray wrote in *Time.* However, he continued, "Gordimer is saying much more than that. Her novel is both richly detailed and visionary, a brilliant reflection of a world that exists and an affirmation of faith in one that could be born."

My Son's Story (FARRAR, STRAUS & GIROUX, 1990) • In what Patrick Parrinder in the *London Review of Books* called "an intricate spider's web of a novel," Gordimer examines several permutations of loyalty and betrayal. Sonny is a "colored" schoolteacher who has become radicalized and now prominently figures in the struggle against apartheid. Will is his son. The tension at the heart of the book is this: Sonny is having an affair with a white human rights activist, Will knows, and Sonny knows that Will knows. "In theory, this is a novel of ambiguity; it's supposed to 'raise questions' about conflicting loyalties," George Packer remarked in *The Nation.* "It would be dishonest to say that…anything like this actually happens."

Jump and Other Stories (FARRAR, STRAUS & GIROUX, 1991) • In these sixteen stories, Gordimer is alternately hopeful and despairing of the possibility that a better world might emerge. In "Keeping Fit," a white jogger caught in a sudden frenzy of township violence is saved by a black woman who shelters him in her shack until the trouble has passed. In "Woe Is Me," a young black girl whose father has lost his job and whose mother can no longer walk breaks down in front of her mother's white mistress. "What could I do for her?" the woman says. "I gave her my handkerchief." As always, reviewers liked some stories more than others, but none thought that Gordimer had lost her touch. "Ms. Gordimer takes upon herself this burden of getting it straight and telling it straight," John Edgar Wideman wrote in the *New York Times.* "Her eloquence breaks through the silence, parses it, shames it."

None to Accompany Me (FARRAR, STRAUS & GIROUX, 1994) • This novel—"one of [Gordimer's] strongest in recent years," according to Merle Rubin in the *Christian Science Monitor*—charts the fortunes of one white family and one black family as power is transferred in South Africa from the white minority regime to a democratically elected government. Gordimer's protagonist, Vera Stark, is a liberal white lawyer who expects to find fulfillment helping rural blacks reclaim their stolen land, yet she can't ignore her increasing sense of cultural displacement. Writing in *The New Republic,* Caryl Phillips wasn't as impressed as Rubin: "Gordimer has produced a broken-backed novel that has the feel of two books. Both [one about the "new" South Africa, the other about Vera Stark] are interesting in themselves, but they do not sit well together."

The House Gun (FARRAR, STRAUS & GIROUX, 1998) • Harald and Claudia Lindgard are good white liberals in the new democratic South Africa. Claudia, a doctor, treats black patients in a free clinic, while Harald, an insurance executive, works to make capital available to black businesses. The Lindgards feel comfortable and—living in a restricted-access condo— safe. Suddenly their son Duncan is arrested for murder, and their sense of safety disappears. Duncan has apparently killed a friend who was having sex with Duncan's lover. He has even hired a lawyer, the brilliant black barrister Hamilton Motsamai, the book's most vivid and interesting character. "Gordimer's portrait of the Lindgards...is masterly," Richard Eder wrote in the *Los Angeles Times.* "She writes, in fact, something like a doctor whose sympathy never clouds a cold knowledge of the patient's lethal disability."

BIOGRAPHY

NADINE GORDIMER WAS BORN IN the mining town of Springs, South Africa, to a working-class Lithuanian father and his middle-class British wife, both of whom were apolitical Jews. When Gordimer was eleven and her doctors diagnosed a minor heart ailment, her parents withdrew her from school. For the next five years she was taught by a private tutor, and her after-school activities were curtailed. Without much peer contact, she became the constant companion of her lonely mother, especially after her older sister left for college. Socializing nearly exclusively with adults, Gordimer became, as she once said, "a little old woman." To compensate for her loneliness, she read voraciously and discovered an alternative world more to her liking: the world of ideas. At age thirteen, she began contributing to the children's page of the *Johannesburg Sunday Express*, and by fifteen she was publishing short stories in *The Forum*, a liberal South African weekly.

For nearly half a century, Nadine Gordimer has written eloquently about her South African homeland and the system of apartheid under which its citizens lived. Her novels and short stories often contain characters who must in some way avoid, confront, or change the oppressive conditions under which they live. Although South Africa produced a number of important antiapartheid writers in the aftermath of World War II, notably Alan Paton, Gordimer was one of the few to remain a resident of her troubled country throughout her career. The most enduring feature of her work, according to Michiko Kakutani in the *New York Times*, has been its focus on "the consequences of apartheid on the daily lives of men and women, the distortions it produces in relationships among both blacks and whites."

Twice married and the mother of two, Gordimer finally won a Nobel Prize in literature in 1991 after a decade of being short-listed. She subsequently donated a portion of her $985,000 prize to support the African National Congress's Department of Arts and Culture.

NEXT ON THE READING LIST: Chinua Achebe, Alice Hoffman, Kazuo Ishiguro, Doris Lessing, Toni Morrison, Iris Murdoch, V. S. Naipaul

David Guterson
(b. May 4, 1956)

"As you know, and as they know, people with soft voices force you to pay attention to them. This is not the same as catching more flies with honey. David Guterson writes with a soft voice and kills his flies with vinegar. You have to watch him like a hawk."
—*Susan Salter Reynolds,* Los Angeles Times

The Country Ahead of Us, the Country Behind (HARPER & ROW, 1989) • Guterson sets these short stories within a Steven Spielberg landscape of suburban homes, shopping malls, and backyard ball fields. Mostly tales of growing up, they evoke, according to *New York Times* reviewer Lois E. Nesbitt, "the mores and dilemmas of middle-class life with a familiarity tinged with nostalgia and tempered with irony." Of particular interest to Guterson are pivotal moments in the childhoods of his protagonists, all of whom are male and nearly all of whom feel some sort of lingering guilt or regret. According to Susan Salter Reynolds in the *Los Angeles Times*, "Guterson, like the best authors, isn't out to satisfy us—we can watch TV and eat frozen Snickers for that. He's out to make us [think]."

* Snow Falling on Cedars (HARCOURT BRACE, 1994) • Guterson's first novel opens in December 1954 at the trial of salmon fisherman Kabuo Miyomoto, who has been accused of murdering fellow fisherman Carl Heine. Kabuo's alleged motive concerns a strawberry farm that Kabuo's father had been buying from the Heine family. The mortgage was nearly paid off in 1942, when the Miyomotos, like the other Japanese Americans on San Piedro Island, were sent to the Manzanar internment camp. Guterson alternates chapters describing the trial with well-researched flashbacks detailing the characters' personal histories as well as the prewar racial climate on San Piedro, a fictional island in the Puget Sound. Although the novel works effectively as a whodunit, it won a PEN/Faulkner Award because it also addresses another mystery: how people who have been neighbors (and lovers) for generations can nevertheless be torn apart by racial bias and hatred.

> *"David Guterson's carefully crafted first novel provides more than just courtroom drama.... Guterson's prose is controlled and graceful, almost detached. But the accretion of small details gives his story weight. He's particularly good at evoking a sense of place—the yellow dust cloaking the barbed wire and barracks of Manzanar, the strawberry-scented summer in San Piedro, the slippery, kerosene-lanterned deck of a fishing boat at night."* (*Nancy Pate*, Chicago Tribune)

BIOGRAPHY

DAVID GUTERSON HAS SPENT most of his life in the Pacific Northwest. Born in Seattle to a criminal defense lawyer and a housewife, Guterson was a troublemaker as a child: "Just petty delinquencies, just flirting with danger," he now says. "It came, in part, out of a critique of mainstream life in the 1960s." Guterson has since abandoned his formerly wild ways but not his penchant for mildly alternative lifestyles.

He first became obsessed with writing at the University of Washington, where he earned a bachelor's degree in 1978. A year later, he married Robin Radwick, whom he had known since high school. Together, they moved to Rhode Island, where Guterson entered, and then dropped out of, the Brown creative writing program. (It was "too experimental," he has said.) For a year, they lived in a cabin on a Rhode Island tree farm, while Robin worked as a speech therapist and Guterson wrote short stories and collected rejections.

The couple then moved back the Northwest, where Guterson pursued a master's degree in writing at his undergraduate alma mater. On completing this program in 1982, he and his wife moved to Bainbridge Island in Puget Sound, later fictionalized as San Piedro in *Snow Falling on Cedars*. In 1984, after the births of two of his four children, Guterson went to work as a high school English teacher, but he didn't give up writing. Rather, he rose every morning at four-thirty so that he could write for two and a half hours before school. Ironically, it was on a class trip to an exhibit about how the Japanese internment affected Bainbridge Island residents that he conceived of the plot for his best-selling novel. With the success of *Snow Falling on Cedars*, Guterson was able to quit his teaching job in 1994 and begin writing full time.

"I write because something inner and unconscious forces me to," Guterson explained in one interview. "That is the first compulsion. The second is one of ethical and moral duty. I feel responsible to tell stories that inspire readers to consider more deeply who they are." Guterson is also the author of *Family Matters: Why Homeschooling Makes Sense* (1992).

NEXT ON THE READING LIST: Ivan Doig, Peter Høeg, Tim O'Brien, Kenzaburo Oe, E. Annie Proulx, Mona Simpson, John Edgar Wideman

Jane Hamilton
(b. 1957)

"Hamilton's special genius lies in blending the quotidian and the mythic. Ordinary details become luminous under her pen as she describes human pain with a rare limpid force, unshackled by melodrama."
—*Viva Hardigg*, U.S. News & World Report

* The Book of Ruth (TICKNOR & FIELDS, 1988) • The heroine of this novel, which won a PEN/Hemingway Award for best first fiction, is a materially, culturally, and emotionally deprived young woman named Ruth Dahl. Considered a failure by almost everyone around her, Ruth is especially miserable because she's trapped between her love for her emotionally disturbed husband and her loyalty to her embittered, abusive mother. With all three living in the same house, it should come as no surprise that domestic violence eventually rips Ruth's world apart.

> *"Jane Hamilton's ambitious and satisfying first novel asks one of literature's biggest questions: What is the meaning of human suffering? In the end, she*

gives the old answer—to expose the truth and teach forgiveness." (*Judith Paterson,* Washington Post)

A Map of the World (DOUBLEDAY, 1994) • Former hippies Alice and Howard Goodwin live on a dairy farm outside Racine, Wisconsin. Their domestic tranquility seems enviable until two traumas upend their lives: First, while baby-sitting her best friend's daughters, Alice inadvertently loses track of the youngest one, who drowns in the farm pond. Then, soon after this tragedy, Alice is accused of sexually abusing students at the elementary school where she works as a nurse. Unable to raise the exorbitant bail, Alice (whom we know is innocent) is jailed pending her trial. "*A Map of the World* is not an easy or light read; indeed, it takes on some of the toughest issues of modern life," Suzanne L. MacLachlan wrote in the *Christian Science Monitor.* "But the writer's skill in describing a community and a way of life, as well as her insights into the hearts of her characters, render this story difficult to forget."

BIOGRAPHY

JANE HAMILTON HAS LIVED her entire life in the Midwest. She grew up in sub-urban Oak Park, Illinois, where her father read her Dickens and Hugo and during high school she pored over E. M. Forster. After graduating from Minnesota's Carleton College in 1979, she took a job with a publishing house in New York City; however, on her way there she stopped off to visit a friend at an apple orchard in Wisconsin—and never left. Hamilton hired on as a picker for a few days but stayed the season, falling in love with Robert Willard, her friend's cousin and one of the orchard's owners. Hamilton and Willard were married in 1982.

In addition to helping out at harvesttime, Hamilton took on some free-lance writing work and began to compose autobiographical short stories. Her novels, though, while making use of the midwestern landscape outside her window, haven't fictionalized her own life. "I wanted to see if I could write about other people besides myself," Hamilton has said. "My mother was horrified when she read [*The Book of Ruth*], because she saw it as having no relation to my life," Hamilton continued. "She wondered how 'Sweet Jane' could have come up with the squalid, squalid people [in that book]." In fact, Hamilton got the idea for the novel in 1983 from a string of murders in which several rural Wisconsin men did away with their mothers-in-law.

According to Hamilton, her chief literary inspirations have been Tolstoy's *Anna Karenina* and E. B. White's *Charlotte's Web,* Tolstoy for his family obsessions and White for his agrarian milieu. "I really believe you can't build a self without books," Hamilton told one interviewer. "You get an inner voice by listening to someone else's words in your ear."

NEXT ON THE READING LIST: Pat Barker, Pat Conroy, Jim Harrison, Barbara Kingsolver, Jane Smiley, Mona Simpson, Melanie Rae Thon

Jim Harrison

(*b. December 11, 1937*)

"Harrison writes the kind of bedrock Americana that Hemingway might have turned out if he had come home from the Great War, moved up to Michigan and stayed there, with occasional side trips to Key West, Idaho, and other points west.... His combination of poetic attentiveness to detail with the exemplary commonplaceness of the life he has continued to lead gives his work a genuine mythopoetic quality that is rare, if not unique, among contemporary American writers."
—*Joseph Coates,* Chicago Tribune

Wolf: A False Memoir (SIMON & SCHUSTER, 1971) • The antihero of Harrison's first novel is Carol Severin Swanson—a bitter, restless thirty-three-year-old drifter who abandons the decadence of urban life for the renewing atmosphere of Michigan's Upper Peninsula. During his stay in the forests of the U.P., Swanson becomes obsessed with spotting a wolf, a creature that he identifies as a kindred spirit. Greeted with generally negative reviews that nonetheless recognized Harrison's promise, *Wolf* was described by Joyce Carol Oates as a novel of initiation for both Swanson and Harrison: "[It's] the kind of diarylike work many writers must publish before they can write their first significant books."

A Good Day to Die (SIMON & SCHUSTER, 1973) • Darker, more unsettling, and even less successful than its predecessor, Harrison's second novel picks up *Wolf's* theme of being out of sync with the twentieth century. In this tale of disaffection, a ne'er-do-well fisherman abandons his wife and child to travel west with a suicidal Vietnam vet and his alienated girlfriend. They plan to dynamite a dam as part of a vague and ill-conceived ecological protest. Curiously, one reviewer noted that this book and *Wolf* both "fail as novels precisely because they triumph as poetry, diatribe and personal memoir."

* Farmer (VIKING, 1976) • Harrison's third and finest novel unfolds slowly against the gracefully etched backdrop of a rural northern town in 1956. Joseph Lundgren, a forty-three-year-old teacher and farmer, is undergoing an identity crisis. The school where he teaches is being closed, his mother is dying of cancer, and he's torn between relationships with his longtime mistress and a racy high school senior. Harrison presents the resolution of Joseph's turmoil within the first two pages of the book, then slowly reveals its development using flashbacks. Critics felt that Harrison's patient unraveling of the plot succeeded in placing the reader inside Joseph's head.

> *"[Harrison] writes beautifully. He sees life going on and on, its meaning in its pattern, its outcome uncertain except in ending. He moves rather than*

overwhelms us. He creates an art small except in its grace." (*Webster Schott,* New York Times)

✻ Legends of the Fall (DELACORTE, 1979) • Each of the three novellas in this collection explores the themes of violence, revenge, and self-realization. "Revenge" tells the story of a retired air force pilot who pays a brutal price for an ill-advised affair with the comely wife of his Mexican criminal associate. The title novella has three parts, all connected by the angry and brooding figure of Tristan Ludlow. Both are among the best known of Harrison's work, having been subsequently adapted into successful movies. Drawing favorable comparisons with the likes of Henry James, Joseph Conrad, and Isak Dinesen, the majority of critics found Harrison to be working at the height of his powers in the format that suited him best.

> *"I can't even begin to do justice to nuances of character and honest complexities of plot in this work.... The writing is precise and careful—and sings withal."* (*Raymond Carver,* Washington Post)

Warlock (DELACORTE, 1981) • Like *Farmer,* Harrison's fourth novel addresses the midlife angst of the American male. John Milton Lundgren, "a goofy fop and terribly intelligent," has been fired from his job as a foundation executive. After relocating to northern Michigan with his wife, an emergency room nurse, Lundgren accepts a job investigating possible business infractions committed by a doctor's spendthrift wife and their gay son. After a series of bumbling adventures, Lundgren discovers the truth, which nearly destroys him. Most critics agreed that Harrison's affectionate detective spoof was marred by its uneven pacing, taking forever to start and no time to finish.

Sundog: The Story of an American Foreman, Robert Corvus Strang (DUTTON, 1984) • The narrator of *Sundog*—an unnamed writer of some renown—travels to Michigan's Upper Peninsula to record the life story of a dying man, the self-taught Robert Corvus Strang, who is meant to embody all the optimism and vitality of an older (now almost defunct) frontier America. Living comfortably in a cabin by a stream, Strang spends most of the book rambling along the byways of his memory and imagination. Unfortunately, most critics agreed that Harrison's characters fail to resonate with meaning and instead lay flat on the page, an assortment of badly rendered clichés.

Dalva (DUTTON, 1988) • This contemplative novel, Harrison's longest and most ambitious work yet, consists of imaginary diaries written by Dalva; her historian-lover, Michael; and her great-grandfather, a passionate supporter of Indian causes. Dalva herself is haunted by the memory of an affair with her Sioux half brother and the loss of the son she gave up for adoption. Harrison's use of a vigorous, independent, tough-minded female protagonist surprised many critics, who didn't think he had it in him. Most reviewers also praised Harrison for his elegant prose and generosity of spirit, but some felt that he'd merely stitched together three novellas (and not all that well).

The Woman Lit by Fireflies (HOUGHTON MIFFLIN, 1990) • The protagonists of Harrison's second collection of novellas have all reached middle age without suffering too many bouts of introspection. Now they find themselves forced, by circumstances or self-doubt, to reassess their lives. In the title story, a forty-nine-year-old woman walks out on her husband at a rest area somewhere along I-80, then spends the night testing her survival skills and reflecting on the events that have brought her to this point. Critics again praised Harrison's newfound ability to write convincingly in a female voice, pointing out that it had noticeably widened the range of his work.

Julip (HOUGHTON MIFFLIN, 1994) • Harrison's third collection of novellas established beyond doubt his comic credentials. He sets each of these stories in a traditionally male proving ground: the fishing waters of the South, the hunting camps of the North, the cattle ranches of the West. As Harrison demonstrates, however, the mythology of maleness often fails. In the war between the sexes that underlies this book, only the women can successfully negotiate the darker paths; they wait on the shore while the men flounder at sea.

BIOGRAPHY

JAMES THOMAS HARRISON WAS BORN IN Grayling, Michigan, the son of an agriculturist. Determined to escape the boredom and meaninglessness of middle-class life, he decided at a young age to become a writer, receiving a B.A. from Michigan State University in 1960 and an M.A. four years later. Although an award-winning poet, he remained almost unknown until the publication of *Wolf: A False Memoir*, which he wrote on a whim while recovering from a hunting accident. Before 1979, when the publication of *Legends of the Fall* raised his income substantially, Harrison made only about ten thousand dollars a year.

Ever since *Wolf*, reviewers have compared Harrison's work to that of Hemingway because of its understated prose and simple sentence structure. Although generally considered an extraordinary talent, Harrison has often been criticized for his harsh, violent subject matter and narrow focus on masculine self-sufficiency. With few exceptions, however, his male protagonists aren't very macho. In fact, the opposite is true: Harrison's sensitive, fallible men feel anxious, get scared, and even doubt themselves. They seem as though they might succumb to the perversions of contemporary society at any minute, yet they survive.

Harrison himself bristles at the "macho" label, saying that "macho is when you throw a rattlesnake in a baby carriage or bite off your mother's toe—some kind of overpowering violence." Being a writer, Harrison feels, "requires an intoxication with language, an obsession with language. You get the meaning later, because you don't have a great sense of meaning when you're first finding this out—it's the hormones again."

NEXT ON THE READING LIST: Harry Crews, Pete Dexter, Richard Ford, Thomas McGuane, Tim O'Brien, Cathie Pelletier, Robert Stone

---

Ursula Hegi
(b. May 23, 1946)

"To read Hegi is a treat, a lesson in linguistic elegance and refinement. Her images are lucid, lyrical, and sad. There is something so innocent, old-fashioned, and bittersweet about [her writing] that it can break your heart."
—*Sabine Reichel*, Los Angeles Times

Intrusions (VIKING, 1981) • With this first novel, according to *Harper's*, Hegi "lets loose a point-of-view experiment that would have been tiresome enough in the classroom." Specifically, Hegi writes about herself writing about Megan Stone, a Connecticut housewife with the typical problems of a Connecticut housewife. The title refers, in part, to the continual intrusions of the author's world into Megan's: Hegi's husband and children appear, as does a fellow writer who urges her to spice up her manuscript with sex. For example, Hegi writes, "Beverly Stone (I might still change her name to Mildred or Eleanor) is very satisfied with her life." *Kirkus Reviews* said, "Admittedly, Hegi serves up the author-character kibbitz routine in a fey and agreeably light manner, but [this doesn't] justify Hegi's recycling of a secondhand, wildly obtrusive literary device."

Unearned Pleasures (UNIVERSITY OF IDAHO, 1988) • This short-story collection apparently came and went with nary a trace until Simon & Schuster republished it in the wake of Hegi's success. Writing in 1990 in the *New York Times*, Edward Hoagland referred to *Unearned Pleasures* as "a [slim] collection of fragmentary apprentice stories...set in New Hampshire or the northwestern United States."

Floating in My Mother's Palm (POSEIDON, 1990) • This "novel" is actually a compilation of loosely connected vignettes describing the residents of Burgdorf, a small town in 1950s Germany (not unlike the one in which

Hegi herself grew up). The stories are linked by the viewpoint of their young narrator, Hanna, whose father is a dentist and whose artist mother likes to swim nude during rainstorms. Among Hanna's acquaintances is Trudi Montag, an obese dwarf who knows all the town's secrets. However, it's Hanna's mother who teaches her the secret that only recklessness can dispel the town's oppressive sense of propriety. "The quality of Hegi's writing is so consistently excellent," Barbara Finkelstein wrote in the *Chicago Tribune*, "that one can easily forget that this is a novel set in a Germany that only a few years before had given rise to Auschwitz."

* Stones from the River (POSEIDON, 1994) • With this novel, nominated for a PEN/Faulkner Award, Hegi revives the town of Burgdorf and many of the characters that she introduced to readers in *Floating in My Mother's Palm*—especially the dwarf, Trudi Montag. The key difference here is the time frame: This novel takes place just before and during the Nazi era, a subject about which Hegi's previous novel was pointedly silent.

> "Thematically, Hegi's story is all over the map, as if she's striving for a unified field theory of human experience. But her sense of place keeps drawing her back, into a portrait of small-town life that is intimate, affectionate, and shadowed by a startlingly accessible cruelty." (*Julie Phillips*, Voice Literary Supplement)

Salt Dancers (SIMON & SCHUSTER, 1995) • When Julia Ives was nine, her mother disappeared. After that, her father beat her repeatedly. As soon as she could, she moved from Spokane to New England, where she married a ski instructor. Their marriage later faltered because, fearing that she might be carrying her father's brutality within her, Julia refused to have children. Now she's forty-one, a successful architect, and—ironically—pregnant by a casual lover. Once she decides that she's going to have the baby, she realizes that she must return home to face her father before her own child is born. Although John Skow in *Time* praised Hegi for the sequence in which Julia realizes that there will be no healing resolution, he faulted her for the plot machinations that follow: "This slack stuff is soap opera, and even a writer as gifted as Hegi can't dress it up as anything else."

BIOGRAPHY

BORN IN WEST GERMANY, Ursula Hegi grew up in a small town outside Düsseldorf. When she was eighteen, she immigrated to the United States to work for a German accounting firm in Fort Lee, New Jersey. "I would have gone anywhere," she recalled. "I wanted to get away from Germany.... My mother died when I was thirteen, and I think if she had lived, my family situation would have been very, very different, But as a result, it just was not very close, and I really wanted to get away."

In 1967, she married management consultant Ernest Hegi, with whom she had two children. In 1970, she became a naturalized citizen, and in

1974, she went back to school at the University of New Hampshire, where she earned a B.A. in English in 1978 and an M.A. in creative writing the following year. She taught at New Hampshire until 1984, when she divorced her husband and moved to the Spokane area to take a job at Eastern Washington University.

Only in middle age did Hegi become interested in writing about her German past: "[When I left Germany] I really believed that you can leave your country of origin behind and start your life anew. The older I get, the more I realize you can't do that." When she was a child, recent German history wasn't taught in the local schools. But "when I came over here," she has said, "I realized that the Americans of my generation knew a lot more about the war than I did. I read, I asked questions, I ran away from what I found, I went back. It's been a process of trying to understand what happened in Germany." Hegi has also written *Tearing the Silence: Being German in America* (1997), a collection of interviews that she conducted with other German-born Americans of her generation.

NEXT ON THE READING LIST: Dorothy Allison, Kaye Gibbons, Amos Oz, Mona Simpson, Jane Smiley, Graham Swift, Anne Tyler

Mark Helprin
(b. June 28, 1947)

"Mr. Helprin's style is odd, mysteriously accented, as if he were a foreigner imperfectly acquainted with English. But then as we follow him, we begin to wonder whether the foreignness is not in things themselves, intrinsic to them.... Nothing is familiar in his stories: He is interested only in the fabulous, the borderline between perception and hallucination."
—Anatole Broyard, New York Times

A Dove of the East and Other Stories (KNOPF, 1975) • Helprin's first collection of stories combines the kind of voice that would become his trademark—"a dreamy, antique style," one reviewer called it—with deep and profound sentiment. The situations bear "the thumb marks of sanctimoniousness and sentimentality," according to *The Spectator*—as when, in the title story, a soldier whose horse treads on a dove determines to return it to health. But there are also glimmers here of real, old-fashioned elegance.

Refiner's Fire: The Life and Adventures of Marshall Pearl, a Foundling (KNOPF, 1977) • In Helprin's careful hands, this bildungsroman explodes into a high romance. Its hero, born to a mother who disappears, is raised by adoptive parents, but as he roams the continent, America itself becomes his hometown. Then, as though this massive nation were not enough to hold him, Marshall Pearl bursts free of its borders and winds up a soldier in the Israeli army. According to Peter Ackroyd of *The Spectator,* the book's "most important, and attractive, quality is its absence of realism on every level. The book is wonderfully egocentric."

✳ Ellis Island and Other Stories (DELACORTE, 1981) • With the publication of this collection, critics began comparing Helprin with such writers as Poe and Isaac Bashevis Singer because of the fantastic variety of settings, times, and life incidents that he portrays. The title novella features the sort of character in which Helprin most delights: one whose personality is too big for reality to hold. A boisterous Russian Jew emigrates to America, where Ellis Island and lower Manhattan become a phantasmagoria painted in Chagall-like tones. Anne Duchene, writing in the *Times Literary Supplement,* thought "Ellis Island" was "a preposterous, touching, and very disarming little essay."

> *"Some of Helprin's...stories, long on mood and short on plot, seem like water-color sketches for more finished work, but the majority of them shimmer with the bright and lavish metaphors of this most accomplished artist." (Rhoda Koenig,* New York)

Winter's Tale (HARCOURT BRACE JOVANOVICH, 1983) • It's hard to know what Helprin had in mind here: a seven-hundred-page fairy tale in which a grim and hopeless New York City transforms, frog-into-prince-like, into "a perfectly just city." One of the main characters, for example, is a flying horse. Helprin's language can be soaringly poetic, but just as often he simply *tells* us that New York is vile rather than *showing* us. "Unfortunately," Seymour Krim wrote in the *Washington Post,* "*Winter's Tale* turns out to be a self-willed fairy tale that even on its own terms refuses to convince."

A Soldier of the Great War (HARCOURT BRACE JOVANOVICH, 1991) • An old Italian named Alessandro Giuliani, riding a trolley, takes pity on a boy who runs behind, trying to catch it. He orders the trolley to stop, with the result that both he and the boy are soon footbound. As they hike to a distant village, the old man tells the boy the story of his service in World War I. Helprin's version of that war is to Hemingway's as the *Iliad* is to a rap song. The scenes, characters, and morals roll out in great thunderclouds, with all the necessary homage paid to the author's vision but not much to historical accuracy. "Research kills a book," Helprin told the *New York Times.*

Memoir from Antproof Case (HARCOURT BRACE, 1995) • Helprin says that he has never tasted coffee, and the narrator of this bizarrely entertaining novel seems to be an extreme personification of this aversion. Helprin's hero is a world-historical individual whose preposterous adventures—childhood in a Swiss lunatic asylum, services as a World War II flying ace, career as a globetrotting investment banker, theft of 2,222 gold bars—can all be traced to his conviction that the brown "malodorous poison" has ruined humanity. The tale has no purpose, but it's a delightful read.

BIOGRAPHY

WHEN MARK HELPRIN WAS a child, his father required him to make up a story before he would be allowed to eat his dinner; if the story wasn't interesting enough, the boy would go hungry. How's that for an episode from a storyteller's life? Too good to be true? Alas, yes. Helprin has developed such a reputation for fictionalizing his own life that journalists now hesitate to believe many remarkable stories about him that actually are true. Helprin later admitted (after his father read the interview and was infuriated) that the infamous story-for-a-meal tale was a tall one. Yet he apparently did show up at the door of an attractive woman who had bought one of his books...and ended up marrying her. Among Helprin's other notable adventures, he was nearly killed by an irate Pakistani in Jamaica, and while skiing down a glacier on Mount Rainier, he zigged when he should have zagged. As Helprin describes the incident, he surely would have perished had he not, amazingly, caught himself on his ski poles before plunging over the precipice.

What seems fairly certain is that he's the child of Morris Helprin, a *New York Times* film critic who later became a movie industry executive. He attended Harvard University and began selling short stories to *The New Yorker* as an undergraduate. His wife, Lisa Kennedy, is a lawyer. They have two daughters.

Helprin is distinguished from many other renowned American writers of his generation by his politics. He is a staunch conservative and an expert on the Middle East but only recently did he achieve wider-than-literary fame when it was revealed that he was the author of the unusually lyrical speech in which Bob Dole resigned from the Senate. Although a contributing editor to the *Wall Street Journal* and a fellow of the conservative Hudson Institute, Helprin has distanced himself from the current Republican leadership by calling himself a "[Theodore] Roosevelt Republican."

NEXT ON THE READING LIST: Paul Auster, T. Coraghessan Boyle, A. S. Byatt, Louis de Bernières, Don DeLillo, E. L. Doctorow, Michael Ondaatje

Oscar Hijuelos

(b. August 24, 1951)

"Once in a great while a novelist emerges who is remarkable not for the particulars of his prose but for the breadth of his soul, the depth of his humanity, and for the precision of his gauge on the rising sensibilities of his time.... Oscar Hijuelos is one of these."
—Marie Arana-Ward, Washington Post

TITTONI

Our House in the Last World (PERSEA, 1983) • Hijuelos's first novel, an immigrant memoir, follows the fortunes of the Santinio family over several decades. The central consciousness is that of Hector, the second son—who, like Hijuelos, was born in New York City in 1951. Unlike his older brother, who emulates their father's machismo, Hector is an overweight and shy "American" teen who views his family's Cuban heritage with a mixture of awe and apprehension. Praising Hijuelos's elegantly accessible style, critics singled out his eloquent description of the Santinio family's attempt to balance the rough realities of Spanish Harlem with the values and personal identities they brought from Cuba.

* The Mambo Kings Play Songs of Love (FARRAR, STRAUS & GIROUX, 1989) • Hijuelos's Pulitzer Prize winner chronicles the lives of two Cuban brothers, Cesar and Nestor Castillo, who immigrate to New York City during the late 1940s. Forming an orchestra called the Mambo Kings, they achieve ephemeral fame when they appear one night as Ricky Ricardo's cousins on an episode of *I Love Lucy*. In general, the novel's relationship to things Cuban is affectionate yet distant; Cesar's Americanized nephew Eugenio provides the book's point of view, as well as its attitudes and values.

> *"Mr. Hijuelos is writing music of the heart, not the heart of flesh and blood that stops beating, but this other heart filled with light and music.... [His is] a world of pure affection, before torment, before loss, before awareness."* (*Margo Jefferson*, New York Times)

The Fourteen Sisters of Emilio Montez O'Brien (FARRAR, STRAUS & GIROUX, 1993) • Whereas *The Mambo Kings* used a single narrator to tell its story of fraternal machismo, this book manipulates a number of viewpoints to create a paean to femininity spanning several generations in the life of a boisterous Cuban-Irish family. The fourteen sisters of the title are born between 1902 and 1923 to an American photographer and his Cuban wife (they meet during the Spanish-American War). Critics praised Hijuelos for handling so many characters so deftly, but a few noted that he did so at the expense of reducing these women to shorthand portrayals that inevitably bog down the book's pacing.

Mr. Ives' Christmas (HARPERCOLLINS, 1995) • Edward Ives, a retired commercial artist, treasures the Dickens first editions that he inherited from the kindly man who rescued him from an orphanage. A mild and blameless character, he has just one principal flaw: his inability to come to terms with the senseless murder of his only son. While most reviewers were indifferent to Hijuelos's ready affirmation of Catholicism, some thought that this parable of good will lost and regained was his best work to date.

BIOGRAPHY

OSCAR HIJUELOS WAS BORN IN New York City in 1951—the son of a hotel worker and a homemaker, both Cuban immigrants eager to achieve the American dream of material success. Hijuelos, who writes exclusively in English, received his B.A. from the City College of New York in 1975 and an M.A. the following year. He worked for seven years as an "advertising media traffic manager" before the successful publication of his first novel relieved him of the need to pursue a nonliterary career.

The first Latino novelist to win a Pulitzer Prize for fiction, Hijuelos is one of an increasing number of Hispanic-American authors who have reached out and found a broad national audience. Although Cuban culture strongly informs his work, the voice that speaks to the reader in Hijuelos's novels is that of a second-generation Cuban-American—in other words, someone whose ties to Cuba are becoming increasingly distant. Hijuelos draws extensively on Hispanic material, yet weaves it into a body of work that's unquestionably Anglocentric. Even so, his novels are a complex and moving tribute to his Cuban parents, their Spanish language, and their uneasy homeland's mores and music.

NEXT ON THE READING LIST: Isabel Allende, Julia Alvarez, Cristina Garcia, Gabriel García Márquez, Naguib Mahfouz

Peter Høeg
(b. 1957)

"Mr. Høeg...is a storyteller [who] eventually [discovered] the local traditions of Selma Lagerlöf, Johannes Jensen, and Hans Christian Andersen, which serve him best—legends tinged with romantic melancholy, fictitious biographies, tall tales told with zest in bold lines. Mr. Høeg's contribution to this kind of storytelling is his tongue-in-cheek humor, notably his lively sense of the absurd."
—John David Morley, New York Times

The History of Danish Dreams (ROSINANTE, 1988; FARRAR, STRAUS & GIROUX, 1995) • Høeg's first novel experiments ambitiously with the genre of the family saga. It begins in 1520 with four families, consolidating them through marriage and chance into two by the end of World War I and then, after World War II, merging them into one. In the meantime, Høeg briefly traces Danish history from feudalism to the present welfare state, along the way suggesting elegantly his contempt for the self-satisfaction of his countrymen. "There are passages," John Skow wrote in *Time*, "in which the reader's eyes slide off the page. And in something like an equal number, or a bit more, there are set pieces, two or three or several dozen pages long, that are among the funniest satirical sketches seen in years."

* Smilla's Sense of Snow (ROSINANTE, 1992; FARRAR, STRAUS & GIROUX, 1993) • This was Høeg's first novel translated into English, and it became a runaway bestseller. Its narrator, a half-Inuit, half-Danish glaciologist named Smilla, lives in a dreary Copenhagen apartment building. One day, a neighbor boy falls off the snow-covered roof. The police don't seem to care, but Smilla's ability to "read" the boy's footprints tells her that he was murdered. As one might expect, her diligent investigation of this small event soon uncovers a large conspiracy that takes her to Greenland—which, according to John Williams in *New Statesman & Society*, "Høeg relieves...of its normal fictional role as an empty, hostile territory [and turns] into a place where people live."

> "Smilla's Sense of Snow *is a thriller, but it's a thriller like no other. Maybe a Le Carré novel comes closest, with its brainy characters enmeshed in deliciously intricate conundrums.... But Le Carré, whose view of women can most charitably be called old-fashioned, could never have created a narrator as daring and self-sufficient as Smilla."* (*Laura Shapiro,* Newsweek)

Borderliners (ROSINANTE, 1993; FARRAR, STRAUS & GIROUX, 1994) • This novel, the second of Høeg's works translated into English, takes place at an authoritarian Danish boarding school, where three orphans have been placed in a secret experiment on mainstreaming problem children. When fourteen-year-old Peter begins to suspect that something sinister is going on, he allies himself with Katarina and the unstable August to subvert the schemes of the headmaster. The real villain, though, is linear time, which constrains "the circular talents and zigzag impulses of human nature," according to *Los Angeles Times* critic Richard Eder. *New York Times* reviewer David Sacks complained that *Borderliners* "suffers from a disjointed, repetitious plot that bogs down under its own philosophical baggage," yet in *New Statesman & Society* Sarah A. Smith praised the book for its "extraordinary intellectual and creative energy."

The Woman and the Ape (FARRAR, STRAUS & GIROUX, 1996) • Høeg's eagerly anticipated fourth novel, his first since *Smilla*, opens with the strong hook of an ecothriller. A smuggler of endangered species transports an ape to London; initially, evil zoologist Adam Burden thinks that Erasmus is a dwarf chimpanzee, but then Burden discovers he's actually a member of an unknown species that might just be capable of high cognitive functions, such as language. Meanwhile, Adam's beautiful alcoholic wife begins to feel a strange attraction for Erasmus and, sensing that Adam has something terrible planned, helps him to escape. At this point, when the novel turns into an interspecies love affair, it falls apart. "For several chapters as his story takes shape, Mr. Høeg has us in his spell," Richard Bernstein wrote in the *New York Times*. "Unfortunately, the promising structure he has built suddenly collapses into a precious, preachy, implausible, even maudlin fairy tale."

BIOGRAPHY

PETER HØEG WAS BORN, RAISED, and lives in Denmark with his wife, a dancer originally from Kenya, and their daughter. During his twenties, he worked as an actor, a dancer, a drama teacher, and a sailor "on rich people's boats." Then he became a writer. "Ten years ago," he has said, "I was much more restless than I am now. I knew all the time, as I was starting other careers, that this was not final, it was a transition, something that would be replaced by something else. I don't have that feeling any longer. One thing that came to me with writing was peace."

In his writing, Høeg repeatedly questions the political and cultural values of contemporary Denmark, especially its tendency to favor social conformity over individuality. He worries about the detrimental effects of this regimentation on children, whom he often uses in his books (most obviously in *Borderliners*) to symbolize human potential. According to Nader Mousavizadeh, writing in *The New Republic*, "Høeg has brought to modern Danish literature an intensity, a worldliness, a love of language, and a depth of learning that entirely on their own have raised the standards for contemporary writing in Denmark."

NEXT ON THE READING LIST: Paul Auster, Madison Smartt Bell, Joan Didion, David Guterson, Mark Helprin, Jane Smiley

Alice Hoffman
(b. March 16, 1952)

"Hoffman's narrative domain is the domestic, the daily. Yet her vision—and voice—are lyrical. She is a writer whose prose style is often praised as painterly, and, indeed, Hoffman's fictional world is like a Vermeer: a beautifully crafted study of the interior life."
—*Alexandra Johnson*, Boston Review

Property Of (FARRAR, STRAUS & GIROUX, 1977) • Hoffman sets her first novel in a world made familiar by urban genre movies: the lawless city ruled by gangs. Her prose, however, is remarkably calm, and it gives the book's jagged plot a mythic feel. Although the heroine falls in with a gang leader, she's determined not to become his "property," the label given to all other girlfriends. The *Times Literary Supplement* called *Property Of* "a sort of punk or pop-Gothic *Jane Eyre*" and noted that Hoffman "artfully reproduces" the "solemn dignities" of the street.

The Drowning Season (DUTTON, 1979) • Hoffman's mythic sensibility reveals itself even more fully in her second novel. In one sense, *The Drowning Season* is the story of a Russian family that immigrates to Long Island. However, it's also the tale of a "white" witch, a "black" witch, and a possibly insane man who insists on drowning himself once a year, only to be saved each time at the last moment. "Alice Hoffman's hallucinatory novel skims along just above the surface of the real like a finely wrought nightmare," Jean Strouse wrote in *Newsweek*.

Angel Landing (PUTNAM, 1980) • A bomb goes off at a nuclear power plant, and when the bad guy who set it wanders into town, Natalie, our heroine, falls in love with him. He becomes her dark knight and she his saving grace. Writing in *Ms.*, Miriam Sagan called the book "vivid and hilarious" and "a novel of character, in which individuals struggle for meaning and control." However, several other reviewers chastised Hoffman for lapsing into prose that often takes on a purplish hue.

White Horses (PUTNAM, 1982) • Teresa's mother once told her tales of the Arias, mythic horsemen who ride off into the retreating sun. Now Teresa is in love with her brother, Silver, whom she fancies is an Aria. As incest awakens, Teresa falls prey to a sleeping sickness. "A lot of very careful Creative Writing has to be got through before Teresa escapes her fate," Hermione Lee warned in *The Observer*. "Any interesting ideas about incestuous love are buried deep beneath the drifts of self-conscious mush and whimsy."

Fortune's Daughter (PUTNAM, 1985) • The mythic and the mundane merge in this story about motherhood as experienced by two women. Ever since Lila gave up her baby years ago, thoughts of it have filled her mind. Now Rae is pregnant, and she needs Lila's help. "To a susceptible reader, at least, *Fortune's Daughter* is something of a tearjerker," and it leaves the reader "with a gullible feeling," Susan Lardner wrote in *The New Yorker.*

* Illumination Night (PUTNAM, 1987) • The setting is Martha's Vineyard, where once a year the old Victorian houses in the town of Oak Bluffs are illuminated with romantic lantern light. Around this event come together the intersecting stories of several characters. *Illumination Night* is less obviously enchanted than Hoffman's earlier works but more masterful.

> *"[Hoffman] practices an unusually fluid form of subjectivity that becomes a kind of total omniscience: She glides from one character's consciousness to another...in a single paragraph or sentence, without breaking the rhythm of her prose or storyline." (Jack Sullivan,* Washington Post)

At Risk (PUTNAM, 1988) • In this novel about AIDS, the dying victim is an innocent young girl. As always, Hoffman writes well, but not well enough to get beyond the pat characterizations inherent in such a subject. As Christopher Lehmann-Haupt pointed out in the *New York Times,* "One can't help being conscious of obligatory scenes being played out," such as the one in which friends of the girl's brother no longer want to play with him.

Seventh Heaven (PUTNAM, 1990) • Nora Silk is a divorcée who arrives in suburbia one day in 1959, looking for a little peace and quiet. Unfortunately, her nice neighbors soon begin projecting their fears and desires onto her, and when her odd eight-year-old son develops a penchant for mind reading, things really get bizarre. Writing in the *New York Times,* Alida Becker praised *Seventh Heaven* for its "wonderful blend of humor, shrewdness, and compassion."

Turtle Moon (PUTNAM, 1992) • It's a hot and humid day in Verity, Florida—every day is. In fact, the heat positively shimmers from the pages of this novel, which knits together the fortunes of a twelve-year-old bad boy and a baby girl whose mother is on the run. On their trail are the boy's mother and a local cop (another fateful couple). According to one reviewer, "Ms. Hoffman writes quite wonderfully about the magic in our lives and in the battered, indifferent world."

Second Nature (PUTNAM, 1994) • A child who survives a plane crash is raised by wolves. Later, as a grown wolf-man, he's captured. Psychiatrists attempt to resurrect his humanity but fail. Finally, a woman attracted to his animal magnetism rescues him and begins to make him human again. The plot may sound hokey, but *Second Nature* was one of Hoffman's most enthusiastically received books. Howard Frank Mosher in the *New York Times* called it "outstanding" and "very possibly her best."

Practical Magic (PUTNAM, 1995) • Sally and Gillian Owens come from a long line of witches. As girls, Sally fights her heredity, while Gillian embraces it. Years later, after Sally has fled to another town, Gillian appears with a dead body in tow. "The witches in this novel are not like Anne Rice witches," Mark Childress explained in the *New York Times*. "They have children they love [and] dinner to get on the table." Hoffman's story, Childress added, is "charmingly told and a good deal of fun."

Here on Earth (PUTNAM, 1997) • Hoffman's twelfth novel, something of a bodice ripper, reads like *Wuthering Heights:* There's a stormy landscape, a secretive family, a troublesome orphan, and an obsessive love affair as bleak and tempestuous as the weather. As a young woman, March Murray, like Brontë's Cathy, fails to join with her soulmate, Hollis, and instead marries next-door neighbor Richard, moving away with him to California. However, nineteen years later—and here's where Hoffman diverges from Brontë— March returns to rural Massachusetts and once again falls under the spell of the now malevolent Hollis. *Here on Earth* is "by turns inspired, profound, and dreadful," Karen Karbo wrote in the *New York Times*. In *Newsday*, however, Daisy Fried called the novel "fascinating...and marvelous storytelling."

BIOGRAPHY

ALICE HOFFMAN HAS THE KIND of life that novelists aren't supposed to live anymore. She avoids big-city life and university writing programs so that she can keep herself focused on events in and around her Brookline, Massachusetts, home. Of greatest interest to her are the lives of her two sons and her husband, screenwriter Tom Martin. In fact, Hoffman had published nine novels before she grudgingly embarked on her first book tour in 1994. She said later that she spent most of the time sitting in hotel rooms dreaming about her next batch of characters, who remained locked in her attic, awaiting her return.

Born and raised in New York City, Hoffman earned a bachelor's degree from Adelphi University and a master's from Stanford before beginning her writing career. She published her first novel, *Property Of*, in 1977, when she was twenty-five. Since then, she has become famous for her effortless blending of mundane suburban settings and mythical, magical themes. In Hoffman's work, for example, it's not unusual to find a wolfman using Tupperware.

Perhaps her favorite type of heroine is the wandering, apparently distracted woman—often a mother, often someone in financial trouble—who turns out to possess a deep reservoir of feeling and sensitivity that allows her to achieve a mystic wisdom. Hoffman once said that she writes about disaffected people because "they're outsiders and to some extent we all think of ourselves as outsiders. We're looking for that other person—man, woman, parent, child—who will make us whole."

NEXT ON THE READING LIST: Amy Bloom, Ellen Gilchrist, Nadine Gordimer, Kazuo Ishiguro, Alice Munro, Joyce Carol Oates, Grace Paley

---

John Irving
(b. March 2, 1942)

"Irving's philosophy is basic stuff: One must live willfully, purposefully, and watchfully. Accidents, bad luck,…and open windows lurk everywhere—and the dog really bites. It is only a matter of time. Nobody gets out alive, yet few want to leave early. Irving's popularity is not hard to understand. His world is the world according to nearly everyone."
—R. Z. Sheppard, Time

Setting Free the Bears (RANDOM HOUSE, 1969) • Irving sets his first novel in Austria, where a young student named Hannes Graff has a number of misadventures with his sidekick, Siegfried. One critic complained that the book, which fills its first hundred pages with prosaic descriptions of Austrian life, reads like a "European translation from an original by a European writer"—presumably not a very good one. In fact, we don't reach the worthwhile heart of this novel until Siegfried begins staking out a zoo in preparation for liberating its animals. Only then do we glimpse Irving's ability to build suspense and his "uncommon imaginative power."

The Water-Method Man (RANDOM HOUSE, 1972) • Fred Trumper develops a rare urinary tract condition that makes both urinating and intercourse painful. His options are an even more painful operation or a long-term water treatment, during which he must urinate frequently. Being an Irving character, Trumper chooses the latter. According to Jan Carew in the *New York Times*, "*The Water-Method Man*, a rambling episodic novel, is held together almost miraculously by the skill of an author who is a born writer…. After putting down the novel and allowing some time to elapse, the characters, the kaleidoscope of events assume a cohesive and even more meaningful form."

The 158-Pound Marriage (RANDOM HOUSE, 1974) • When two married couples swap partners, jealousy and hostility (rather than excitement and pleasure) result. The unnamed narrator of this book, a historical novelist displaced from Massachusetts to Vienna, and his wife, Utch (her name means "cow" in Russian), are persuaded to "swing" by another couple who want to get even with each other for past infidelities. Irving himself described this novel, his shortest and perhaps most hilarious, as one "about lust and rationalization and restlessness: I decided I wanted to write a really dark tale of sexual intrigue; in the end nobody would know anything about each other."

* The World According to Garp (DUTTON, 1978) • Winner of an American Book Award, this is Irving's finest, most original, and most successful work. Writer, wrestling coach, and sexual adventurer T. S. Garp obsesses about protecting his family and friends from harm, yet his eccentric world—inhabited by his mother, Jenny, a feminist icon, and his best friend, Roberta, a transsexual football player—is quite beyond his control. This zany episodic novel spans Garp's entire lifetime, from before his conception until after his death.

> "The World According to Garp...*contains almost intolerable pain. It is a bloody package, and if [Irving] had flung this in front of us, we would have backed away in horror. As it is, we read on, at first entertained, then puzzled, then trapped, wanting to look away, but by this time unable to avert our eyes."*
> (*Margaret Drabble,* Harper's)

The Hotel New Hampshire (DUTTON, 1981) • This novel, another family saga, recounts forty years in the lives of the Berry family, presenting yet more of Irving's peculiar takes on such extreme issues as incest, suicide, and gang rape. As the Garps did, the Berry family experiences a series of bizarre, implausible, and mostly tragic events that critics soon began to describe as "Irvingesque." For example, Franny Berry, after being gang-raped by a prep school football team, has an affair with a woman in a bear costume. Although *The Hotel New Hampshire* sold well, obviously buoyed by the success of *Garp*, most critics deplored its obsession with cruelty, not to mention Irving's poor writing. "*The Hotel New Hampshire* is crammed with exotic characters and fantastic events that spill from the pages of his other novels," James Atlas wrote in the *New York Times*. "But Irving isn't here just to entertain. There are a number of serious messages in *The Hotel New Hampshire*, among them the conviction that life is a pretty dreary affair."

The Cider House Rules (MORROW, 1985) • The gentle ether addict Dr. Larch—who runs an orphanage in St. Cloud, Maine—performs illegal abortions so that future orphans might be saved from an existence that he considers bleak. Larch is hopeful that his protégé, orphan Homer Wells, will assume leadership of the orphanage (and take over his abortion duties) when the time comes. Instead, Homer, who believes that fetuses have souls, runs away to a nearby apple orchard. Despite the book's weighty moral overtones, Susan Brownmiller, writing in the *Chicago Tribune*, called *The Cider House Rules* "a heartfelt, sometimes moving tract in support of abortion rights."

A Prayer for Owen Meany (MORROW, 1989) • In this novel, Irving renders all of Owen Meany's speech in capital letters to suggest Meany's unusual-sounding voice (he has a fixed larynx) and to remind readers of the way in which the words of Jesus are differentiated in certain editions of the New Testament. Johnny Wheelwright tells the story of the adolescent Owen, who accidentally kills Johnny's mother with a foul ball. Owen believes that he's an "instrument of God" and eventually persuades Johnny to believe as well. Although some reviewers criticized Irving for being too "cute," Brigitte Weeks in the *Washington Post* defended the book: "John Irving is a reader's writer, and *A Prayer for Owen Meany* is a reader's novel, a large, intriguing grab bag of characters and ideas that moves the spirit and fascinates the mind."

Son of the Circus (RANDOM HOUSE, 1994) • Spanning three continents and twenty years, *Son of the Circus* features transsexuals, transvestites, eunuchs, twins separated at birth (a film star and a Jesuit), a potentially HIV-positive child prostitute, a serial killer, a dildo filled with Deutsche marks, and, of course, a circus! It's the circus that brings neurosurgeon Farrokh Darruwalla to Bombay to test the blood of several dwarf clowns so that he might find the cause of achondroplasia (dwarfism). Although Robert Towers in the *New York Times* found the book "superficial...and inadequately dramatized," Michael Harris in the *Los Angeles Times* called it a "three-ringer of a novel," whose teeming Indian setting "makes Irving's convoluted plot seem natural."

Trying to Save Piggy Sneed (ARCADE, 1996) • This collection, which contains three decades' worth of Irving leftovers, contains several short stories, including "The Pension Grillparzer," originally published in *The World According to Garp*. Dismissed by Dan Cryer of *Newsday* as a "between-novels collection that only the most famous and best-selling authors can persuade anyone to publish," *Trying to Save Piggy Sneed* offers a few worthwhile surprises, but much too much wrestling commentary.

BIOGRAPHY

BORN IN EXETER, MASSACHUSETTS, to a Russian history teacher and his wife, John Irving was an average student in high school. He prepped at Exeter, where he learned to write, and attended the University of Pittsburgh, where he dreamed of becoming a star wrestler. Instead, he learned that he had a greater talent for fiction. After transferring to the University of New Hampshire, he moved to Austria and attended the University of Vienna for a year before returning to New Hampshire and graduating cum laude in 1965. While abroad, he married artist Shyla Leary (they were divorced in 1981).

After New Hampshire, Irving attended the Iowa Writers' Workshop, where he studied with Kurt Vonnegut Jr. and earned an M.F.A. in 1967.

Two years later, Random House published Irving's first novel, *Setting Free the Bears*. Like the two novels that followed, *The Water-Method Man* and *The 158-Pound Marriage*, it earned him neither great sums of money nor great renown. However, all that changed following the 1978 publication of *The World According to Garp*. *Garp* sold three million copies, became a cult classic, and was made into a 1982 film starring Robin Williams and Glenn Close. (Two years later, *The Hotel New Hampshire*, starring Jodie Foster and Rob Lowe, followed *Garp* into theaters.)

Irving's deeply ironic worldview and perverse love for black humor have led him to construct elaborate jokes about subjects that many people don't find funny, such as speech impediments, dwarfism, prostitution, rape, castration, transsexuality, disfigurement, and reckless driving. Although none of his post-*Garp* novels has matched that book's success, Irving continues to receive good reviews. He lives in Vermont with his second wife, Janet Turnbull, whom he married in 1987, and their son, Everett. He also has two sons from his previous marriage. When he can, he still keeps up his interest in wrestling.

NEXT ON THE READING LIST: Beryl Bainbridge, T. Coraghessan Boyle, Harry Crews, Terry McMillan, Lorrie Moore, V. S. Naipaul, Jane Smiley

---

Kazuo Ishiguro
(b. November 8, 1954)

"Masks are what Ishiguro's novels are about, and he himself always chooses the mask of first-person narrator. All the narrators are sedate and formal people so he never needs to drop into any kind of vulgar slang or colloquialism, and hardly to change gear when he allows them to call up a landscape or an atmosphere. Descriptions are as factual and plain as a Morandi still life, but they exude powerful moods and mostly sad ones: nostalgia, regret, resignation."
—*Gabriele Annan*, New York Review of Books

A Pale View of the Hills (PUTNAM, 1982) • Ishiguro's first novel is narrated by Etsuko, a middle-aged Japanese woman living in England. The suicide of her troubled daughter awakens in her somber memories of the summer that the daughter was born in war-ravaged Nagasaki. Through Etsuko, Ishiguro depicts the incineration of a culture and the disjointed lives of those who survive. Some critics enjoyed his portrayal of the survivors' hope, courage, and tenacity; others remarked on the great evocative power produced by his delicate layering of the book's themes and images.

An Artist of the Floating World (PUTNAM, 1986) • In this winner of a Whitbread Award, Ishiguro again explores a Japan in transition. The story, set in a provincial town during the late 1940s, revolves around Masuji Ono, a painter who once worked as a propagandist for the prewar imperialist regime. While showing how the traditional Japanese virtue of loyalty was distorted and exploited, Ishiguro also allows deep reservations to surface about the wholesale Americanization of Japan after the war. Once again, critics noted his flawless control—every incident, every comma, seems to be exactly in its proper place—and they also praised his gently oblique manner of storytelling.

* The Remains of the Day (KNOPF, 1989) • The narrators of Ishiguro's first two novels each lived according to the ethos of "knowing one's place." Likewise the English butler Stevens in *The Remains of the Day*. After years of faithful service to Lord Darlington, he finds himself suddenly in the employ of a congenial American who has purchased Darlington Hall and kept on Stevens as part of the furniture. Described as a "tragedy in the form of a comedy of manners," *The Remains of the Day* met with a highly favorable critical response.

> *"Just below the understatement of the novel's surface is a turbulence as immense as it is slow.... [Stevens's] whole life has been a foolish mistake; his only defense against the horror of this knowledge is that same facility for self-deception which proved his undoing. It's a cruel and beautiful conclusion to a story both beautiful and cruel."* (*Salman Rushdie,* The Observer)

The Unconsoled (KNOPF, 1995) • Ishiguro's ambitious fourth novel also explores the ways in which a disingenuous public facade can eviscerate the private self behind it. In a fresh and unusual (for Ishiguro) way, *The Unconsoled* details the Kafkaesque journey of Ryder, a famous pianist who travels to a small Central European city to give a concert. The local citizenry has organized for him a number of social functions that he seems obliged to attend, although he can't remember agreeing to any of it. While not as critically embraced as his earlier work, *The Unconsoled* did show Ishiguro's willingness to set aside his earlier successes and try something new.

BIOGRAPHY

THE SON OF A SCIENTIST and a homemaker, Kazuo Ishiguro was born in Japan but raised in England from the age of five. He graduated with honors from the University of Kent in 1978, earning a master's degree in creative writing from the University of East Anglia two years later. Prior to the 1982 publication of *A Pale View of the Hills,* Ishiguro held jobs as a social worker in Renfrew, Scotland, and then West London.

Ishiguro has insisted that he doesn't really write about Japan, but about a country he has invented that merely resembles Japan. He wrote his two "Japanese" novels, for example, without ever revisiting his birthplace. Similarly, his "English" novel is about an England he never knew.

Ishiguro's books deal with issues of memory, self-deception, and codes of etiquette, which lead his characters to subtle yet wrenching realizations about the relative success or failure of their lives. According to Ishiguro, "What I'm interested in is not the actual fact that my characters have done things they later regret.... I'm interested in how they come to terms with it."

NEXT ON THE READING LIST: A. S. Byatt, Nadine Gordimer, Mark Helprin, Alice Hoffman, V. S. Naipaul, Kenzaburo Oe, Graham Swift

---

Charles Johnson

(b. April 23, 1948)

"[Johnson's] language is an invigorating interweaving of hieratic and demotic English and everything in between. His tales are peopled by characters who, by virtue of their all-too-human wit unwitting itself, for good or ill, tumble into surreal existential trick-bags; and whoever they were, their heretofore quotidian lives are never to be the same again."
—*J. J. Phillips*, Los Angeles Times

Faith and the Good Thing (VIKING, 1974) • Faith, a poor black girl from the South, heads north to Chicago in search of "the good thing," which her dying grandmother promised her could be found there. This scenario may sound quaint, but Johnson isn't a straightforward tale spinner. The plot quickly veers into surreality, as both witchcraft and Western philosophy inform Faith's journey. In *Time*, John Skow called *Faith and the Good Thing* "a tricky mixture of down-home storytelling and faculty-lounge chitchat."

Oxherding Tale (INDIANA UNIVERSITY, 1982) • This book employs a conceit similar to the one that Johnson used in his first novel, with the journey taking place a century earlier as a slave makes his way to freedom. Yet the slim tale of Andrew Hawkins isn't so much about the evils of slavery as the conundrum of choice, for Hawkins is a mulatto who can pass for white. "Andrew's growth is thrilling because Johnson skillfully avoids melodramatic platitudes while creating suspense and comedy, pathos and nostalgia," Stanley Crouch wrote in the *Village Voice*.

The Sorcerer's Apprentice (ATHENEUM, 1986) • In these stories, as in his previous works, Johnson mixes low speech with high philosophy, as though he was testing various combinations of Western intellectual ideas and African-American reality in search of a winning match. As a result, these stories "aren't for pleasure cruising," according to Jonathan Penner in the *Washington Post.* "They're stripped models, the vehicles of ideas."

✳ Middle Passage (ATHENEUM, 1990) • Johnson's third novel, winner of a National Book Award, is a hilarious, dense, and yet very readable tale of a highly educated freed slave who winds up boarding a slave ship headed back to Africa. Some reviewers had problems with Johnson's mixture of modern and old-fashioned idiom ("All the characters sound as if they're double majors in classics and philosophy," wrote one), but the result is a delightfully fresh story.

> *"Johnson transforms [Ralph] Ellison's black victim of white society...into a laughing, sensual rogue, fully equipped intellectually, who exults in his difference from white Americans and from black Americans who stereotype themselves in the white image."* (*Joseph Coates,* Chicago Tribune)

BIOGRAPHY

AFTER SEEING HIS SON'S early drawings, Charles Johnson's father encouraged him to become a cartoonist, which he did on entering Southern Illinois University. By the time of his graduation, however, Johnson had switched to journalism. Then, abruptly, he switched again, this time pursuing a master's degree in philosophy. Yet even this field couldn't adequately sustain Johnson's restless intellect.

During his student years, he wrote six novels. Although none was published, it was while studying creative writing under John Gardner that Johnson began to understand the possibilities of the novel. He has said that, like Gardner, he believes that fiction should have a moral purpose. Johnson has also credited Gardner with helping him conceive of ways to blend the black experience with the concepts of Western philosophy.

Johnson has distinguished himself from other black novelists by his refusal to tell straightforward tales of white oppression and black struggles for equality. His studies in philosophy and his commitment to Buddhism have, he has said, deepened his appreciation for the complexity of racial and social issues.

Johnson is currently a professor of English at the University of Washington. He's married and the father of two children. In addition to his novels and short stories, he has published two collections of cartoons and written several television scripts.

NEXT ON THE READING LIST: Bebe Moore Campbell, Toni Morrison, Gloria Naylor, Mario Vargas Llosa, John Edgar Wideman

William Kennedy

(b. January 16, 1928)

"In [Kennedy's] fictional world, good deeds are not automatically rewarded, love is not eternal, and death is frequent, offhand and cruel. He demurs at the suggestion that he is preternaturally unkind to the gangsters, hoboes, has-beens and almost-were athletes and would-be entertainers who populate his fiction: 'I don't see how you can say that I'm crueler than God. God is the cruelest cat in town.'"
—Michael Ryan, People

The Ink Truck (DIAL, 1969) • Kennedy's first novel is loosely based on a 1964 walkout at the *Albany Times-Union*, where he was working at the time. As the book opens, most of the strikers have either capitulated or been wooed back to work—except for Bailey, Irma, Rosenthal, and Jarvis. Bailey presages Kennedy's later Irish Catholic protagonists, who generally fall before they rise. Originally dismissed by critics, *The Ink Truck* was republished in the aftermath of *Ironweed*, at which time Anne Tyler noted that it had served Kennedy as a "finger-exercise for the Albany cycle."

Legs (COWARD, MCCANN & GEOGHEGAN, 1975) • When an editor bought Kennedy's second novel based on a few sample chapters, the author left journalism to immerse himself in exhaustive research. Written over six years, the resulting "fictional biography" of John T. "Legs" Diamond reinvents this vicious Irish-American gangster (killed in Albany in 1931) as an almost Gatsby-like character, reviled by the public yet pressed for autographs. A handful of critics noted Kennedy's maturing skills, but this first novel in Kennedy's Albany Cycle wasn't a commercial success.

Billy Phelan's Greatest Game (VIKING, 1978) • Through the eyes of reporter Martin Daugherty, we watch Billy Phelan—pool shark, bowling ace, and saloon-wise hustler—prowl the underside of Albany circa 1938. When kidnappers abduct the only child of a powerful local family, Billy is pressured to inform. Like *Legs* before it, this second novel in Kennedy's Albany cycle received a smattering of mildly favorable reviews but didn't sell particularly well. In fact, Kennedy's first three novels together sold only a few thousand copies.

* Ironweed (VIKING, 1983) • Kennedy's third Albany novel was rejected by thirteen publishers before Viking, at the insistence of Saul Bellow, reconsidered its decision. Bellow was right: The book went on to win both a National Book Critics Circle Award and a Pulitzer Prize. Its protagonist is former big-league ballplayer Francis Phelan, who returns home to depression-era Albany, where ghosts lead him on a Dantean tour of the hobo underworld. (Francis had left town in 1916 shortly after the accidental death of his infant son.) Widely considered Kennedy's most outstanding work, *Ironweed* was praised for its command of time and place, its blend of lyrical and colloquial prose styles, and its compassionate humanism.

> *"Herman Melville probably had it right. It's impossible to write a great work of fiction about the life of a flea. Until now, one might have thought it equally impossible to write a lyric work of fiction about the life of a bum. But William Kennedy has done it with this beautifully sorrowful novel."* (Webster Schott, Washington Post)

Quinn's Book (VIKING, 1988) • The action here spans 1849 to 1864, a tumultuous period for both the city of Albany and the country at large. The Underground Railroad, the Civil War, and the New York draft riots are all part of this book's backdrop. Its Dickensian narrator is adolescent orphan Daniel Quinn. After Daniel saves twelve-year-old Maud Fallon from drowning, the two of them begin a relationship that becomes central to Daniel's life and to the book's development. While some critics felt that Kennedy's fifth novel occasionally faltered under the weight of its historical content, most agreed that the story itself was consistently fascinating.

Very Old Bones (VIKING, 1992) • Variously damned for being "thin and mechanical" and praised as his best work yet, Kennedy's sixth novel, set in 1958, is narrated by Orson Purcell. This thirty-four-year-old aspiring writer is also the caretaker of Peter Phelan, his unacknowledged father. Phelan was a successful artist in Greenwich Village during the 1930s; he painted, with exuberant charm, American vignettes not unlike those found in Kennedy's own fiction. While documenting the life of his famous father, Orson drifts off to write, at greater length and with greater panache, of his own troubled career and marriage.

The Flaming Corsage (VIKING, 1996) • The main characters in this novel first appeared in *Billy Phelan's Greatest Game* and *Ironweed*. The son of working-class immigrants, Edward Daugherty is a reporter turned playwright who jeopardizes his marriage when he writes a play parodying his patrician wife's father. While praised for keeping his characters consistent with their actions in his earlier works, Kennedy was criticized for his lack of skill in writing about women: good on virgins and whores, yet weak on all the women in between.

BIOGRAPHY

BORN IN 1928 IN ALBANY, New York, to a deputy sheriff and a secretary, William Kennedy received a B.A. from Siena College in 1949. Following his 1952 discharge from the army, he worked as a journalist for such newspapers as the *Puerto Rico World Journal* and the *Miami Herald;* he was also the founding managing editor of the *San Juan Star.* While living in Puerto Rico, he attended a fiction writing course taught by Saul Bellow. After trying unsuccessfully to use San Juan as a setting for his stories, Kennedy realized that his hometown of Albany made much more sense as a fictional locale, so he moved back there during the early 1960s.

Although his journalism was respected, as a tenderfoot novelist Kennedy didn't command much attention. He once admitted that for more than a decade after the publication of *The Ink Truck,* he and his family "lived on credit and promises to pay. It was a good life, and we had a lot of fun. But we never had an extra nickel." Kennedy's economic woes ended on his fifty-fifth birthday, when he received a $264,000 "genius" grant from the MacArthur Foundation. Then came the triumph of *Ironweed* and finally the republication of his first three novels, which all became belatedly profitable.

Kennedy's ongoing Albany Cycle explores the lives of the disaster-prone Phelan family, a fictive Irish clan that immigrated to America in the 1820s to work on the Erie Canal. Although each of the Albany novels can stand on its own, Kennedy has, like William Faulkner, created a precisely detailed fictional world that he reenters in each book at a different angle. His themes, however, remain the same: human vice, bigotry, politics, sexual desire, and survival.

NEXT ON THE READING LIST: Pat Conroy, Pete Dexter, Joan Didion, E. L. Doctorow, Louise Erdrich, Richard Ford, Larry McMurtry, E. Annie Proulx

---

Jamaica Kincaid
(b. May 25, 1949)

"Cynthia Ozick, Mary Gordon, and Susan Sontag have sighed over Kincaid's virtuosity with language, and they were right. Her language recalls Henri Rousseau's painting: seemingly natural, but in reality sophisticated and precise. So lush, composed, direct, odd, sharp, and brilliantly lit are Kincaid's word paintings that the reader's presuppositions are cut in two by her seemingly soft edges."
—*Jacqueline Austin,* Voice Literary Supplement

At the Bottom of the River (FARRAR, STRAUS & GIROUX, 1984) • Kincaid's first book contains ten stories set in Antigua, seven of which previously appeared in *The New Yorker.* Most recount life's mundane aspects in great detail: "Girl," for example, consists almost entirely of a mother's instructions to her daughter: "Wash the white clothes on Monday and put them on the stone heap; wash the color clothes on Tuesday and put them on the clothesline to dry." In "The Letter from Home," a character explains her daily chores in such a manner that the story becomes an incantation: "I milked the cows, I churned the butter, I stored the cheese, I baked the bread, I brewed the tea," Kincaid begins. Although some reviewers, notably *New Republic* critic Anne Tyler, found Kincaid's writing to be solipsistic and "almost insultingly obscure," David Leavitt, writing in the *Village Voice*, praised her ability to "articulate the internal workings of a potent imagination without sacrificing the rich details of the external world on which that imagination thrives."

* Annie John (FARRAR, STRAUS & GIROUX, 1985) • Although *Annie John* was originally published as a series of short stories in *The New Yorker*, most critics considered it a bildungsroman because the stories, presented here as chapters, are so interrelated. At first, young Annie John and her mother are inseparable: She follows her mother everywhere and even dresses like her. However, when Annie John enters puberty, her mother's attitude toward her changes, and the two women begin to compete. In the final chapter, Annie John leaves Antigua, a heaven that has become too small for her.

> *"[Annie John's] story is so touching and familiar...so inevitable [that] it could be happening to any of us, anywhere, anytime, any place. And that's exactly the book's strength, its wisdom, and its truth."* (*Susan Kenney*, New York Times)

Lucy (FARRAR, STRAUS & GIROUX, 1990) • Kincaid's first book set outside Antigua begins where *Annie John* left off: Nineteen-year-old Lucy travels from her Caribbean home to New York City, where Lewis and Mariah, an upper-class couple, employ her to care for their three children. When Lewis and Mariah's marriage collapses, Lucy moves out to begin life on her own. Although Lucy's anger alienated some reviewers, not so Richard Eder in the *Los Angeles Times:* "This harsh and graceful book tells us in the only possible way...what it is to be a colonized subject, a third world sensibility in the United States, a child battling with her past and a woman battling with her identity."

* The Autobiography of My Mother (FARRAR, STRAUS & GIROUX, 1995) • The narrator of this novel, a National Book Critics Circle Award finalist, is a megalomaniacal seventy-year-old woman whose Carib Indian mother died in childbirth. Raised on the island of Dominica, young Xuela has no hatred for her foster mother, a washerwoman who treats her decently, but no love for her either. When Xuela's father, a policeman of mixed African and European heritage, remarries, his new half-French, half-African wife abuses Xuela. Although Xuela rises to the challenge, her own self-hatred ultimately becomes twisted into what one reviewer called "willed nihilism."

"This is a shocking book. Elegantly and delicately composed, it is also inhuman, and unapologetically so. Jamaica Kincaid has written a truly ugly meditation on life in some of the most beautiful prose we are likely to find in contemporary fiction." (*Cathleen Schine*, New York Times)

BIOGRAPHY

JAMAICA KINCAID WAS BORN out of wedlock in St. John's on the Caribbean island of Antigua. Her given name was Elaine Potter Richardson, Richardson being the surname of her formidable mother, Annie, who—like Xuela in *Autobiography of My Mother*—had immigrated to Antigua from Dominica. Soon after the birth of her daughter, Annie Richardson married David Drew, a carpenter and cabinetmaker whom Kincaid has used as the model for her fictional fathers. Annie Richardson Drew taught her daughter to read when she was three years old and, and on Kincaid's seventh birthday, presented her with the *Concise Oxford English Dictionary*.

Although Kincaid has said that she would have preferred to remain in Antigua and become a teacher or librarian there, the lack of such opportunities forced her seek work in the United States. After her arrival in New York City, she took a job as an au pair for a wealthy couple in Westchester County. "When I first started [to write]," Kincaid recalled, "among the things I wanted to do was to say, 'Aren't you sorry that no greater effort was made over my education? Or over my life?'"

Between 1966 and 1973, Kincaid held several different jobs while completing her high school work and taking a few college courses. "Everyone thought I had a way with words, but it came out as a sharp tongue," Kincaid once told an interviewer. "No one expected anything from me at all. Had I just sunk into the cracks, it would not have been noted." Instead, a mutual friend introduced her to George W. Trow, who wrote *The New Yorker*'s "Talk of the Town" column. At first, Trow began incorporating Kincaid's quips into his column; later, he introduced her to editor William Shawn, who became another important mentor. In 1976, Shawn hired Kincaid as one of his staff writers.

Kincaid's books have been admittedly autobiographical. "I am writing for solace," Kincaid has said. "I consider myself the reader I am writing for, and it is to make sense of something, even if to repeat to myself what has happened. Character and ideas are not separate from me." More explicitly, Kincaid has written the National Book Award nominee *My Brother* (1997), a brutally honest account of her younger brother's aimless life and death from AIDS. Anna Quindlen called *My Brother* "a lesson in constructing a memoir that resembles not a neat narrative but the meandering river of human memory." Kincaid's short fiction continues to appear in *The New Yorker*, and since 1991 she has also published essays there relating to her interest in gardening. She lives in North Bennington, Vermont, with her husband, composer Allen Shawn (son of William), and their two children.

NEXT ON THE READING LIST: Julia Alvarez, Edwidge Danticat, Cristina Garcia, Toni Morrison, Gloria Naylor

Barbara Kingsolver
(b. April 8, 1955)

"[Kingsolver's] most memorable characters are women or girls becoming women, single mothers mostly, living in the mall world in trailer parks and townhouses, just getting by economically and trying, against all odds, to make moral sense of their lives. This is what ennobles them, makes them more than mere case histories."
—*Russell Banks,* New York Times

* The Bean Trees (HARPER & ROW, 1988) • A strong-willed Kentuckian named Taylor Greer narrates Kingsolver's first novel, which explores the mutually sustaining friendships among an otherwise disparate group of women. While traveling west in search of a better life, Taylor becomes the unlikely caretaker of an abandoned Cherokee girl. The pair settle in Tucson, where they form a nontraditional family with Lou Ann Ruiz, a dejected mother, and Mattie, a warmhearted widow who runs the Jesus Is Lord Used Tire Company. Critics responded to *The Bean Trees* with enthusiasm, noting the book's sensitivity and humor. Some also observed that, for all its political correctness, Kingsolver's prose was remarkably free of cant.

> *"The Bean Trees is hilariously funny. You laugh out loud. I literally fell off my chair. You turn the pages and wheeze, empathetically amazed and delighted by the characters who people these pages; by their perceptions of themselves and the world and by the decisions they make for their moral as well as physical survival."* (*Margaret Randall,* Women's Review of Books)

Homeland and Other Stories (HARPER & ROW, 1989) • This collection of short stories focuses on individuals, mainly women, who struggle to find homes for themselves. Of particular note is the title story, which explores the disappointment of an aged Indian woman whose beloved Cherokee homeland has been transformed into a tourist trap. Once again, critics were lavish in their praise for Kingsolver, applauding her poetic language, realistic portrayals of human nature, and genuinely engaging plots.

Animal Dreams (HARPERCOLLINS, 1990) • In Kingsolver's second novel, Codi Noline returns to her agricultural hometown of Grace, Arizona, after her urban career track "had run straight down to the weedy lots on the rough side of town." But she finds little stability in Grace. Instead, she's forced to deal with grief, bigotry, disease, environmental pollution, and even the political brutalities in Central America. Though some critics felt that Kingsolver never really resolved the large questions she raised, Ursula K. Le Guin, writing in the *Washington Post,* called *Animal Dreams* "aesthetically rich and of great political and spiritual significance."

Pigs in Heaven (HARPERCOLLINS, 1993) • In this sequel to *The Bean Trees,* Taylor Greer discovers that she has no legal claim to her adopted Cherokee daughter because she didn't first receive the formal approval of the Cherokee nation. Demanding that the girl be returned, lawyer Annawake Fourkiller argues that only the tribe can instill in Turtle a proper understanding of her heritage and identity. Although faulted for its sentimental predictability, overly eccentric characters, and fawning treatment of popular liberal social issues, *Pigs in Heaven* was praised for its insightful examination of the bond between parent and child.

BIOGRAPHY

A HUMAN RIGHTS ACTIVIST and self-proclaimed pantheist, Barbara Kingsolver was born in Annapolis, Maryland, to a physician and a homemaker. For several years during her twenties, she labored as a research assistant and technical writer at the University of Arizona, where she'd earned a master's degree in 1977. In 1985, at age thirty, she embarked on a career as a freelance journalist. Two years later, after winning an award from the Arizona Press Club for her feature writing, Kingsolver turned to fiction full time.

A firm believer in the dignity and worth of all humanity, Kingsolver returns time and again to themes of inspiration, love, strength, and endurance. A divorced mother of one, she has described herself as being "horribly out-of-fashion: I want to change the world. I write because I have a passion for storytelling, but also because I believe fiction is an extraordinary tool for creating empathy and compassion."

NEXT ON THE READING LIST: Andrea Barrett, Harry Crews, Louise Erdrich, Jane Hamilton, Thomas McGuane, John Nichols, Anne Tyler

Milan Kundera
(b. April 1, 1929)

"Czech author Milan Kundera is a harem master of his own mind. An idea man with the soul of a sensualist, he makes servants of all he surveys. Dolling up even his darkest ideas in diaphanous gauze, he puts on a floor show for the reader—a fleshy symposium."
—*James Wolcott,* Vanity Fair

The Joke (CZECHOSLOVAK WRITERS UNION, 1967; COWARD, MCCANN & GEOGHEGAN, 1969; HARPER & ROW, 1982; HARPERCOLLINS, 1992) • Communists have no sense of humor: Thus might one summarize Kundera's first novel, widely considered one of the great comic indictments of socialism. ("You have first to assume that the hacks in the Czech government believe they have created a Socialist paradise," wrote Paul Theroux; "after that, everything they do is funny.") Ludvik, a wry Czech student, sends his unironic girlfriend a joking postcard: "Optimism is the opium of the people!... Long live Trotsky!" What does she do? Turns him in to the party, of course, which sends him to the mines.

Life Is Elsewhere (GALLIMARD, 1973; KNOPF, 1974) • On the surface, Kundera's second novel is a comedy about a young man, Jaromil, whose mother pushes him to become a poet because, in the old Czechoslovakia, poetry was a noble and heroic profession. However, *Life Is Elsewhere* is also, as John Skow wrote in *Time,* "a sly and merciless lampoon of revolutionary romanticism."

Laughable Loves (KNOPF, 1974) • Sex, for Kundera, is a perfect metaphor for politics because the root of sex is control. Thus the sexual interplay in this collection of stories always has a sinister, shadowy quality. In one story, a man keeps meticulous files of his conquests and hopes, mimicking the secret files maintained by the government. The stories are amusing, but their humor has a moody edge, not warmth.

The Farewell Party (KNOPF, 1976) • Klima, a trumpeter, gets Ruzena, a nurse at a fertility clinic, pregnant. Meanwhile, women who have come to the clinic in search of a miracle cure seem to find it...until we learn that the director has been inseminating them with his own sperm. At first glance, one might be tempted to dismiss this novel as merely a clever bedroom farce, but in Kundera hand's, according to the *New York Times,* comedy and farce "are always subverted and transformed by darker, more ambiguous tones."

The Book of Laughter and Forgetting (GALLIMARD, 1979; KNOPF, 1980; HARPERPERENNIAL, 1996) • The Communist party removes a fallen leader from history by retouching him out of a famous photograph. This act sets the theme for Kundera's fourth novel, in which several sets of characters use sex and forgetfulness as weapons to escape the Communist-constructed prisons of their lives. The surrealistic prism through which Kundera tells his story is, according to *New York Review of Books* critic Janet Malcolm, "somewhat pathetic and outdated." However, David Lodge in *Critical Quarterly* called *The Book of Laughter and Forgetting* "a masterpiece of post-modernist fiction."

* The Unbearable Lightness of Being (HARPER & ROW, 1984) • Using two couples living in Prague, Kundera explores life under the burden of totalitarianism, but this narrow core doesn't limit the book's subtext, which explodes into a rainbow of themes, most particularly lightness (lack of connectedness, of responsibility, of meaning) versus heaviness (density of associations, contacts, loves). Although cleaner and more taut than its predecessor, *The Unbearable Lightness of Being* is just as daring in form.

> "*The Unbearable Lightness of Being has a kind of charmed life. It is like a performance that has gotten off on the right foot. Every door Kundera tries opens for him.*" (*Janet Malcolm,* New York Review of Books)

Immortality (GROVE, 1991) • Superficially, *Immortality* is the story of Agnes; her husband, Paul; and their daughter, Brigitte. Agnes dies, and Paul marries Agnes's sister. But the plot really isn't the thing here. Rather, Kundera gives free rein to his philosophizing and annotating, so much so that, as Jonathan Yardley observed in the *Washington Post,* "The novel's energy wanes, and the reader finds himself restlessly turning the page in hope of relief."

Slowness (HARPERCOLLINS, 1996) • A very apt title, even though the book is only 156 pages long. Kundera's usual authorial presence (often named Milan Kundera) swells here to engulf the entire work, in which edgy denizens of gray cityscapes are replaced by a well-to-do middle-aged couple who decide on a lark to "spend the evening and night in a chateau." Slowed down by the country air to a more civilized pace, they recognize that the rush of modern life obscures much that is fine. This epiphany might do for another novelist, but coming from Kundera it's small beer.

BIOGRAPHY

MILAN KUNDERA'S WAS A PROTOTYPICAL European artistic upbringing. The son of a classical pianist, he tried following his father into music but later shifted to writing. In college during the postwar years, he studied filmmaking, wrote poetry, and became an idealistic young Communist. (More than one observer has noted that Kundera's novels reflect not merely anger at the socialist system but more pointedly the bitterness of an apostate.)

During the 1950s and 1960s, Kundera wrote several plays and volumes of poetry that earned him a measure of prominence among the Czech literati. Events surrounding the publication of his first novel, however, set an ironic tone for his later career: The young Czech writer who falls afoul of the system in *The Joke* became a prophetic figure when, after the book's publication, the Czech government removed Kundera from his teaching position and suppressed his writings. Kundera emigrated to France in 1975 and has lived there ever since.

Recently, Kundera has been attacked by other Czechs for continuing to live as an expatriate despite the fall of the Communist government in his homeland. As evidence of Kundera's "sellout," his detractors have pointed to the shift in the settings of his novels (from Prague to Paris) and, most damning of all, to the fact that his latest novel, *Slowness*, was written not in Czech but in French.

NEXT ON THE READING LIST: Stephen Dixon, Francisco Goldman, Doris Lessing, V. S. Naipaul, Amos Oz, Philip Roth, Salman Rushdie

---

David Leavitt
(b. June 23, 1961)

"Leavitt has the wonderful ability to lead the reader to examine heterosexist assumptions without becoming polemical. In prose that is often spare and carefully honed, he sensitizes us to the daily difficulties of homosexual life—of negotiating public spaces, for example, where holding hands or a simple embrace becomes problematic."
—*Wendy Martin, New York Times*

* Family Dancing (KNOPF, 1984) • Leavitt's first collection of short stories, published at age twenty-three, showcased his precocious insights into some of the more offbeat and troubling aspects of domestic life. The stories in *Family Dancing* describe individuals isolated from one another through illness and divorce as well as through differences in sexual orientation. The stories include "Radiation," about a slowly dying cancer victim; "Out Here," which concerns sibling guilt; and "Aliens," about a young girl who thinks that she's an extraterrestrial. A finalist for both a National Book Critics Circle Award and a PEN/Faulkner Award, *Family Dancing* immediately vaulted Leavitt to the forefront of the gay literature movement in the United States.

"David Leavitt has a genius for empathy. I say 'genius' because this twenty-three-year-old writer can't possibly have had time to acquire the kind of knowledge that emerges from the best stories in Family Dancing. *When Mr. Leavitt writes about a middle-aged woman with cancer, or a single mother of a problem child, or a wife whose husband lies paralyzed in a hospital, he becomes that character."* (*Wendy Lesser,* New York Times)

The Lost Language of Cranes (KNOPF, 1986) • The protagonist of Leavitt's first novel, twenty-five-year-old Philip Benjamin, holds a lowly editorial job at a Manhattan publishing house specializing in "bodice rippers." His parents, Rose and Owen, don't know that he's gay. And Rose and Philip don't know that Owen has been leading a secret homosexual life for the past fifteen years. Critics noted Leavitt's stylistic competence and his ability to evoke the tensions and turmoil, as well as the fulfillment and ecstasy, of love. But *The Lost Language of Cranes* was nonetheless savaged for being experientially thin, intellectually timid, contrived, and immature.

Equal Affections (WEIDENFELD & NICOLSON, 1989) • Leavitt's second novel received a mixed critical response, ranging from "gritty and passionate" to "distinctly soggy." The plot centers around Louise Cooper, who is dying of cancer. Louise's husband, Nat, is a computer visionary whose ideas have never amounted to much; her son, Danny, is a gay lawyer living in bland, immaculate suburban monogamy. As Louise's struggle with her illness draws to a close, her bitterness over lost opportunities in life, her crisis of faith, and her impending death all color her interactions with both husband and son.

A Place I've Never Been (VIKING, 1990) • Unlike his acclaimed debut, Leavitt's second collection of short stories focuses nearly exclusively on gay characters and their relationships. "Houses" chronicles the psychological upheavals of a real estate agent, in love with another man, who doesn't want to leave his wife. "My Marriage to Vengeance" depicts a lesbian character who undertakes the emotional challenge of attending her former lover's heterosexual wedding. Most critics hailed this book as a return to form for Leavitt. "Short stories, unlike novels, have to be perfect," Harriet Waugh noted in *The Spectator.* "*A Place I've Never Been...*very nearly is."

While England Sleeps (VIKING, 1993) • Set in the 1930s against the backdrop of the Spanish Civil War, *While England Sleeps* introduces Brian Botsford, a literary aristocrat, and his lover, Edward Phelan, a lowly ticket taker on the London Underground. After discovering Brian's involvement with a young lady of similarly high social standing, a despondent Edward joins the International Brigade and goes off to fight in Spain. Leavitt's ambitious work, however, turned out to be a little too ambitious. He included several scenes lifted from Sir Stephen Spender's 1951 memoir, *World within World,* which infuriated Spender and prompted a well-publicized lawsuit. Ironically, even with the borrowed passages, the novel was widely panned by the mainstream press.

Arkansas (HOUGHTON MIFFLIN, 1997) • The three novellas in the follow-up to *While England Sleeps* take liberties with Leavitt's own identity rather than someone else's. In "The Term Paper Artist," a gay male author, suffering from writer's block in the wake of a literary scandal, begins to write term papers for young UCLA students in exchange for sex. His name? David Leavitt. Called "sly, knowing, and hilarious," "The Term Paper Artist" was hailed as the best writing of Leavitt's career, but he once again found himself at the center of a controversy when *Esquire* abruptly yanked the sexually explicit story from its April 1997 issue.

BIOGRAPHY

ALTHOUGH BORN IN PITTSBURGH, David Leavitt grew up in Palo Alto, California, where his father was a professor of organizational behavior at Stanford. While attending Yale University, his story "Territory" was published in *The New Yorker* in 1982. It was the magazine's first short story to deal openly with a gay theme. After receiving his B.A. from Yale, Leavitt worked briefly as an editorial assistant at Viking before the publication of *Family Dancing* in 1984. The book's success made him a star of the literary youth movement and one of the few mainstream writers whose work dealt primarily with gay subjects.

In 1985, Leavitt was chosen to write the decennial "My Generation" essay for *Esquire*, an honor previously accorded to such writers as F. Scott Fitzgerald and William Styron. The result, entitled "The New Lost Generation," presented Leavitt's premise that his generation didn't inherit the sense of family stability that previous generations took for granted. As a result, one of his generation's primary concerns was the pursuit of security.

Although Leavitt has described the experiences of gay men and women in a manner that has allowed him to reach a broad audience, he remains one of the most poignant communicators of what it means to be gay in a world not entirely accepting of sexual differences. His detractors, however, argue that, far from the "sexual outlaws" celebrated by John Rechy and Jean Genet, Leavitt's ordinary preppy Everymen are so well behaved and nice that they court blandness. Leavitt currently lives in Rome.

NEXT ON THE READING LIST: Dorothy Allison, Amy Bloom, Mary Gaitskill, Joyce Carol Oates, Michael Ondaatje, Grace Paley, Reynolds Price

Doris Lessing
(b. October 22, 1919)

"Of all the postwar English novelists, Doris Lessing is the foremost creative descendant of that 'great tradition' which includes George Eliot, Conrad, and D. H. Lawrence: a literary tradition that scrutinizes marriage and sexual life, individual psychology, and the role of ideology in contemporary society."
—Richard Locke, New York Times

The Grass Is Singing (CROWELL, 1950) • Mary Turner lives on an impoverished farm in Southern Rhodesia with her husband, whom she married late in life. Not surprisingly, she has a few problems, which Lessing skillfully explores: One is the difficulty she has adapting to the isolation of her farm life; another is the psychological strain that apartheid places on her, even though she's white. Never having had much direct contact with blacks, Mary feels compelled by social and psychic forces beyond her awareness to treat her black servants cruelly, and she provokes violence in return. *New York Review of Books* contributor J. M. Coetzee called this "an astonishingly accomplished debut."

This Was the Old Chief's Country (JOSEPH, 1951; CROWELL, 1953) • Set in the fictional nation of Zambesia, these ten stories expose the injustices of racial and gender inequality in rural Africa. Perhaps the best known of them is "The Old Chief Mshlanga," which describes the gradual realization of a fourteen-year-old white girl that her father's farm originally belonged to a black African tribe and her very presence there makes her somewhat culpable in its theft. Other stories about Africa's polarized society explore conflicts between men and women and children and adults. In the *Saturday Review*, Edward Hickman called these stories "astonishingly mature and consistent."

Martha Quest (JOSEPH, 1952; SIMON & SCHUSTER, 1964) • Lessing's autobiographical Children of Violence series tells the story of Martha Quest and her intellectual development, from her childhood in Africa at the turn of the twentieth century to her later years in London at the century's end. In *Martha Quest*, the first volume in the five-book series, Lessing's young disaffected heroine struggles to throw off the yoke of her possessive, domineering mother and find her own place in the world. "Through Martha," one critic observed, "Lessing accurately states the problem of women in the modern world: They do not have images and models of self with which to...chart their experiences." Another, however, pointed out that the writing in *Martha Quest* was "undistinguished, artisan rather than artistic."

Five: Short Novels (JOSEPH, 1953; BANTAM, 1961) • In these five novellas, an African boy journeys from the country to the city to better his condition but learns instead the benefits of community, a family of liberal white immigrants discovers that it must adopt prevailing racist values in order to assimilate, a father and son search for gold, the half-caste son of a millionaire mine owner turns against his father, and a dutiful daughter achieves independence. "Much as Lessing experiments with new forms in this collection," one critic remarked, "her protagonists struggle to come to terms with new modes of living and social structures."

A Proper Marriage (JOSEPH, 1954; SIMON & SCHUSTER, 1964) • The second novel in Lessing's Children of Violence series finds young Martha Quest and her husband, Douglas Knowell, living in Zambesia during the early years of World War II. Martha, now pregnant, becomes active in left-wing politics, and as her consciousness expands, she begins to find married life stifling. Critics weren't especially impressed with this book, which many faulted for its several long dull passages. "[Lessing's] politics are one-sided, her characters are limited in conception, and her world revolves in a simple pattern," one critic complained.

A Retreat to Innocence (JOSEPH, 1956; PROMETHEUS, 1959) • Lessing later disowned this uncritically pro-Communist novel, which she has since blocked from publication. Although committed to Marxism during the 1940s and early 1950s, she abandoned the Communist party in 1956, when Khrushchev denounced Stalin and the Soviet Union invaded Hungary. The book's propagandistic plot concerns Julia Barr, who tries to emancipate herself through a sexual and political relationship with a Jewish Czech Communist but eventually returns to the fold of middle-class conventionality.

The Habit of Loving (CROWELL, 1957) • Lessing's third collection of short fiction includes seventeen transitional pieces set in both Africa and England. The stories about Africa generally make use of themes already well developed in Lessing's work, such as her disappointment with marriage and the difficulties faced by Europeans adjusting to life in Africa. The stories set in England are a bit more varied, though reviewers weren't much interested in Lessing's plots; it was her execution that they adored. "With these short stories," Pamela Hansford Johnson wrote in *The New Statesman*, "I am no longer in any doubt whatsoever that Mrs. Lessing is one of the best writers in England, male or female."

A Ripple from the Storm (JOSEPH, 1958; SIMON & SCHUSTER, 1966) • In Lessing's third Children of Violence novel, Martha Quest continues her progress from self-centered concerns to a greater awareness of the world around her: She marries a Jewish refugee from Germany principally to save him from deportation. Martha knows this man, Anton Hesse, because he's the leader of her leftist political group. The group's gradual disintegration into moderate and militant factions, however, doesn't bode well for their marriage. Most reviewers thought that this installment didn't measure up very well against the earlier books in the series. "Just as *Martha Quest* fairly shimmers with allusions to romantic love," one critic wrote, "*A Ripple from the Storm* reeks with Marxist jargon, as various 'comrades' try to impose their vision of the future on a basically indifferent society."

* The Golden Notebook (SIMON & SCHUSTER, 1962) • In Lessing's masterpiece, novelist Anna Wulf attempts to define her life as a woman in a man's world by writing about it in four special notebooks. In a black notebook, she records her youthful experiences in colonial Africa. In a red notebook, she writes an account of her years as a Communist. Into a yellow notebook goes material for a new novel about an alter ego named Ella. And, finally, a blue notebook contains an empirical account of her daily life. Thus, in one notebook or another, Anna subjects virtually all of her life to critical scrutiny. "The 'golden notebook' of the title," one critic explained, "is Anna's desperate attempt through art to integrate her fragmented experiences and to become whole in the process."

> "The Golden Notebook *is Doris Lessing's most important work and has left its mark upon the ideas and feelings of a whole generation of young women."* (*Elizabeth Hardwick,* New York Times)

A Man and Two Women (SIMON & SCHUSTER, 1963) • This collection of nineteen stories, written while Lessing composed *The Golden Notebook,* shows her interest in the private psychologies of her lonely, bewildered characters. Stories such as "England versus England," "Outside the Ministry," and "Notes for a Case History" depict class and racial conflict, while others, notably "One off the Short List," portray the war between the sexes from a strongly feminist point of view. "Sometimes..., where she seems to be struggling with material not wholly congenial, her prose reflects the strain and goes flat-footed," the *Times Literary Supplement* noted. "And yet sometimes one of these, at first sight unrewarding, expeditions of hers turns out to be full of illumination."

African Stories (JOSEPH, 1964; SIMON & SCHUSTER, 1965) • This volume brings together all of Lessing's stories about Africa, including those published in *This Was the Old Chief's Country* and four not previously collected in book form. "On the basis of this book alone, Doris Lessing must be counted as one of the most important fiction writers of our times," J. M. Edelstein declared in *Commonweal.*

Landlocked (MACGIBBON & KEE, 1965; SIMON & SCHUSTER, 1966) • This novel, the fourth in the Children of Violence series, opens near the end of World War II. Martha and Anton are still married but living separate lives. Martha becomes romantically involved with a Jewish refugee from Poland, who subsequently leaves Africa for Israel. Meanwhile, Martha's life is touched by multiple tragedies—including, finally, her second divorce—and she prepares to emigrate to England. Perhaps because of the seven-year gap between this novel and *A Ripple from the Storm*—or because of Lessing's emerging interests in telepathy, ESP, and Sufism—most reviewers seemed to be tiring of the series. "*Landlocked*," one critic wrote, "reflects in its stylistic experiments not only Martha's impatience with a life without a future, but Lessing's own impatience with her medium."

The Four-Gated City (KNOPF, 1969) • This concluding volume in the Children of Violence series takes place in postwar London, which Martha discovers is hardly the ideal place for which she has been searching all these years. After wandering the city for a few months, she takes a job as an assistant to the noted writer Mark Coldridge and soon becomes his mistress. Eventually Martha settles into a relatively calm routine, although the book ends with a much-discussed apocalyptic climax. *Commonweal* reviewer Linda Kuehl called *The Four-Gated City* "the most intelligent novel to come out of England since [Lessing's] own *Golden Notebook*," but other critics were glad that the series was finally over.

Briefing for a Descent into Hell (KNOPF, 1971) • Lessing's only novel with a male protagonist, *Briefing for a Descent into Hell* recounts the unusual efforts of Charles Watkins, a classics professor at Cambridge, to regain his psychic health. After a spaceship abducts his companions, leaving him behind, Watkins navigates the Atlantic on a raft until he reaches an island on which he finds the ruins of a prehistoric city. He then witnesses a war between apes and half-rat, half-dog creatures before a great white bird carries him away to safety. Later found wandering the streets of London, Watkins is admitted to a mental hospital and treated by two psychiatrists who have obviously never read R. D. Laing. "In this, her quasi-science-fiction novel, [Doris Lessing] rings changes on themes from her earlier books: her concerns for feminism and Marxism, her distrust of psychiatry, the possibility of visitors from other worlds," Peter S. Prescott wrote in *Newsweek*. "Unfortunately, in this story Mrs. Lessing's thinking is fuzzy; her symbols are shopworn, and her ideas dull."

The Temptation of Jack Orkney (KNOPF, 1972) • This collection of thirteen stories includes two about Africa, others set in Britain, and one science-fiction piece in which a group of aliens travel to Earth to save humanity from disaster. In the title novella, leftist author Jack Orkney experiences a midlife crisis following his father's death—he toys with religious commitment and confronts the threat of madness. "Little in...*The Temptation of Jack Orkney* is going to wind up part of [Lessing's] most admired work," Roger Sale wrote in the *New York Review of Books*, "but no one can make being dead serious seem so interesting, and she stamps herself in her slightest work as a major writer." (This collection was published in Britain as *The Story of a Non-Marrying Man.*)

* The Summer Before the Dark (KNOPF, 1973) • Often compared with *The Golden Notebook* because of its woman-in-a-man's-world theme, *The Summer Before the Dark* explores the psychology of forty-five-year-old Kate Brown, whose awareness of aging and death has grown as she enters middle age. The novel, Lessing's most popular if not most praised work, begins and ends with Kate in the bosom of her family, yet the middle section describes a series of adventures—an overseas job, a love affair, a mental breakdown—that reveal how submitting to social norms of marriage and motherhood can leave a woman such as Kate feeling cheated by life.

> "*I think* The Summer Before the Dark *is not only Doris Lessing's best novel, but the best novel to have appeared here since García Márquez's* One Hundred Years of Solitude." (*John Leonard*, New York Times)

The Memoirs of a Survivor (OCTAGON, 1974; KNOPF, 1975) • This novel, another of Lessing's grimly cautionary tales, presents the story of an unnamed middle-aged woman living in a large British city after a terrible war. She becomes guardian to a twelve-year-old girl named Emily and observes Emily's passage into adulthood even as their city disintegrates around them. "There is much one could criticize in *The Memoirs of a Survivor*—the heaviness of the symbols, the total lack of humor, the murkiness, the repetition, the awkwardness of so much of the prose—yet in the end the book has a power that works on the reader's mind," Leslie Garis wrote in the *Washington Post.* "It is as if a huge, cumbersome beast came to you and put his paw on your forehead—it might not feel good, but you will probably never forget it."

Shikasta (KNOPF, 1979) • Less a novel than a tedious series of documents, this first volume in Lessing's Canopus in Argos: Archives series recounts the history of the planet Earth from a cosmic point of view. It turns out that Shikasta (as the aliens call Earth) is a battleground, where the benevolent Canopeans and the wicked Shammats have been mucking about in the gene pool since the Pliocene Epoch. Lessing's narrator, the Canopean agent Johor, takes earthly form as Englishman George Sherban in an attempt to counteract the evil influence of Shammat and turn humanity from its destructive course. Writing in the *New York Review of Books,* Gore Vidal called *Shikasta* "the work of a formidable imagination" but one that "is never quite real enough."

The Marriages between Zones Three, Four, and Five (KNOPF, 1980) • The second of the Canopus in Argos: Archives novels takes the much lighter form of a medieval romance. In Zone Three, the peaceful and harmonious realm of Queen Al•Ith, relations between the sexes are marked by equality, tranquility, and delight. Such is not the case in militaristic Zone Four, where King Ben Ata wages war against the even more barbarous Zone Five. However, when Al•Ith marries Ben Ata, Zone Four is transformed, raising hopes for a peaceful resolution of its war with Zone Five. Writing in *The New Republic,* Ursula K. Le Guin called Lessing's effort "finer-grained and stronger than *Shikasta*" and noted that "what might have been a fable enacted by wooden puppets twitching on the strings of allegory becomes a lively and lovable novel."

The Sirian Experiments (KNOPF, 1981) • Unfortunately, the third Canopus in Argos: Archives novel reverts to the didactic format of *Shikasta,* collecting reports about ancient human history written by Ambien II, a high official in the Sirian colonial administration. More intriguing, though, are the passages describing Ambien II's changing perceptions of humanity as, under Canopean influence, she slowly begins to care about us. "Doris Lessing has always been a fine storyteller, and she demonstrates her skills in this book as much as in any other," Penelope Lively observed in *Encounter.* "The obstacle is Ambien's soul-searching and her earnest and overlong conversations with her colleagues. Eavesdropping in the corridors of power is never as gripping as you think it is going to be."

The Making of the Representative for Planet 8 (KNOPF, 1982) • This brief but heartbreaking novel continues the Canopus in Argos: Archives series with the story of a planet slowly freezing to death. Doeg, the narrator, is one of forty Representatives informed by Johor, the Canopean agent of *Shikasta,* that the inhabitants of Planet 8 must prepare for transport to the more hospitable world of Rohanda. Later, as Planet 8 grows colder, it turns out that the mass evacuations won't take place after all. Lessing's superb description of the doomed planet's physical and psychological circumstances recalls Robert Scott's ill-fated Antarctic expedition of 1910–13, which Lessing herself discusses in a lengthy afterword. According to R. L. Widmann in the *Washington Post,* "Those who are Sufists will gobble [this novel] up. Adolescent males eager to read science fiction will surely be fascinated. Lessing fans, like myself, will read anything she writes.... Other readers, though, are quite likely to be disappointed."

Documents Relating to the Sentimental Agents in the Volyen Empire (KNOPF, 1983) • The final volume in the Canopus in Argos: Archives series is an Orwellian satire on the decay of language and its exploitation for political purposes. The novel presents the reports of the Canopean agent Klorathy on the fall of the Volyen Empire, where things have gotten so bad that people are being hospitalized for "rhetorical diseases." Meanwhile, Klorathy teaches his younger colleague Incent not to get too sentimental about the poverty and oppression that he sees. While Rosemary Herbert was guardedly positive in her *Christian Science Monitor* review, calling the novel "the most approachable of Lessing's Canopean fare," Edward Rothstein wrote in the

New York Times that "whatever promise it offers of satire and enlightened vision dissipates into cliché and platitude. The humor falls flat, the rhetorical jests become tiresome, and the political insights seem derivative."

The Diaries of Jane Somers (VINTAGE, 1984) • This volume combines two works that Lessing originally published in 1983 and 1984 under the pseudonym Jane Somers. Her intention, she later admitted, was to dramatize the problems faced by unknown writers and to be "reviewed on merit, as a new writer, without the benefit of a 'name.'" *The Diary of a Good Neighbor* introduces Janna Somers, a fashionable but guilt-ridden London magazine editor whose unlikely friendship with Maudie, an angry and elderly destitute widow, transforms her life. In the sequel, *If the Old Could...*, Lessing picks up the story after Maudie's death, when Janna (now calling herself Jane) has an unconsummated affair with a married man named Richard. Jane's life becomes further complicated when her unstable niece Kate arrives unannounced to live with her. Although Pearl K. Bell noted in *The New Republic* that the "Jane Somers" novels had been swiftly rejected by ten British publishing houses "and deserved to be," Doris Grumbach wrote in the *Washington Post* that *The Diary of a Good Neighbor* "extends one's comprehension of the possibilities life offers, and does it with wit and compassion."

The Good Terrorist (KNOPF, 1985) • Alice Mellings, the thirty-six-year-old protagonist of this novel about bumbling radicals squatting in a condemned London house, is a "good terrorist" because she really wants to help people. Unable to relinquish her bourgeois sense of propriety, Alice steals from her parents in order to provide for the members of her political cell, most of whom are on the dole. "*The Good Terrorist* is bound to give comfort to the middle classes," Denis Donoghue wrote in the *New York Times*, "if only because their enemies, Alice and her friends, are so ludicrously inept." In the *New York Review of Books*, Alison Lurie objected to the "makeshift, sharp-edged, and unfinished" nature of the characters but called *The Good Terrorist* "one of the best novels in English I have read about the terrorist mentality."

The Fifth Child (KNOPF, 1988) • Harriet and David Lovatt are happily married with four children, a large Victorian house in the suburbs, and plenty of friends—until their fifth child is born. Not like his siblings, Ben is a freak of nature, a genetic error, a malevolent Neanderthal who single-handedly destroys the Lovatts' harmonious family life. Through the bars of his crib he badly sprains his brother's arm; then he strangles a guest's small terrier and murders the family cat. David and the other children want Ben institutionalized, but his mother won't have it. "In *The Fifth Child* [Lessing] has given us what is destined to become a minor classic," Carolyn Kizer wrote in the *New York Times*.

The Real Thing (HARPERCOLLINS, 1992) • In this collection of eighteen "stories and sketches" (published in Britain as *London Observed*), the British capital becomes "a character in its own right," according to *Maclean's* reviewer John Bemrose. Along with shorter descriptive pieces, Lessing includes a handful of longer stories in which, Bemrose wrote, "[her] imagination is working at full throttle." The best of these is "The Pit," in which Sarah is approached by her former husband, James, who left her for a woman named Rose. Now that Rose is herself having an affair, James wants to have a fling with Sarah.

Love, Again (HARPERCOLLINS, 1996) • The unexpected femme fatale of this regrettably humorless novel is Sarah Durham, a sixty-five-year-old theatrical producer whose business experience and matronly manner make her the backbone of her company. *Love, Again* concerns the development of Sarah's new play, a romance about a doomed love affair, and its mood soon arouses a great deal of amorous longing in the cast—a surprising amount of which is directed toward Sarah. Unfortunately, according to *Los Angeles Times* reviewer Maria Flook, the characters "seem airbrushed like familiar TV types and at times become farcical.... Lessing seems unwilling to fully explore the terrain of sex and instead submerges the reader in Sarah's swooning symptoms. The best we get is repetitive descriptions of this 'whirlpool,' until the whole things washes over the dam."

BIOGRAPHY

DORIS LESSING'S PARENTS MET during World War I, when her father was a wounded British army officer and her mother the nurse assigned to care for him. When Lessing was born in 1919, the country of her birth was still known as Persia. Five years later, her father moved the family to Southern Rhodesia (now Zimbabwe), where he planned to grow corn and tobacco while prospecting for gold. In the remote Southern Rhodesian bush, however, life turned out to be much harder than Taylor had expected and gold much less plentiful. Lessing suffered from both dysentery and malaria, but she enjoyed the feelings of freedom and solitude with which the open African landscape provided her.

Lessing's mother schooled her at home until 1927, when she was sent to a Catholic boarding school in Salisbury. After four years, Lessing transferred to a girls' high school, but dropped out at age fourteen. In between odd jobs, she read voraciously such authors as Woolf, Proust, Mann, Lawrence, Tolstoy, Dostoevsky, Chekhov, and Turgenev. In 1939, Lessing married Frank Wisdom, a civil servant in Salisbury. Four years later, shortly after becoming involved in leftist politics, she divorced Wisdom, giving him custody of their two children. Meanwhile, working as a typist in a law firm, she met German immigrant Gottfried Lessing, a Communist active in a local Marxist group. They were married in 1945 to save him from internment as an enemy alien. "It was my revolutionary duty to marry him," Lessing later said. The couple had one son, Peter, before divorcing in 1949.

Lessing left Africa for London that same year, taking her two-year-old son with her. Determined to launch a literary career, she published her first novel in 1950 to excellent reviews. The Children of Violence series later secured her reputation as a first-rate novelist of politics and ideas, but it was *The Golden Notebook* that made her famous, especially outside England.

NEXT ON THE READING LIST: Nadine Gordimer, Milan Kundera, Naguib Mahfouz, Iris Murdoch, Amos Oz, Richard Powers, Muriel Spark

---

Penelope Lively
(b. March 17, 1933)

"She writes as she finds the condition of man and woman to be, from her own vision, unafraid. The world as it is, not as it would be nice if only it were so."
—*Fay Weldon*, Los Angeles Times

The Road to Lichfield (HEINEMANN, 1977; GROVE, 1991) • After years of writing juvenile fiction, Penelope Lively based her first novel for adults on a single loaded event that contrasts a child's and a grown-up's realities. On her father's death, heroine Anne Linton discovers that throughout her childhood, her father wasn't the devoted husband that she thought him to be. This sets in motion an elegant musing on the meaning of that seemingly straightforward concept: the past.

Nothing Missing But the Samovar and Other Stories (HEINEMANN, 1978) • Lively's short stories for adults seem like many of her children's stories: elegant little tales of everyday life. Yet what works well in juvenile fiction can be a trifle wan when applied to the grown-up world. The stories in this collection hint at layers below the surface—sexual longing, for example, and generational tension—but Lively's language is occasionally stilted, and in the end she seems too tactful for her own good.

Treasures of Time (HEINEMANN, 1979; DOUBLEDAY, 1980) • Once again Lively digs into the past, this time using the device of a TV documentary being made about a famous archaeologist. As the participants work on the film, we receive conflicting images—not only of the archaeologist, but also of his family and friends, and even of the historic site that he excavated. At the center of the book is a young researcher who joins the film project thinking that he already understands the concept of history but soon learns that he was mistaken. One reviewer concluded that *Treasures of Time* "is enjoyable, perceptive, shrewd, but it collapses badly, and scurries towards a rather arbitrary conclusion."

Judgement Day (HEINEMANN, 1980; DOUBLEDAY, 1981) • Residents of an ancient English village attempt to restore their equally ancient church; meanwhile, Clare Paling explores the church's grim history and poses to the vicar difficult questions about its purpose. Although Clare loses her faith, the story keeps its vision, developing into a sharp meditation on fate and accident.

Next to Nature, Art (HEINEMANN, 1982) • Lively's fourth novel satirizes the recent phenomenon of conceptual art. Its protagonists are a gang of artistic types, short on talent but long on didactic artspeak ("the poet is the message"). They confuse their naive students while simultaneously maintaining one another's illusions. "Penelope Lively writes elegant, incisive prose which often conceals the genuine savagery of her attack," one reviewer noted.

Perfect Happiness (HEINEMANN, 1983; DIAL, 1984) • Middle-aged Frances is mourning her husband's death; meanwhile, her daughter, Tabitha, is suffering the initial agonies of love. Lively gives both stories such a light, readable treatment that when raw emotion finally comes to the fore, it's truly shocking, almost embarrassing—just as it ought to be in a proper middle-class English family.

According to Mark (HEINEMANN, 1984; BEAUFORT, 1985) • Biographer Mark Lamming takes on the task of writing a life of one of England's greatest men of letters. Some careful inspection of books and furniture is to be expected, but Lamming gets a little too close to his subject when he has an affair with the dead man's granddaughter. As a result, Lamming's perspective on the old man keeps changing, which gives Lively yet another avenue to approach the riddle of human identity and, as an aside, to question the notion of biography and its relation to "truth." Lively's language is occasionally stuffy, but as the characters shake off their stiffness, their interactions become compelling.

Corruption and Other Stories (HEINEMANN, 1984) • These short stories, even more than Lively's other work, revolve around terribly English characters living out their lives in terribly English surroundings. The stories range broadly in theme and artistry, and Lively takes chances with them, meaning that sometimes they don't work.

✳ **Moon Tiger** (DEUTSCH, 1987; GROVE, 1988) • The novel that won a Booker Prize centers on a dying historian who looks back on her busy life in a series of beautifully disjointed scenes. Locating her emotional core in Egypt, she focuses on an affair she had with a soldier during World War II. As her death approaches, she hones her memory even further, zeroing in on a particular image: a moon tiger, a green coil of incense used in the tropics to keep away mosquitoes. It burns through the night, leaving only ashes behind.

> *"Its red eye glows beside the hotel bed in wartime Luxor in which the heroine, Claudia, lies contented beside her army officer lover, so soon to be killed in the desert. But, at a deeper level, its gradual, inevitable disintegration symbolizes the transitoriness of all human happiness and indeed of all human life, which is here the author's main preoccupation, as it is Claudia's."* (Francis King, The Spectator)

Passing On (DEUTSCH, 1989; GROVE, 1990) • When Dorothy's coffin gets stuck and won't come out of the house at the beginning of Lively's eighth novel, the snafu is a clear storyteller's signal that here was a recalcitrant woman. The death of this cruel and domineering old lady finally frees her middle-aged children, Helen and Edward—but how does one begin to grow again after five decades of stasis? And why did the children never rebel? Aren't they in part to blame for their missed opportunities? *Passing On* is one of Lively's most scathing, elegant, and successful books.

City of the Mind (HARPERCOLLINS, 1991) • Lively had a promising concept: using a renowned architect in modern-day London to explore the city's many facets and eras; letting facades lead us into bygone days and a symphony of forgotten voices sing the city's history. However, Lively stretches too far in her attempt to pull off this daring narrative tactic, and the result is an awkward species of time travel.

Cleopatra's Sister (HARPERCOLLINS, 1993) • The premise of *Cleopatra's Sister* is simple: Howard and Lucy meet on a flight from London to Africa. But Lively quickly puts it through the mill of chaos theory as she charts the seemingly random chains of events leading her characters to this moment in time. The technique is a bit overwhelming in its omniscience, yet "if Ms. Lively is playing God here," Scott Spencer wrote in the *New York Times*, "she is doing it with fine high spirits."

Heat Wave (HARPERCOLLINS, 1996) • Fifty-five-year-old Pauline has divorced Harry, her staggeringly unfaithful husband, and now lives with her daughter and son-in-law and their infant son. Slowly she begins to detect familiar signs in Maurice, the son-in-law, suggesting that he too is unfaithful and that her daughter will soon be experiencing the same life-shattering turmoil that she has had to endure. Fay Weldon called *Heat Wave* "a very English novel, indeed, in its ability to disturb by understatement.... [It's] well-behaved, a trifle Austenish, a fraction insular, perfect in its manners,

[and] courteous to the reader in its carefulness, the sharpened paper knife well hidden beneath the elegant sleeve."

The Five Thousand and One Nights (FJORD, 1997) • The fourteen stories in this collection feature mild-mannered people thrust into unfamiliar or uncomfortable situations: Former lovers meet at a wedding; an elderly woman outwits a salesman who has come to rob her; a woman attending a literary conference in a Yugoslavia on the brink of civil war becomes lost in the woods. Reviewers, however, disagreed as to whether the stories were any good: *New York Times* critic Claire Messud dismissed them as "elegant but insubstantial," while Michael Upchurch in the *San Francisco Chronicle* praised the collection for its "mischievous wit" and called it "Penelope Lively at her finest."

BIOGRAPHY

THE SURFACE OF PENELOPE LIVELY'S fiction suggests a typically English upbringing, but the deeper layers—which question, mock, and probe her characters in quite un-English ways—hint at something else. In fact, Penelope Green was born and spent her childhood in Cairo, where she was schooled by a governess until age twelve. At the end of World War II, her parents remanded her to England to be raised by her grandmother and educated at a boarding school. Although she quickly adjusted to the dramatic change in climate, she later remarked that the "absolutely appalling" boarding school she attended marred her intellectual development.

Oxford University cured that—renewing her love of history, which the sight of wartime London had instilled in her as a child, and introducing her to a young student of politics named Jack Lively. The couple were married in 1957 and have two children.

Lively commenced her literary career as a reviewer of children's literature; in 1970, she began writing it, publishing the novel *Astercote*, the first of some two dozen works for children. In 1977, after establishing a worldwide reputation in the field of children's fiction, she embarked on a second career as an adult novelist. In appearance, Lively is a quiet cardigan-wearing English mother, yet professionally she has been widely praised for a vision that cuts through the apparent and the mundane.

NEXT ON THE READING LIST: Beryl Bainbridge, Anita Brookner, A. S. Byatt, Kazuo Ishiguro, David Lodge, Muriel Spark, Fay Weldon

David Lodge
(b. January 28, 1935)

"[Lodge's] acerbic observations are leavened by [his] customary playfulness and by his contagious empathy for his characters' complicated lives and fates. He has a wonderful way of surprising and enchanting his readers with whimsical, fairy-tale-like resolutions to problems that might have ended tragically in the hands of a less upbeat author."
—*Susan Miron,* Christian Science Monitor

The Picturegoers (MACGIBBON & KEE, 1960; PENGUIN, 1993) • Lodge's first novel, begun during his final months in the army, records a year in the lives of a dozen people who frequent the same South London cinema. The book focuses, in particular, on the gradual return to the faith of literature student (and lapsed Catholic) Mark Underwood, who's regularly frustrated by his conflicting physical and spiritual desires. In *The New Statesman,* Maurice Richardson called the novel "arbitrarily constructed but lively."

Ginger, You're Barmy (MACGIBBON & KEE, 1962; DOUBLEDAY, 1965) • Lodge wrote this story of two army conscripts as an "act of revenge" following his own difficult army experience. The book's narrator, plucked out of a sheltered university existence, finds himself thrust into a crude, dehumanizing world where, in the words of one critic, "his assets—intelligence, critical judgment, and culture—become liabilities." In *Commonweal,* Thomas P. McDonnell observed, "Some reviewers have passed off *Ginger, You're Barmy* as the same old thing about life in the army, but it is a much better book than they are readers."

The British Museum Is Falling Down (MACGIBBON & KEE, 1965; HOLT, RINEHART & WINSTON, 1967) • The life of postgraduate English student Adam Appleby takes on a Joycean quality when he arises one morning to discover that the papally sanctioned rhythm method may have failed him once again. His planned day of quiet study in the Reading Room of the British Museum shortly becomes one of pandemonium. The first of Lodge's highly satiric novels, *The British Museum Is Falling Down* pursues to great comic effect a recurring theme in Lodge's work: the plight of sincere Catholics struggling against unreasonable and rigid church doctrine. Paul West, writing in *The New Statesman,* called the *The British Museum Is Falling Down* "a pert fable, discomfiting yet warm."

Out of the Shelter (MACMILLAN, 1970; REVISED, SECKER & WARBURG, 1985; PENGUIN, 1989) • In this fictionalization of his own wartime childhood,

Lodge tells the story of Timothy Young in two parts: The first covers Timothy's experiences in London during the Blitz; the second recounts a trip that the sixteen-year-old takes in 1951 to visit his sister in Germany, where she works for the American army and he struggles with his own emerging sexual identity. "The book lacks intensity," one critic complained. "It has no sharply drawn conflict or dramatic tension, and, for most of the story, the only real suspense has to do with the question of how and when Timothy will learn about sex."

* Changing Places: A Tale of Two Campuses (SECKER & WARBURG, 1975; PENGUIN, 1979) • *Changing Places* introduced that Odd Couple of literary theory, timid Philip Swallow and bombastic Morris Zapp (reportedly modeled on Duke literary critic Stanley Fish). As the novel opens, Swallow of the University of Rummidge (Lodge's own Birmingham) and Zapp from Euphoria State University (Berkeley) trade jobs for six months as part of an academic exchange program. Set during 1969, when the author was himself a visiting professor at Berkeley, this book made Lodge's reputation as a skillful and humorous writer of "campus novels."

> "I hope nobody will be put off buying David Lodge's hugely funny new novel by hearing that it has some quite serious things to say about some quite serious things. I cannot remember having laughed aloud so much at a book since Lucky Jim." (*Neil Hepburn,* The Listener)

How Far Can You Go? (SECKER & WARBURG, 1980; PUBLISHED IN THE U.S. AS *SOULS AND BODIES,* MORROW, 1982) • Beginning with a Valentine's Day service in 1952, Lodge follows a group of enlightened Catholics as they experience a quarter century of spiritual turmoil. *How Far Can You Go?* covers much the same contraceptual territory as *The British Museum Is Falling Down,* but with much greater bitterness. (During the five years between these two books, the 1968 papal encyclical *Humanae Vitae* had made it clear that, despite the rumors, the church wouldn't be loosening its prohibition on birth control.) In the *New York Times,* LeAnne Schreiber wrote that *How Far Can You Go?* "does not cohere, but each of its parts offers enough satisfactions to make that normally damning statement a quibble."

* Small World: An Academic Romance (MACMILLAN, 1984) • This magnificent sequel to *Changing Places* picks up the lives of Philip Swallow and Morris Zapp ten years later. Its hero, however, is a much lesser literary light: Persse McGarrigle, a junior lecturer at an Irish agricultural college. The novel opens at a conference hosted by a provincial British university, at which chaste Persse first espies the beautiful, enigmatic Angelica Pabst, a literary conference groupie. The rest of the story, written in the form of a Grail quest and filled with sly lit-crit references, follows Persse as he jets in and out of conferences from Tokyo to Jerusalem, striving for another glimpse of the fair Angelica.

"As in all David Lodge's novels, the characters in Small World *are instantly forgettable. There is no savagery in his satire or real malice in his wit. Instead, his novels engender a flowing sense of fun. The reader is given a very enjoyable time at nobody's expense."* (*Harriet Waugh,* The Spectator)

Nice Work (SECKER & WARBURG, 1988; VIKING, 1989) • Robyn Penrose, temporary lecturer in English literature at the University of Rummidge, is the sort of fashionable semiotician who believes that "character" is a bourgeois myth. She is, therefore, less than thrilled when Philip Swallow assigns her to shadow Vic Wilcox, managing director of a local engineering firm, as part of a partnership program to encourage town-gown amity. In the course of the novel, however, Robin learns much about the workings (or nonworkings) of modern British industry, while Vic develops a passion for scholarship. "It would be hard to have a better time than we do with this funny, intelligent, superbly paced social comedy," Christopher Lehmann-Haupt wrote in the *New York Times*.

Paradise News (SECKER & WARBURG, 1991; VIKING, 1992) • The hero of this novel is a familiar Lodge type: Bernard Walsh, a failed priest who now teaches theology at a small drab college in Britain. As fate would have it, Bernard accompanies his father on a package tour to Hawaii so that they can visit a dying relative. There he meets Yolande Miller, who has run over his father with her car. With Yolande's help, lonely Bernard overcomes his metaphysical doubts and soon discovers his own resourcefulness. *"Paradise News* isn't as uproariously funny as Mr. Lodge's academic satires," Michiko Kakutani explained in the *New York Times*. "Its humor is kinder and gentler, though just as sharply observed."

Therapy (VIKING, 1995) • Fifty-eight-year-old screenwriter Laurence "Tubby" Passmore seems to have it all—a sexually fulfilling marriage, a hit TV sitcom, and a fancy car (he calls it the Richmobile). But Tubby can't help feeling unhappy in a vague sort of way, and none of his therapists seems able to help. Written as a diary, *Therapy* is a typically humorous and satisfying Lodge romp, yet Martha Duffy did note pointedly in *Time* that Lodge doesn't seem to know nearly as much about prime-time television as he does about academia.

BIOGRAPHY

DAVID LODGE WAS THE ONLY child of a lower-middle-class suburban couple: His father played saxophone in dance-hall bands, and his Roman Catholic mother was a housewife. Born in South London, Lodge lived there through the Blitz before moving to the Surrey countryside for the remainder of the war. After attending a Catholic grammar school and University College, London, he began his national service in 1955. By all accounts, he resented this obligation and hated the tedium and brutality of military life.

After leaving the army, Lodge returned to University College, where he earned a master's degree with the thesis "Catholic Fiction Since the Oxford Movement." In 1960, he accepted a job teaching English literature at the University of Birmingham, later satirized in his novels as the University of Rummidge. In 1966, he published *The Language of Fiction*, the first of his five books of criticism. Lodge's prominent place among literary critics was confirmed in 1976, when he was made Professor of Modern English Literature at Birmingham. Lodge retired from the university in 1987 at the unusually young age of fifty-two.

Lodge's characters are, for the most past, weak and awkward. As such, they immediately evoke the reader's sympathy, and Lodge seems to care for them, too. According to one reviewer, "It is as though Lodge...has abandoned the specific tenets of Catholicism while retaining at least one of its basic moral principles for his artistic vision: The meek shall inherit the earth. These short, fat, bumbling characters usually end up okay, often even better off than they were at the beginning." Lodge has described himself as "a believing Catholic of a very liberal kind theologically."

NEXT ON THE READING LIST: Beryl Bainbridge, Alison Lurie, Lorrie Moore, V. S. Naipaul, Cathie Pelletier, Graham Swift, Fay Weldon

Alison Lurie
(b. September 3, 1926)

"Lurie's protagonists are always academics or writers; well-read and well-controlled, thoughtful and successful, people of good taste—and hence people especially susceptible to the Call of the Wild and the perfectly rational processes of self-deception."
—Sara Sanborn, New York Times

Love and Friendship (MACMILLAN, 1962) • Like so many of Lurie's later works, her first novel is a comedy set in the world of academia, specifically elite Convers College, a bastion of "order, reason, and upper-class New England Protestantism." Enter a young academic couple, Emily and Holman Turner, who seem the model of middle-class respectability but soon become embroiled in adulterous misadventures. The *Atlantic Monthly* compared Lurie's wit to "Jane Austen's, wicked and delicious," but the *New York Times* thought that "the over-all strength of the novel lacks the grace and strength of its many well-handled episodes."

The Nowhere City (COWARD, MCCANN & GEOGHEGAN, 1965) • Lurie's second novel, which received poor reviews, was called by one critic a "textbook on the moral geography of California." A Northeast academic couple, Paul and Katherine Cattleman, relocate to Los Angeles—the mysterious Oz, or "nowhere city," of the title. At least L.A. seems like a nowheresville to Katherine, who's delicate, frigid, highly strung, and afflicted with sinus trouble made all the worse by the smog. Her husband, a former Harvard professor now writing a corporate history, fits in more easily, especially once he forms a romantic liaison with the bohemian Ceci.

Imaginary Friends (COWARD, MCCANN & GEOGHEGAN, 1967) • Lurie's satiric insight into intellectuals informs the story of Tom McCann and Roger Zimmern, sociologists who investigate the Truth Seekers, a millennarian cult of rustics in upstate New York. The Truth Seekers insist that they're in touch with the planet Varna—and its flying saucers—through the auspices of a local sybil. As Tom and Roger are drawn deeper into the cult, they abandon their clinical detachment and start to question their narrowly circumscribed role as "participant observers." *The Observer* called the novel "a crisp, dry comedy," but the *New York Review of Books* disagreed: "Miss Lurie, hesitating between seriousness and farce, settled for the trivial."

Real People (RANDOM HOUSE, 1969) • In her fourth novel, Lurie satirizes Illyria, a pastoral retreat, or "creative park," for writers, musicians, and painters. Janet Belle Smith, a forty-two-year-old fiction writer and the wife of an insurance executive with whom she shares a distressingly conventional existence, arrives at Illyria, hoping that the weeklong experience will spice up her life. It does, but not in the way she expects. In its review, the *Times Literary Supplement* praised Lurie for "creeping nearer the knuckle."

* The War between the Tates (RANDOM HOUSE, 1974) • This comic novel, set in 1969, made Lurie famous. The Tates—"exceptionally handsome, intelligent, righteous, and successful people"—are Brian and Erica. He's an ambitious and prominent professor and she his intelligent, bored wife. Their adulterous "war" becomes a metaphor for the greater conflict, Vietnam, which has made a battlefield of the idyllic college campus (modeled on Cornell) where Brian teaches.

> *"There are a great many pleasures to be found in* The War between the Tates. *There is, for one thing, the faultless prose, like an English lawn. One could play polo on such prose, swatting ideas with a mallet up and down the pastoral field. There are brilliant scenes, dozens of them…[and] a detachment so profound that we might be looking at tropical fish in a tank instead of people in extremis."* (John Leonard, The New Republic)

Only Children (RANDOM HOUSE, 1979) • This tautly structured novel, set during the Great Depression, explores the interactions of two families who spend the Fourth of July holiday together on a farm. The musings of the book's child protagonist, Mary Ann, which open and close the narrative, unmask the failings of the adults around her, particularly in their intersexual relationships. Critics praised Lurie's precision in evoking the details of her characters' lives yet found her satiric distance from them condescending and somewhat off-putting.

* Foreign Affairs (RANDOM HOUSE, 1984) • Lurie won a Pulitzer Prize for this best-selling and richly comic portrait of two American professors—one a middle-aged Plain Jane and the other a handsome young man—who share a sabbatical year in London. Their adventures, told in alternating chapters, intertwine in surprising and ingenious ways.

> *"High and low, this is a* very *literary comedy.... It's an ingenious book and, surprisingly for Lurie, a touching one. She has not been famous for mercy.... I'll be surprised if another novel this year amuses and bothers me so."* (*Walter Clemons,* Newsweek)

The Truth about Lorin Jones (LITTLE, BROWN, 1988) • In this clever send-up of both feminism and contemporary biography, Manhattanite Polly Alter takes a year off from her job at a museum to research and write a life of painter Lorin Jones, who died prematurely in 1969. On a quest to discover what really happened to Jones, Polly interviews the many people who figured in her life, above all the men whom Polly assumes brought Jones to her ruin. The story unfolds smoothly, but the ends tie up too neatly, muffling the satiric force of the opening chapters.

Women and Ghosts (DOUBLEDAY, 1994) • Reviewing Lurie's first short-fiction collection, David Leavitt likened its highly unconventional ghost stories, at once witty and scary, to a hybrid of Dorothy Parker and Edgar Allan Poe. He found those tales strongest "in which Ms. Lurie uses the ghost story genre as an occasion for some larger investigation." One such tale is "The Double Poet," in which a writer becomes aware that a doppelgänger has been shadowing her from stop to stop on a reading tour.

BIOGRAPHY

BORN IN CHICAGO AND educated at Radcliffe, Alison Lurie has earned herself a reputation as one of America's most cerebral and sophisticated writers. Married for many years to a professor of English, John Peale Bishop Jr. (the son of a well-known poet), Lurie has flourished in the groves of academe and since 1968 has taught English at Cornell, in the same department as Bishop, from whom she was divorced in 1985.

Critics have compared Lurie's fiction to that of Jane Austen and Henry James. They cite the classic formality of its structure; its elegant, witty prose; and its comic (more often satiric) depiction of middle-class characters and their milieux. Most of Lurie's novels—including her best-known works, *The War between the Tates* and *Foreign Affairs*—explore the delusively ordered lives of academic intellectuals. One of her favorite themes has been the havoc wrought on these lives by adultery.

The mother of three sons, Lurie has written a number of children's books and one acclaimed critical study, *Don't Tell the Grown-Ups: Subversive Children's Literature* (1990). Her criticism and essays have appeared in a number of literary publications, including the *New York Review of Books* and the *New York Times*.

NEXT ON THE READING LIST: Beryl Bainbridge, David Lodge, Terry McMillan, Lorrie Moore, Edna O'Brien, Muriel Spark, Fay Weldon

Naguib Mahfouz
(b. December 11, 1911)

"With Mr. Mahfouz's fiction, comparisons are particularly odious, because he has in his lifetime...virtually invented the novel as an Arab form. He has done so not by drawing on foreign models but by relying on poetry and storytelling, the key strengths of indigenous Arab and Egyptian culture. Mr. Mahfouz excels at fusing deep emotion and soap opera."
—Peter Theroux, New York Times

Midaq Alley (MAKTABAT MISR, 1947; AMERICAN UNIVERSITY IN CAIRO, 1966; THREE CONTINENTS, 1977) • Mahfouz's sixth novel, the earliest of his works translated into English, describes the daily life of an impoverished Cairene alley during World War II. The central character, the haughty beauty Hamida, longs to rise above the limitations of her squalor. She becomes engaged to a barber, but when he leaves to work for the British army, she becomes a prostitute catering to Allied soldiers. Writing in the *Times Literary Supplement*, P. J. Vatikiotis observed that "the dialogue is vital and spontaneous,...the tension is constant, the precise detail and meticulous description of foods, smells, and the like absolutely superb."

The Beginning and the End (MAKTABAT MISR, 1949; AMERICAN UNIVERSITY IN CAIRO, 1985; DOUBLEDAY, 1989) • In this novel, which *Times Literary Supplement* reviewer J. M. Coetzee called "as bleak and relentless as anything in Dreiser," a lower-middle-class Egyptian family that has fallen on hard times makes ultimately ruinous sacrifices to help its ambitious, ungrateful youngest son earn a prestigious military commission. According to *New York*

Times reviewer Carol Bardenstein, "Mr. Mahfouz poignantly, and with great sympathy and pathos, captures the family's tragic circumstances."

* Palace Walk (Maktabat Misr, 1956; Doubleday, 1990) • This first novel in Mahfouz's Cairo Trilogy, considered a masterpiece of Middle Eastern literature, introduces readers to Egyptian life during a period of dramatic change: the turbulent months between the end of World War I and the beginning of the 1919 revolt against British rule. The stern but philandering family patriarch, al-Sayyid, holds his family together through intimidation. In contrast, his submissive wife, Amina, uses warmth, kindness, and piety. Al-Sayyid has instructed Amina never to venture beyond the walls of the family home, yet one day her sons persuade her to visit a local mosque. Although this disobedience is punished, it leads to an awareness that triggers irrevocable changes in the family.

> *"For all its family intrigues, the novel is more than a domestic saga. It is the story of the awakening of an entire generation to the social and political realities of the twentieth century.... The universal appeal of Mr. Mahfouz's characters and his insight into the role of religion in their lives will go a long way toward demystifying Western readers' views of the Middle East."* (*Howard Hower,* New York Times)

Palace of Desire (Maktabat Misr, 1957; Doubleday, 1991) • The second novel in Mahfouz's celebrated Cairo Trilogy opens a few years after the close of the first, during the early 1920s. It features the second generation of the family introduced to readers in *Palace Walk*—the children of al-Sayyid. The dual themes of this book, illustrating Cairo's public and private life, are the transition from British rule to an independent monarchy and the psychological damage caused by a string of extramarital affairs among the older characters. "Mr. Mahfouz's success in conveying the color and fascination of the social life of Cairo in one of its richest and most turbulent periods, and the breadth of his canvas, lead to inevitable comparison to Charles Dickens," Peter Theroux wrote in the *New York Times.* "But *Palace of Desire*, both in itself and in the dimension of time it adds to the previous volume, shows a greater kinship with Marcel Proust."

Sugar Street (Maktabat Misr, 1957; Doubleday, 1992) • In this final volume of the Cairo Trilogy, the activities of al-Sayyid's grandsons—one a Communist, another an Islamic fundamentalist—reflect Egyptian politics during World War II, when the monarchy of King Farouk was nearing its end. The central character, however, is al-Sayyid's son Kamal, an indecisive writer (and the closest Mahfouz has ever come to creating an autobiographical persona). Louis Werner, writing in the *Christian Science Monitor,* called *Sugar Street* "the best social study of Cairo yet to appear in English." (Although publication was delayed several years, Mahfouz completed the Cairo Trilogy in 1952, the year of the military coup that ousted King Farouk.)

Children of Gebelaawi (AL-AHRAM, 1959; DAR AL-ADAB, 1967; THREE CONTINENTS, 1981; PUBLISHED BY DOUBLEDAY IN 1996 AS *CHILDREN OF THE ALLEY*) • This novel was originally serialized in 1959, seven years after both the completion of the Cairo Trilogy and the emergence of the Nasser dictatorship. It marks an important shift in style for Mahfouz, from objective realism to symbolism and allegory. Each of its five chapters is named for a descendant of Gebelaawi, the godlike patriarch for whom the book's setting (Gebelaawi Alley) is named. The first four of Gebelaawi's "children" are obvious incarnations of Adam, Moses, Jesus, and Mohammed, and their stories critique religion in the broadest sense. However, Cairo's Islamic establishment interpreted Mahfouz's novel very narrowly and pronounced it heretical, blocking its publication in Egypt and throughout much of the Arab world. Although noting that *Children of Gebelaawi* was "an impressive, though imperfect, landmark in the development of [Mahfouz's] art," M. M. Badawi in the *Times Literary Supplement* complained that the novel was "too repetitive" and "lacking in the poetic spirit."

The Thief and the Dogs (MAKTABAT MISR, 1961; AMERICAN UNIVERSITY IN CAIRO, 1984; DOUBLEDAY, 1989) • Using stream-of-consciousness narrative for the first time in Arab fiction, Mahfouz tells the story of a thief who, upon his release from prison, sets out to avenge himself on those who have betrayed him. Said Mahran, however, is no ordinary thief: He stole—in the words of his mentor, ideologue Rauf Ilwan—"to relieve the exploiters of some of their guilt." Moreover, while Said has been in prison, the political situation has changed: Nasser has come to power, and Rauf, with a stake in the new regime, wants nothing to do with Said. Mahfouz's theme is thus the relationship between radical intellectuals and the masses who carry out their political directives. In the *Times Literary Supplement*, Ivan Hill called *The Thief and the Dogs* "a fast-moving psychological study" with a "strongly critical tone."

Autumn Quail (MAKTABAT MISR, 1962; AMERICAN UNIVERSITY IN CAIRO, 1985; DOUBLEDAY, 1990) • Isa al-Dabagh, a senior official in King Farouk's government, loses his job, his fiancée, and his self-esteem in the aftermath of the 1952 coup. Dismissed for taking bribes (an accepted practice at the time), Isa drifts from Cairo to Alexandria, where he gradually descends into decadence and despair. Reviewers pointed out that this novel's ending, which takes place during the 1956 Suez crisis at the height of Nasser's nationalistic glory, was for Mahfouz strangely optimistic. Ivan Hill in the *Times Literary Supplement* even suggested that it might have been the result of political pressure applied after the publication of Mahfouz's previous novel. From a purely literary standpoint, *World Literature Today* reviewer John Haywood called the ending "vague" and Isa "a truly tragic figure, beyond redemption."

The Search (MAKTABAT MISR, 1964; AMERICAN UNIVERSITY IN CAIRO, 1987; DOUBLEDAY, 1991) • Like Mahfouz's previous two novels, this one is short, fast paced, and focused on a single character: Saber, the prodigal son of a recently deceased madam. Rather than money, his mother has left him two bequests: a marriage certificate and a photograph of his allegedly wealthy father. As Saber's search for his father drags on, however, he and his mistress plot to murder her aged husband for his money. According to Mahfouz, "[Saber's] mother had afforded him a brief life of luxury; when that inevitably collapsed, he had to find a father or kill." Pointing out the ways in which this "very good" novel recalled film noir, Michael Wood wrote in the *Times Literary Supplement* that "Mahfouz's Egypt bears more than a passing resemblance to Raymond Chandler's California and Elmore Leonard's Florida."

The Beggar (MAKTABAT MISR, 1965; AMERICAN UNIVERSITY IN CAIRO, 1986; DOUBLEDAY, 1990) • Unlike his earlier novels, which charmingly and compassionately evoke the details of life in the old quarters of Cairo, Mahfouz's work after 1959 seemed obsessed with the betrayal of the ideals of social justice by those, especially the intellectuals, who came to power after the 1952 coup. In this short novel, the wealthy lawyer Omar has a midlife crisis: For no apparent reason, he loses interest in money and his wife and begins seeking enlightenment, first through sex and then via mysticism. "Imagine an unlikely blend of Trollope's feline social nuance with Camus's visions of emptiness, and you might approach [*The Beggar*'s] unique, bittersweet flavor," suggested Boyd Tonkin in *The Observer*.

Adrift on the Nile (MAKTABAT MISR, 1966; DOUBLEDAY, 1993) • This novel's protagonist, civil servant Anis Zaki, owns a houseboat aboard which a group of his friends meets in the evening to smoke hashish, discuss Camus and Sartre, and declare their indifference to political and social reality. They're the last of the pre-Nasser bourgeoisie and are dying out, yet on a drug-induced expedition away from the houseboat, something happens that makes them confront the reality that they've been denying. "Although this kind of existential awakening could seem dated," Christopher Walker wrote in *The Observer*, "Mahfouz's writing has a liveliness and grace that makes the book's philosophical concerns still seem immediate and real."

* Miramar (MAKTABAT MISR, 1967; AMERICAN UNIVERSITY IN CAIRO, 1978; THREE CONTINENTS, 1983) • Called by *World Literature Today* reviewer Michael Beard "the most appealing Mahfouz yet translated," *Miramar* describes the ups and downs of life in an Alexandria boarding house. Five single men—four of whom narrate the story—live in the Miramar along with the maid, Zohra, a peasant girl who has escaped an arranged marriage. All the men are interested in Zohra in one way or another, and their interrelationships form a microcosm of Egyptian society. "What intrigues us," according to Beard, "is the kind of endless variation and witty restatement which keeps us interested in village gossip once we are attuned to its rhythms."

"Like all novels worth their salt, Miramar *allows us the rare privilege of entering a national psychology in a way that a thousand journalistic articles or television documentaries could not achieve; and perhaps more important, beyond that, we can encounter in it a racial temperament that has been widely misunderstood in the West." (John Fowles)*

Mirrors (MAKTABAT MISR, 1972; BIBLIOTHECA ISLAMICA, 1977) • Even more so than Mahfouz's other work of this period, *Mirrors* is an experiment: It presents, in alphabetical order, fifty-five capsule portraits of Egyptians who are the narrator's friends and acquaintances. The characters are a mix of radicals, conservatives, rogues, and idealists, carefully created to "mirror" Egyptian society at large. "Its experimental form makes it an unrepresentative text," Michael Beard wrote in *World Literature Today,* "but as a portrait of society in cross-section, with its frequent references to political history..., it has a greater concentration of the elements for which a Western reader will study [Mahfouz]." Beard also pointed out that the book's strange format made its translation (by Roger Allen) somewhat awkward.

God's World (BIBLIOTHECA ISLAMICA, 1973) • This collection of twenty stories was the first Mahfouz short-fiction anthology published in English. Its contents were selected to demonstrate the ways in which Mahfouz's traditional, pious characters relate to the modern world. In the extremely surreal and symbolic "Under the Bus Shelter," written in the aftermath of the 1967 Six-Day War, a group of pedestrians waiting in the rain under a bus shelter are confounded by what they see: a wild car chase, naked people fornicating in the street, and a bizarre character who appears to be directing a film. They huddle together, wondering aloud what's going on, but none of them investigates. Then a policeman appears and asks them why they're holding a meeting. When they fail to respond, he kills them—apparently, this is the penalty for those who "stand and stare." According to one reviewer, the Egypt described in *God's World* is a place "where modern ideas and technologies are in conflict with tradition, faith, and even reason."

Al-Karnak (MAKTABAT MISR, 1974; PUBLISHED BY YORK IN 1979 AS PART OF *THREE CONTEMPORARY EGYPTIAN NOVELS*) • Written after Anwar el-Sadat's public criticism of his predecessor, this "relentlessly political" novel, according to Saad el-Gabalawy in the *International Fiction Review,* reveals Nasser's gruesome excesses and the hollowness of his revolutionary rhetoric. During their university days, two innocent lovers, Ismail and Zeinab, become "children of the revolution." Based on their blind faith in Nasser, they expect the 1952 coup to produce a new era of freedom, justice, and equality. However, as intellectuals they pose a threat to Nasser, so one night the secret police drag them barefoot from their bed. In his dark prison, the head of the secret police threatens to torture Zeinab unless Ismail admits (falsely) to being a Communist. Of course, Zeinab is raped anyway, yet both she and Ismail maintain their faith in the revolution until the regime is humiliated during the Six-Day War. According to el-Gabalawy, Mahfouz "reveals here a deep insight into the psychology of revolutionary idealism."

Fountain and Tomb (MAKTABAT MISR, 1975; THREE CONTINENTS, 1988) • This volume has been variously described as a collection of short stories, a novel, and in the introduction to the English translation "a novel disguised as a collection of tales." In any case, all the vignettes contained in *Fountain and Tomb* take place within the same quarter of old Cairo during the early twentieth century. They're loosely linked by the viewpoint of the first-person narrator—clearly a boy in some of the stories and apparently a young adult in others. The denizens of this quarter, a slum trapped against the walls of Cairo's cemetery, include the same sort of colorful riffraff that one finds in Mahfouz's earliest realistic novels. "Although *Fountain and Tomb* is clearly not one of the author's more outstanding contributions to modern Arabic fiction," Roger Allen wrote in *World Literature Today*, "it can provide Western readers with a 'slice of life,' Egyptian style, which is pleasant enough to read."

Respected Sir (MAKTABAT MISR, 1975; AMERICAN UNIVERSITY IN CAIRO, 1986; DOUBLEDAY, 1990) • *Respected Sir* chronicles the bureaucratic career of Othman Bayyumi, an ambitious civil servant who enters the government sometime after the 1919 revolt against British rule. The novel, which moves briskly, carries Othman through to the eve of the 1952 revolution. Along the way, Mahfouz pays close attention to Othman's motivation, especially his obsession with promoting his career—which, Mahfouz implies, may be at the cost of his soul. "Mr. Mahfouz's dexterity in shunting us along the corridors of Othman's career is so subtle that we may want to see *Respected Sir* as a simple cautionary tale—a latter-day *Bleak House* in Arabic," Michael Beard noted in the *New York Times*. "But Mr. Mahfouz also makes it clear that his protagonist is talented, sensitive, and not without charm." Because the book is "sparing in detail and less anchored in social specifics" than most of Mahfouz's other novels, Beard suggested, it may help attune readers "to Mahfouz's subtleties as a writer."

The Harafish (MAKTABAT MISR, 1977; DOUBLEDAY, 1994) • The title of this historical novel refers in a positive sense to the "common people," the menial laborers who once inhabited the poorer districts of Cairo and lived under the clan system that prevailed in much of the urban Middle East well into the twentieth century. Under this system, young men organized themselves into vigilante groups that protected their neighborhoods and administered populist justice within them. To tell their story, Mahfouz uses the idiom of the folk tale, the traditional medium for recording the exploits of clan leaders: how they struggled to become leader, how they chivalrously defended the clan, and how some became tyrants. In this case, Mahfouz presents the history of one clan over the course of several centuries. "Imagine *Buddenbrooks* stripped down, speeded up, and multiplied by ten,"

Maureen Freely wrote in *The Observer*, "and you have an idea of [this novel's] pacing, its preoccupations, and the size of the cast."

Wedding Song (MAKTABAT MISR, 1981; AMERICAN UNIVERSITY IN CAIRO, 1984; DOUBLEDAY, 1989) • In this novel about the relationship between life and art, Mahfouz presents the same series of events from four distinct perspectives, each account differing subtly from the others. The principal characters are a troupe of actors rehearsing a play that apparently reflects the dishonesty, treachery, corruption, and sexual intrigue of their own lives. While noting that Mahfouz used a similar multiple-narrator technique in *Miramar*, Roger Allen in *World Literature Today* added pointedly that "*Wedding Song* is no equal of the earlier novel, either in the subtlety of its presentation...or in its brilliant use of style to convey the differing attitudes."

Arabian Nights and Days (MAKTABAT MISR, 1982; DOUBLEDAY, 1995) • This collection of modernist fairy tales picks up the story of Shahrzad (or Scheherazade) where the medieval *Thousand and One Nights* left off. She has persuaded her despotic husband, King Shahriyar, to give up his evil ways (particularly his habit of beheading his wives), but she remains uneasy: Can he be trusted to reform himself and the wicked city over which he rules? Against this backdrop, thirteen more tales are told. In one, a good genie orders a corrupt police chief to kill a bad governor. In another, a bad genie torments a pure-hearted virgin with dreams of forbidden love. According to Merle Rubin in the *Christian Science Monitor*, "*Arabian Nights and Days* retains the timeless settings and miraculous atmosphere of the original while raising timely questions about crime and punishment, political reform and corruption, and the role of storytelling in the search for truth and justice."

The Journey of Ibn Fattouma (MAKTABAT MISR, 1983; DOUBLEDAY, 1992) • Although modeled on the *Rihlat*, the classic fourteenth-century travel narrative by Moroccan journeyman Ibn Battuta, this novel also recalls *Gulliver's Travels*, but without the broad satire. Disappointed by his own culture, Ibn Fattouma journeys to five mythical lands, each representing a different political system (for example, theocracy, democracy). None proves tolerant enough to suit him, however, and at the novel's end, we leave Ibn Fattouma on the road to Gebel, a "land of perfection" that one critic has suggested stands for death. "Mahfouz is notoriously reluctant to travel abroad," Robert Irwin observed in the *Times Literary Supplement*, "and indeed it does not seem that he has traveled very far in this book, even in the imagination."

The Time and the Place and Other Stories (DOUBLEDAY, 1991) • Although the novels of Naguib Mahfouz are now famous both within and without the Arab world, his short stories remain little known in the West. Of the twenty selected for this volume by Denys Johnson-Davies (the translator of

Mahfouz's most recent works), sixteen appear here in English for the first time. "Each reader will have his own favorite," John Haywood wrote in *World Literature Today*. "To me, 'Zaabalawi' and 'By a Person Unknown' stand out. Both reflect that air of mystery which is a characteristic of Mahfouz's short stories as a whole."

BIOGRAPHY

KNOWN VARIOUSLY AS the Dickens, Proust, Tolstoy, Dostoevsky, and Balzac of Egyptian fiction, Naguib Mahfouz was born in al-Gamaliya, one of the older quarters of Cairo. Although his father, a successful merchant, moved the family from al-Gamaliya when Mahfouz was twelve, his memories of the quarter's diverse, bustling alleyways stayed with him. Mahfouz received a degree in philosophy from the University of Cairo in 1934 and worked there as a secretary until 1938, when his first collection of short stories, *Hams al-junun*, was published. A year later, he began his lengthy bureaucratic career with a job in Egypt's Ministry of Islamic Affairs.

Mahfouz's first three novels, *Abath al-aqdar* (1939), *Radubis* (1943), and *Kifah Tiba* (1944) were all set in ancient Egypt, though each contained allusions to modern society. His first novel with a twentieth-century setting, *Khan al-Khalili* (1945)—and the seven that followed, including *Midaq Alley*, *The Beginning and the End*, and the Cairo Trilogy—established Mahfouz as a master of social realism and the greatest Arab novelist of his time. However, although esteemed throughout the Arab world, Mahfouz remained virtually unknown to Westerners until 1988, when he became the first Arab to win a Nobel Prize in literature. Only then did many of his novels become widely available in English translation through a publishing and translation program championed by Doubleday editor Jacqueline Kennedy Onassis.

The Nobel Prize, however, had its drawbacks as well. Remembering the heresy of *Children of Gebelaawi*, many fundamentalists criticized the selection of Mahfouz as a subtle Western conspiracy to discredit Islam. Death threats against Mahfouz were renewed, and in 1994, on his way to a weekly literary gathering that he had been attending for decades, Mahfouz was stabbed in the neck with a kitchen knife. He survived the attack, and several Islamic militants were put on trial for the crime.

NEXT ON THE READING LIST: Chinua Achebe, Jorge Amado, Oscar Hijuelos, Doris Lessing, Toni Morrison, V. S. Naipaul, Salman Rushdie

Cormac McCarthy
(b. July 20, 1933)

"McCarthy resembles the ancient Greek dramatists and medieval moralists—a strange, incompatible mixture.... He is a novelist of religious feeling who appears to subscribe to no creed but who cannot stop wondering in the most passionate and honest way what gives life meaning."
—Robert Coles, The New Yorker

The Orchard Keeper (RANDOM HOUSE, 1965) • The judges who awarded *The Orchard Keeper* the William Faulkner Foundation's prize for best first novel called McCarthy "a young writer of dark vision" who had shown himself able to "transmute that vision into an art which is strong and vital for all its darkness." In this auspicious debut, McCarthy tells the coming-of-age story of John Wesley Rattner, a young man with two mentors who function as surrogate fathers. One of these men, a bootlegger, unknowingly killed John Wesley's real father when John Wesley was six. The other, the orchard keeper of the title, discovered the body but kept it hidden for years. Walter Sullivan, writing in the *Sewanee Review*, called the prose "magnificent, full of energy and sharp detail and the sounds and smells of God's creation."

Outer Dark (RANDOM HOUSE, 1968) • After abandoning his infant son in the woods, Culla Holme tells his sister, still weak from the delivery, that it has died. But she doesn't believe him. Later, the incestuous siblings set out separately in search of the child, undertaking parallel but very different quests. Reviewers were divided over the merits of this allegory in which the characters eerily resemble figures from Greek tragedy. Detractors called it too Gothic, too murky, and too inconsistent in tone, but *New Yorker* reviewer Robert Coles observed that McCarthy rewards the reader "with an astonishing range of language—slow-paced and heavy or delightfully light, relaxed or intense, perfectly plain or thoroughly intricate."

Child of God (RANDOM HOUSE, 1974) • Based on actual events that took place in Knoxville, Tennessee, *Child of God* tells the story of Lester Ballard, an alienated outcast who gradually strays so far from accepted human behavior that he becomes a killer and a necrophiliac—not by inclination, McCarthy implies, but seemingly by necessity. This book received more critical attention than McCarthy's previous work, both positive and negative. The favorable reviews contained liberal praise, and even the negative ones, which criticized the lack of depth in Ballard's character and motivation, acknowledged the compelling nature of the story and McCarthy's beautiful prose.

Suttree (RANDOM HOUSE, 1979) • McCarthy's only book to date with an urban setting concerns Cornelius Suttree, scion of a prominent Knoxville family, who lives on a houseboat near the seamy neighborhood of McAnally Flats. Fearing both life and death, Suttree withdraws into himself, only to be drawn into the world again by the humanity of his drunkard and derelict neighbors. These marginal characters also serve as the basis for much of the book's sardonic humor, which McCarthy uses to great ironic effect. "I cannot see how anyone...can avoid the deep-rocking belly laughs I found on almost every page of this evocative and highly poetic examination of what is admittedly the bottom stratum of our society," Shelby Foote wrote in the *Memphis Press-Scimitar.*

Blood Meridian; or, The Evening Redness in the West (RANDOM HOUSE, 1985) • In this revisionist Western, described by *New Republic* reviewer Sven Birkerts as "Louis L'Amour rewritten with a bloody pen," McCarthy moves from the Tennessee landscape of his previous novels to the desert Southwest. An extensively researched historical novel, *Blood Meridian* describes several nineteenth-century scalp-hunting expeditions staged by a bounty hunter against the local Apache. "*Blood Meridian* must be the most beautifully written, unrelievedly ghastly chronicle of violence, carnage, torture, rapine, plunder, murder, and every other conceivable variety of barbarism to be found anywhere in our literature," John W. Aldridge declared in the *Atlantic Monthly.*

＊ All the Pretty Horses (KNOPF, 1992) • McCarthy's sixth novel is the story of two teenagers who leave home on horseback in 1949, bound for Mexico. It won a National Book Award and a National Book Critics Circle Award and stayed on the *New York Times* best-seller list for twenty-one weeks. Considered more accessible than McCarthy's previous books, this novel received both critical and popular acclaim. Like *The Orchard Keeper, All the Pretty Horses* is a coming-of-age story whose central character, John Grady Cole, chases a vanishing western way of life. His trip to Mexico, in fact, becomes a trip back in time to a place where horses—and the cowboy way of life—are still valued.

> *"In the hands of some other writer, this material might make for a combination of* Lonesome Dove *and* Huckleberry Finn, *but Mr. McCarthy's vision is deeper than Larry McMurtry's and, in its own way, darker than Mark Twain's." (Madison Smartt Bell, New York Times)*

The Crossing (KNOPF, 1994) • This novel, the second book of the proposed Border Trilogy (*All the Pretty Horses* being the first), introduces another questing teenager, Billy Parham, who travels to Mexico three times during the course of the story—the first time to free a wolf he has trapped, the second to seek revenge, and the third to retrieve the body of his brother. The natural world figures prominently in *The Crossing*, so much so that several reviewers were prompted to describe Nature as an additional character. Another described the novel as "philosophically challenging, darker than *All the Pretty Horses*, and infused with McCarthy's soaring and delving prose."

BIOGRAPHY

ALTHOUGH CORMAC MCCARTHY was born in Rhode Island, when he was four years old he moved with his family to a small rural community outside Knoxville, Tennessee. His father was a Yale-educated lawyer who served in the late 1930s as a special assistant to FDR's first attorney general. During his youth, McCarthy fished, rode horses, and met many of the people who would later populate his novels. "We were considered rich because all the people around us were living in one- or two-room shacks," he told one interviewer. McCarthy's college career at the University of Tennessee was interrupted between 1953 and 1957 by service in the air force. Back at Tennessee, he published two short stories in a university literary magazine and began work on several novels before quitting school in 1960 to pursue a full-time writing career. "Teaching writing is a hustle," he later observed.

Most critics consider McCarthy's writing to be extraordinarily original and superbly crafted. Saul Bellow, for instance, has praised McCarthy's "absolutely overpowering use of language, his life-giving and death-dealing sentences." Yet McCarthy's detractors have complained that his style owes too great a debt to William Faulkner. McCarthy has also been compared to Mark Twain, Herman Melville, Flannery O'Connor, and even Shakespeare. Yet none of his first five books sold more than twenty-five hundred copies in hardcover, which led one critic in 1988 to call McCarthy "our best unknown major writer by many measures."

McCarthy's commercial doldrums, blamed on the difficulty of his writing style, ended with the 1992 publication of *All the Pretty Horses*. Even so, McCarthy has never been very interested in popularity or its financial rewards. At the time he won a $236,000 MacArthur Foundation "genius" grant in 1981, the twice-divorced writer was living in a motel room in Knoxville. By all accounts, his circumstances didn't change terribly much even after he got the money. Throughout his career, McCarthy has studiously avoided media attention, and he habitually refuses requests for speaking engagements with the comment that everything he has to say can be found in the pages of his books.

NEXT ON THE READING LIST: Russell Banks, Larry Brown, Pete Dexter, Larry McMurtry, Tim O'Brien, E. Annie Proulx, Melanie Rae Thon

Thomas McGuane
(b. December 11, 1939)

"Thomas McGuane likes dogs, horses, Indians, golf, the road, hawks, rocks, peppery food and outdoor sex. For characters he has a soft spot for loony old men; hateful, dead or vanished fathers; hot-blooded, sharp-tongued women; struggling protagonists with high-stakes, dangerous male friends.... Mr. McGuane is concerned with irony, voice, lingo, dialogue that cries to be read aloud, descriptive passages that are never coy or sloppy.... What he's really after is language—fully extended and at serious play."
—Beverly Lowry, New York Times

The Sporting Club (SIMON & SCHUSTER, 1969) • Set in the woods of Michigan, his native state, McGuane's first novel describes the members of a tony sporting club and their wild carryings-on, which escalate during the course of the novel from the hilarious to the chaotic. At the story's center is a confrontation between Vernon Stanton, who's determined to destroy the Centennial Club, and James Quinn, Stanton's rival and alter ego. A third principal character, Earl Olive, a criminal hired by Stanton as the club's caretaker, instigates much of the looniness. The book won praise for its satire of American machismo, its exuberant absurdism, and its rowdy, flamboyant, "amphetamine-paced" prose.

The Bushwhacked Piano (SIMON & SCHUSTER, 1971) • McGuane's second novel, winner of the prestigious Rosenthal Award from the National Institute of Arts and Letters, is a black comedy told in energetic, virtuousic prose. Protagonist Nicholas Payne—hip, wised up, but utterly confused—goes around on crutches "for no reason." He also carries a pistol and believes in "horses that will not allow themselves to be ridden." Payne joins C. J. Clovis, a builder of "bat towers" that repel mosquitoes, on a road adventure following the trail of Payne's girlfriend, a compulsive photographer whose pictures are meant to capture the many experiences that she doesn't always live.

* Ninety-Two in the Shade (FARRAR, STRAUS & GIROUX, 1973) • With this acclaimed novel, a finalist for a National Book Award, McGuane emerged as one of his generation's most accomplished novelists. The tightly narrated story, set in the Florida Keys, concerns a pair of fishing guides: one a marine biology student and the other a grizzled outdoorsman with a taste for brutish pranks. Their conflict begins lightheartedly but soon spirals into violence. Reviewers noted McGuane's large debt to Hemingway, both in his tactile rendering of an exotic landscape and in his fine descriptions of male characters at work in the outdoors.

"Ninety-two in the Shade *is a short, tight, dense tale of the classic American confrontation between waste of time, waste of life, and death, on the one hand, and sublime mastery of a talent, gift, skill, or trade, on the other.... The book is a black comedy that has the grinding inevitability of tragedy."* (L. E. Sissman, The New Yorker)

Panama (FARRAR, STRAUS & GIROUX, 1978) • This somewhat autobiographical work combines self-indulgent excess with emotional honesty. Narrator Chester Hunnicutt Pomeroy, a burned-out rock star, has plummeted from overnight fame and wealth into an abyss of dissolution and despair. He limps home to Key West in the hope of reuniting with his estranged wife, only to sink further into cocaine, madness, and moral anarchy. McGuane relates this story disjointedly, but his prose, critics noted, was vivid, energetic, and at times deliciously funny.

Nobody's Angel (RANDOM HOUSE, 1982) • This dark fable, less frantic in the telling than McGuane's previous work, relates the story of Patrick Fitzpatrick, "a fourth-generation cowboy outsider, an educated man, a whiskey addict and until recently a professional soldier." Having left the military, he returns to his family's ranch outside Deadrock, Montana, where he hopes to find order and stability. Instead, he's pulled into a dangerous relationship with a wealthy Oklahoma oilman and his alluring wife. A few critics thought that McGuane had matured some and become more contemplative; others found the story clichéd and its hero uninteresting.

* Something to Be Desired (RANDOM HOUSE, 1984) • Lucien Taylor gives up his career as a diplomat in Latin America and abandons his wife and son in order to rescue a former girlfriend who has gotten into some serious trouble. He acquires the title to her Deadrock, Montana, ranch, which he converts into a flashy spa. Meanwhile, he struggles with his inner demons and gropes toward self-knowledge. The story is implausible in places, though McGuane's description of Montana is superb, as is his rendering of the effect of this landscape on the inner lives of its inhabitants.

"*What makes* Something to Be Desired *remarkable is its setting, the mountains and flatlands of Montana that Mr. McGuane so lovingly describes."* (Ronald Varney, Wall Street Journal)

To Skin a Cat (DUTTON, 1986) • All the stories in this uneven collection, McGuane's first, are set in the West, often the "new" West with its glass-walled skyscrapers and nouveau-riche millionaires. Some of the tales are introspective character studies; some are touching memory pieces; some are fast-paced adventure stories written in the high-voltage prose that made McGuane famous. Many feature the familiar McGuane protagonist: restless, skeptical, and appalled by the excesses of an increasingly vulgar civilization.

Keep the Change (HOUGHTON MIFFLIN, 1989) • The setting of McGuane's seventh novel is again Deadrock, Montana, which by now had emerged as the author's universal symbol of the American West. This time, however, McGuane offers the sort of conventional plot that one might expect in a TV drama. Although the teenage Joe Starling once helped manage his family's ranch, the adult Joe, a Yale graduate, now works as a successful artist in New York City. Even so, when his alcoholic father dies, only Joe can save the ranch from being sold off to a greedy neighbor. But some reviewers liked the book: "In these days of hot early starts and quick nasty fall-offs," one remarked, "it's encouraging to see a good writer getting better."

Nothing But Blue Skies (HOUGHTON MIFFLIN, 1992) • Frank Copenhaver, a real estate developer in Deadrock, is careening toward a midlife crisis. He drinks too much, his twenty-year marriage is unraveling, and he can't find common ground with his daughter. Soon he begins speeding downhill, and so does business, even as he hatches a grand scheme to transform a decrepit landmark building into an expensive luxury hotel. Critics tended to agree that the story was less interesting than either the Montana backdrop or the joys of the outdoor life that McGuane so masterfully evokes.

BIOGRAPHY

BORN IN WYANDOTTE, MICHIGAN, Thomas McGuane spent some of his early years in Florida. McGuane, of Irish background, grew up among accomplished storytellers and embarked early on a writing career. He attended several Michigan colleges, eventually earning a degree from Michigan State in 1962. He then studied writing at Yale and Stanford and wasn't yet thirty when *The Sporting Life* was published to wide acclaim. Four years later, with the publication of *Ninety-Two in the Shade*, McGuane established himself as a leading contemporary novelist. Critics observed that he pursued classically American themes of manhood, but that he brought to them a unique verbal energy as well as a flair for loopy humor.

McGuane devoted himself monastically to his craft until a near-fatal 1972 car accident—he was speeding at 120 miles an hour—profoundly transformed his outlook. As he told one interviewer, "It was getting unthinkable to spend another year sequestered like that, writing, and I just dropped out." He embarked on a second career, writing screenplays, the best known of which are *Rancho Deluxe* (1975) and *The Missouri Breaks* (1976). He also became involved with a succession of prominent actresses—one of whom, Margot Kidder, he briefly married. As a result, his name began to appear in tabloids—much to his dismay, though he has admitted that he "had a lot of fun drinking and punching people out for a while." He has said that his current wife, Laurie Buffett, the sister of singer Jimmy Buffett, brought stability and order to his life after their marriage in 1977.

For many years now, McGuane has lived in Livingston, Montana. An expert horseman, he has competed in rodeos and written about them in his nonfiction collection *An Outside Chance: Essays on Sport* (1980). In his recent fiction, McGuane has emerged as a chronicler of the West during its current period of transformation. He has also become the literary custodian of an exclusively masculine world of outdoor athleticism once the stomping ground of Ernest Hemingway.

NEXT ON THE READING LIST: Martin Amis, Harry Crews, Ivan Doig, Jim Harrison, Barbara Kingsolver, Larry McMurtry, Cathie Pelletier

---

Terry McMillan
(b. October 18, 1951)

"How critics will ultimately judge McMillan is a good question. Will she turn out to be, like Danielle Steel and Judith Krantz, just one more queen of the steamy, scented stuff that the publishing industry calls 'commercial'? It's possible. But so far McMillan has not written formula glop. And most of the time her characters…have a brassy realism that saves them from the trash bin."
—*John Skow, Time*

Mama (HOUGHTON MIFFLIN, 1987) • The heroine of McMillan's first novel is poor black Mildred Peacock, whose weaknesses for rotten whiskey and rotten men are offset by her devotion to her five children. Set in a small Michigan industrial town, the story opens in 1964, when Mildred throws out her no-good husband. Then she moves from job to job and man to man as she experiences both failure (her son goes to jail) and success (her eldest daughter goes to college) as a parent. Among the book's crowded ensemble of funny, earthy characters, Mildred stands out as not a monolithic black "mama" but a complex woman capable of both deceit and tenderness. "McMillan is a master of black humor in both senses of the phrase," Elizabeth Alexander wrote in the *Village Voice*. "Her details and names are exact and telling."

Disappearing Acts (VIKING, 1989) • With this novel, McMillan examines a subject that had become a staple of black women's magazines: relationships between professional black women and working-class black men. Zora Banks is a music teacher who dreams of landing a recording contract. Franklin Swift is a high school dropout who takes construction work when it's available. When they meet outside Zora's Brooklyn apartment building (Franklin is helping out with some renovations there), it's love at first sight, and they move in together. However, the tension arising from their class differences, especially Franklin's frustration with not being able to find regular work, puts a great deal of strain on the relationship. Although some reviewers complained that *Disappearing Acts* was too predictable, nearly all agreed with Louise Bernikow, writing in *Cosmopolitan*, that "the stunning achievement here is the creation of Franklin, whose voice on the page rings with authenticity, whose intimidation, anger, even violence are unforgettable."

✱ Waiting to Exhale (VIKING, 1992) • In this female buddy story, the four characters "waiting to exhale" are professionally successful black women in their midthirties. They all live in Phoenix, and each is holding her breath until she finds Mr. Right. As they wait, they enjoy good times and bad and work through such contemporary hot-button issues as high blood pressure, homelessness, nail care, and Xanax dependency. According to Darryl Pinckney, writing in the *New York Review of Books*, *Waiting to Exhale* is "a book that knows to whom it is addressed."

> *"Terry McMillan's heroines are so well drawn that by the end of the novel, the reader is completely at home with the four of them. They observe men—and contemporary America—with bawdy humor, occasional melancholy, and great affection.... Reading* Waiting to Exhale *is like being in the company of a great friend. It is thought-provoking, thoroughly entertaining, and very, very comforting." (Susan Isaacs, New York Times)*

How Stella Got Her Groove Back (VIKING, 1996) • Stella Payne is a forty-two-year-old investment analyst and single mother who makes a lot of money and likes to shop—but guess what? No man. So she takes a vacation to Jamaica, where she meets Winston Shakespeare, a handsome, gentle man who's half her age. Next thing you know, Winston's on a plane to California, where he moves in with Stella and is instantly accepted by her son and her family. This slight plot might seem implausible were it not for the fact that it closely resembles McMillan's own romantic life. Writing in the *New York Times*, Richard Bernstein compared the novel to a sitcom, although it's "a good deal more raunchy than anything that would be allowed on television." (All of McMillan's books make extensive use of profanity.) In *Newsday*, Beth Gutcheon called *Stella* "a serious sex-and-shopping novel."

BIOGRAPHY

TERRY MCMILLAN'S BOOKS read like a road map to her life. *Mama* takes place in Point Haven, Michigan, where Mildred raises five children, the eldest of whom goes to college in California. McMillan was born in Point Huron, Michigan, the eldest of her mother's five children. She also survived a hardscrabble childhood to attend college in California.

In *Disappearing Acts*, Zora, an aspiring professional, has a relationship (and a child) with Franklin, a working-class carpenter. During the early 1980s, McMillan had a similar affair with Leonard Welch, the father of her son, Solomon. In fact, Welch saw so much of himself in the character of Franklin that he filed a $4.75-million defamation suit against McMillan (and lost). McMillan later transformed another romantic episode into *How Stella Got Her Groove Back*. Like Stella, McMillan returned from a Jamaica vacation in 1995 with a live-in companion half her age. "I don't care what anybody thinks," McMillan told *Time*. "Men have been doing this shit for years."

A determined woman, McMillan promoted her first novel largely on her own, writing thousands of letters to bookstores, colleges, and newspapers to drum up interest. She even arranged her own book tour. As a result, her first two novels were surprisingly successful, yet neither prepared her for the impact of *Waiting to Exhale*, which earned her a devoted following among black women readers (and proved that they made up quite a lucrative market). The book's paperback rights sold for $2.64 million, and the 1996 film version starring Whitney Houston and Angela Bassett was a surprise hit at the box office, too. As a result, the advance for *Stella* was a staggering $6 million, part of which McMillan has spent on a luxurious new home in Danville, California, across the bay from San Francisco. According to *Time*, she grumbles when reporters write about her wealth: "What's their point?... Why are they so fucking surprised?"

NEXT ON THE READING LIST: Bebe Moore Campbell, John Irving, Alison Lurie, Toni Morrison, Gloria Naylor, Alice Walker, Fay Weldon

---

Larry McMurtry
(b. June 3, 1936)

"McMurtry's fiction sometimes leans toward what a friend of mine calls 'the dirty sock novel,' that alienated masculine genre where men are men and they don't do emotional responsibility or laundry. But it's redeemed by the author's extraordinary way with women. His heroines are the kind you want to love, listen to forever, or at least move in next door."
—*Barbara Kingsolver*, New York Times

Horseman, Pass By (HARPER, 1961) • An outbreak of hoof-and-mouth disease in a small Texas town provides the backdrop for this novel in which adolescent Lonnie Bannon loses his innocence and becomes a man. McMurtry, who was just twenty-five years old when he published *Horseman, Pass By*, has since called the book "immature." However, it inspired the Oscar-winning 1963 film *Hud* and brought McMurtry a great deal of critical attention. One reviewer described the novel as "the starkest, most truthful, most terrible, and yet beautiful treatment of [ranching country] I've seen. It will offend many...but it is a true portrait of the loneliness and pervading melancholy of cowboying."

Leaving Cheyenne (HARPER & ROW, 1963) • Returning to the fictional town of Thalia, Texas, in which he set *Horseman, Pass By*, McMurtry tells the story of Molly Taylor and her two lovers, Gideon and Johnny, and the sons she has with each of them (both boys are later killed during World War II). As the narration shifts among the three principal characters, we learn about their lives from youth through middle age to their later years. "*Leaving Cheyenne* is a rarity among second novels in its exhilarating ease, assurance, and openness of feeling," Walter Clemons wrote in the *New York Times*.

* The Last Picture Show (DIAL, 1966) • This novel, which completed McMurtry's Thalia Trilogy, features a romantic triangle: Sonny, his friend Duane, and Jacy, the girl for whom they both lust. Its racy portrayal of small-town sexuality—including exhibitionism, bestiality, masturbation, and homosexuality—caused some excitement in McMurtry's hometown of Archer City, Texas, yet few critics found the book offensive or sensational. The *New York Times* called the sex scenes "sad, funny, touching, sometimes horrifying, but always honest, always human."

> "*A sorrier place is hard to find. [Thalia] is desiccated and shabby physically, mean and small-minded spiritually. Mr. McMurtry is expert in anatomizing its suffocating and dead-end character.*" (*Thomas Lask*, New York Times)

Moving On (SIMON & SCHUSTER, 1970) • Fearing that their marriage is disintegrating, Jim and Patsy Carpenter test it against the relationships of four other married and unmarried couples. The first few hundred pages of this novel are set in rodeo locations, but then McMurtry shifts the action to the Rice University campus in Houston, causing reviewers to note that *Moving On* has a much more urban feel than McMurtry's previous works. They also pointed out that, at 794 pages, it's his most tedious book. *New York Times* critic John Leonard compared *Moving On* to "turning on the radio and leaving it on for years."

All My Friends Are Going to Be Strangers (SIMON & SCHUSTER, 1972) • Houston novelist Danny Deck shuffles from one pathetic situation to another: His wife, pregnant with their child, leaves him for a blind man, so he takes up with a passionless cartoonist. Apparently, after the bad reviews of *Moving On*, McMurtry tried to inject some humor back into his work—for example, Danny's uncle's ranch has camels rather than cattle. Most critics were pleased with the result. "Unlike the panting ladies-magazine prose of *Moving On* (particularly the sex scenes), *[All My Friends Are Going to Be Strangers]* is crisp, lean, and forceful," Ruth Prigozy wrote in

Commonweal. "This is a novel of high comedy, rich pathos, and what is rare, genuine charm."

* Terms of Endearment (SIMON & SCHUSTER, 1975) • This novel, though well liked, didn't command much popular acclaim until the 1983 film starring Shirley MacLaine, Debra Winger, and Jack Nicholson won five Academy Awards. Irascible, overbearing Aurora Greenway, a widowed New Englander transplanted to Houston, has a busy social life filled with potential suitors— oil magnates, retired army officers—but she always has enough time to meddle in the affairs of her daughter, Emma, whose marriage self-destructs shortly before she dies of cancer.

> *"Maybe what keeps one entertained is the sympathy with which Mr. McMurtry writes about these people.... One laughs at the slapstick, one weeps at the maudlin, and one likes all of Mr. McMurtry's characters, no matter how delicately or broadly they are drawn."* (*Christopher Lehmann-Haupt*, New York Times)

Somebody's Darling (SIMON & SCHUSTER, 1978) • The first McMurtry novel set outside Texas, *Somebody's Darling* resurrects Jill Peel, a minor character in *All My Friends Are Going to Be Strangers.* She's a young film director with a smash hit who's currently the "darling" of the industry. Her sudden success ruins her friendship with aging screenwriter Joe Percy but leads to an affair with football-player-turned-producer Owen Oarson. According to Jonathan Yardley in the *Washington Post,* "Mr. McMurtry's characters are real, believable, and touching; his prose has life and immediacy; and he is a very funny writer."

Cadillac Jack (SIMON & SCHUSTER, 1982) • Former rodeo cowboy Jack McGriff drives around the country in his Cadillac, collecting antiques and making car-phone calls to his ex-wives and "girlfriends du jour." For a week, we follow Jack as he attends several Washington, D.C., parties; heads back to Texas for fifty pairs of cowboy boots; and visits two teenagers who give Jacuzzi massages. Although Jack's narration holds the story together, the constant motion can make one a little carsick. "It is difficult for a reviewer to know quite what to do when a favorite author disappoints so keenly," Peter Prince admitted in *The Nation.* "Probably the best thing to do is to bow the head, avert the gaze, and hope for better things—perhaps a swift, safe return to Texas."

The Desert Rose (SIMON & SCHUSTER, 1983) • McMurtry began this well-received mother-daughter story as a screenplay but finished it as a novel. Harmony is an aging Las Vegas showgirl whose life seems to be falling apart. Her boyfriend wrecks her car and then leaves her (but not before he steals her insurance checks); meanwhile, she loses her job. On the other hand, the life of her sexpot daughter, Pepper, seems to be on the upswing: Pepper first takes over her mother's job and then accepts a marriage proposal from an older man. "When I finished the novel, I was left rooting for Harmony to hold on to her humanity...and for the desert to spread and take over Las Vegas," Steve Tesich wrote in the *New York Times*.

* Lonesome Dove (SIMON & SCHUSTER, 1985) • This eight-hundred-page magnum opus, which won McMurtry a Pulitzer Prize, tells the epic tale of cowboys Augustus McCrae and Woodrow Call and the 1870s cattle drive they lead from Texas to Montana. Although McMurtry made use of standard Western conventions—his characters include an Indian villain named Blue Duck and a heart-of-gold whore named Lorena—reviewers praised him for presenting the Old West in all its grimy, dusty shabbiness.

> *"McMurtry's...refusal to glorify the West works to reinforce the strength of the traditionally mythic parts of* Lonesome Dove *by making it far more credible than the old familiar horse operas. These are real people, and they are still larger than life." (Nicholas Lemann, New York Times)*

Texasville (SIMON & SCHUSTER, 1987) • This melancholy satiric novel, set in modern-day Texas, features the central characters from *The Last Picture Show*, now in middle age. Sonny still owns the pool hall bequeathed to him at the end of the last book—as well as half of downtown Thalia. Duane, who returned safely from Korea, has won and lost a fortune in the oil business. Jacy—more sympathetic and less self-absorbed than in the first book—has become famous playing a jungle queen in Italian movies. "*Texasville* often reads like a movie script, all dialogue and situation," Louise Erdrich wrote in the *New York Times*. "The individual scenes are sharp, spare, full of longhorn humor and color, but motivation is sketchy, rarely described, clued by action rather than reflection."

Anything for Billy (SIMON & SCHUSTER, 1988) • In this somewhat heavy-handed retelling of the story of Billy the Kid, McMurtry drops Sheriff Pat Garrett and the Lincoln County War and turns Billy into a Western-ized version of Eliza Doolittle. Dime novelist Benjamin Sippy abandons his domineering wife and their nine daughters to roam the Wild West with the cowboys and gunslingers that he writes about. After botching a train robbery that nearly lands him in jail, Sippy meets simpleminded, bucktoothed Billy Bone, reputed to be a ruthless gunfighter (though he's never fired a gun). Using his writing skills, Sippy transforms Bone into legend. "The book's greatest strength," M. George Stevenson wrote in the *Village Voice*, "is in Sippy's accounts of how his dime novelist's expectations of the West were either too grand or too mundane."

Some Can Whistle (SIMON & SCHUSTER, 1989) • For his thirteenth novel, McMurtry brings back Danny Deck, last seen in *All My Friends Are Going to Be Strangers*. Now fifty-one, Deck has made a fortune in Hollywood creating sitcoms for television. Returning to Texas, he works lethargically on his next novel as he carries on relationships with the answering machines of his European-actress paramours. Then his twenty-two-year-old daughter appears. The kicker is: He's never seen her before. Barbara Kingsolver pointed out in the *New York Times* that writing a novel about a novelist was somewhat narcissistic, but she admitted that "McMurtry's prose stands up and kicks fence posts."

Buffalo Girls (SIMON & SCHUSTER, 1990) • Here McMurtry examines the twilight years of Wild West legends Sitting Bull, Calamity Jane, Wild Bill Hickok, and Buffalo Bill Cody. Now drunken, exhausted has-beens, they relive their glory days as part of Buffalo Bill's Wild West Show. "*Buffalo Girls* is truly operatic," Susan Fromberg Schaeffer wrote in the *New York Times*. "Although something happens on every page...this book is really composed of interwoven arias, death songs in which each character sings about what he remembers best of his soon-to-be-ending life."

The Evening Star (SIMON & SCHUSTER, 1992) • With this effort, reviewers finally wearied of McMurtry's sequels. Here he revives Aurora Greenway and the other surviving characters from *Terms of Endearment*. Now in her seventies, Aurora has raised Emma's children, but they have all turned out flawed in some important "McMurtry-like way," wrote one reviewer. Tommy is in prison for killing his ex-girlfriend, Teddy is a former mental patient working at a convenience store, and Melanie is pregnant, unsure of her baby's father. "It is damning praise to be termed a 'cinematic writer' and McMurtry certainly is," jabbed *Los Angeles Times* critic Julia Cameron. "More script than novel," complained Mack Starr in *Newsweek*.

Streets of Laredo (SIMON & SCHUSTER, 1993) • This sequel to *Lonesome Dove* also failed to impress reviewers, who suggested that McMurtry's larger-than-life characters had grown smaller with the passage of time. Call is old, McCrae is dead, and the prostitute Lorena has become a schoolteacher and mother of five. One critic did praise McMurtry's vision of an Old West grown older as "more vicious than ever," but H. H. Harriman in the *Detroit News* described the novel as "a Pulitzer Prize-winner...reduced to pandering." He added, "Sequels are a kind of exhumation, a dishonor to the memory of the dead."

Pretty Boy Floyd (SIMON & SCHUSTER, 1994) • Reviewers were mystified by this novel, cowritten by McMurtry and his screenwriting partner, Diana Ossana. Why would McMurtry, ostensibly a "cowboy novelist," choose to write about the gangster who became Public Enemy Number One after John Dillinger's death? McMurtry has hinted that Floyd's appeal was his legend, the same blend of fact and fiction that drew McMurtry to Billy the Kid and other heroes of the Old West. Yet according to Sidney Zion of the *New York Times*, "Floyd comes out flatter than a Depression pancake in the meanest Okie truck stop."

The Late Child (SIMON & SCHUSTER, 1995) • "McMurtry's career as a serious novelist is becoming checkered fast," Verlyn Klinkenborg wrote in a *New York Times* review of *The Late Child* that described the novel as "a lesser suffix" to *The Desert Rose*. This sequel opens with former Vegas showgirl Harmony reads a letter informing her that her daughter, Pepper, has died of AIDS. Harmony then takes off with her five-year-old son for New York City, where she meets a large cast of characters, including Pepper's lover. "McMurtry is at his best when he delves into Harmony's fragile psychological state," David L. Ulin observed in the *Los Angeles Times*, but that's not very often in this "substantially flawed novel, with plot lines that go nowhere and a contrived flavor to much of the action."

Dead Man's Walk (SIMON & SCHUSTER, 1995) • After a string of four critical flops (three of them sequels), McMurtry tried a prequel. This novel features Gus McCrae and Woody Call of *Lonesome Dove* as teenaged Texas Rangers during the days when Texas was still an independent republic. With a couple of hundred soldiers and a dozen wagons, they trek hundreds of difficult miles across the desolate Jornada del Muerto to take Santa Fe from the Mexicans. Some reviewers, including John Milius in the *Los Angeles Times*, liked the book even better than *Lonesome Dove*: "In *Dead Man's Walk*, McMurtry uses a simple, wry storyteller's voice, immensely accessible, and with it he ponders the same questions that Melville and Conrad did."

Zeke and Ned (SIMON & SCHUSTER, 1997) • McMurtry and his cowriter, Diana Ossana, set this tale in the Indian Territory just after the end of the Civil War. Zeke Proctor, a Cherokee, accidentally shoots and kills the woman whom he intends to make his second wife. Her death triggers a series of events that lead to a showdown between Zeke and his son-in-law. "The writers favor a slow, leisurely pace to their storytelling: small talk about livestock and whiskey, crops, hunting, minor family feuds, and women," Joyce Maynard wrote in the *Los Angeles Times*. "You know as McMurtry and Ossana go into their windup that pretty soon hearts will break and bullets will fly. But the writers are in no hurry to get there."

Comanche Moon (SIMON & SCHUSTER, 1997) • McMurtry's fourth novel in the hugely successful series that began with *Lonesome Dove* takes place sometime before the action in that original book but later than the events in *Dead Man's Walk*. Epic buddies Gus McRae and Woodrow Call are at the height of their powers in this sprawling picaresque adventure; however, as they boldly tame the West and the still fearsome Comanche, Texas prepares for the Civil War. Most reviewers agreed that this was the best of the three "subsidiary" *Lonesome Dove* novels. In *People*, Kyle Smith called it "a joy even if you haven't read the previous books." and Andy Solomon noted in the *New York Times* that, as usual, "the characters are the novel's strength."

BIOGRAPHY

LARRY MCMURTRY WAS BORN into a family of Texas cattle ranchers, from whose elders he learned about cowboying, the pioneer spirit, self-reliance, and the heartache of loss. McMurtry developed his particular passion for the Old West during his childhood in Archer City, Texas, the small town that inspired the setting of his Thalia novels. He received a bachelor's degree from North Texas State College in 1958 and a master's degree from Rice University two years later. In between, he married Josephine Ballard, with whom he had a son (the folksinger James McMurtry) before their divorce in 1966. After taking a few courses at Stanford University, where he became friendly with fellow writing student Ken Kesey, McMurtry accepted a teaching job at Texas Christian University, moving to Rice in 1963.

From the very start, McMurtry's novels generated a great deal of attention. His first book, *Horseman, Pass By*, became *Hud*, the first of many films or television miniseries based on McMurtry's work. McMurtry himself received an Academy Award nomination for his 1971 screen adaption of *The Last Picture Show*. His other major award is the 1986 Pulitzer Prize that he won for *Lonesome Dove*, his most popular work (and later the basis of a highly successful 1989 CBS-TV miniseries).

Although McMurtry lives on and off in Arizona and Washington, D.C., where he owns and operates a rare-book store called Booked Up, his "home" has always been Texas. He often wears a sweatshirt emblazoned with the phrase MINOR REGIONAL NOVELIST. "Being a writer and a Texan is an amusing fate," McMurtry wrote in his 1968 collection of essays, *In a Narrow Grave*, "especially when one is a regionalist from an unpopular region." That sense of self-mocking irony pervades all of McMurtry's work.

NEXT ON THE READING LIST: Pat Conroy, Ivan Doig, William Kennedy, Cormac McCarthy, Thomas McGuane

Steven Millhauser
(b. August 3, 1943)

"Mr. Millhauser...has all the precision of the careful realist, but that quality is coupled with passages of metaphor and description whose source is not naturalistic observation but the inwardness of an original and mysterious imagination."
—*Frederic Tuten,* New York Times

✳ Edwin Mullhouse: The Life and Death of an American Writer, 1943–1954, by Jeffrey Cartwright (KNOPF, 1972) • This smart satire of literary biography describes the brief career of child novelist Edwin Mullhouse, as told by his Boswell (and erstwhile best friend), twelve-year-old Jeffrey Cartwright. Millhauser's book is also an unsentimental portrait of American childhood that most reviewers praised for its brilliantly recaptured images of youth and its playful humor, located primarily in Jeffrey's precociously pompous narrative. *New York Times* critic George Stade called *Edwin Mullhouse* "probably the best Nabokovian novel not written by the master himself."

> *"Don't be put off by the apparent whimsy of the title and the youth of the characters; this is a mature, skillful, intelligent, and often very funny novel."* (The New Republic)

Portrait of a Romantic (KNOPF, 1977) • In this novel, darker than *Edwin Mullhouse*, Millhauser concerns himself with adolescence, specifically with the years between twelve and fifteen. His narrator, twenty-nine-year-old Arthur Grumm, looks back on those years and remembers in particular the two friends who fed his then-split personality: William Mainwaring, a devoted realist, and Philip Schoolcraft, an equally devoted Romantic. Drawing parallels between Romanticism and adolescence, Millhauser mixes in suicide pacts and games of Russian roulette with discussions of Poe, boredom, and other aspects of literary despair. According to Sheldon Frank in *Saturday Review*, "Millhauser is blessed with spectacular descriptive gifts.... Yet he also overwrites with a vengeance." William Kennedy, writing in the *Washington Post*, noted that the novel's pace was "snailishly slow" but called Millhauser's "overall achievement [one] of a high order."

In the Penny Arcade (KNOPF, 1986) • The seven short stories in this collection feature themes similar to those found in Millhauser's novels, such as the role of the artist in society and the special imaginative powers of children. In these stories, however, especially the four about human-made imitations of life, magical things happen, leaving the reader with a perception

of the marvelous even after the magical acts have been "explained."
"Though [Millhauser's] art can be hampered by too rigid conceits and occasional bad choices of subject," Robert Dunn observed in the *New York Times*,
"he is a true original when he draws us into his precise, luminous awareness,
when he makes our world turn amazing."

From the Realm of Morpheus (MORROW, 1986) • While watching a baseball
game, sleepy Carl Hausman chases a foul ball into the woods, where he falls
down a hole into a netherworld presided over by Morpheus, the god of
sleep and dreams. Morpheus offers Carl a tour, and the two of them move
from one set piece to another as Millhauser parodies and pays homage to
Alice in Wonderland, Gulliver's Travels, The Divine Comedy, and many classics
you probably haven't read. In the *New York Times*, Michiko Kakutani called
the novel "somewhat idle" and lacking in originality: "For all his manipulation of old myths, Freudian theories, and literary allusions, Mr. Millhauser
seems less interested in satirizing society or scoring esthetic points than in
simply exercising his imagination and his facility with language."

The Barnum Museum (POSEIDON, 1990) • The subject of these ten stories is
the imagination, especially its limits (or lack thereof). In the title story,
for example, the Barnum Museum itself embodies the imagination, its
endless halls filled with every manner of imaginary beast and object.
Another tale describes secret apartments in a movie theater, where film
characters continue their lives offscreen. Although admirers of Millhauser's work generally liked *The Barnum Museum*, Carlin Romano panned
it in the *Philadelphia Inquirer:* "Convinced of the meaningfulness of his
every burp and cough, [Millhauser] serves up aesthetic gimcrackery
while...displaying an arrogant unwillingness—or philosophical inability—
to articulate the point, or why we should care about it."

Little Kingdoms (POSEIDON, 1993) • This collection of three novellas, according to Dan Cryer in *Newsday*, "demonstrates anew [Millhauser's] wonderfully
fluid storytelling and his fascination with the nature of art and the creative
process." The first of these novellas concerns a 1920s cartoonist who sacrifices everything for his art. The second is a medieval fairy tale, complete with
princess, mysterious nobleman, and lustful dwarf. The final work, "Catalogue
of the Exhibition: The Art of Edward Moorash, 1810–1846," uses the format
of a museum catalog and the language of twentieth-century art criticism to
tell the story of four nineteenth-century American Romantics. "There was no
such artist and there are no such paintings," Frederic Tuten wrote in the *New
York Times*, "but Mr. Millhauser makes you wish there were."

* Martin Dressler: The Tale of an American Dreamer (CROWN, 1996) • Millhauser won a Pulitzer Prize for this story of a shopkeeper's son who rises,
by virtue of his ambition and imagination, to become a real estate mogul in
a delightfully evoked turn-of-the-century New York City. In Millhauser's

world, however, the American Dream is a "perilous privilege, which the gods guard jealously." More interested in creation than in wealth, Martin keeps striving for larger and better—until finally he reaches too far.

"The unique appeal of Martin Dressler *is perhaps best captured in the author's phrase from a previous book—'lavish awareness.' This Zen-like expression strikes all the right notes found here—a brilliantly intense focus on the wondrous hum and whirl of everyday." (Dan Cryer,* Newsday)

BIOGRAPHY

STEVEN MILLHAUSER WAS BORN IN New York City, where his German Jewish father taught English at City College. When Milton Millhauser became an assistant professor at the University of Bridgeport, the family moved to Connecticut. Millhauser himself returned to New York City in 1961 to attend Columbia, earning his B.A. in 1965 and subsequently spending three years in a graduate program at Brown before deciding that he didn't want an academic career after all. At this point, he asked his parents if he could move back home.

Sleeping and working in the book-lined attic of his parents' home, Millhauser struggled to produce his first novel. "I had a novel in me [that] I had to get out," he remembered, "but I was blocked. I couldn't proceed. It was a terrifying time." According to his mother, Charlotte, "The years were going by, Steven was getting older, and he was still writing in the attic. But his father had complete faith in him." Yet when Millhauser finally produced a novel, no one would publish it. Then he wrote another one, *Edwin Mullhouse,* which was critically acclaimed but sold modestly, earning Millhauser only four thousand dollars. Because Millhauser's books still sell poorly, since 1988 he has supplemented his income by teaching creative writing part time at Skidmore College in Saratoga Springs, New York.

Superstitious about the creative process, Millhauser wrote all his books on his father's Remington manual typewriter until it died. Since then, he has used a pencil and an IBM Selectric. His typical workday includes seven hours at a library carrel with his pencil and a notebook. "Being a writer is a very peculiar endeavor," Millhauser has said. "You spend tremendous amounts of your waking hours dreaming thoughts and writing them down. It seems like you're tricking the world to allow you to do that."

Millhauser met his wife, Cathy, playing anagrams at a friend's dinner party. He was forty when they married, and they have since had two children. Cathy Millhauser herself enjoys a national reputation as a crossword puzzle creator, regularly working up puzzles for the *New York Times* and the *Washington Post,* among other publications.

NEXT ON THE READING LIST: Paul Auster, Don DeLillo, Umberto Eco, Gabriel García Márquez, Richard Powers, Thomas Pynchon, Philip Roth

Lorrie Moore
(b. January 13, 1957)

"In her wry, precise remarks, she sometimes seems like a witty foreigner describing American life—like English novelist David Lodge, for example, though Moore has more pointedly lyric areas in her work. And in the way she mixes comedy and sadness, wisecracks and poignancy, there's a resemblance to the Woody Allen of Annie Hall *and* Manhattan.*"*
—*John Casey,* Chicago Tribune

* Self-Help (KNOPF, 1985) • The self-help manual is the structuring gimmick behind Lorrie Moore's first collection of short stories, but the clarity and steely ring of her prose makes this gimmick more than a ruse. Stories such as "How to Talk to Your Mother" and "How to Be an Other Woman" sting with wit and lightly lambaste the yuppie class.

> *"In* Self-Help, *the collection of short stories that is her first book, Lorrie Moore examines the idea that lives can be improved like golf swings and in so doing finds a distinctive, scalpel-sharp fictional voice."* (*Jay McInerney,* New York Times)

Anagrams (KNOPF, 1986) • Moore's first novel has "creative writing program" written all over it. It's so packed with writerly tricks—most notably, the conceit of having her four main characters change places in each chapter (and only two of them are real!)—that it loses contact with the authentic emotions that are the basis of good fiction. "Because of its form, the novel is episodic, often seeming like a series of one-liners," Laura Furman wrote in the *Los Angeles Times.*

Like Life (KNOPF, 1990) • It's an older, wiser sensibility that pervades Moore's second collection of stories, and yet the stories themselves skip along just as glibly as the ones in *Self-Help.* The puns and palindromes are still here, as are the characters who obsess about love and then run the other way when they find it. "*Like Life* is Moore's toughest work," Ralphe Sassone wrote in the *Voice Literary Supplement.* "It shows human vulnerability in various contours, and with heightened sympathy, while never dropping its cynicism."

Who Will Run the Frog Hospital? (KNOPF, 1994) • Previously Moore's fiction either gleamed or seemed bloated with postmodern nonconventions, but this novel is a true departure, a casting off of tricks. There's a real story here, told in a mostly straightforward way, and the result is that Moore's voice comes through all the more clearly. A husband and wife venture to Paris, where they discover that they're no longer in love. Mentally retracing her life, the wife looks for a time when "the future" was an exciting concept. "It is a small book," the *Christian Science Monitor* noted, "but its impact is quite big."

BIOGRAPHY

MARIE LORENA MOORE WAS BORN and raised in upstate New York, the daughter of an insurance executive. While a student at St. Lawrence University in 1976, she sent a piece to *Seventeen* and won the magazine's short-story contest. After earning her B.A., she went on to Cornell, where she received an M.F.A. in creative writing in 1982. *Self-Help*, most of which was written during her Cornell days, made her an instant literary star. The second-person perspective she used in those stories grew out of her desire to mimic how-to prose. Said Moore, "I was interested in whatever tensions resulted when a writer foisted fictional experience off of the 'I' of the first person and onto the more generalized 'you' of the second—the vernacular 'one.'"

Although her subsequent books haven't achieved the renown of her first, Moore is still regarded as an important voice in American literary fiction. She is currently a professor of English at the University of Wisconsin in Madison.

NEXT ON THE READING LIST: Ann Beattie, Amy Bloom, John Irving, David Lodge, Alison Lurie, Mona Simpson, Anne Tyler, Fay Weldon

---

Toni Morrison
(b. February 18, 1931)

"From book to book, Morrison's larger project grows clear. First, she insists that every character bear the weight of responsibility for his or her own life. After she's measured out each one's private pain, she adds on to that the shared burden of what the whites did. Then, at last, she tries to find the place where her stories can lighten her readers' load, lift them up from their own and others' guilt, [and] carry them to glory."
—*Ann Snitow*, Voice Literary Supplement

The Bluest Eye (HOLT, RINEHART & WINSTON, 1970) • Morrison's debut novel, which grew out of a story that she wrote while teaching at Howard University in 1962, is a wrenching account of how the Western ideal of beauty converts self-esteem into self-loathing within the black community. This process manifests itself in Pecola Breedlove, a young black girl who believes that having blue eyes will make her pretty and win her love. *The Bluest Eye* was faulted for a "fuzziness born of flights of poetic imagery," but many critics nevertheless noted the beauty of Morrison's prose and suggested that she might be a major talent in the making.

Sula (KNOPF, 1974) • Set in a midwestern hilltop community (ironically known as The Bottom), *Sula* focuses on the relationship between Nel Wright and Sula Mae Peace, childhood friends who grow apart when one marries and the other goes off to college. Sula rejects the traditional gender roles embraced by Nel, but both women, neither white nor male, have to struggle to forge their own identities. Although *Sula* was nominated for a National Book Award, reviewers were divided once again in their opinion of Morrison's prose poetry, narrative construction, and moral vision of black life.

* Song of Solomon (KNOPF, 1977) • Heading south in search of gold, Milkman Dead arrives in Shalimar, a town that boasts no commerce, no government, and no transportation. In this sequestered setting, he undergoes a rite of passage—not from innocence to experience, but from one history to another. Milkman's journey from spiritual death to rebirth is symbolized in Morrison's widely acclaimed third novel by his discovery of the secret power of flight. A Book-of-the-Month Club main selection, *Song of Solomon* found an exuberant audience and won a National Book Critics Circle Award.

> *"Here the depths of the younger work are still evident, but now they thrust outward, into wider fields, for longer intervals, encompassing many more lives. The result is a long prose tale that surveys nearly a century of American history as it impinges upon a single family. Few Americans know, and can say, more than [Morrison] has in this wise and spacious novel."* (*Reynolds Price*, New York Times)

Tar Baby (KNOPF, 1981) • No longer focusing exclusively on black life, Morrison sets this novel on the tiny Caribbean Isle de Chevaliers. As in *Song of Solomon*, she invokes the supernatural, this time as a way to fend off a reality in which whites are set against blacks, women against men, civilization against primitivism, and culture against nature. Only the heroic Son, a handsome roustabout with a strong aversion to whites, emerges as a human being capable of spiritual, emotional, and intellectual growth. Although reviews were generally mixed, *Tar Baby* spent three months on national best-seller lists.

* Beloved (KNOPF, 1987) • Set in Cincinnati during Reconstruction, Morrison's Pulitzer Prize–winning fifth novel introduces Sethe, a former slave who fled the South with her children eighteen years earlier. She now lives with her youngest daughter, Denver, and a supernatural presence: the ghost of her murdered two-year-old. How that tragedy came to pass and just who was responsible are the mysteries at the center of *Beloved*, which is as much about the dynamics of mother-child relationships as it is about the haunting legacy of slavery.

"[Readers] experience American slavery as it was lived by those who were its objects of exchange—both at its best, which wasn't very good, and at its worst, which was as bad as can be imagined." (*Margaret Atwood,* New York Times)

Jazz (KNOPF, 1992) • Morrison's sixth novel contains parallel narratives set during Reconstruction and the Jazz Age. Continuing her ongoing investigation into the debilitating impact of history on black families, she weaves together the stories of Joe, a middle-aged cosmetics salesman; his childless wife, Violet; and his teenage mistress, Dorcas—with the history of their predecessors. Another character in the novel is New York City, whose concrete and steel protect black residents from the constant scrutiny of a racist society. Reviewers praised *Jazz* for its rich language and intricate plot construction but tended to admonish Morrison for her use of an unreliable narrator.

* Paradise (KNOPF, 1998) • Morrison's first novel since winning her Nobel Prize presents the utopian paradise of Ruby, Oklahoma, a small all-black town founded just after World War II by descendants of former slaves who had founded a similar town, Haven, during Reconstruction. The residents of Ruby are proud of their heritage and their prosperity but extraordinarily wary of strangers because they know that the price they must pay for paradise is isolation. All proceeds well until the 1970s, when a group of odd young women gathers at the Convent, an old mansion just outside town. Soon the residents of Ruby come to see the Convent as the source of an encroaching evil—with frightening consequences.

"With Paradise, *Morrison has brought it all together: the poetry, the emotion, the broad symbolic plan. Not that the novel is free of awkward elements,...and* Paradise, *like Morrison's other fiction, is not an easy read.... But the novel richly rewards the reader's efforts."* (*Brooke Allen,* New York Times)

BIOGRAPHY

TONI MORRISON WAS BORN Chloe Anthony Wofford in Lorain, Ohio—the second of four children raised in a family that endured both economic and social adversity. Although her family couldn't afford many books, Morrison was still encouraged to read and did so voraciously, her interests ranging from classic Russian novels to the works of Jane Austen. "Those books were not written for a little black girl in Lorain, Ohio," she has explained, "but they were so magnificently done that I got them anyway. They spoke directly to me out of their own specificity." After graduating with honors from high school, she went on to earn a bachelor's degree from Howard University in 1953 and a master's degree from Cornell two years later. She then taught English at Texas Southern University in Houston for two years, beginning a teaching career that she continues to this day.

In 1957, while teaching at Howard, Morrison began to meet and influence several young men—among them Amiri Baraka, Andrew Young, and

Claude Brown—who would soon become prominent in black politics and literature. She also married architect Harold Morrison. Toni Morrison has been reticent to discuss her brief and troubled union, which produced two sons, but during this unhappy period she did begin to write. "It was as though I had nothing left but my imagination. I had no will, no judgment, no perspective, no power, no authority, no self—just this brutal sense of irony, melancholy, and a trembling respect for words." By the time *The Bluest Eye* was published in 1970, Morrison had taken a job as a senior editor at Random House, where she established herself as a mentor to such aspiring black women writers as Toni Cade Bambara, Gayl Jones, and Angela Davis.

In an effort to redefine the black experience not as marginal or peripheral but as fully American, Morrison has experimented with both narrative and language forms, producing a unique blend of fantasy and reality, history and myth. Along the way, she has been chastised for her fabulistic visions of black life, her lack of strong male characters, and her characterizations of white people. Yet Morrison ignores this criticism. "I really think the range of emotions and perceptions I have had access to as a black person and a female person are greater than those of people who are neither," she told the *New York Times*. "My world did not shrink because I was a black female writer. It just got bigger." In 1993, Morrison became the first black (and only the eighth woman) to win a Nobel Prize in literature, the world's most prestigious literary honor.

NEXT ON THE READING LIST: Isabel Allende, Nadine Gordimer, Charles Johnson, Jamaica Kincaid, Naguib Mahfouz, Gloria Naylor, Alice Walker

Alice Munro
(b. July 10, 1931)

"Like her similarly gifted contemporaries Peter Taylor, William Trevor, Edna O'Brien, and some few others, the Canadian short-story writer Alice Munro writes stories that have the density—moral, emotional, sometimes historical—of other writers' novels."
—*Joyce Carol Oates*, New York Times

Dance of the Happy Shades (RYERSON, 1968; MCGRAW-HILL, 1973) • "The short story is alive and well in Canada" the *New York Times* declared in its review of Munro's first collection. The fifteen stories here overflow with small details of life in southern Ontario. Their photographic intensity makes the action so real that, according to *The New Yorker*, "a reader who has never heard of Canada would understand, and perhaps even half recognize, the world Alice Munro is describing."

Lives of Girls and Women (MCGRAW-HILL RYERSON, 1971) • Its stories are so interconnected that this collection could be read as a novel. The overarching subject is the coming of age of Del Jordan, whose struggles with family members augur her sexual awakening. Writing in the *Times Literary Supplement*, Patricia Beer complained that Munro "often explains too much" but admired the way she "draws a clear distinction between youthful and adult emotional attitudes even when exactly the same things are happening."

Something I've Been Meaning to Tell You (MCGRAW-HILL RYERSON, 1974) • Munro expands her range with these stories about older, more experienced people. Most of the protagonists are sophisticated city dwellers who understand and appreciate irony. "Material" describes the process by which a male writer turns bits of his life into fiction. When this man's wife skewers him for permitting publication of jacket copy that gives him a false biography, we know that Munro has entered a new, more biting phase. Joyce Carol Oates, writing in the *New York Times*, was most impressed by "the evocation of emotions, ranging from bitter hatred to love, from bewilderment and resentment to awe."

Who Do You Think You Are? (MACMILLAN OF CANADA, 1978; PUBLISHED IN THE U.S. AS *THE BEGGAR MAID*, KNOPF, 1979) • Another story collection cum novel, *Who Do You Think You Are?* focuses on an Ontario woman named Rose: We meet her first as a schoolgirl and then follow her life as she marries, divorces, and builds a career as a modestly successful actress. According to Ted Morgan in the *Saturday Review*, Rose "is immensely likable, and there is gallantry in her willingness to take risks, open herself up to the chance of love, and measure herself against what she was and fled from."

The Moons of Jupiter (MACMILLAN OF CANADA, 1982; KNOPF, 1983) • This collection examines people in middle age (one critic called it "menopausal"). Its characters wrestle with the demise of their ideals, particularly those concerning love. Some spar with psychiatrists, others with lovers, friends, and strangers. Writing in *The New Republic* that the book has "a vision of life customarily reserved for poets," Mary Jo Salter particularly admired the story "Accident" for its sense "that we are all both irreplaceable and dispensable."

* The Progress of Love (KNOPF, 1986) • The title story of this collection opens with an image guaranteed to warp a child's life: A girl finds her mother standing on a chair with a rope around her neck. The mother tells her to go and get her father. As the girl races off, we wonder what she'll find when she returns. All of the stories are similarly harrowing.

"The book is aptly named. In every story, love takes its circuitous, enigmatic route—not only passionate love, but the faintly absurd, faintly perilous self-love that animates adolescent longings, the ambiguous, self-denying love of family, and the corrosive obligatory love that makes [one character] his weird, quasi-retarded brother's keeper." (*Lynne Sharon Schwartz,* Washington Post)

Friend of My Youth (KNOPF, 1990) • The title story of Munro's seventh collection presents a confrontation between a dying woman and her enraged daughter, who objects to the way the mother has selectively altered the past in order to support her present self-image. We expect the story to end with some shocking scene in which the mother is forced to face reality. Instead, it's the daughter who comes to appreciate the reality created by one's own sense of self. According to Carol Shields in the *London Review of Books*, one finds "on every page the particular satisfactions of prose that is supple, tart, and spare, yet elegant and complex."

Open Secrets (KNOPF, 1994) • Munro's later stories have more shock value than her earlier ones: They leap backward and forward in time and change scenes suddenly. These stories in particular focus on confession, such as the one in which a prim woman meets a stranger in a hotel dining room just after World War I. She tells him about the soldier who made love to her via letters, only to marry someone else after the war. The stranger offers her sympathy...and then his bed. Ann Hulbert wrote in the *New York Review of Books* that this collection shows Munro to be "a regional writer without borders."

BIOGRAPHY

THE CHARACTERS IN ALICE MUNRO'S fiction often inhabit a nether zone somewhere between the city and the countryside, which is precisely where Alice Anne Laidlaw grew up—on her parents' farm outside the town of Wingham in southwestern Ontario. She was graduated from the University of Ontario in 1952, promptly married bookseller James Munro (whom she divorced in 1976), and began raising children. However, the artist in her wasn't satisfied with this arrangement, so, when not keeping house, she wrote short stories, continuing a habit that she had formed in high school. For several years Munro published stories in regional journals while enduring a steady stream of rejections from book publishers. When her first collection finally appeared in 1968, it was widely praised by critics, won Canada's prestigious Governor General's Award for fiction, and transformed Munro into a major Canadian voice.

Although distinctly Canadian, Munro also identifies herself with writers of the American South, notably Eudora Welty and Flannery O'Connor, who share her interest in small-town concerns and the oddities of rural hamlet life. Curiously, she has no interest in writing novels. "I no longer feel attracted to the well-made novel," she has said. "I want to write the story that will zero in and give you intense, but not connected, moments of experience."

NEXT ON THE READING LIST: Margaret Atwood, Alice Hoffman, Edna O'Brien, Michael Ondaatje, Grace Paley, Carol Shields, William Trevor

---

Iris Murdoch
(b. July 15, 1919)

"Iris Murdoch careens around the curves of her art, ringing it with fictions that coil inside each other. Like most conical labyrinths, the entrance to Miss Murdoch's world is less impressive than the interior. The threshold is so familiar with its cuckolds, mousy wives, and clamoring mistresses that it hardly seems worth crossing. Yet one must to reach the nether world and watch the archetypes at play."
—*Bernard F. Dick*, Sewanee Review

Under the Net (VIKING, 1954) • An infatuation with existentialism underlies Murdoch's first novel. The "net" is the structure of language that we build to make sense of the world—and which, perhaps inevitably, separates us from it. Despite being heavily philosophical, *Under the Net* was an immediate success: Jake, the hero, wanders around London and Paris, having long conversations with his friend Hugo; they discuss Jake's attempts to build fortifications against "contingency" in life. Malcolm Bradbury called *Under the Net* "a good book about virtue though also a good book about contemporary life."

The Flight from the Enchanter (VIKING, 1956) • Nearly all of Murdoch's novels involve an enchanter of some sort, to whom other characters are drawn or from whom they want to flee. The surface of this book is light comedy, centered on a charismatic man's effort to take over a magazine, but the comic patina cracks when one attempted suicide leads to another, successful one. One critic wrote that *The Flight from the Enchanter* "should be explored simultaneously on the levels of psychology, social commentary, and myth."

The Sandcastle (VIKING, 1957) • While Rain, a young woman, is painting an old man's portrait, another man, Mor, falls in love with her. Mor plans to leave his wife and children for Rain, but Mor's wife is too wily for him, and she executes a brilliant counterstrike to keep her man. Murdoch makes much of the symbolism of the painter as a depicter of reality; her twist is that the subject of the painting tells the other characters where they're going wrong in their lives. A fair-to-middling example of a Murdoch novel, *The Sandcastle* is swathed in intellectual allusiveness and deeply plotted.

The Bell (VIKING, 1958) • A group of Christians in rural 1950s England has the task of hoisting a bell onto a church tower as a testament to their devotion...but the bell comes crashing down. This novel has been called both "anti-Christian allegory" and, more broadly, an effort to show that the symbols of the past cannot sustain modern man. It's one of Murdoch's drier and more anemic studies.

A Severed Head (VIKING, 1961) • Martin has a wife, Antonia, and a mistress, Georgie, but he loves Honor. Antonia loves Martin's brother, Alexander. Alexander loves Georgie, who loves Martin. Although the strong authorial presence makes this a better novel than it sounds, Murdoch is nonetheless constrained by her own heavy plotting. "The characters dress, talk, act like ourselves," Anthony Burgess wrote, "but they are caught up in a purely intellectual pattern, a sort of contrived sexual dance in which partners are always changing."

An Unofficial Rose (VIKING, 1962) • Randall grows roses; when a lovely flower named Lindsay comes along, he abandons his wife for her. Curiously, his father supports his action, and eventually we learn why. The atmosphere Murdoch creates here is oppressively and unconvincingly Gothic; one might say that the effect is too floral and too close to romance literature.

The Unicorn (VIKING, 1963) • This very good novel, with its high Gothic tone, shows the influence that nineteenth-century fiction, especially the novels of Wilkie Collins, has had on Murdoch. And yet *The Unicorn* is also very knowing: The book keeps winking at you, letting you know that the complex events unfolding in this archly romantic setting are contrived for someone's amusement. Or are they? We follow a pair of outsiders as they venture into the self-imposed medieval isolation of a group of oddballs living in a castle—and, like the outsiders, we struggle to understand what force binds them together.

The Italian Girl (VIKING, 1964) • The characters in *The Italian Girl*—a son who returns home to attend his mother's funeral, his older and younger female relatives, the cad who seduces them, the eponymous servant with whom the son becomes infatuated—all seem made of cardboard, which is why this novel is often considered among Murdoch's weakest.

The Red and the Green (VIKING, 1965) • *The Red and the Green* concerns the Irish Easter Rebellion of 1916, and it's a departure for Murdoch in that it is her first historical novel. The characters are members of an extended Anglo-Irish family, and the novel charts meticulously the effects of the uprising on each of them. At the center of the group is Barney, one of Murdoch's more engaging heroes, who comes to a poignant realization that the world around him is at least as real and important as his own internal life. The *Times Literary Supplement* called *The Red and the Green* "implausible," but another journal thought it a novel of "great neatness."

The Time of the Angels (VIKING, 1966) • Religion and incest, unnaturally natural bedfellows, conjoin exquisitely here as the chief themes in *The Time of the Angels*. The characters in this novel include a rector, his daughters, and his lover-maid—all of whom are pretty seriously deranged. Living together in the rector's bombed-out church, they serve as perfect foils for Murdoch's rich mix of ideas and dense plotting.

The Nice and the Good (VIKING, 1968) • On the first page of this novel, a pistol is fired: A man named Radeechy has shot himself. Murdoch subsequently delves into the affairs of Radeechy's family and associates, only very slowly coming around to the point that underlies the plot—the reason for the pistol shot. Although the happy ending feels forced, this book is otherwise a pleasantly nasty novel about niceness.

Bruno's Dream (VIKING, 1969) • Here Murdoch achieves an odd combination of domestic comedy and deep philosophy. The book's theme is utterly simple: Who will win the girl? The answer: Bruno. To some critics, *Bruno's Dream* ranks among Murdoch's best books, while others thought that it contained little more than philosophical propositions decked out as characters. According to Linda Kuehl in *Commonweal*, "While *Bruno's Dream* can be viewed as an attempt to scale universal ambiguity down to human proportions, it is an undistinguished novel of ideas, with only a few vestiges of the Murdoch flair and wit and scarcely a breath of life."

A Fairly Honorable Defeat (VIKING, 1970) • A familiar Murdoch figure occupies the focus of this novel: the enchanter, the magus, the man (it's usually a man) who holds others in his thrall. The twist here is that Murdoch seems to be setting up the evil genius for a fall, yet he may still have the last laugh. Rubin Rabinovitz, writing in the *New York Times*, thought that the book was "not an unqualified success. Melodramatic incidents and transparent stratagems, useful as they are as indicators of the novel's philosophical aspects, strain the reader's belief."

An Accidental Man (VIKING, 1971) • The accidental man is an American living in England during the Vietnam War. Because he happens to have English citizenship, he's able to remain abroad and avoid U.S. military service. But should he? Intent on exploring this theme of accidency to its fullest, Murdoch presents the reader with all sorts of other seemingly random events: love affairs, sudden deaths, and so on. And, as in her first novel, she allows her preoccupation with Sartrean existentialism—

especially its search for personal meaning and morality—to come to the fore. But what was somewhat lively in *Under the Net* comes across as a bit heavy handed here.

The Black Prince (VIKING, 1973) • Bradley Pearson, as he approaches old age, falls in love with the college-aged daughter of a friend, subsequently whisking her off to Lolita-land. In fact, *The Black Prince* has much in common with Nabokov's classic, especially its pleasantly dark corners, yet its tone is curiously detached. "*The Black Prince* is a very good book," Alison Lurie wrote in the *New York Review of Books*, but "it does not seem to be taking place in the modern world."

The Sacred and Profane Love Machine (VIKING, 1974) • This book has possibly the perfect 1970s title for a novel about sex. Unfortunately, a middle-aged philosophy professor turned novelist isn't the ideal character to make good on it. Instead, what we get is more akin to a discourse than to a flesh-and-blood tale. "The book contains as many elegant paragraphs as slovenly ones and for somebody who writes so fast Miss Murdoch writes dismayingly well," Martin Amis wrote in *The New Statesman*. "But it is bloated, and it sags."

A Word Child (VIKING, 1975) • Hilary Burde, a linguistically gifted child from a poor family, wins a place at Oxford, then loses everything. This would provide plenty of material for the plot of an ordinary novel, yet Murdoch has to go it one better, bringing Hilary into adulthood and letting the entire tragedy happen again under different circumstances. A typically challenging Murdoch product, filled to brimming with story and morals, *The Word Child* is easy to get lost in but hard to love.

* Henry and Cato (VIKING, 1977) • Henry is a goof, Cato a stern and moralizing priest. The two friends seem to know what life will dish out to each of them: maundering and disappointment to Henry, respect and success for Cato. But exactly the opposite happens in this novel, which Joyce Carol Oates called "at once deeply moving and entertaining." As the story unfolds, we begin to understand why each friend gets exactly what he deserves.

> *"The interweaving of the parallel stories is endless and fascinating, and it is a measure of Murdoch's superb craft that the effect, like that of classical ballet, is one of effortless grace, the labor and the discipline quite hidden."* (*Brigitte Weeks*, Washington Post)

* The Sea, the Sea (VIKING, 1978) • This is Murdoch's Booker Prize winner. Charles loved Hartley, but Hartley dumped him. Now, years later, they both live in the same town. Although Hartley has become a sad and dowdy middle-aged woman, Charles still holds a girlish picture of her in his mind and remains determined to have her, even to the point of being willing to invoke some magical assistance.

"The Sea, the Sea is a kind of Tempest on its own account, a book that explores the art of the novel and of magic, and also the need to elicit from life's facts and fantasies a meaning, a sense of the things that matter." (Malcolm Bradbury, The New Statesman)

Nuns and Soldiers (VIKING, 1981) • As Guy Openshaw lies dying, his wife and friends begin to align themselves into new sexual formations that, of course, have not only moral and financial but also religious ramifications. With this book, the *Washington Post* declared, Murdoch "exhibits an unflagging technical mastery and seems to have entered a mature phase, sounding ever deeper currents of the human condition."

The Philosopher's Pupil (VIKING, 1983) • A philosopher is a difficult character for a novelist to pull off; an evil man, a relatively easy one. And yet in *The Philosopher's Pupil,* Murdoch gives a skillful portrait of the philosopher, Rozanov, and a poor one of his evil understudy. The eponymous pupil, George, comes off as a wandering mass of nasty characterizations that don't quite add up to a human being. The story also wanders, as does the narrator in lengthy asides. "There were moments when I wished that it could be infinitely extended," Robertson Davies wrote in the *Washington Post.* "There were other moments (such as the 4,000 words that intervened between a character reaching a door and crossing the threshold) when I found myself mentally shouting, 'Get on with it!'"

The Good Apprentice (VIKING, 1986) • Edward, a student, secretly slips his friend Mark some drugs. After Mark jumps out a window and dies, Edward spends the rest of this book alternating between anguish at Mark's death and a desire to be reunited with his own father. "I found myself reading it late into the night, and woken early by the excitement of it, I continued to read at dawn," A. N. Wilson wrote in *The Spectator.* "It is the sort of book which takes hold of you completely."

* The Book and the Brotherhood (VIKING, 1988) • The book is a political tract being written by young David Crimond. The brotherhood is an odd group of university friends who, to honor one of their deceased number, decide to sponsor Crimond's project. However, Crimond's ideas and theirs soon come into conflict. This is a long, densely philosophical book, but it has a good deal of the verve that distinguishes Murdoch's best work.

> *"[It] is that rarest of fictions these days: a social and political novel that is not journalistic, a novel of ideas that is not ideological, and a deep exploration of national character that is not parochial." (Charles Newman,* New York Times)

The Message to the Planet (VIKING, 1990) • Murdoch's preoccupation with philosophy is so all-consuming here that it gives her little room to breathe. The characters are a mathematician-philosopher, a priest, and a historian.

Their concerns are such things as "pure thought." Uh-huh. In this novel, Anatole Broyard wrote in the *New York Times*, Murdoch "sounds like Henry James on crack."

The Green Knight (VIKING, 1993) • As her model for this work, Murdoch used the medieval romance *Sir Gawain and the Green Knight*, in which chivalry is put to magical tests. In her latter-day version, a man who kills a mugger is overcome with guilt. But the mugger returns, insisting that he didn't die, and offers a bizarre promise of new life for the main characters. Linda Simon, writing in the *New York Times*, said that *The Green Knight* "offers a keen satire on the way we create fantasies and diversions to protect ourselves from moral complexities and spiritual vacuity."

Jackson's Dilemma (VIKING, 1996) • Murdoch's twenty-sixth novel centers on a disappearing bride. When Marian leaves Edward stranded at the altar, the search is on, and foremost among the searchers is Edward's butler, Jackson, who turns out to control just about every character in the novel. "At this point in her illustrious career," Brad Leithauser wrote in the *New York Times*, "Dame Iris…may well be deemed above editing by her publishers. If so, it's a judgment that disserves her prose, which is strewn with imprecisions and blatant redundancies."

BIOGRAPHY

JEAN IRIS MURDOCH WAS BORN IN Dublin, but her upbringing was purely English: Her father was a civil servant who sent her to private schools in London from the age of thirteen. At Oxford she became fascinated with continental philosophy; and when she met Jean-Paul Sartre, Simone de Beauvoir, and other French intellectuals after leaving Oxford, she developed what would become her lifelong preoccupations: the need to define one's sense of morality and the certainty that this task must be accomplished not in isolation but in the round, giving others' lives their due.

At first, while teaching philosophy at Oxford, Murdoch published a critical study of Sartre, but then she abruptly changed her course. In 1954, she came out with her first novel, *Under the Net*, which placed her work in the somewhat inglorious tradition of novels by philosophers. Some critics noted that *Under the Net* was particularly reminiscent of Samuel Beckett's darkly comic *Murphy*.

Murdoch has become one of the most prolific novelists in history. In addition to her twenty-six novels, most of which run to five hundred pages or more, she has produced seven plays, eight books of nonfiction, and even a volume of poetry. Queen Elizabeth named her a peer of the realm in 1987. She now lives in Oxford with her husband, John Bayley, a literary critic.

NEXT ON THE READING LIST: A. S. Byatt, Kazuo Ishiguro, Edna O'Brien, Muriel Spark, Graham Swift, William Trevor, John Updike, Fay Weldon

V. S. Naipaul

(b. August 17, 1932)

"For sheer abundance of talent, there can hardly be a writer alive who surpasses V. S. Naipaul. Whatever we may want in a novelist is to be found in his books: an almost Conradian gift for tensing a story, a serious involvement with human issues, a supple English prose, a hard-edged wit, a personal vision of things. Best of all, he is a novelist unafraid of using his brains."
—Irving Howe, New York Times

The Mystic Masseur (DEUTSCH, 1957; VANGUARD, 1959) • Naipaul's first published work tells the story of Ganesh Ransumair, an impoverished native of Trinidad who rises to fame and wealth through the skillful exploitation of his dubious talents as a masseur, literary fantasist, publicist, and religious mystic. Ganesh's entry into Trinidadian politics, however, proves to be his downfall. Naipaul's deft use of dialect and sardonic yet affectionate tone were widely praised by critics.

The Suffrage of Elvira (DEUTSCH, 1958; KNOPF, 1982) • The small Trinidadian town of Elvira suffers the attentions of a political candidate from the island's capital, Port of Spain, when he moves to Elvira in an attempt to purchase a seat in Trinidad's Legislative Council. Naipaul's second novel was praised for its colorful characterizations though criticized for its uneven narrative and episodic structure.

Miguel Street (DEUTSCH, 1959; VANGUARD, 1960) • Actually Naipaul's earliest work of fiction, this book was withheld by Naipaul until he was satisfied as to its completeness. It's a collection of seventeen stories whose characters Naipaul modeled on people he knew as a youth in Port of Spain. Reviewers faulted *Miguel Street* for some abruptness in the unfolding of its plot, but in general they saluted Naipaul for improvements in his sense of narrative tone and perspective.

* A House for Mr. Biswas (DEUTSCH, 1961; McGRAW-HILL, 1962; REVISED, KNOPF, 1983) • Naipaul's great comic novel chronicles the story of Mr. Biswas, a journalist and would-be fiction writer whose lifelong struggle to own his own house comes to represent a universal human predicament. A sympathetic character loosely modeled on Naipaul's own father, Mr. Biswas struggles to assert himself against the formidable influence of his wife's extended family. Teeming with exotic characters and played out in both rural and urban settings on Trinidad, this novel catalyzed Naipaul's growing reputation as a literary master. Some reviewers of Naipaul's later books, with their increasingly restricted scope and somewhat bitter tone, came to regard the exuberant Dickensian nature of *A House for Mr. Biswas* with nostalgic affection. Naipaul himself appears to share this view, writing in a foreword to the 1983 edition that he has "no higher literary ambition than to write a piece of comedy that might complement or match this early book."

> *"If the silting-up of the Thames coincided with a freak monsoon, causing massive flooding in all parts of South London, the first book I would rescue from my library would be* A House for Mr. Biswas." (*Paul Theroux*, New York Times)

Mr. Stone and the Knights Companion (DEUTSCH, 1963; MACMILLAN, 1964) • Written while Naipaul was living in India, this is his first novel with an English setting. It tells the story of Mr. Stone, a London bachelor who attempts to renew his life through marriage and also a good-works project called the Knights Companion, which aids retired employees of his company. The book's narrow focus on Stone's internal thoughts and feelings, however, makes it a slow read.

The Mimic Men (MACMILLAN, 1967) • This novel of colonial politics is written as the memoir of Ralph Singh, a politician from the small Caribbean island of Isabella who's exiled to London after his tenure in office comes to a disgraceful end. Praised for its astute analysis of the personal and political consequences of imperialism, *The Mimic Men* signaled a new direction in Naipaul's writing, away from the comic mode of his earlier work and toward more overtly political themes.

A Flag on the Island (MACMILLAN, 1967) • This collection of short stories written between 1950 and 1962 includes Naipaul's earliest work of published fiction, "The Mourners," written while he was still in his teens. It also features some satires from the 1960s that reveal his early talent for irony and deadpan comedy.

In a Free State (KNOPF, 1971) • This Booker Prize winner contains a prologue, an epilogue, and two short stories in addition to the title novella. Each part develops the principal theme that had, by this time, come to dominate Naipaul's mature vision: displacement in the postcolonial world. The novella follows two British expatriates who flee by car from the capital of an East African nation in political turmoil. Its violent conclusion demonstrates Naipaul's willingness to consider the sometimes ugly consequences of revolutionary ideology. The simple plot and straightforward narrative make for a unified and consistent tale but also one that lacks some of the colorful and vivid characterization one expects to find in a Naipaul story.

Guerrillas (KNOPF, 1975) • This widely praised novel, which did much to expand Naipaul's readership in the United States, examines nationalist and racial politics in the Caribbean using three protagonists: a white liberal, Roche; his British girlfriend, Jane; and a black nationalist, Jimmy Ahmed, whom Naipaul modeled on the controversial Trinidadian revolutionary leader Abdul Malik. Praised for its penetrating psychological profiles yet faulted for its bleak vision, Naipaul's novel provides a portrait of liberal European outsiders trying—unsuccessfully—to negotiate the often paranoid politics of the Caribbean. According to Paul Theroux in the *New York Times,* "*Guerrillas* is one of Naipaul's most complex books; it is certainly his most suspenseful, a series of shocks, like a shroud slowly unwound from a bloody corpse, showing the damaged—and familiar—face last."

✳ A Bend in the River (KNOPF, 1979) • Critics generally consider this novel the best of Naipaul's later fiction. It's the first-person account of Salim, an Indian merchant in East Africa who becomes yet another casualty of imperialism when the world falls apart around him. Suffused with melancholy and peopled with a cast of typically Naipaulian characters—disaffected expatriates, survival-hardened outsiders, native sons with grandiose nationalist visions—*A Bend in the River* has been described by critics as a postcolonial *Heart of Darkness,* with Africans assuming the roles Conrad had earlier assigned to Europeans. In particular, the enigmatic character of the African president, said to be modeled on Mobutu, becomes a particularly chilling latter-day Kurtz.

> "A Bend in the River...*proves once more that Naipaul is incomparably well situated and equipped to bring us news of one of the contemporary world's great subjects—the mingling of its peoples.*" (*John Updike,* The New Yorker)

The Enigma of Arrival (KNOPF, 1987) • According to Salman Rushdie, "it is impossible not to see" the first-person narrator of this book as the author himself. He's a writer, an immigrant to Britain, who leaves London to live on the grounds of a decaying estate in Wiltshire, from whose pastoral setting he looks back on his life. *The Enigma of Arrival* weaves together excellent landscape descriptions with sardonic assessments of the writer's often lonely life and those of his Wiltshire neighbors. "It is one of the saddest books I have read in a long while," Rushdie wrote, "its tone one of unbroken melancholy."

A Way in the World: A Sequence (KNOPF, 1994) • This isn't a traditional work of fiction but rather an extended series of nine narratives ranging from personal reflection to historical inquiry. The first traces the rise and tragic demise of Blair, a gifted black Trinidadian who becomes a financial adviser to newly independent (but enduringly corrupt) third-world governments. Other narratives chronicle the lives of three historical figures: Christopher Columbus, Sir Walter Raleigh, and the Venezuelan revolutionary Francisco Miranda. The book's complex structure and unorthodox blend of themes made for a mixed critical reception. Some reviewers said the book lacked coherence, while others enjoyed its shifting perspective and overall sophistication. Writing in the *New York Times,* Brent Staples called *A Way in the*

World "a distinguished book even by Naipaulian standards, a bewitching piece of work by a mind at the peak of its abilities."

BIOGRAPHY

VIDIADHAR SURAJPRASAD NAIPAUL was born in 1932 at Lion House, his mother's ancestral estate in rural Trinidad. His youth was spent in the small town of Chaguanas and in Trinidad's capital, Port of Spain. An excellent student, Naipaul won a scholarship to attend University College, Oxford. He left for England in 1950 and has lived there ever since. After earning a degree in English in 1954, he set to work, determined to make a living as a writer. He worked at the BBC while penning his first few fictional works, all based on his life in Trinidad.

Naipaul's breakthrough came in 1961, with the publication of *A House for Mr. Biswas*, the comic novel that secured his reputation as a major novelist. Just after completing work on this novel, Naipaul made the first of several extended trips, beginning a pattern that would find him making such journeys—and writing about them—every other year or so. Naipaul's seven-month trip to the West Indies produced the nonfiction account *The Middle Passage* (1962). A yearlong trip to India in 1962, however, proved to be a great disappointment. Naipaul had expected to rediscover his Indian roots but instead became disillusioned with the poverty, squalor, and stultifying rigidities of the Indian caste system. In 1964 he published an extremely critical account of his Indian trip, *An Area of Darkness*. At this critical juncture in his life, Naipaul felt that he didn't quite belong anywhere—not in London, where he had made his home, or in India, and certainly not in his native Trinidad.

Following yet another trip, this one to Uganda in 1965, Naipaul wrote a short novel, *The Mimic Men*, that transformed his own "homelessness" into what would become the principal theme of his mature work: the political and psychological alienation prevalent in newly independent third-world nations. His acclaimed works of the 1970s—*In a Free State, Guerrillas*, and the masterful *A Bend in the River*—all developed various dimensions of this central theme. Naipaul's dedication to such a politically charged subject has brought him both controversy and acclaim. Some critics have objected to what they see as his excessively pessimistic assessment of third-world possibilities, yet supporters praise his incisive intelligence, which punctures all pretensions, and his relentless exploration of the sentiments and ideas that motivate his characters to act as they do.

NEXT ON THE READING LIST: Nadine Gordimer, Kazuo Ishiguro, Milan Kundera, Doris Lessing, David Lodge, Naguib Mahfouz, Salman Rushdie

Gloria Naylor
(b. January 25, 1950)

"Naylor is not afraid to grapple with life's big subjects: sex, birth, love, death, grief. Her women feel deeply, and she unflinchingly transcribes their emotions.... Naylor's potency wells up from her language. With prose as rich as poetry, a passage will suddenly take off and sing like a spiritual."
—Deirdre Donahue, Washington Post

* The Women of Brewster Place (VIKING, 1982) • Set in a poor urban housing project, Naylor's debut novel introduces seven women of varying ages and backgrounds who are nonetheless equally burdened because they're all black and female. The tenants' association that they form provides them with a badly needed sense of community, but the consequences of a brutal hate crime soon test their collective resolve. Reviewers quickly recognized Naylor's talent, and the novel won an American Book Award.

> *"Even if Gloria Naylor's first novel were not the emotionally satisfying and technically accomplished book that it is, her decision to set it on Brewster Place, a [stereotypical] one-street 'ghetto,' would have been courageous. What is marvelous, however, is that she doubled her own dare by leaving in the predictable landmarks, the archetypal characters, the usual clues, and made the whole thing work."* (Susan Bolotin, New York Times)

Linden Hills (TICKNOR & FIELDS, 1985) • In this novel, Naylor comments allegorically on decadence among the upwardly mobile black middle class. Founded during the early nineteenth century as a sanctuary for prosperous blacks, Linden Hills has become an affluent suburb controlled by the founder's satanic great-great-grandson. In fact, the town's vertical geography intentionally mimics that of Dante's Hell. As Lester and Willie make their way, working at odd jobs, from the top of the town to the bottom, they observe residents who are increasingly emotionally and morally bankrupt, particularly in their rejection of their racial heritage. "Although Miss Naylor has not been completely successful in adapting the *Inferno*," Mel Watkins wrote in the *New York Times*, "she has shown a willingness to expand her fictional realm and to take risks. *[Linden Hills]* is a fascinating departure for Miss Naylor, as well as a provocative, iconoclastic novel about a seldom-addressed subject."

Mama Day (TICKNOR & FIELDS, 1988) • Protected by the sea, the black inhabitants of Willow Springs, an isolated island on the border between South Carolina and Georgia, have retained a great deal of their ancestor's African culture, especially their religious traditions. When Cocoa and her husband, George, both jaded New Yorkers, come to Willow Springs to visit Cocoa's grandmother—and Cocoa becomes seriously ill—only her great-aunt, a witch known as Mama Day, can save her. Reviewers admired Naylor's rendering of southern idiom and her use of folklore to advance the plot, which reminded many of *The Tempest.* According to *Publishers Weekly*, Naylor "illustrates with convincing simplicity and clear-sighted intelligence the magical interconnectedness of people with nature, with God, and with each other."

Bailey's Cafe (HARCOURT BRACE JOVANOVICH, 1992) • Inspired by Edith Wharton's *The House of Mirth*, Naylor's fourth novel explores female sexuality and the ways in which women are defined by social standards. Most of the customers who frequent Bailey's Cafe hope to find some measure of solace there despite the racial and sexual injustice with which they're daily confronted. Eve, who runs the boarding house next door, is famous for healing desperate yet strong-willed female boarders. The most memorable character, however, is Miss Maples, a male transvestite who arrives at Bailey's Cafe with a doctorate in mathematics from Stanford but few career prospects. Dan Wakefield, writing in the *New York Times*, called *Bailey's Cafe* a "virtuoso orchestration of survival, suffering, courage, and humor."

BIOGRAPHY

THE OLDEST OF THREE DAUGHTERS, Gloria Naylor was born in Queens, New York. Her father, a transit worker, and her mother, a telephone operator, had worked as sharecroppers in Mississippi before relocating to New York City, where they hoped to find better educations for their children. Although quiet as a child, the precocious Naylor grew into a strong-willed teenager who, after graduating from high school, defied her father by refusing to attend the college he had chosen for her.

After spending seven years as a missionary for the Jehovah's Witnesses, Naylor moved back to New York City, working as a telephone operator at several Manhattan hotels. Meanwhile, she enrolled at Brooklyn College, graduating in 1981 with a bachelor's degree in English. Naylor's first published fiction, "A Life on Beekman Place," appeared in *Essence* in March 1979. Another story, "When Mama Comes to Call," appeared in August 1982. Both later became chapters in *The Women of Brewster Place.* Between 1981 and 1983, Naylor continued her academic career at Yale, where she earned a master's degree in African-American studies while simultaneously finishing her second novel, *Linden Hills.*

Naylor has been a persistent critic of what she calls "the historical tendency to look upon the output of black writers as not really American literature." Her own work, she told *Publishers Weekly*, attempts to "articulate experiences that want articulating—for those readers who reflect the subject matter, black readers, and for those who don't, basically white middle-class readers."

NEXT ON THE READING LIST: Bebe Moore Campbell, Charles Johnson, Jamaica Kincaid, Terry McMillan, Toni Morrison, Amy Tan, Alice Walker

John Nichols
(b. July 23, 1940)

"[Nichols] reminds us of the love and laughter, the courage it takes to be honest, caring human beings in an age when greed and self-fulfillment seem synonymous."
—*Norbert Blei,* Chicago Tribune

The Sterile Cuckoo (McKay, 1965) • In Nichols' first novel, a collegiate love story, narrator Jerry Payne falls for the funny, unpredictable, and quite mixed-up Pookie Adams. As Nichols follows the blossoming and eventual dissolution of their romance, he pays particular attention to the then-topical issue of should we or shouldn't we? Critics were divided: In the *Saturday Review*, Granville Hicks called *The Sterile Cuckoo* "the best of many novels I have recently read about sex and the younger generation." Meanwhile, Charles Shapiro, also writing in the *Saturday Review*, tossed the book aside as "possibly the feeblest pop college novel to date."

The Wizard of Loneliness (Putnam, 1966) • The title character, a precocious eleven-year-old named Wendall Oler, is wrenched away from his friends and shipped to a small town in Vermont to spend the later years of World War II with his grandparents. Eventually, Wendall's loneliness subsides as he becomes integrated into the life of the community, which seems to have more than its share of oddball, offbeat characters. Praising the early chapters of the novel, *New York Times* reviewer Thomas J. Fleming wrote that "Mr. Nichols has remarkable insight into life's crazy blend of comedy and tragedy," yet Fleming also pointed out that Nichols loses control after the first hundred pages or so. "It is too bad the author did not hang on for another rewrite," Fleming concluded.

* The Milagro Beanfield War (Holt, Rinehart & Winston, 1974) • In Nichols's best-known novel, a small act—Joe Mondragon's impulsive decision to divert water into a beanfield once owned by his father—has momentous consequences. Mondragon's subsequent assertion of his right to that water provokes a latter-day peasant rebellion in the New Mexico town of Milagro, where corrupt politicians and greedy developers have been carving up the land for years.

> *"Nichols has written a bawdy, slangy, modern proletarian novel that is [consistently entertaining] while at the same time it manages to make funny-serious sense out of a contemporary situation of endured injustice and imminent violence."* (Choice)

The Magic Journey (HOLT, RINEHART & WINSTON, 1978) • The second novel in Nichols's New Mexico Trilogy takes place in Chamisaville, a small southwestern town that has been transformed by real estate developers into "the playground of the Land of Enchantment." Its original Chicano inhabitants are, of course, less than enchanted. "Unlike *The Milagro Beanfield War*, in which humor and absurdity prevailed, this work asks to be taken seriously," Jeffrey Burke wrote in *Harper's*. Most reviewers found it too preachy.

A Ghost in the Music (HOLT, RINEHART & WINSTON, 1979) • A B-movie production company hires stuntman Bart Darling to make a difficult parachute jump into a rugged gorge of the Rio Grande. His pregnant girlfriend, Lorraine, can't stand the pressure, so Bart flies in his son, Marcel, from New York to help Lorraine cope. The author's primary focus, however, is on the problematic father-son relationship. "Nichols has dropped the fantasy, polished the eye-popping phrases..., and returned to his roots," Joel Swerdlow wrote in the *Washington Post*, mildly praising the novel. But Al Barozzi, writing in *Best Sellers*, hated it: "Nichols's talents have failed him.... The book has nothing to offer: no plot, no characters, no style, no elevating ideas."

The Nirvana Blues (HOLT, RINEHART & WINSTON, 1981) • The final volume of Nichols's New Mexico Trilogy chronicles four days in the life of Chamisaville garbageman Joe Miniver. When a box of pure cocaine falls into his hands, Joe thinks that he's finally found the sixty thousand dollars he needs to buy land that he covets. Sadly, the illicit nature of Joe's sudden wealth corrupts his relationships with both the land and other people. Reviewers had mixed opinions: Lois Bragg in *Best Sellers* called the book "much ado about nothing." However, in the *Fort Worth Star-Telegram*, Frank Wilson hailed *The Nirvana Blues* as "the best novel published in America this year.... The trilogy itself can only be regarded as the greatest literary effort by an American in decades."

An Elegy for September (HOLT, 1992) • This short novel encompasses the love affair that results when a nineteen-year-old woman writes a fan letter to a fifty-one-year-old author going through his second divorce. The nameless protagonists ("he" and "she") enjoy a passionate month of September, but the man, although rejuvenated, ultimately resists further commitment. *Chicago Tribune* reviewer Nicholas Delbanco offered qualified praises for the book, noting that "there's a certain edge to some of the dialogue, and much of the nature writing is first-rate." However, he added, "the language of the love affair is often simply silly."

Conjugal Bliss: A Comedy of Marital Arts (HOLT, 1994) • Roger and Zelda get married, but they don't get along. From Roger's point of view, Zelda the sexy siren has become Zelda the wife from Hell. For example, she stops working and instead spends her time spending his money, mostly on garish redecorating. When Roger visits a former lover dying of cancer, Zelda explodes in a jealous rage. Sometimes the antics are funny and sometimes— as when Roger stops visiting the hospital and the friend dies—they're not. "Despite its intimate subject matter, *Conjugal Bliss* feels generic—in fact, it feels as if we've read it before—and the mocking note on which it concludes raises the unsettling possibility that the author himself doesn't take it all that seriously," Wendy Smith wrote in the *New York Times*.

BIOGRAPHY

AFTER JOHN NICHOLS'S MOTHER died when he was two, his father, a professor of psychology, moved around a lot—from Berkeley, California, where Nichols was born, to Vermont, Connecticut, New York, Virginia, and Washington, D.C. The only place that Nichols felt at home, he has said, was his grandparents' house in Mastic, Long Island, where boxes full of treasured artifacts made him deeply aware of his family history. Furthermore, the house's surrounding landscape of ocean, forest, and field awakened in him a love for the natural world that became an ongoing source of artistic inspiration.

Nichols spent the summer that he turned seventeen in and around Taos, New Mexico, where he worked at a number of odd jobs and learned Spanish. So affected was he by this experience that he found it difficult to return east. But he did, finishing prep school in Connecticut and then earning his B.A. from Hamilton College in Clinton, New York. Following his college graduation in 1962, Nichols spent a year living with some relatives in Barcelona, where he improved his Spanish, became acquainted with the work of leftist Mexican muralists Diego Rivera and David Siqueiros, and worked on his first novel. *The Sterile Cuckoo* was published in 1965 and made into a popular film starring Liza Minnelli three years later.

The late 1960s were a tumultuous time for a dissatisfied and restless Nichols. His close involvement with the anti–Vietnam War movement and various other social causes resulted, he later said, in the disintegration of his writing into "shrill, polemical, nihilistic tracts." In 1968, on the day that Martin Luther King Jr. was shot, Nichols fled to the Southwest to reestablish his ties with the region that had so affected him as a youth. A year later, he settled in the small New Mexican town of Upper Ranchitos, where he still lives. Nichols spent a great deal of time fishing for trout, remodeling his house, and chopping wood—while making repeated, and often unsuccessful, attempts to write a novel representative of his New

Mexican experiences. The 1974 publication of *The Milagro Beanfield War* (later the basis of a 1988 feature film directed by Robert Redford) was the greatest artistic fruit of that period.

NEXT ON THE READING LIST: Joan Didion, Louise Erdrich, Carlos Fuentes, Barbara Kingsolver, Thomas McGuane, Leslie Marmon Silko

---

Joyce Carol Oates
(b. June 16, 1938)

"Joyce Carol Oates is a 'popular' novelist because her stories are suspenseful (and the suspense is never fake: The horror will really come, as well as, sometimes, the triumph), because her sex scenes are steamy, and because when she describes a place, you think you're there."
—*John Gardner*, New York Times

By the North Gate (VANGUARD, 1963) • Oates sets these stories, written during her undergraduate years, in Eden County, New York. The name is meant to be ironic because Eden County is certainly not paradise. As one critic pointed out, the collection, which was generally praised, "borrows its title from the point of view of an Ezra Pound character condemned to service at a bleak outpost."

With Shuddering Fall (VANGUARD, 1964) • Back in town to bury his hated father, stock-car racer Shar Rule begins a destructive romance with eighteen-year-old Karen Herz. Oates then introduces religion as an important theme when Karen's father, like Abraham, receives a message from God instructing him to sacrifice his (potential) son-in-law. In the *New York Times*, John Knowles praised the "clarity, grace, and intelligence of the writing," but in *Harper's* H. G. Jackson called Oates's prose "hysterically incoherent."

Upon the Sweeping Flood (VANGUARD, 1966) • These psychological stories confirm Oates's taste for independent, sometimes violent young heroines of limited means and opportunity. Because many of these tales feature men from the city preying on country girls, critics began to view Oates as a regional writer in the manner of William Faulkner and Flannery O'Connor.

A Garden of Earthly Delights (VANGUARD, 1967) • Clara, a migrant worker, finally escapes the hardships of that itinerant seasonal life to settle down in

Eden County. However, when her lover abandons both her and their child, she's forced to become the mistress (and later the wife) of the county's most wealthy and powerful man. "*The Garden of Earthly Delights* has its narrative so overlaid by patterns and inevitabilities," complained the *Times Literary Supplement*, "that its account of real life is distorted."

Expensive People (VANGUARD, 1968) • Richard Everett writes this first-person memoir just prior to killing himself. We learn soon enough that Richard's relationship with his mother, Nada, has driven him mad and sent him on a killing spree, culminating in his mother's murder. Despite the admittedly odd plot, Martin Price wrote in the *Yale Review* that "this vision of the American family and the larger patterns of our suburban subculture has a somewhat tiresome familiarity."

✱ them (VANGUARD, 1969) • This winner of a National Book Award chronicles three decades in the lives of Loretta Wendall and her children, Jules and Maureen. The story, set mostly in Detroit, opens with the murder of sixteen-year-old Loretta's lover (by her brother) and her subsequent marriage to policeman Howard Wendall, who helped her cover up the crime. Later, Howard, too, meets his maker, after which the novel focuses on Loretta's children as they struggle to free themselves from the limitations of their poverty.

> "*Miss Oates writes a vehement, voluminous, kaleidoscopic novel, more deeply rooted in social observation than current fiction usually tends to be.*" (*Robert M. Adams*, New York Times)

The Wheel of Love (VANGUARD, 1970) • In this collection of stories, Oates writes of marriage and its viability in the modern world. For example, "I Was in Love" presents the first-person account of a woman, stuck in an unsatisfying marriage, who has an affair that distresses and confuses her. According to Charles Lam Markmann in *The Nation*, "Every one of these twenty stories is at the very least a respectable creation, and a surprising number deserve to be called accomplished in every sense of that word."

Wonderland (VANGUARD, 1971) • As well as marriage and love, Oates is fond of murder and suicide. Jesse Harte's father slaughters his family (Jesse is only wounded), then kills himself. Subsequently, Jesse overcomes drug addiction, alcoholism, homosexuality, cannibalism, castration, and the assassination of President Kennedy to finish medical school and become a brilliant neurosurgeon. *Partisan Review* called *Wonderland* the "painful unpeeling" of a quintessentially American hero; however, other critics found this novel's pessimism nearly unbearable.

Marriages and Infidelities (VANGUARD, 1972) • In this collection, Oates is apparently hard at work redefining marriage. Yet, given the unfortunate circumstances of her characters, one suspects that she secretly wants to do away with the institution entirely. "To read Oates is to cross an emotional minefield, to be stunned to the soul by multiple explosions, but to emerge to safety again with the skull ringing with shocked revelation and clarity," S. K. Oberbeck wrote in the *Washington Post.*

Do with Me What You Will (VANGUARD, 1973) • The first two sections of this novel recount the early lives of introspective Elena Howe, married to criminal lawyer Marvin Howe at seventeen years of age, and Jack Morrissey, son of Marvin's most famous client. In the third section, of course, Jack and Elena fall in love. "The novel has its flaws, like most big efforts," Sara Sanborn wrote in *The Nation,* "but they are scarcely worth discussing next to its achievement."

The Hungry Ghosts: Seven Allusive Comedies (BLACK SPARROW, 1974) • Here Oates viciously satirizes writers, critics, poets, and other denizens of the intellectual underworld. Even her story titles—"Democracy in America," "The Birth of Tragedy"—suggest the profoundness of her vitriol. "*The Hungry Ghosts* crackles with tension and wit, and its subjects—the foibles of academia and the literati—are tantalizing," John Alfred Avant wrote in *The New Republic.*

The Goddess and Other Women (VANGUARD, 1974) • "I looked forward to another big book of Oates's stories," John Alfred Avant wrote in *The New Republic* just seven months after his glowing review of *The Hungry Ghosts* appeared, "but *The Goddess and Other Women* is Oates at her worst." Most reviewers found only three of its twenty-five stories about molestation, adultery, rape, and rage worth reading. "There's no artistic growth to witness and little impetus to finish the book," Avant added.

* Where Are You Going, Where Have You Been?: Stories of Young America (FAWCETT, 1974; REVISED, RUTGERS UNIVERSITY, 1994) • The title story in this anthology is one of Oates's best-known works. Originally published in 1966, it tells the story of fifteen-year-old Connie and her sexual awakening courtesy of thirty-year-old Arnold Friend, who wants to take her for a ride in his convertible. Although she declines, the story ends with the suggestion that Arnold will rape and possibly murder her.

> "It has been left to Joyce Carol Oates, a writer who seems to know a great deal about the underside of America, to guide us—splendidly—down the dark passages and [she] returns to tell us what we have known but never wanted to admit: Women also have dark hearts." (Marian Engel, New York Times)

The Poisoned Kiss and Other Stories from the Portuguese (VANGUARD, 1975) • Oates has suggested that she was compelled to write these short stories— "thoroughly uncharacteristic," according to Phoebe-Lou Adams in the

Atlantic Monthly—by the spirit Fernandes, a Portuguese writer from an alternate reality. "Fernandes appears to have read a bit of Borges," Adams continued, "but the business is otherwise quite unaccountable." According to Julian Barnes, writing in *The New Statesman*, "Some of the pieces are not so much brief as fugitive. But the longer ones…have scale enough and a spare, intriguing power."

The Assassins: A Book of Hours (VANGUARD, 1975) • The assassination of ultra-right-winger Andrew Petrie dislocates the lives of his young wife, Yvonne, and his brothers, Hugh and Stephen—all in different ways. The plot, already confusing, is made even more so by the awkward use of dreams and flashbacks. In the end, two of the three central characters die (one commits suicide, the other is murdered) and the third wanders off on a religious quest. "Joyce Carol Oates has subtitled her novel *A Book of Hours*," J. D. O'Hara wrote in the *New York Times*. "And painfully exasperating hours they are, every one of them."

Childwold (VANGUARD, 1976) • The impoverished Bartletts eke out a meager existence on their deteriorating Eden County farm. Their situation appears to improve when Fitz John Kasch falls in love with fourteen-year-old Laney Bartlett—then he subsequently marries Laney's mother, Arlene. In Oates's novels, these changes are always for the worse. In *The New Republic*, Irene H. Chayes called *Childwold* "comparable to the best of [Oates's] short stories," yet in *The New Yorker* Susan Lardner wrote that the novel was "distinctly languid."

Crossing the Border (VANGUARD, 1976) • The first fourteen stories in this collection depict the struggles of Evan and Renée Maynard to keep their sinking marriage afloat. The final story, "River Rising," reveals their fate. "Oates has produced another fine set of tales—witty, wily, and variegated," Harold Beaver wrote in the *Times Literary Supplement.*

Night-Side (VANGUARD, 1977) • The paranormal tales in this collection demonstrate Oates's affection for the eerier work of Poe and Hawthorne. Although her characters are all haunted people, they suffer less from troublesome ghosts than from madness and mental disorder. According to *Commonweal* critic Robert Phillips, "[These] are interior tales—stories of individuals haunted by their own uneasiness and anxieties. What is striking is how Ms. Oates manages to reconstruct the dreams and nightmares which afflict us all."

Son of the Morning (VANGUARD, 1978) • Eden County evangelist Nathan Vickery believes that God has chosen him to become one with the Christ of the Second Coming. His faith gives him a fanatic energy, but that isn't enough to overcome the sins of the flesh that cause his downfall and the death of his only friend. Writing in the *Yale Review*, Maureen Howard complained of "too many sermons so much like the Sunday morning fare on television," but Victoria Glendinning in the *New York Times* called *Son of the Morning* "a rich dish that will be devoured by the hungry [Oates] faithful.... Clearly well-researched, it could serve as the basis for a sociological study of the...Pentecostal religion."

Unholy Loves (VANGUARD, 1979) • Described by A. G. Mojtabai in the *New York Times* as a "ferocious comedy," this satire of academic life opens with the arrival at Woodslee College of septuagenarian British poet Albert St. Dennis. We soon learn that St. Dennis's appointment as Distinguished Professor of Poetry has made the rest of the Woodslee faculty insanely jealous. "Miss Oates...is not a careful craftsman and, I suspect, has no great desire to be one," Mojtabai continued. "[Yet] it is a tribute to Miss Oates that even her lightly sketched characters seem so interesting."

Bellefleur (DUTTON, 1980) • This huge novel marked the beginning of Oates's experimentation with the Gothic genre. The Bellefleur family, cursed with passion and greed, settles in the Adirondack Mountains of New York, where the second of six generations builds a castle (also called Bellefleur) to celebrate the family's power. There are frighteningly vivid scenes of violence, such as the stoning of a young boy, and cameo appearances by real historical figures (Oates's Lincoln fakes his own assassination to escape the pressures of public life). "*Bellefleur* is simply brilliant," John Gardner wrote in the *New York Times*, "a medieval allegory of *caritas versus cupiditas*, love and selflessness versus pride and selfishness."

A Sentimental Education (DUTTON, 1980) • Although all the characters in these stories attempt to shield themselves from one truth or another, they cannot, and each story ends with a revelation. Sadly, nobody liked them. "All six stories are plotless rambles through emotional terrain as bleak and autumnal as the settings in which they are cast," David Bell wrote in the *Saturday Review*. Robert Kiely, writing in the *New York Times*, agreed: "Their extraordinary and often violent behavior notwithstanding, the characters in these stories are not very interesting.... One looks in vain for motivation, for reasoning or feeling of even the most rudimentary kind."

Angel of Light (DUTTON, 1981) • The Halleck children, Owen and Kirsten, believing that they're instruments of God's justice on earth, conclude that they must avenge their politician father's death. The plot is an old one—Aeschylus used it for the *Oresteia*—and in Oates's hands it's just as violent and tragic. "*[Angel of Light]* is a complex, dense, multilayered work that unfolds with all the profound implications of a Greek tragedy," Susan Wood observed in the *Washington Post*. "Yet Oates seems at last to have in control two of the weaknesses that have sometimes been the result of her considerable ambition and energy—a feverish, overwritten prose style and a heavy-handed use of symbolism."

A Bloodsmoor Romance (DUTTON, 1982) • This evocation of nineteenth-century Romanticism, which many reviewers took to be a six-hundred-page joke, follows the five Zinn sisters of Bloodsmoor, Pennsylvania, as their lives unfold during the 1870s. "The book is a feminist romance with a lot of axes to grind," Diane Johnson wrote in the *New York Times*, "and it grinds them wittily till their edges are polished to a fine sharpness." However, Denis Donoghue in the *New York Review of Books* found the novel "almost unreadable."

Mysteries of Winterthurn (DUTTON, 1984) • Brilliant young nineteenth-century detective Xavier Kilgarvan, who modestly considers himself an American Sherlock Holmes, investigates three cases during the course of this novel. Meanwhile, he becomes increasing skeptical about human nature and his old-fashioned moralistic notion that the "numerous forces for Good" will inevitably prevail. "It is easy enough to identify the typical lurid three-decker novel of the last century as Miss Oates's starting point," Patricia Craig pointed out in the *New York Times*. "But at times it's unclear to the reader whether she's reproducing a nineteenth-century detective novel, overturning it, expanding it, or sending it up."

Last Days (DUTTON, 1984) • Most of the stories in this collection feature characters who have been abandoned by men. The fathers here are particularly predatory and frightening, especially to their children. *Publishers Weekly* called these tales "excessive, overdone, and overwrought.... At the same time, however, they are often compelling in a way that sets the author distinctively apart." In the *Washington Post,* Jay Parini singled out "The Witness" and "My Warszawa: 1980," which won an O. Henry Award, as "equal to [Oates's] best previous work."

Solstice (DUTTON, 1985) • Hoping to escape the pain of her failed marriage, Monica Jensen accepts a job as an English teacher at a prep school in Bucks County, Pennsylvania. She soon becomes friendly with the capricious and aloof Sheila Trask, an older artist who eventually comes to overshadow all the other people in Monica's life, including the young lawyer whom she's been dating. Michael F. Harper in the *Los Angeles Times* compared reading *Solstice* to "the illusion of being trapped in someone else's mind, and Oates has made it a powerful and vertiginous experience." However, Jonathan Yardley in the *Washington Post* noted that "it's characteristic of the book's disorganization and carelessness that it is littered with parenthetical asides, some of them running to a paragraph or more, that seem to have been injected as hasty afterthoughts by a writer too hurried to pause and weave things together."

Marya: A Life (DUTTON, 1986) • The title character, a writer and teacher in her thirties, searches for the alcoholic mother who abused and then abandoned her when she was eight. Through flashbacks we learn that Marya's mother left her with a negligent aunt and uncle, in whose home she was sexually assaulted by her cousin until excellent grades earned her a scholarship to a state university. The critical reaction to this novel, as to much of Oates's recent work, was extremely mixed: In the *New York Times,* Mary Gordon called *Marya* Oates's "strongest book in years, uglier, grittier, less literary than *Solstice.*" On the other hand, Dorothy Allison in the *Village Voice* found it "disappointing" and "very dry."

Raven's Wing (DUTTON, 1986) • The characters in these stories are pathetic, even hopeless people, mostly of the working class, who seek control in a threatening world but never find it. In the title story, Billy quits his job rather than pay child support. After failing to get it back, he becomes fixated on a racehorse that miraculously returned to the sport after suffering a broken leg. Billy hopes that the horse will bring him luck. "Perhaps [Oates's] greatest gift—and it seems also to be the spark of her energy—is to catch a cresting emotion and ride it," Stephen Goodwin wrote in his *Washington Post* review of *Raven's Wing.*

* You Must Remember This (DUTTON, 1987) • Reviewers described this novel, Oates's seventeenth, as her most erotic yet. The characters—three generations of the Stevick family—copulate at all times of day and in all manner of setting. Moreover, this being an Oates novel, there's plenty of emotional and physical violence. The principal character is Enid, whose prizefighting uncle Felix seduces her at age fourteen.

> *"Writing in powerful, meticulous prose, Ms. Oates conjures up for the reader the physical passion shared by Felix and Enid with the same brutalizing immediacy that she lavishes on the scenes of Felix boxing in the ring. We are made to see the dark, chaotic currents of guilt, anger, and eroticism that run beneath the seemingly placid surface of the Stevicks' lower-middle-class existence." (Michiko Kakutani,* New York Times)

The Assignation (ECCO, 1988) • These "short short" stories are snapshots of characters taken at revealing moments. Some are as short as a paragraph, none more than six pages long. Of course, there's violence in them, but mostly their "plots" are mundane: prostitutes preparing for work, wives drinking with their lovers. One critic called the sketches "poetic," but *New York Times* reviewer James Atlas dismissed them as "ephemera."

American Appetites (DUTTON, 1989) • Most people simply assume that historian Ian McCullough and his wife, Glynnis, a cookbook author, are happily married. They have a college-bound daughter and a gregarious social life in their hometown of Hazelton-on-Hudson, New York. However, Ian's fiftieth birthday party reveals that all is not as it appears, and soon he's charged with Glynnis's murder. According to Robert Towers in the *New York Times,* "Oates handles all this material with the authoritative ease of an experienced novelist.... But for all of its accomplishments...*American Appetites* left me oddly disengaged."

Because It Is Bitter, and Because It Is My Heart (DUTTON, 1990) • Tormented by a bully, fourteen-year-old Iris Courtney, who's white, seeks the help of sixteen-year-old Jinx Fairchild, who's black. After Jinx accidentally kills the bully, he and Iris cover up the "crime." Subsequently, Jinx accepts a basketball scholarship and Iris marries into a wealthy academic family, but they nevertheless remain bonded to each other in unique and powerful ways. According to *New York Times* reviewer Marilynne Robinson, "The novel cherishes what is unuttered, uncountenanced, undivulged—the heart's darkness and bitterness.... Only fiction of extraordinary imaginative power could propose such a vision."

I Lock My Door upon Myself (ECCO, 1990) • Oates took the title of this novel from an 1891 painting by Belgian symbolist Fernand Khnopff that depicts a woman sitting on the porch of a farmhouse staring off into space. Oates has named this woman and given her a story: One day, uncharacteristically, Calla, a mother of three and wife of a prosperous farmer, begins an affair with trespasser Tyrell Thompson. Later, she abandons her family to accompany Tyrell on a personal quest. "A small, carefully crafted book, *I Lock My Door* possesses the same qualities as the painting that inspired it: beauty, strangeness, and the capacity to disturb," Michiko Kakutani wrote in the *New York Times*.

Heat and Other Stories (DUTTON, 1991) • Called by one critic a "study in serious literary horror," this collection of short stories reveals the frightening side of middle- and working-class domestic life. In "House Hunting," the marriage and sanity of a yuppie couple fracture after the death of their newborn. In the title story, winner of an O. Henry Award, a set of identical eleven-year-old twins want to be a single person. "Nothing has perplexed critics more about Joyce Carol Oates than her inclination to turn her prodigious talents toward the rendition of gloomy, gruesome, and macabre narratives," Mary Warner Marien wrote in the *Christian Science Monitor*.

The Rise of Life on Earth (NEW DIRECTIONS, 1991) • The year is 1961, the place Detroit, and a severe beating by her father puts eleven-year-old Kathleen Hennessy into the hospital. Befriended by nurses, she resolves to become one herself when she grows up. She does, compassionately serving others, yet she cannot escape her abuse-filled childhood, which inclines her dangerously toward violence of her own. "The cards are so thoroughly stacked against Kathleen," Jane Smiley observed in the *New York Times*, "that her case seems too extreme to be instructive. [She] seems to be struggling as hard against the author's bleak and unredeemed vision of her life as she is against that life itself."

* Black Water (DUTTON, 1992) • One might call this Oates's Chappaquiddick novel: A U.S. senator picks up a girl at a party, accidentally drives his car off a bridge, and leaves her to drown. The twist is that Oates tells the story from the drowning girl's point of view.

> *"[Oates] has never been more in control of her material than in* Black Water, *a tight, taut volume. The novel reads as though Oates went into a sustained meditative trance about the implications of the incident and emerged, a brief 160 pages later, with a stunning and singular portrait of a young woman's dying moments."* (*Judith Timson,* Maclean's)

Where Is Here? (ECCO, 1992) • These thirty-five stories, like those in *The Assignation*, are "short shorts," most but a few pages in length. Oates keeps to her usual subjects—murder, madness, heartbreak, death—and her usual characters, the down and nearly out. For example, one mother murders her children, while another simply neglects them. *New York Times* reviewer Randall Kenan liked the bits and pieces very much: "In 193 pages, Joyce Carol Oates's *Where Is Here?* serves up a dazzling assortment of fictional hors d'oeuvres. But it's not my intent to be misleading—many of these stories are quite a meal in themselves."

Foxfire: Confession of a Girl Gang (DUTTON, 1993) • In this novel, set during the 1950s, a destructive sisterhood of teenagers visits sex and violence on teachers, father figures, and other men of authority. The girls mark themselves with shoulder tattoos and rumble with the best of them until their leader, Legs Sadovsky, gets sent to reform school. Most reviewers remarked that *Foxfire* was Oates's most overtly feminist book. However, as Cynthia Kadohata pointed out in the *Los Angeles Times*, the girls "become demons themselves—violent and conniving and exuberant in their victories over the opposite sex."

Haunted: Tales of the Grotesque (DUTTON, 1994) • According to Michael Upchurch's *New York Times* review, "*Haunted*...pulls off what this author does best: exploring the tricky juncture between tattered social fabric and shaky psyche, while serving up some choice macabre moments that should please both devotees of her early stories and fans of her pseudonymous Rosamond Smith mystery novels." Some of these stories feature ghosts as sympathetic characters; others are simply "grotesque" (in Poe's sense of the word), such as "Martyrdom," which some critics have called Oates's most gruesome story yet.

* What I Lived For (DUTTON, 1994) • Jerome (Corky) Corcoran has his ego shattered when he learns that his mistress, Christina, has been conducting their affair with the knowledge and permission of her crippled husband. During the drunken weekend that follows this discovery, Corky careens through Union City (a stand-in for Buffalo), slowly becoming caught up in the mystery of why a young black woman committed suicide. His investigation into her death soon develops into a moral quest for truth.

> *"What writer in her right mind would dare to compose a novel that would allow the reader to compare it, even for a fleeting moment, to [Ulysses]? Only the audacious, pugnacious, and triumphant Joyce Carol Oates. She's pushed her art to the limits here and shown us, to paraphrase old Hemingway, that she can go a few rounds with the champion of us all."* (Alan Cheuse, Los Angeles Times)

Zombie (DUTTON, 1995) • Given Oates's fascination with gruesome, bizarre brutality, we should've expected this one: a book based on the case of Jeffrey Dahmer, the Milwaukee man who dismembered and then ate his victims. Presented as the killer's original manuscript, complete with crude line drawings and eccentric typing errors, Oates's twenty-fifth novel tells the first-person tale of Quentin, who tries to create a zombie by performing ice-pick lobotomies on his squirming victims. Writing in the *Atlanta Journal and Constitution*, Greg Johnson called *Zombie* "a virtuoso piece of literary art"; however, Steven Marcus complained in the *New York Times* that "the idea of this narrative…is more interesting than its execution."

Will You Always Love Me? (DUTTON, 1996) • All the characters in this short-story collection can expertly identify their pain, yet none has the power to relieve it. In the title story, Andrea McLure, obsessed by the rape and murder of her sister, sleeps with a man who's excited by the prospect that she might be thinking about the rape during intercourse. Kathryn Harrison in the *New York Times* called these stories "tortured examinations of crime and culpability."

First Love: A Gothic Tale (ECCO, 1996) • Given Oates's prolific output, it shouldn't be too surprising that a few of her plots get recycled—but how many stories of older male family members abusing their pubescent cousins will she write? In this one, eleven-year-old Josie, left with a great-aunt by her negligent mother, suffers ritualistic abuse at the hands of cousin Jared, a violent and disturbed seminary student. Most reviewers passed this novel off as a minor work, one calling it "trite."

We Were the Mulvaneys (DUTTON, 1996) • The Mulvaneys hail from western New York, familiar Oates territory. They seem to be the perfect family: Parents Michael and Corinne are still embarrassingly in love with each other; their children are all popular, bright, and athletic. Then daughter Marianne, a pretty cheerleader, is raped by a local boy. For the next seventeen years, the ineffectual Mulvaney men plot their revenge, yet they never achieve it. In the meantime, the family falls apart. In the *Los Angeles Times*, Beverly Lowry wrote that *We Were the Mulvaneys* "is a book that, because it fulfills its promise to 'set down the truth,' will break your heart, heal it, then break it again every time you think about it."

Man Crazy (DUTTON, 1997) • Like *The Bell Jar* and *I Never Promised You a Rose Garden, Man Crazy* charts the descent into madness of a despairing young woman. Pretty, passive, and starved for love, eighteen-year-old Ingrid Boone learns from her mother to seduce men to get what she wants. However, her express train to the Good Life is derailed when she becomes involved with Satan's Children, a cult that kidnaps and rapes juveniles. Although *Publishers Weekly* called the story "gripping," Michiko Kakutani in the *New York Times* wrote that *Man Crazy* read like a "perfunctory exercise tossed off to fill some sort of self-imposed quota."

BIOGRAPHY

JOYCE CAROL OATES GREW UP outside Buffalo, New York, in rural Erie County (later fictionalized in her novels as Eden County). She began her education in a one-room schoolhouse, later attending Williamsville Central High School, from which she graduated in 1956. In most interviews, Oates has dismissed her childhood as "dull and ordinary," yet occasionally she has contradicted herself, admitting that it was difficult and that "a great deal frightened me." She has never been more specific.

Possibly as an escape from these fears, Oates began using pictures to create an imaginary world even before she could write. Later she wrote stories that she collected in books, which she bound herself. At age fifteen, she submitted her first novel to a publisher. It was rejected as too bleak for young readers.

While majoring in English and minoring in philosophy at Syracuse University, she churned out a novel every semester and published short stories in several undergraduate literary magazines. One of these won *Mademoiselle*'s 1959 college fiction contest. A year later, Oates graduated as her class's valedictorian and began graduate work in English at the University of Wisconsin. There, she met and married Raymond Smith. When another of her stories was anthologized in *Best American Short Stories of 1961*, she chose to dedicate herself to writing rather than to the pursuit of a doctorate.

Perhaps the most prolific author of this century, Oates has composed more than one hundred books of fiction, nonfiction, poetry, and drama. She has even transformed one of her novels, *Black Water*, into an opera, albeit a poor one. Meanwhile, she has served on the English faculties of the University of Detroit (1961–67) and the University of Windsor (1967–78). Since 1978, she has been a writer-in-residence at Princeton. In 1970, when she was honored for *them*, she became the youngest writer ever to win a National Book Award for fiction. She has also been twice nominated for Pulitzer Prizes, once for *Black Water* and once for *What I Lived For*.

Notable among Oates's nonfiction work is her 1987 collection of essays, *On Boxing*, describing her fascination with the sport. She has since called a number of fights as a ringside television announcer. However, even that hasn't been enough to keep her busy. Since 1988, she has also published four mystery novels under the pseudonym Rosamond Smith, a feminization of her husband's name.

NEXT ON THE READING LIST: Margaret Atwood, Anita Brookner, E. L. Doctorow, Alice Hoffman, David Leavitt, Cormac McCarthy, Susan Sontag

---

Edna O'Brien
(b. December 15, 1936)

"Miss O'Brien's outlook is intemperate, like Irish weather. She's fond of blarney, but a bleak, literary kind, more in the mood of the later Yeats than of Celtic charm.... Her people's houses are always damp; their teeth are bad; they have no charity; their pleasures are tainted."
—*Anatole Broyard*, New York Times

* The Country Girls (KNOPF, 1960) • O'Brien's first novel—and according to many, her best—is a sort of female version of Joyce's *Portrait of the Artist as a Young Man:* a heavily autobiographical story of an Irish girl's sexual awakening and her abandonment of home. The style is plain and direct, the setting rural, and the time the 1940s—all of which make the sexual directness, when it comes, a shock.

> *"The narrowness of her life forces Kate to conceive, in self-defense, a sad roman-ticism, like a stillborn baby.... Like Kate, Miss O'Brien too sees the world through 'wronged eyes.'"* (*Anatole Broyard*, New York Times)

The Lonely Girl (RANDOM HOUSE, 1962) • O'Brien's first novel left her hero-ine, Kate, in Dublin, having recently abandoned her family's rural home-stead. This book picks up the story with Kate narrating the sexual escapades on which she and her friend Baba embark. Here, as elsewhere, O'Brien skillfully combines a prose style that would suit the *Ladies Home Journal* with a reading of life's nuances that approaches the realm of world-class literature.

Girls in Their Married Bliss (JONATHAN CAPE, 1964; SIMON & SCHUSTER, 1968) • Baba takes over the narration in this final volume of O'Brien's Country Girls Trilogy. Wilier and nervier than Kate, Baba gives a tangy reading of their married lives spiced with a few tawdry affairs: "Kate Brady and I were having a few gloomy gin fizzes up London, bemoaning the fact that nothing would ever improve, that we'd die the way we were—enough to eat, married, dissatisfied." O'Brien paints these characters, according to Mary Rourke in the *Los Angeles Times*, "with love and outrage, compassion and contempt."

August Is a Wicked Month (SIMON & SCHUSTER, 1965) • This is arguably the weakest of O'Brien's novels, perhaps because she took such great pains to break away from the style of her Country Girls Trilogy. Most noticeably, there's none of the dry, seemingly guileless wit that marked her earlier work. Ellen, an Irish divorcée, goes on holiday to the Mediterranean, where she finds herself torn between sexual longing and guilt. Meanwhile, a child's death hovers in the air like bad weather.

Casualties of Peace (SIMON & SCHUSTER, 1966) • This heavy-handed tale reads as though O'Brien had decided to adapt the central characters of *The Country Girls* to a potboiler. At its core are two women whose lives and sexual escapades intertwine violently when Willa, mistaken for Patsy, is murdered. Along with *August Is a Wicked Month*, this novel belongs to a difficult transitional stage in O'Brien's career, during which she moved from the bildungsromans of her youth to more mature works.

The Love Object (JONATHAN CAPE, 1968) • In the title story of this collection, Martha longs to be needed, but her husband no longer needs her, so she takes a lover who does. Then she finds out that the lover, rather than needing her, merely finds her pleasant. This is tough stuff to make engaging, and O'Brien not surprisingly falls short. "The tone and mood," Julian Moynahan wrote in *The New Republic*, "approach barely controlled hysteria as the man starts finding other ways of spending his free afternoons. It is all so stereotypically British." The other stories aren't much better.

A Pagan Place (KNOPF, 1970) • Another departure in style for O'Brien, this tale is told in the second person, as though by an adult talking to a younger self who is the book's protagonist. Amid a dense, utterly Irish clutter of sex and Catholicism, the young girl is beset by the revelation that her older sister is pregnant. Then the local priest begins to make advances; when she succumbs, disaster ensues. An obscure O'Brien work, but a very good one.

Zee & Co. (WEIDENFELD & NICOLSON, 1971) • This isn't a novel so much as a novelization of one of O'Brien's teleplays. In a precursor to the genre that Fay Weldon would make her own, O'Brien gives us a wife determined to take revenge on her cheating husband. "She fails at suicide," Janet Burroway wrote in *The New Statesman*, "and finally succeeds, in an orgy of improbability, with lesbianism."

Night (KNOPF, 1973) • The experimental, almost stream-of-consciousness form that O'Brien appropriates from her idol, James Joyce, works very well in this story that takes place during a single night. Mary, the caretaker of a gloomy house, is spending that night alone when her mother's ghost appears. Scenes and characters from her life float by; and, at the end of what John Updike called a "brilliant and beautiful book," Mary experiences a scaled-down version of the Scrooge epiphany, learning that life is indeed worthwhile.

A Scandalous Woman and Other Stories (HARCOURT BRACE JOVANOVICH, 1974) • In this collection, O'Brien gives us a number of takes on the grand disappointment that occurs when one's childish dreams for the future fall into decay. The title story—in which a feisty woman's spark transmutes, under the pressure of a dull marriage, into madness—is especially poignant. Writing in the *New York Times*, Julia O'Faolain said that these stories offered "the brisk and deadly pleasures of fairy tale."

Johnny I Hardly Knew You (WEIDENFELD & NICOLSON, 1977; PUBLISHED IN THE U.S. AS *I HARDLY KNEW YOU*, DOUBLEDAY, 1978) • The typical O'Brien heroine, who suffers male brutishness and longs for sexual and emotional gratification, gets some revenge here when Nora, the narrator of this pleasantly vile tale, murders her lover. For all its ugliness, the *Times Literary Supplement* thought that *Johnny I Hardly Knew You* retained "a fluency which celebrates the failure of love, and the belief that 'even the blights of love have in them such radiance that they make other happiness pale indeed.'"

Mrs. Reinhardt and Other Stories (WEIDENFELD & NICOLSON, 1978) • After enduring a great deal of hardship at her husband's hand, Mrs. Reinhardt does something rare for an O'Brien heroine: She goes back to him and finds a bit of happiness. Such is the new ground in these stories—an apparent break in O'Brien's gloom—but it's just a chink, as several of the heroines don't even get a qualified happiness. Although many reviewers considered *Mrs. Reinhardt* one of O'Brien's best collections, Frank Tuohy complained in the *Times Literary Supplement* that "a certain decorousness" often creeps into the prose.

A Rose in the Heart (DOUBLEDAY, 1979) • This collection of love stories has a hurried, harried feel; even the grammar is messy in places. But O'Brien's delicate, natural sense of ordinary pain comes through strongly, as does her appreciation for the sensory details that relieve it: the hues of flowers, the taste of beer. "What she has, and what many more highly educated, self-consciously literary writers would give their eyeteeth for," Victoria Glendinning wrote in the *New York Times*, "is a direct line between her own yeasty, mazy imaginings and her pen."

Returning (WEIDENFELD & NICOLSON, 1982) • O'Brien takes a step back in time with these stories—back to the settings and preoccupations of her own youth and her earliest stories. We visit pre- and postwar rural Ireland, peopled with peaty eccentrics, and we learn that you can't quite go home again. In several of the stories, a middle-aged woman returns to her village of birth, where she has an experience that casts a crucial childhood incident in a new light. Sara Maitland, writing in *The Spectator*, said that O'Brien "keeps her details so specific and material—smells, colours, objects rendered with a hard precision—that she saves them from soft mistiness."

A Fanatic Heart (FARRAR, STRAUS & GIROUX, 1984) • What we have here is a handful of previously published stories, a foreword by Philip Roth, and four new works by O'Brien that investigate the subject of manic love. The adulterous passion in the new stories, which are notably less vibrant than the older ones, seems especially scripted. "In these stories of English passion among top people," Julian Moynahan wrote in *The New Republic*, "Edna O'Brien manages to make the game of adultery dull and predictable."

The Country Girls Trilogy and Epilogue (FARRAR, STRAUS & GIROUX, 1986) • Appended to this collection of O'Brien's first three novels is a new epilogue in which Baba looks back on the girls' doings from a distance of twenty years. The epilogue's prose, however, is oddly forced—written, according to *New York Times* critic Anatole Broyard, with "slang, verbal jitters, and epithets—in what seems a retrospective attempt to modernize the trilogy."

The High Road (FARRAR, STRAUS & GIROUX, 1988) • It's difficult to tell whether this book is a spotty collection of stories that have been linked together or the remains of a failed episodic novel. Its plot involves an Irish woman vacationing with several other haughty, imperialist Northern Europeans on a Spanish island. There's a plot of sorts about the woman's attempt to relocate her emotions, but the work's structure prevents it from coming together. "The language here is often infused with an intense energy," Marilynne Robinson wrote in the *New York Times*, "but the form of the novel makes it difficult to know what these energies arise from or tend toward."

Lantern Slides (FARRAR, STRAUS & GIROUX, 1990) • In this collection of stories, O'Brien introduces us to a much broader set of Irish types than we usually find in her work. Here she shows us not only bog-bound widows and lunatic priests but also modern, affluent wives who engage in lifelong affairs and Irish families who go on European vacations. "O'Brien continues to display acute powers of observation in a prose that is always neat and often immaculate," wrote Louise Doughty in the *Times Literary Supplement*.

Time and Tide (FARRAR, STRAUS & GIROUX, 1992) • Nell is a middle-aged Irish woman for whom nothing ever goes right. Her husband is a monster, her lover not much better, and her parents twin specters in her life. The climax of all this misery occurs when her child dies. *Time and Tide* is an elegantly written book but an unremittingly bleak one. Writing in the *New York Times*,

Joel Conarroe observed that it "will offer shocks of recognition to anyone who has ever had a difficult parent—or been one."

House of Splendid Isolation (FARRAR, STRAUS & GIROUX, 1994) • Although O'Brien is one of the few Irish writers whose work largely ignores "the troubles," here she takes on her country's history of political violence in a story about a Republican whose wife and baby were killed before his eyes and his attempt to start life anew with another woman. Unfortunately, as Susan Salter Reynolds wrote in the *Los Angeles Times*, "all this violence will not evaporate, it gets passed on, and this is what O'Brien captures so unobtrusively: the senseless continuation of pain."

Down by the River (FARRAR, STRAUS & GIROUX, 1997) • Incest in rural Ireland is the subject here. When teenager Mary MacNamara's mother dies of cancer, her father becomes no longer able to control his emotions and longings—with disastrous results for Mary. Dan Cryer, writing in *Newsday*, called this book "psychologically astute, morally outraged and, yes, thrillingly crafted."

BIOGRAPHY

EDNA O'BRIEN'S FIRST SEVEN novels were banned in her native Ireland because of what was then considered their graphic sexual content. Yet this rejection didn't dissuade O'Brien from continuing to pursue the prevailing theme of her fiction and her life: the emotional and sexual frustrations of women, especially women in rural Ireland.

O'Brien was born and raised in Taumgraney, County Clare, in the west of Ireland. She remembers the men there as drunken and domineering, the women as saintly sufferers. Dismissing her Catholic education as suffocating and "medieval," she recalls a childhood during which she alternated between passionate, incessant prayer and gleefully committed sins. As described in *The Country Girls*, O'Brien broke free from this emotional and intellectual confinement at age fourteen when she left Country Clare for Dublin. Her discovery of the work of James Joyce led to her decision to become a writer. She took a job with the *Irish Press* in 1948; her first novel was published to wide acclaim twelve years later. Since then, she has been credited with giving first fictional expression to the psychological and physical hardships faced by women in rural Ireland.

O'Brien has been married twice and has two sons. She has lived in London for many years but has also spent significant time in New York, where she has taught creative writing at the City College of New York. Like Joyce's, however, her fictive persona remains among the green hills and stone walls of the Ireland that she left behind.

NEXT ON THE READING LIST: Beryl Bainbridge, Pat Barker, Roddy Doyle, Alison Lurie, Alice Munro, Iris Murdoch, William Trevor

Tim O'Brien
(b. October 1, 1946)

"His contribution to the literature of the [Vietnam] war has been exceptional, partly because his own experience has led to an almost unbearable share of...American guilt and shame and anguish."
—*H. Bruce Franklin,* The Progressive

If I Die in a Combat Zone, Box Me Up and Ship Me Home (DELACORTE, 1973) • Bookstores were uncertain whether to stock this title under fiction or autobiography. The first of many attempts by O'Brien to make literary sense of his experiences in Vietnam, it self-consciously blurs the distinction between truth and invention. *If I Die in a Combat Zone* has an impressionistic, postcards-from-the-front feel and "a style which is lucid, relaxed, razor-sharp, and consciously dispassionate," according to Chris Waters in *The New Statesman.*

Northern Lights (DELACORTE, 1975) • Several reviewers have remarked that O'Brien's early work suggests that he was reading too much Hemingway. In *Northern Lights* O'Brien brings the Vietnam War (literally) home, following a young soldier as he returns to his family in Minnesota. Using a style that one critic called "heavily naturalistic," O'Brien describes how the soldier, Harvey, becomes locked into a confrontation with his brother Paul, who didn't go to war. "Is it possible to read *The Sun Also Rises* too often?" asked Roger Sale in the *New York Review of Books.* He concluded in the end that O'Brien had, in fact, let Hemingway's prose "sink into him too deeply."

✳ Going After Cacciato (DELACORTE, 1978) • O'Brien's breakout book, *Going After Cacciato* won a National Book Award and established him as a writer with a unique voice. Writing in the *Chronicle Review,* Doris Grumbach said that it was, "without reservation, one of the most challenging and powerful novels to find its way into print in some time." An American soldier named Paul Berlin is assigned to a detail searching for a man named Cacciato, who went AWOL in Vietnam after declaring that he was heading for Paris. O'Brien's lost-generation-at-war theme and his phantasmagorical prose make for a challenging work that reads like a hybrid of Hemingway and Gabriel García Márquez.

"By bringing to the stark facts of war the subtle style of peace, with its layers of ambiguity, O'Brien has written a modern novel old-fashioned in its wish to be

morally exhaustive, to purge: not a war but a postwar novel." (*John Updike,* The New Yorker)

The Nuclear Age (KNOPF, 1985) • What better focus for the postwar obsession of a Vietnam vet than nuclear war? O'Brien's standard shell-shocked, daydreaming soldier-hero has here successfully worked his way back into society—with one tiny exception: He's positively nuts with bomb worry. After building an elaborate shelter, William kidnaps his family and shoves them into it. However, "Mr. O'Brien never makes William's hysteria real or convincing," Michiko Kakutani wrote in the *New York Times*. Rather, "he strikes us as little more than an aberration—a kook, and a pretty boring kook at that."

The Things They Carried (HOUGHTON MIFFLIN, 1990) • "They," of course, are soldiers, and what they carry with them into combat is what we all carry into our daily battles: dreams, loves, anguish, chewing gum, photographs, rings. These interconnected short stories and sketches, some of which include graphic depictions of battle, are variously brilliant and half baked. But according to Robert Harris in the *New York Times*, "The overall effect of these original tales is devastating."

In the Lake of the Woods (HOUGHTON MIFFLIN, 1994) • The Lake of the Woods is ideal vacation spot on the U.S.-Canadian border; it's big and wild, a place to get lost in. Unfortunately, when John and Kathleen Wade travel to the Lake of the Woods to relax, Kathleen actually does get lost. As John searches for her, the sudden loss of his wife forces into his consciousness certain things that he had long since buried. We learn both who he is (a failed Senate candidate) and who he was (a participant in the My Lai massacre). O'Brien was himself in My Lai following the massacre. "Without a doubt," the *Christian Science Monitor* wrote of this exceptionally striking book, "O'Brien has been walking around inside John Wade's head for years, trying to discover where a man who was at My Lai would have hidden his memories."

BIOGRAPHY

A MIDWESTERN UPBRINGING, according to one truism, gives a person a solid, commonsense approach to life. According to another, the straight, unironic tone of such a life can drive a person to distraction. "My dominant recollection," Tim O'Brien has said of his childhood in Worthington, Minnesota, "is one of a kind of seething rage." The son of a life insurance salesman, he had no particular ambition for the writing game and might have remained on an apparently steady keel were it not for the Vietnam War. O'Brien was drafted immediately on his graduation from college in 1968, and after anguishing over whether or not to skip to Canada, he made what he later considered the morally inferior decision to answer his nation's call. He served a little more than a year in one of the most hellish theaters of the war; when he returned home in 1970, it was with a need to write his way out of the horrors that he had experienced.

Like Hemingway, with whom he's often compared, O'Brien put in some time as a newspaper correspondent, spending parts of 1973 and 1974 as a reporter with the *Washington Post;* he later summarized what he learned from that experience, in appropriately Hemingwayesque reduction, as "discipline" and an appreciation for active verbs. (O'Brien doesn't deny the Hemingway influence, but he has expressed the belief that Joseph Conrad, particularly *Lord Jim*, has had a greater effect on his work.)

O'Brien did some graduate work at Harvard University shortly after his return from Vietnam, and he has lived in Cambridge, Massachusetts, ever since. His wife, Ann, is a magazine production manager.

NEXT ON THE READING LIST: Madison Smartt Bell, Robert Olen Butler, Jim Harrison, Gabriel García Márquez, Cormac McCarthy, Robert Stone

Kenzaburo Oe
(b. January 31, 1935)

"Until recently, Japanese literature had remained in hermetic isolation.... [No] major writer had appeared to describe the hope, anger, and despair that followed VJ Day. Then came Kenzaburo Oe, [who] has apparently become the literary hero of Japan's young intellectuals."
—James Toback, New York Times

Nip the Buds, Shoot the Kids (KODANSHA, 1958; MARION BOYARS, 1995) • Oe's first novel tells the disturbing tale of a group of reform school boys who are evacuated to a remote mountain village during World War II. The villagers subsequently flee to escape a plague, leaving the boys to survive on their own. Generally praised as a dark parable of postwar Japanese society, Oe's novel was, according to *Kirkus Reviews*, "more shaded, more graphic, and angrier than *Lord of the Flies*, but the fierce anger is transmuted by Oe's art into literary gold—an anguished plea for tolerance more wrenching than any rant could ever be."

A Personal Matter (SHINCHOSHA, 1964; GROVE, 1969) • Oe based this novel, one of his best known, on his own experience raising a son born with a brain defect. His alter ego, Bird, is an unconventional delinquent forced to accept middle-class Japanese values. Through the course of the novel, Bird struggles to decide whether or not to allow his mentally impaired son to live. Most reviewers liked the opening chapters of *A Personal Matter* but complained about its ending—a happy resolution tacked onto a disturbing story. In the *Washington Post*, Geoffrey Wolff wrote that Oe's characters "trick themselves with hopeless dreams of a new life."

* The Silent Cry (KODANSHA, 1967; KODANSHA INTERNATIONAL, 1974) • Praised by the Nobel Prize committee as "Oe's major mature work," *The Silent Cry* presents an allegorical tale in which two brothers return to their ancestral home. Mitsuzaburo must accept his friend's suicide and the birth of a retarded son, while Takashi incites the locals to attack a Korean entrepreneur, called the Emperor of the Supermarkets, who controls the village. The *Times Literary Supplement* called the book "a major feat of the imagination," while other journals compared its "grotesque realism" to the magical realism of Latin American novelists such as Gabriel García Márquez.

> "The Silent Cry *is a particularly potent distillation of the somber themes that haunt [Oe's] work."* (*Merle Rubin,* Christian Science Monitor)

The Pinch Runner Memorandum (SHINCHOSHA, 1976; M. E. SHARPE, 1993) • In this Rabelaisian satire, a nuclear engineer and his eight-year-old brain-damaged son take on an underworld boss who wants to control Japan by manufacturing two atomic bombs. *The Pinch Runner Memorandum* demonstrates both Oe's increasing use of fantasy and his growing preoccupation with nuclear war. Describing Oe's writing as "bold, savage, and often very funny," *The New Yorker* called *The Pinch Runner Memorandum* "a heartening display of the explosively constructive power of imagination."

Teach Us to Outgrow Our Madness (GROVE, 1977) • The four long stories in this collection make use of many themes to which Oe has repeatedly returned: madness, suicide, physical deformity, and disease. As in *A Personal Matter*, the title work explores the close bond that develops between a father and his brain-damaged son. "The Day He Himself Shall Wipe My Tears Away" presents a man in a hospital who obsessively analyzes his past as he succumbs to liver cancer. Comparing Oe favorably with Norman Mailer and John Updike, one reviewer called the stories in *Teach Us to Outgrow Our Madness* "original, well-plotted tales with vivid, if not likable characters and memorable scenes."

An Echo of Heaven (SHINCHOSHA, 1989; KODANSHA INTERNATIONAL, 1996) • In *An Echo of Heaven*, Marie Kuraki plunges into depression after the double suicide of her two children and her husband's death from cancer. She briefly studies Catholicism and then joins a Japanese religious cult before fleeing to California. Finally, she journeys to a Mexican commune, where the members draw inspiration from her experience as a "sorrowing mother" and venerate her as a saint. According to John L'Heureux in the *Los Angeles Times*, the book's relentless intellectualism makes it a "taut and forceful" work, yet it "does not succeed in touching the heart."

A Quiet Life (KODANSHA, 1990; GROVE, 1996) • This novel takes the form of a diary kept by Ma-chan, the daughter of a famous Japanese writer. Her closest relationship is with her mentally retarded brother, Hikari, whose nickname is Eeyore. When Ma-chan's mother suggests that her father read Ma-chan's diary, the exercise gives the writer an opportunity to reacquaint himself with his neglected family. In the *New York Times*, John David Morley praised *A Quiet Life* for its "intimate domestic portrait in the form of Ma-chan's diary" but complained about the book's unsatisfactory ending and its use of improbable plot devices.

Seventeen & J (BLUE MOON, 1996) • The two novellas in this volume were written by Oe when he was just twenty-five years old. "Seventeen," which dramatizes the 1960 murder of Japan's Socialist party leader, caused a scandal and generated a number of right-wing death threats. "J" is the story of a wealthy man who dedicates himself to debauchery. Comparing the two works, Richard Eder of the *Los Angeles Times* described "Seventeen" as "written with rough urgency" and "J" as "rough but more complex and accomplished."

BIOGRAPHY

KENZABURO OE WAS BORN into a prominent samurai family. He grew up in Ose, a small mountain village on the Japanese island of Shikoku. Later, Oe credited his literary preoccupation with eccentric outsiders to a childhood spent in this remote locale. One of his earliest and most powerful memories concerns the emperor simultaneously announcing Japan's surrender and renouncing his own godhood. Oe was so astonished, he has said, that he turned to literature in order to comprehend Japan's defeat and the collapse of its belief system.

Studying French literature at the University of Tokyo, Oe immersed himself in the writings of existential philosopher Jean-Paul Sartre. In 1958, he won the prestigious Akutagawa Prize for his short story "The Catch," which described the friendship between a Japanese schoolboy and a captured black American pilot. During the 1960s, Oe became involved in international antiwar and ban-the-bomb movements, traveling to China, Russia, and Western Europe. This left-wing activism, combined with his controversial subject matter, made Oe Japan's literary enfant terrible.

Oe has often said that the 1963 birth of his brain-damaged son, Hikari, was an important milestone in his life. Although Hikari's doctors predicted that he'd be a "human vegetable," Oe and his wife decided to care for their son rather than allow him to die. Thereafter, Oe's fiction repeatedly returned to the question of how a father should treat his mentally retarded child. (Although he still suffers from language impairments, Hikari Oe is now a successful composer of music.)

In 1994, Oe became the second Japanese writer (after Yasunari Kawabata) to win a Nobel Prize in literature. According to the award citation, "Oe has blazed literary trails with his poetic force, and his works create an imaginary world where life and myth condense to powerfully portray the human predicament." A few days after the Nobel Prize was announced, Japan's cultural establishment hurriedly conferred on Oe its highest artistic honor, the Imperial Order of Culture, but Oe refused to accept the award, calling it a relic of Japan's undemocratic past and causing a sensation.

NEXT ON THE READING LIST: Stephen Dixon, Gabriel García Márquez, David Guterson, Kazuo Ishiguro, Susan Sontag

---

Michael Ondaatje
(b. September 12, 1943)

"Michael Ondaatje's special gift as a novelist is to keep all the elements of a story in suspension, up in the air, seeming still yet buzzing with life, like a juggler's dinner-service. You can see space round the edge of each episode, too, which is doubtless an effect he borrows from his other self, the poet. His materials are realistic...but he picks and chooses them for their eccentricity and brittleness and the suggestive butterfly sheen that comes off them."
—*Lorna Sage*, Times Literary Supplement

Coming through Slaughter (NORTON, 1976) • Grounded in the history of early-twentieth-century New Orleans, Ondaatje's first "novel" both documents and invents the tragic life of jazz pioneer Buddy Bolden, who suffered a debilitating mental collapse prior to the spread of recorded music. Drawing on interviews with people who knew Bolden, historical records, and his own richly imagined conception of Bolden's troubled inner thoughts, Ondaatje re-creates Bolden's early career in New Orleans, barbering during the day and playing cornet at night, as well as his subsequent descent into madness at age thirty-one. Most reviewers agreed with one critic's complaint that Bolden "never emerges clearly from the desert of facts, real or fictional, which comprises his life." As Anatole Broyard pointed out in the *New York Times, Coming through Slaughter* is "made up of shards of various techniques.... The author gives us all the broken pieces and leaves it to us to infer the final form."

In the Skin of a Lion (KNOPF, 1987) • In this novel, which more closely resembles traditional historical fiction, Ondaatje chronicles the oppressed lives of the immigrant workers who modernized the city of Toronto during the early twentieth century. However, Ondaatje's literary techniques remain thoroughly untraditional: He uses both a nonlinear plot and a surreal, collagelike narrative style to trace the growing social awareness of his protagonist, Patrick Lewis. Many reviewers, while expressing admiration for Ondaatje's technical daring and the exceptional quality of his prose, felt that *In the Skin of a Lion* was too convoluted and Patrick too passive a lead character. As Tom Marshall observed in *Books in Canada*, "Reading this novel is rather like watching some overambitious and overlong Stanley Kubrick film that has, however, absolutely wonderful moments."

✻ The English Patient (KNOPF, 1992) • It's spring 1945, and the Allied forces in Italy are advancing on Central Europe. Despite the danger, an emotionally scarred Canadian nurse named Hana chooses to remain behind in the ruins of a villa near Florence so that she can care for a mysterious English soldier who has been severely burned. David Caravaggio, a spy and thief whom Hana knew during her childhood, stumbles into the makeshift hospital, where he's treated for wounds inflicted by the Germans. A fourth character, Kirpal "Kip" Singh, has been recruited by the English army to defuse bombs left by the retreating Nazis. As the novel progresses, the relationships among these four characters metamorphose in response to the stress of their situation and the secrets that they reveal. Although some critics found fault with Ondaatje's convoluted plot and all-too-precious prose, the novel won Britain's esteemed Booker Award.

> *"The writing is so heady that you have to keep putting the book down between passages so as not to reel from the sheer force and beauty of it. Color and landscape are evoked with such vividness that whole chunks of description become assimilated into the reader's mind—when I finished the book I felt as dazed as if I'd just awoken from a powerful dream."* (*Cressida Connolly*, The Spectator)

BIOGRAPHY

MICHAEL ONDAATJE WAS BORN IN Ceylon (now Sri Lanka), where his paternal grandfather owned a successful tea plantation. Ondaatje's parents separated in 1948, when he was five, and four years later he left Ceylon for England with his mother, brother, and sister. After attending Dulwich College in London, Ondaatje became dissatisfied with the English educational system and emigrated to Canada in 1962, joining his brother, Christopher, who was already living in Montreal. After several years at Bishop's University in Lennoxville, Quebec, he transferred to the University of Toronto, from which he received a bachelor's degree in 1965. Two years later, he earned a master's degree from Queen's University, Kingston, Ontario.

During the late 1960s Ondaatje emerged as one of Canada's most respected young poets. In such volumes as *The Dainty Monsters* (1967) and *The Man with Seven Toes* (1969), he examined the dichotomy between rational intellect and disorderly reality and suggested—à la Heisenberg—that the poet's efforts to relate personal experience necessarily results in distortion. Early on, critics praised Ondaatje's humor and flamboyance, yet few foresaw the brilliance that he exhibited in *The Collected Works of Billy the Kid: Left Handed Poems* (1970). This fictionalized biography—stitched together from poems, prose, photographs, illustrations, interviews, and even comic-book panels—won a Governor General's Award, Canada's highest literary honor, and catapulted Ondaatje to the front rank of North American writers.

NEXT ON THE READING LIST: Pat Barker, A. S. Byatt, Stephen Dixon, Mark Helprin, David Leavitt, Alice Munro, Leslie Marmon Silko

Amos Oz
(b. May 4, 1939)

"A veteran of Israel's 1967 and 1973 wars and a prominent advocate for peace, Amos Oz is also one of Israel's best-known novelists, an intelligent and venturesome writer with a gift for illuminating the complex interweavings of the personal and the political in his characters' lives."
—*Merle Rubin,* Christian Science Monitor

Where the Jackals Howl (MASADAH, 1965; HARCOURT BRACE JOVANOVICH, 1981) • This collection of short stories, Oz's first book, was published in the United States well after his reputation was made. Reviewers generally found the stories superior to the writing in Oz's first novel, *Elsewhere, Perhaps.* A. G. Mojtabai in the *New York Times* particularly admired "a consistent inwardness, and a curious, but necessary, lack of resolution to all these tales" and called *Where the Jackals Howl* "a strong, beautiful, disturbing book."

Elsewhere, Perhaps (SIFRIYAT PO'ALIM, 1966; HARCOURT BRACE JOVANOVICH, 1973) • Oz's first novel, about the institution of the kibbutz, doesn't give it a very easy time. Externally, Oz's fictional kibbutz, which lies close to the Israeli border, has to endure the constant threat of Arab attack. Internally, it suffers from friction between older and younger members, who have very different views regarding the ideal Jewish state. The book "was well-written but conventional," Pearl K. Bell commented in *The New Leader*, "and Oz's satiric detachment was too often short-circuited by sentimentality."

My Michael (AM OVED, 1968; KNOPF, 1972) • *My Michael*, the first Oz novel published in the United States, describes the life of an unhappy Israeli housewife whose woes are magnified by the Arab-Israeli conflict. One critic called the book an "Israeli *Madame Bovary*," while David Stern wrote in *Commentary* that the novel "succeeded in transforming a political 'fact'—the Arab-Israeli dilemma—into a genuine metaphor of the imagination."

Unto Death (SIFRIYAT PO'ALIM, 1971; HARCOURT BRACE JOVANOVICH, 1975) • This volume contains two novellas, both of which represent stylistic departures for Oz. "Crusade," a historical fiction, recounts the despoilment of Jews by marauding European crusaders. "Late Love," a self-consciously shrill tale, concerns a Jewish intellectual who travels about Israel lecturing on the need for an attack against Moscow. "What makes both of these novellas so compelling," Ivan Sanders wrote in *The New Republic*, "is that the author fully understands his fanatics' paltry delusions."

Touch the Water, Touch the Wind (AM OVED, 1973; HARCOURT BRACE JOVANOVICH, 1974) • Two different facets of the modern Jewish experience are embodied here by a husband and wife who, having separated, follow different paths. The man escapes Nazi persecution in Poland to become a hero in Israel, while his wife flees to the Soviet Union, where she rises within the governing bureaucracy there. "Though *[Touch the Water, Touch the Wind]* never quite slows down enough to become very profound," *The New Yorker* observed, "its youthfulness and energy are exhilarating."

The Hill of Evil Counsel (AM OVED, 1976; HARCOURT BRACE JOVANOVICH, 1978) • Not so much a novel as a trio of interlocking novellas, *The Hill of Evil Counsel* is set during the period immediately preceding the founding of the Israeli state. This lesser work recounts the lives of three middle-aged Jewish men, all of whom live in the same Jerusalem neighborhood. Lis Harris in *The New Yorker* wrote that Oz "seems unwilling or unable to come to grips with his characters' feelings about the fragility of either their past lives or their present ones."

* A Perfect Peace (AM OVED, 1982; HARCOURT BRACE JOVANOVICH, 1985) • In this thick novel about the conflict between a proud, powerful kibbutz leader and his disillusioned son, Oz tackles the great generational struggle being waged in modern Israel. When the son leaves the kibbutz, his father adopts a surrogate son as a replacement. Not to be outdone, the original son bequeaths his wife to the newcomer.

> *"[This is] Oz's strangest, riskiest, and richest novel to date. He writes in his usual clean, blunt prose, his characters' voices ring true, and he creates a world*

which makes perfect sense, except that at its core is a series of impenetrable mysteries. " (*Rita Kashner,* Washington Post)

Black Box (AM OVED, 1986; HARCOURT BRACE JOVANOVICH, 1988) • In this epistolary novel, a complex family situation unfolds through a transcontinental exchange of letters. Alec, a sociologist and Israeli war hero now living in the United States, corresponds with his ex-wife, Ilana, about how their juvenile delinquent son should be raised. However, the book's underlying truth, according to Mary Gordon in the *New York Times,* is that "the bond between Alec and Ilana—a combination of sadomasochism and simple lust—has never been broken." Gordon added that *Black Box* "extends [Oz's] impressive range."

To Know a Woman (KETER, 1989; HARCOURT BRACE JOVANOVICH, 1991) • This story of a retired Israeli spy fumbling for a sense of meaning in life has a realistic mundaneness that pleasantly challenges what one expects of spy-related fiction. "Part of the novel's power derives from Oz's ability to invest the ordinary with mystery," Thomas D'Evelyn wrote in the *Christian Science Monitor.*

Fima (KETER, 1991; HARCOURT BRACE, 1993) • Fifty-four-year-old Fima has a brilliant mind, but it has never taken him anywhere. All his schoolmates have gone on to lead rich, interesting lives, yet Fima remains a receptionist at a medical clinic, trying to sort out what went wrong. Writing in the *Christian Science Monitor,* Merle Rubin praised "Oz's fine sense of balance," calling the novel "a seamless creation."

Don't Call It Night (KETER, 1994; HARCOURT BRACE, 1995) • In this slight, modest novel, a well-to-do Israeli couple in late middle age begin asking themselves delicate questions about their lives, their nation, and their love for each other. "This novel is a piece of sweet but melancholy chamber music—light but not necessarily insubstantial," Lorrie Moore wrote in the *New York Times.*

Panther in the Basement (KETER, 1995; HARCOURT BRACE, 1997) • The unnamed Israeli narrator of this gentle novel looks back on the summer of 1947, the last summer of the British mandate, when he was twelve years old and nearly bursting with patriotic intensity. Inspired by his parents, both active members of the resistance, Proffy (the boy's nickname) forms an underground cell of his own with two of his friends. These same friends later turn on him when he befriends a lonely British military policeman who wants only to learn how to speak Hebrew. Some reviewers read the book as a justification of Oz's own dovish politics, but most agreed that its story was genuine and tender. In *Newsday,* Dan Cryer called *Panther in the Basement* "minor Oz [but] still far better than the best of many other writers."

BIOGRAPHY

AMOS OZ WAS BORN IN Jerusalem into a family of staunch Zionists named Klausner, but he quit his father's house soon after his mother's suicide and changed his last name to Oz. At age fourteen, he joined a kibbutz. He fought in both the Six-Day War of 1967 and the Yom Kippur War of 1973. He has spent most of his life living on a kibbutz. Thus, as John Bayley pointed out in the *New York Review of Books*, he "has no alternative in his novels but to tell us what it means to be an Israeli." Oz once said, "It's my thing in the same sense that William Faulkner belonged to the Deep South. It's my thing and my place and my addiction."

The straightforward realism of Oz's prose reflects his lifelong attempt to grasp the circumstances of Israeli life. Beyond his fiction, however, he has become, in the words of one writer, "Israel's best-known peacenik." Oz began lobbying for peace during the high-tension days of the 1960s, when he and his family were often attacked as traitors. Today, some hail him as a prophet of peace, while others still consider him a dangerous left-winger.

Oz and his wife, Nily, whom he married in 1960, have three children and numerous grandchildren. They continue to live at Kibbutz Hulda, where Oz fled as a young man to escape his father's right-wing politics. Rather than identify himself with Israel's Labor party, Oz simply calls himself "a social democrat Zionist dove."

NEXT ON THE READING LIST: Joan Didion, Francisco Goldman, Ursula Hegi, Milan Kundera, Doris Lessing, V. S. Naipaul, Philip Roth

---

Grace Paley
(b. December 11, 1922)

"American short-story writers are a tough breed in any event—standing firm in a country where the average reader prefers a novel—but Grace Paley must be one of the toughest.... She continues to speak in a voice so absolutely her own that a single line, one suspects, could be identified as hers among a hundred other lines. She is resolute, stalwart, vigorous. She is urban to an unusual degree, cataloging both the horrors and the surprising pockets of green in her native New York City."
—Anne Tyler, The New Republic

* The Little Disturbances of Man (DOUBLEDAY, 1959) • This volume of ten stories introduced Grace Paley as a short-story writer in the classic sense: Her prose is terse and her characters and settings closely circumscribed and precisely rendered. But they also marked her as one who wasn't afraid to experiment. Mostly they're stories of Jewish women in New York, and her mastery of their Yiddish dialect is unerring.

> *"She doesn't merely use words. She kites them, skitters them, schoons them along the frozen surface of our minds.... She has a wonderful faculty of making everything in her stories seem new and unused."* (*Thomas Lask*, New York Times)

Enormous Changes at the Last Minute (FARRAR, STRAUS & GIROUX, 1974) • Where her first collection merely leaned toward the experimental in its intense focus on character, these highly regarded stories almost dispense with plot altogether. In "A Conversation with My Father," the heroine's father asks her to write a story, but she argues that plot is an outmoded convention. Although Paley ran the risk of annoying both traditionalists and the avant-garde, her goal seemed to be the forging of a new traditionalism. "I would nominate *Enormous Changes* for whatever fiction honors this country can bestow," William Peden wrote in the *Sewanee Review*.

Later the Same Day (FARRAR, STRAUS & GIROUX, 1985) • Paley's third collection doesn't break new ground, though it does continue her close observation of downtown New York characters—especially liberals, intellectuals, and political radicals. At times, as in "This Is a Story about My Friend George, the Toy Inventor," Paley becomes too precious. But Michiko Kakutani, writing in the *New York Times*, called the tales "sad, funny, elliptical stories" about "how we continue to seek, even after disappointment and loss, some approximation of our youthful dreams."

BIOGRAPHY

GRACE PALEY IS A MEMBER OF a vanishing breed: writers of fiction who confine themselves to the short story. Why not tackle a novel? Because, she once said, "Art is too long and life is too short." Paley is further distinguished by her narrow focus on the personalities associated with her Greenwich Village neighborhood and the liberal politics that she (and many of her characters) espouse.

Born Grace Goodside, Paley grew up in the Bronx, the daughter of Russian Jewish parents. She attended both Hunter College and New York University but graduated from neither. Her first husband, Jess Paley, was a cameraman, and it was during her marriage to him that she turned from writing poetry to the short story. Although her first collection was favorably reviewed, she didn't publish a second until fifteen years later, a delay Paley attributes to the demands of raising her two children and taking part in protests against the Vietnam War.

With the publication of *Enormous Changes at the Last Minute*, Paley was recognized—despite her modest output—as one of America's foremost practitioners of the short story. In 1994, her *Collected Stories* was nominated for a National Book Award. Recently, she has served on the faculty of Sarah Lawrence College. She's currently married to poet and playwright Robert Nichols.

NEXT ON THE READING LIST: Amy Bloom, Mary Gaitskill, Alice Hoffman, David Leavitt, Alice Munro, Susan Sontag, William Trevor, John Updike

---

Cathie Pelletier
(b. 1953)

"What makes Pelletier's work so engaging is that she is absolutely, inherently, funny. She doesn't crack wise, and she doesn't resort to one-liners. She just sees the essential weirdness of life—and walks the tightrope between humor and grief without... losing her balance."
—*Karen Stabiner,* Los Angeles Times

* The Funeral Makers (MACMILLAN, 1986) • It's 1959, and elderly spinster Marge McKinnon is dying. Her sister Pearl, a mortician's wife, returns to Mattagash to "make" the funeral, but it's upstaged by news that Amy Joy, their fourteen-year-old niece, is having an affair with Chester Lee Gifford, a scruffy thirty-two-year-old delinquent who prefers cars to women as sex objects. The focus of this charmingly raucous novel, however, is Mattagash itself, an isolated hamlet in northern Maine where there aren't many people and even fewer toilets. Mattagash is literally where the road ends.

> *"Lest you think that* The Funeral Makers *is merely funereal, let me tell you that it is terribly funny and terribly sad, large and wide and deep and finally reassuring as an order of sorts is restored and the survivors become reconciled to one another and the limits of geography."* (*Susan Kenney,* New York Times)

* Once upon a Time on the Banks (VIKING, 1989) • Reviewers wondered whether this sequel to *The Funeral Makers* would live up to the original—until they read it. Pelletier returns to Mattagash ten years later for the wedding of Amy Joy, now twenty-three, to Jean Claude Cloutier, an inept local whose English isn't too great. ("You're going to marry a *Frog?*" her outraged mother exclaims.) The wedding, however, is just an excuse for Pelletier to bring together and play with an assortment of ludicrous characters, including the thieving Gifford brothers, with whom neither one's daughters nor one's hubcaps are safe.

"Funny doesn't begin to describe these shenanigans, and yet, as in most first-rate comic fiction, there's a powerful undercurrent of humane wisdom running straight through the novel from beginning to end." (*Howard Frank Mosher,* Washington Post)

The Weight of Winter (VIKING, 1991) • Life in Mattagash isn't quite so funny once the snows come, and this novel reads like *Once upon the Banks* with its comedy-to-tragedy ratio flipped. Beginning with the first snowfall of 1989, the weight of winter bears down particularly heavily on Amy Joy, still unmarried at forty-four, and Pike Gifford, who divides his disability checks (for a fraudulent ailment) between his family and a local bar. It seems that the six-month snow cover brings out the worst in Mattagash's mostly mean and stupid residents—until the promise of spring offers a bit of hope. "This novel's mystical evocation of nature and history," *The New Yorker* observed, "does not balance with its more prosaic and rewarding emotional life, but the book…is so funny and wrenching that one happily skates over the rough patches."

The Bubble Reputation (CROWN, 1993) • As this novel opens, thirty-three-year-old Rosemary O'Neal is mourning the death of her artist husband, who killed himself during a trip to London. Her crazy family, including a three-hundred-pound gay uncle, soon moves in with her—so that she shouldn't feel alone in the world—yet it's immediately obvious that they need her help more than she needs theirs. Again using humor to lighten a sad story, Pelletier alternates between descriptions of Rosemary's emerging inner life and set pieces involving her uproarious houseguests. Calling *The Bubble Reputation* "more exploratory and personal" than Pelletier's other books, Bruce Allen wrote in the *Chicago Tribune* that "Pelletier…redeems a redundant plot by plunging whole-hog into her characters' sheer human imperfectibility."

A Marriage Made at Woodstock (CROWN, 1994) • Pelletier's fifth novel reads like a staged debate: the unrealistic expectations of the 1960s versus the hollow reality of the 1990s. As the title suggests, Freddy and Chandra met at Woodstock, fell in love, and got married. Twenty years later, Chandra leads New Age seminars (and still joins picket lines), while Freddy has become a nerdy accountant. Early on in this novel, Chandra walks out—and who can blame her? At first, Freddy falls apart, but then slowly he learns how to make peace with his imperfect self. "Frederick's slouch toward divorce and possible renewal seems inevitable [and] predictable," Stephen McCauley noted in the *New York Times.* "Still, the smart vitality of Ms. Pelletier's prose and of her keen observations carries the book."

Beaming Sonny Home (CROWN, 1996) • After John Lennon appears to Sonny Gifford during a TV program about famine in Africa, Sonny takes two young women and a poodle hostage at a trailer park in Bangor, Maine.

Meanwhile, back in Mattagash, his mother, Mattie, watches the tragedy unfold on CNN. In fact, the entire novel takes place inside Mattie's house, where her three unpleasant daughters gather to watch gleefully the downfall of their brother, whom they know is their mother's favorite. Mattie has had a tough life—her husband cheated on her with every woman in town, including her best friend—"but at the same time that one feels with and for Mattie," according to Beth Gutcheon in *Newsday*, "it is impossible not to be hugely entertained" because of Pelletier's "unique ability to be simultaneously sympathetic and wickedly funny."

BIOGRAPHY

CATHIE PELLETIER WAS BORN IN rural Allagash, Maine, a small mill town near the Canadian border that, fictionalized as Mattagash, has become the setting for most of her books. Like the McKinnons of Mattagash, the Pelletiers of Allagash can trace their ancestry back to the town's original settlers. Pelletier herself was the youngest of six children born to a French-Canadian lumber contractor and his Irish wife. Always a precocious child, she enrolled at the University of Maine when she was just seventeen but was soon expelled for her role in some campus hijinks.

Pelletier then hitchhiked across the country but later returned to Maine to finish her degree. After that, she decided to move to Nashville and pursue a career as a songwriter. At first, she lived with a family of morticians who were "crazy as loons," she told *People*. Then she moved in with her longtime companion, Jim Glaser, a country music singer-songwriter.

Pelletier's work has often been compared to the Southern Gothic novels of Eudora Welty, Erskine Caldwell, and Flannery O'Connor. However, as *New York Times* critic Tim Sandlin has pointed out, the South no longer produces that sort of fiction. His theory as to why the genre has moved so far north has to do with air-conditioning. "Laughter-among-the-suicides books simply don't work in towns with malls," Sandlin declared in his review of *The Weight of Winter*.

NEXT ON THE READING LIST: Roddy Doyle, Louise Erdrich, Jim Harrison, David Lodge, Thomas McGuane, Reynolds Price, Anne Tyler, Fay Weldon

Richard Powers

(b. 1957)

"Richard Powers has staked out a unique place for himself, one that straddles our technological and literary cultures. He may be the last humanist with a scientific competence, an invaluable thing when the notion that humans may be just another variety of complex system haunts our sense of ourselves.... He is one of the few younger American writers who can stake a claim to the cerebral legacy of Pynchon, Gaddis, and DeLillo."
—Howard George, The Nation

Three Farmers on Their Way to a Dance (BEECH TREE, 1985) • A photograph of three farmers triggers three overlapping narratives in Powers's first novel, which was nominated for a National Book Critics Circle Award. The first narrative is an engaging account made up by Powers to explain the quarrelsome demeanor of three farmers photographed by August Sanders in 1914 (Sanders was trying to produce a catalog of faces). The second involves a contemporary first-person narrator who manages to connect one of the farmers to Henry Ford; and the third focuses on computer writer Peter Mays, who discovers that the farmer is his ancestor. "It isn't often that a novelist makes a debut with a work as ambition and dazzling as *Three Farmers on Their Way to a Dance*," George Kearns wrote in the *Hudson Review*.

Prisoner's Dilemma (BEECH TREE, 1988) • While dying of a mysterious illness, history teacher Eddie Hobson creates a fantasy world called Hobbstown, a kind of insanely abstract Disneyland. When Eddie Jr., the youngest of Hobson's precocious children, tries to reconstruct his father's life and his reasons for creating Hobbstown, the son discovers that his father was once radiated during an atomic test. Regarding this somewhat inaccessible novel, Tom LeClair remarked in *The New Republic* that Powers is among "the most accomplished practitioners of what I call the 'systems novel,' a fiction that uses postmodern techniques to model the dense and tangled relations of modern history, politics, and science."

* The Gold Bug Variations (MORROW, 1991) • Powers's most confident and rewarding novel yet made him once again a finalist for a National Book Critics Circle Award. The title of this book, an allusion to a similarly named Poe short story, also refers to Glenn Gould's recitation of Bach's *Goldberg Variations* and the structure of DNA. Around this triad, Powers structures a metaphysical detective story set to music. Stuart Ressler, a reclusive scientist once on the brink of cracking the DNA code, befriends the information-obsessed librarian Jan O'Deigh and her commitment-challenged lover,

Franklin Todd. To this couple, Ressler recounts his story of failed love, which threatens to parallel their own.

> *"This enormous book may be the most lavishly ambitious American novel since* Gravity's Rainbow. *That it succeeds on its own intricate intellectual terms (that will not be every reader's) is a considerable triumph; that it also functions as an invitingly readable story is an outright marvel."* (*Curt Suplee,* Washington Post)

Operation Wandering Soul (MORROW, 1993) • The increasingly reclusive Dr. Richard Kraft cares for a coterie of dying children at a hospital in a dystopian Los Angeles of the near future. Although longing to trust someone, he repeatedly sabotages his relationship with nurse Linda Espera; meanwhile, he reconstructs his own childhood in Asia. Sven Birkerts, writing in the *Chicago Tribune,* called this novel, nominated for a National Book Award, "an early entry into what will surely become its own sub-genre soon: the millennial novel." Though praising its clever intricacies, some critics faulted *Operation Wandering Soul* for its dour self-absorption.

✱ Galatea 2.2 (FARRAR, STRAUS & GIROUX, 1995) • Confessing that his last book was too pessimistic and that he had written himself into a corner, Powers recasts himself as a protagonist for this retelling of the Pygmalion myth. An extremely private young writer named Richard Powers returns to the United States after a failed long-term relationship to begin a writing project funded by a genius grant, only to find that he has nothing to write. Enter Phil Lentz, an irritable scientist who wants to construct a machine that can be taught to interpret literature. Though typically dense, *Galatea 2.2* presents a simpler narrative than Powers's previous works, making it his most accessible book, with the fewest multiple narratives to sort out and reintegrate.

> "Galatea 2.2 *is not merely a novel about science, nor science fiction; it's an elegant attempt to use cutting edge research on cognition to explore the nature of memory and literary creation."* (*Steven Moore,* Washington Post)

BIOGRAPHY

RICHARD POWERS GREW UP IN what he calls the midwestern "I" states, in which he set parts of *The Gold Bug Variations* and *Galatea 2.2* and for which he retains a certain fondness. Critics have speculated that most of Powers's novels contain some autobiographical elements, but none know for certain because Powers has zealously guarded both his personal life and his personal history in a manner reminiscent of Thomas Pynchon's.

Wary of the way people can fixate on personality to the exclusion of the work, Powers lived "offstage" in the Netherlands for much of the 1980s, a part of his life hinted at in *The Gold Bug Variations* and centrally incorporated into *Galatea 2.2*. Like the fictional Richard Powers in *Galatea 2.2*, he did win a MacArthur Foundation "genius grant," but not much else is known.

One thing we do know is that Powers is a polymath fond of scientific, literary, and historical references. He also likes to focus on two areas of interest in which he's apparently self-trained: music and computers. In his best novels, Powers's characters try to connect disparate historical circumstances to specific historical events that are seemingly unrelated to, yet always impinge on, lives in the present. It has been suggested that the "butterfly effect" of chaos theory—in which two seemingly random actions or ideas turn out to be linked—best describes Powers's range of writing. Readers who enjoy highly intellectual detective fiction will find Powers's work almost incomparable.

NEXT ON THE READING LIST: Paul Auster, Don DeLillo, Umberto Eco, Doris Lessing, Steven Millhauser, Thomas Pynchon, Salman Rushdie

---

Reynolds Price
(b. February 1, 1933)

"Reynolds Price ought to be as well known and admired among us as Updike or Bellow. That he isn't may have something to do with the gentleness and detachment of his authorial voice, all the more remarkable at a time when so much American writing strains after nudging sophistication or strident jocularity."
—*Jonathan Keates,* The Observer

✳ A Long and Happy Life (ATHENEUM, 1962) • Set in rural North Carolina, Price's debut novel relates Rosacoke Mustian's efforts to snare the heart of Wesley Beavers, for whom she has longed since childhood. Rosacoke's romantic ambitions are dashed when Wesley proposes only after he has impregnated her, and she considers rejecting him. But then, while playing the Virgin Mary in a Christmas pageant, she experiences an epiphany.

> *"I have seldom read a first novel that [has] such sustained lyric power as Reynolds Price's* A Long and Happy Life: *not pretty, pseudo-poetic prose but a vigorous, joyful outburst of song."* (*Granville Hicks,* Saturday Review)

The Names and Faces of Heroes (ATHENEUM, 1963) • These short stories share the same concerns and settings as *A Long and Happy Life*. In "A Chain of

Love," Price's first published work, Rosacoke and her retarded brother, Rato, visit their ailing grandfather in a Raleigh hospital. Rosacoke shows concern for a dying stranger in the next room, but her goodness goes unnoticed and unthanked. Most critics were unimpressed with Price's efforts to make the worn and familiar seem new and his own, yet in the *Saturday Review* Granville Hicks wrote that even "if not all the stories reach the high level of *[A Long and Happy Life]*, the volume is [nonetheless] a considerable satisfaction."

A Generous Man (ATHENEUM, 1966) • Price's second novel relates the sexual and emotional awakening of Rosacoke Mustian's fifteen-year-old brother, Milo. When another brother (the retarded Rato), Rato's dog, and a circus python named Death all go missing in the woods, Milo helps a local posse hunt them down. Along the way, he falls in love with the snake's mysterious handler, Lois. "Price seems to have gone off now in quest of strange gods," Robert Drake wrote in the *Southern Review* of Milo's apparently allegorical search for Death. "What to make of it all remains finally, at least for this reviewer, something of a mystery."

Love and Work (ATHENEUM, 1968) • Thirty-four-year-old novelist Thomas Eborn has forsaken all his emotional relationships—even his marriage—so that he can pursue his literary ambitions undistracted. However, while examining papers left behind by his late mother, he finds a cache of letters that reveal the love his parents shared despite the compromises necessitated by marriage. These letters help Eborn to recognize his own selfish nature, and he begins to look to others, especially his dutiful but disenchanted wife, for fulfillment. Although some critics commended Price for venturing beyond the Mustian clan, they found his new characters to be regrettably smaller than life. Even Granville Hicks in the *Saturday Review* admitted that he was "not so excited by this novel as…by the other two."

Permanent Errors (ATHENEUM, 1970) • These stories describe the effects of past mistakes on current events. Most of the errors to which the title refers are committed by writers who use solitude and detachment to camouflage their vanity, timidity, and selfishness. Chief among them is Charles Tamplin, a young American living in England who is featured in four of these pieces. An aesthete and a prig, Tamplin apparently acquires his knowledge of life primarily through the happiness and suffering of others. "By and large," one critic noted, "the stories are fine, intense, complex, sterner stuff than those in *The Names and Faces of Heroes*." Henry Sloss, writing in *Shenandoah*, agreed: "The tales may turn your head, but the voice is worth attending to. Nobody I know writes better prose."

The Surface of Earth (ATHENEUM, 1975) • This lengthy and ambitious narrative, which spans 1903 to 1944, tracks four generations of the Kendal and Mayfield families, each generation passing on to the next its problems and mistakes. The saga begins with the elopement of sixteen-year-old Eva Kendal and Forrest Mayfield, a Latin teacher twice her age. After Eva's disgraced mother commits suicide, she returns to her father's house in a belated attempt to atone for her errant behavior. In doing so, however, she gives up Forrest, who won't tolerate a wife more devoted to her sense of guilt than to him. Price's admirers called *The Surface of Earth*, which took ten years to plan and three to write, his most mature work yet, but most reviewers agreed with *Newsweek* critic Peter S. Prescott's assessment that the novel was a "lumbering Southern Gothic melodrama." As Christopher Ricks observed in the *New York Review of Books*, "Mr. Price's style can ripen with fatal fluency, and then the rot sets in."

The Source of Light (ATHENEUM, 1981) • In this sequel to *The Surface of Earth*, Hutchins Mayfield, now a twenty-five-year-old aspiring poet, says farewell to his kin in North Carolina and leaves for Oxford. The rest of the novel mostly describes Hutch's experiences during his first year at Merton College, where he indulges in various heterosexual and homosexual liaisons. During a trip home, however, following his father's death, Hutch realizes that the tangled family history he has tried to escape is exactly the stuff of which great writers are made. Although Joyce Carol Oates, writing in the *New York Times*, called *The Source of Light* a "somber, rather beautifully muted work," most reviewers found it no less self-conscious and grim than its predecessor. According to Benjamin DeMott in the *Saturday Review*, "The overall impression left is that of a fictional world rendered indistinct by the spreading shade of the great Faulkner tree; no action or person or style of utterance quite manages to achieve energetically independent being."

∗ Kate Vaiden (ATHENEUM, 1986) • Price revived his dwindling critical reputation with this coming-of-age tale set in the South during the Great Depression and World War II. Departing from his usual third-person narration, Price tells this story from the point of view of his protagonist, Kate Vaiden, an extraordinary fifty-seven-year-old woman who recounts her experiences as an orphaned child, a teenage mother, and a wandering free spirit. Winner of a National Book Critics Circle Award, *Kate Vaiden* was praised for its expertly rendered portrait of life in the modern rural South and the singularity of its heroine, loosely based on both Moll Flanders and Price's own mother.

> *"Kate is superbly in control of her own tale. The informality of her voice, its southern storyteller's love of vivid metaphor, takes precedence over the depressing facts she has to relate, and her tendency toward conciseness and irreverence lets her render the tragic with the poise of distance."* (*Rosellen Brown*, New York Times)

Good Hearts (ATHENEUM, 1988) • Price's seventh novel is a sequel to his first, but unlike the characters in *A Long and Happy Life*, those in *Good Hearts* live very much in the demanding modern world. Although Rosa is still in love with him, fifty-year-old Wesley considers himself a failure, and in the book's opening pages, when Rosa playfully rejects his sexual advances, Wesley misunderstands and abruptly moves out. His departure, Price's omniscient narrator implies, makes him indirectly responsible for Rosa's subsequent rape during a break-in. Using diary entries and letters, the book then follows Rosa and Wesley's slow progress toward reconciliation. Some reviewers criticized Price for attempting to portray Rosa's "gentle rapist" as benign; yet, as Jefferson Humphries declared in the *Southern Review*, "There can be no mistake that we are in the hands of a master who has attained perfect ease in his art."

The Tongues of Angels (ATHENEUM, 1990) • In this first-person reminiscence, a successful middle-aged artist reflects on his role in the death of a teenage boy thirty-four years earlier. During his last summer as a college student, twenty-one-year-old Bridge Boatner accepts a job as counselor at Camp Juniper, where he develops an intense relationship with a fourteen-year-old camper. Described by one reviewer as "chastely visionary," *The Tongues of Angels* was widely faulted for its ambiguous central relationship: Writing in *The Nation*, Reginald Ollen, who compared Bridge and his charge to Verlaine and Rimbaud, suggested that "Price seems to be playing a game with commitment—am I or am I not? Are these symbols or are they not? Will there be love or not? For most of the read this literary dance is intriguing; but ultimately, it is exasperating."

The Foreseeable Future (ATHENEUM, 1991) • Two of the three "long stories" in this volume, "The Fare to the Moon" and "The Foreseeable Future," are set in or near Raleigh, North Carolina, during World War II. The former introduces Leah, the black true love of Kayes Paschal, who's both married and white. In the title story, Whit Wade, wounded in France, returns to his wife, his daughter, and his job as an insurance adjuster. He brings back with him, however, certain suicidal tendencies. The final story, "Back Before Dawn," about a football coach who suspects his wife of infidelity, takes place a decade or so later. Although "the best that can be said about ['Back Before Dawn'] is that it takes up only a fifth of the book," Edward Hower observed in the *Miami Herald*, "it does send you back to the previous two stories to see if they really are as admirable as you first thought them to be. Yes, they are, emphatically."

Blue Calhoun (ATHENEUM, 1992) • Loquacious sixty-five-year-old Bluford "Blue" Calhoun works as a salesman at a music store in Raleigh. When his teenage granddaughter blames him for failing to prevent her father's suicide, Blue writes her a long letter relating the major events of his life. He singles out the year 1956, when, at age thirty-five, he fell recklessly in love with a sixteen-year-old girl. The consequences of this infatuation reverberate to the novel's end. Although reviewers in the past had generally praised Price for his keen insight into the female psyche, not so this time around.

Even his portrayal of Blue was attacked: "Although Blue is allowed to talk his head off about his feelings, he is seldom able to convey their reality," Robert Towers wrote in the *New York Times*. "Whatever is potentially dramatic or psychologically revealing in a situation is buried under a lava flow of some pretty dreadful language."

The Promise of Rest (SCRIBNER'S, 1995) • In this sequel to a sequel, Hutchins Mayfield, now a respected poet and professor, must come to terms with the certain death of his estranged AIDS-afflicted son. Making matters worse is the fact that his wife has left him for reasons that he can't quite grasp (but should). The theme of homosexuality—present but not explicit in *The Surface of Earth*, explicit but undeveloped in *The Source of Light*—dominates this book, especially in the relationship between Hutch and his longtime best friend. However, as John Gregory Brown complained in the *Los Angeles Times*, "the grand, sweeping lyricism of the prose, which shines so brightly in Price's earlier novels, seems to overwhelm the events of this one."

BIOGRAPHY

SINCE THE 1962 PUBLICATION of *A Long and Happy Life*, Reynolds Price has been regularly compared with William Faulkner, if only because he has become the South's most conspicuous contemporary author. Price's novels and short stories, which are frequently set in his native North Carolina, are complex character studies that address such universal themes as the consequences of love and the need for independence. Yet Price has been thoroughly regionalized.

The only son of a dapper traveling salesman and his eccentric wife, Price won a scholarship to Duke University, graduating summa cum laude in 1955. After attending Merton College, Oxford, on a Rhodes Scholarship, he returned to the United States and took a teaching position at Duke in the English department. He has remained there ever since, becoming James B. Duke Professor of English in 1977. His students over the years have included novelists Anne Tyler and Josephine Humphries.

Price dislikes the "southern" label that has often been applied to his work. "The number of times my novels have been described as being about hillbillies is amazing," Price has said. "Well, there's not a hillbilly anywhere in my work." He does, however, acknowledge the influence of such venerable southern authors as Eudora Welty. "One of the things [Welty] showed me as a writer was that the kinds of people I had grown up with were the kinds of people one could write marvelous fiction about," Price told the *Washington Post*. By focusing on those aspects of his rural southern upbringing, Price has been able to create a body of work noted for its unique sense of place and offbeat assortment of characters.

The initial volume of Price's memoirs, *Clear Pictures* (1989), was nominated for a Pulitzer Prize (as was his 1993 anthology *Collected Stories*). The second volume, *A Whole New Life*, published in 1994, recounted Price's ten-year battle with, and recovery from, cancer of the spinal cord (it left him permanently paralyzed from the waist down). In addition, Price has published several volumes of poetry: *Vital Provisions* (1982), *The Laws of Ice* (1986), and *The Use of Fire* (1990), as well as the anthology *Collected Poems* (1997).

NEXT ON THE READING LIST: Dorothy Allison, Larry Brown, Kaye Gibbons, Ellen Gilchrist, David Leavitt, Cathie Pelletier, Anne Tyler

E. Annie Proulx
(b. August 22, 1935)

"Possessor of a weird, quixotic vision, master of a certain rough-hewn poetry, E. Annie Proulx is not a writer for the faint of heart…. Hers is a treacherous but memorable landscape where bad things happen to all kinds of people, whether they deserve them or not…. Proulx has a passion for storytelling and the precision of a diamond cutter, not to mention being wickedly funny."
—*Gail Caldwell*, Boston Globe

Heart Songs and Other Stories (SCRIBNER'S, 1988) • Against a New England background of failing farms, run-down cabins, and lonely places, Proulx sets stories that *New York Times* critic Kenneth Rosen called "shy, battered, depleted." Other reviewers noted Proulx's sharp humor, lyrical imagery, and rather unusual choice of character names. Because Proulx describes emotional hardship unflinchingly and often pushes her characters to the limits of their endurance, these stories can make for difficult reading.

Postcards (SCRIBNER'S, 1992) • Each chapter in this PEN/Faulkner Award winner begins with a postcard that evokes either the novel's main character, Loyal Blood, or the family he leaves behind when he flees their New England farm. While Loyal Blood wanders aimlessly for thirty years, the family farm declines in his absence. Proulx has called this her "road book," because she researched it during several trips across the United States. "Story makes this novel compelling; technique makes it beautiful," David Bradley wrote in the *New York Times*.

✻ The Shipping News (SCRIBNER'S, 1993) • After his wife dies, Quoyle, an awkward and unfortunate lump of a man, returns to his ancestral homeland of Newfoundland with his two young daughters. There he struggles to make a new life in this vigorous, amusing novel about the foibles of humanity, which won both a National Book Award and a Pulitzer Prize.

"Newfoundland is the real subject of Proulx's stunning novel, in which the reader is assaulted by a rich, down-in-the-dirt, up-in-the-skies prose full of portents, repetitions, bold metaphors, brusque dialogues, and set pieces of great beauty. The characters are radiant with life." (*Nicci Gerrard,* The Observer)

Accordion Crimes (SCRIBNER'S, 1996) • Like *Postcards*, this novel ranges in time and place across the American landscape. It follows the hundred-year history of an accordion as immigrants reverentially pass it from hand to hand. In each of the book's nine chapters, Proulx portrays a different ethnic group. Although the novel has a "relentless existential bleakness," according to Michael Dirda in the *Washington Post*, it isn't depressing. "Instead it seems properly clear-eyed, even shrewd with peasant wisdom.... We must, it seems, find pleasure where we can, while we can—in food and drink, love, music, stories. All these, of course, *Accordion Crimes* supplies with the exuberant and loving excess of a good Polish wedding."

BIOGRAPHY

ON HER MOTHER'S SIDE, E. Annie Proulx's ancestors were farmers, mill workers, inventors, and artisans who had lived in Connecticut since 1635. Her father, however, was a textile executive who often moved the family around, and Proulx has herself adopted that lifestyle—traveling North America with, as she has said, "favorite stops" in Newfoundland and Wyoming. During the early 1970s, she worked toward a Ph.D. in history and even passed her oral exams, but she quit academia in 1975 because of the lack of teaching jobs in her field and began a career as a freelance writer instead.

As a self-described "brutally poor" freelancer, she published several nonfiction books, including *What'll You Take for It?: Back to Barter* (1981) and *The Fine Art of Salad Gardening* (1983). Raising three sons as a single mother kept her focused on these projects to earn money. In a 1993 interview, Proulx said, "That was my bread and butter; my dessert was to write one or two stories a year, for which I was paid about ten dollars." She began writing fiction full time in 1989. Now, with her head "jammed with stories," she's "racing against the clock to get everything down."

The research Proulx does for her books is varied and detailed. It includes studying maps, reading local newspapers, and (for *The Shipping News*) roaming beaches and collecting the litter that washes up there. She takes many of her unusual character names from telephone books, directories of fishery officials, and mortuary lists. The long acknowledgments section in *Accordion Crimes* lists over twenty accordion scholars and musicians. Proulx has often complained of the "unpleasant trend that one should only write about one's own personal experience.... If only people would write about what intrigues them, what they *don't* know, would do a little research, would become questioning as well as observant. That's the pleasure in writing."

Thomas Pynchon
(b. May 8, 1937)

"I don't see how anyone who cares the least bit seriously about modern fiction can deny Pynchon's richness of imagination, his mastery of craft, or his power of vision. Attention must be paid to him as an artist of the very first—and most dangerous—quality."
—*Richard Schickel,* The World

V. (LIPPINCOTT, 1963) • This first novel introduces Pynchon's brazenly difficult fictional universe. Even before one starts the book, its title puzzles: Who or what is V.? This question, never answered, suggests the pervasive ambiguity of the work. Briefly, *V.* follows two main narrative paths: The first centers on Benny Profane and his gradual dissipation as he deliberately avoids meaning and worth. The second records Herbert Stencil's quest to discover the history of the mysterious V. Reading this novel can be frustrating, yet Pynchon's genius is obvious. As Richard Locke pointed out in the *New York Times,* "*V.* is more a wonderful, concatenated jigsaw puzzle than an esthetically coherent literary structure."

The Crying of Lot 49 (LIPPINCOTT, 1966) • Considered the most accessible of Pynchon's works, this short novel narrates the discovery by Southern California housewife Oedipa Maas of an ancient and covert postal system known as Tristero. As she struggles to prove the existence of Tristero, Maas encounters many concerns central to all of Pynchon's work, including paranoia, the role of information in society, and the potential disintegration of Western culture. Reviewing the novel in *Commonweal,* Erik Wensberg wrote, "Knowing yet lyric, *The Crying of Lot 49* stands in the line of *The Great Gatsby* in its concise attempt to capture the dangerous exaltations, and the loneliness, of this strange land."

* Gravity's Rainbow (VIKING, 1973) • Simply put, in its nearly eight hundred pages, *Gravity's Rainbow* attempts to contemplate the entirety of Western civilization as we know it. Geographically and chronologically fluid in scope, Pynchon's third novel features over three hundred substantial characters and refers to almost every aspect of our culture—from comic books to astrophysics to opera—in a display of mind-boggling intellectualism. The novel takes place for the most part in Europe at the close of World War II; however, it also takes us into dreamscapes, the sewage pipes of a large city, and the inner life of a lightbulb, as well as to a multitude of imagined and historical places and events. Reviewers immediately hailed this National Book Award winner as a masterpiece, comparing it favorably with such modern classics as James Joyce's *Ulysses*. However, a noticeable exception was the Pulitzer Prize committee, which deplored the book's scatological and sexually explicit aspects.

> *"Few books in this century have achieved the range and depth of* [Gravity's Rainbow], *and even fewer have held so large a vision of the world in a structure so skillfully and elaborately conceived. This is certainly the most important novel to be published in English in the past thirty years, and it bears all the lineaments of greatness."* (*Edward Mendelson,* Yale Review)

Slow Learner (LITTLE, BROWN, 1984) • This volume combines five short stories that Pynchon published early in his career with a introduction offering an insightful assessment of the early Pynchon by the later one. As a whole, the stories foreshadow many of the themes and techniques that Pynchon used later to more profound effect in his novels. These include his use of scientific metaphors to illuminate and define human behavior and his deep suspicion of bureaucracies. Some reviewers thought that the stories had aged well, while others agreed with Peter Prescott of *Newsweek*, who called the collection "a minor disaster" and said that the stories should never have been resurrected.

Vineland (LITTLE, BROWN, 1990) • The publication of *Vineland* was highly anticipated, coming as it did nearly two decades after Pynchon's last novel, the masterful *Gravity's Rainbow*. However, few critics, once they'd read *Vineland*, considered it a major work. "What's at stake in *Vineland*," James Mathus wrote in the *Chicago Tribune*, "is smaller [than in Pynchon's previous novels] and participates less fully in our hubris and grief." However, as Edward Mendelson pointed out in *The New Republic*, *Vineland* has "a deliberately gawky tenderness for the ordinary." Set in contemporary Northern California, the novel follows the exploits of aging hippie Zoyd Wheeler, his daughter, and his ex-wife as they battle the evil federal prosecutor Brock Vond. Although many of the book's scenes are playful, such as one in which we tour a Japanese city recently stomped by a monster, Pynchon also creates many domestic moments between parents and children that make the novel "luminous and undeniably authentic," according to Mendelson.

* Mason & Dixon (HOLT, 1997) • Comparable to *Gravity's Rainbow* in its size, scope, and whimsical inventiveness, *Mason & Dixon* may be even harder for some people to read, despite its many comic anachronisms, because it's written entirely in the vernacular of the eighteenth century. As told by the Rev. Wicks Cherrycoke one extremely long night twenty years after the fact, the novel re-creates the known deeds of astronomer

Charles Mason and surveyor Jeremiah Dixon from their first meeting in 1761 until Mason's death twenty-five years later—and then adds some. Along the way, Mason and Dixon survey their famous line, which both come to view as something sinister, an unjustifiable blemish on a wilderness once natural and free. As Paul Gray pointed out in *Time*, Pynchon "loves the intellectual purities of science and understands them better than any American novelist ever, [yet he] loathes the power that science bestows, since it always ends up in the wrong hands."

> *"What is remarkable about this book, aside from its sheer entertainment value, is how well this method [of mixing accepted with invented history] works. For all its profuse detail, its jokes and songs and absurdities, the book nonetheless evokes its time and place better than any historical novel I can recall." (T. Coraghessan Boyle,* New York Times)

BIOGRAPHY

THE LAST TIME THAT Thomas Pynchon was photographed, as far as anyone knows, was for his high school yearbook. No other author of his stature, with the possible exception of J. D. Salinger, has been so vigilant in guarding his privacy. With Pynchon, there is a Berlin Wall between his books and his life outside his work: We know that he was born on Long Island and attended Cornell University, where he majored in engineering. (This may explain the scientific sensibility that informs his work.) After Cornell, he served for two years in the U.S. Navy (an experience possibly recast in *V.*). However, beyond these few facts, we know little—and, after the publication of *V.*, almost nothing.

Much of what we do know about the later Pynchon he revealed himself in his introduction to *Slow Learner*. For instance, he wrote that *The Crying of Lot 49* was a story "marketed as 'novel,' and in which I seem to have forgotten most of what I'd thought I'd learned up till then." In another introduction, this one to Richard Fariña's novel *Been Down So Long It Looks Like Up to Me*, Pynchon also exposed a bit of himself, writing, "When we speak of 'seriousness' in fiction, ultimately we are talking about an attitude toward death—how characters may act in its presence."

In Pynchon's work, malevolent systems and their life-deadening functionaries labor to absorb characters who are trying, desperately and often without success, to avoid being conscripted. These struggles take place within a fictional realm of incredible complexity, remarkable detail, and labyrinthian plots, all recounted in a language so supple that it bends from the lowest joke to the highest tragedy—sometimes within the space of a single paragraph.

NEXT ON THE READING LIST: Martin Amis, Paul Auster, T. Coraghessan Boyle, Don DeLillo, Steven Millhauser, Richard Powers, Susan Sontag

Philip Roth
(b. March 19, 1933)

"What distinguishes Roth's [fiction] is its outrageousness. In a world where it is increasingly difficult to be 'erotically' shocking, considerable feats of imagination are required to produce a charge of outrage adequate to his purposes. It is therefore not easy to understand why people complain and say things like 'this time he's gone over the top'.... For if nobody feels outraged the whole strategy has failed."
—*Frank Kermode*, New York Review of Books

* Goodbye, Columbus, and Five Short Stories (HOUGHTON MIFFLIN, 1959) • Roth's impressive debut won a National Book Award. The title novella describes the summerlong affair between Neil Klugman, a poor Jew from Newark, and Brenda Patimkin, a nouveau-riche JAP from Short Hills. Critics have long since pointed out that Roth's obsession with the individual-in-search-of-an-identity theme began here. Yet, at the time, the big fuss was about Roth being an anti-Semitic Jew. Although "Goodbye, Columbus" is essentially a satire on conspicuous consumption, the brilliant short stories that follow it strongly challenged the Hadassah party line.

"There is blood here and vigor, love and hate, irony and compassion.... Mr. Roth has written a perceptive, often witty, and frequently moving piece of fiction. He is a good storyteller, a shrewd appraiser of character, and a keen recorder of an indecisive generation. [He] seems to know his people inside and out." (*William Peden*, New York Times)

Letting Go (RANDOM HOUSE, 1962) • This bleak, overwritten comedy of manners features graduate student Gabe Wallach, who's certainly a Jew, but that's quite beside the point. Set in the academic communities of Chicago and Iowa, *Letting Go* is intentionally nonethnic and self-consciously literary. (Roth appears to be emulating Henry James, the subject of Gabe's dissertation.) At the core of the book are Gabe's relationships with three women: a student with whom he has an affair; a divorcée to whom he can't commit; and his Jewish friend's troubled Gentile wife, whom he should sleep with but doesn't. As with many Roth characters, life hasn't given Gabe enough trouble, so he has to create some of his own. In general, reviewers didn't like the book. In the *New York Times*, Dwight Macdonald called it "turgid with angst and alienation."

When She Was Good (RANDOM HOUSE, 1967) • This is the only Roth novel with a female protagonist—and a Gentile one at that! Like Gabe Wallach in *Letting Go*, Lucy Nelson is so obsessed with her own perfection that she's constantly trying to improve others. The story's main action concerns the collapse of her marriage to Roy Bassett, an ineffectual man whom she married only because she was pregnant. Reviewers pointed out that by setting the story in the Midwest, Roth seemed to be trying to prove—not very successfully—that he could write about something besides urban Jews. In *London Magazine*, Paul Bailey derisively called *When She Was Good* "the work of a Herman Wouk with a university education."

* Portnoy's Complaint (RANDOM HOUSE, 1969) • Self-loathing, guilt-ridden Alexander Portnoy actually has many complaints, most of them having to do with his overbearing Jewish mother, and he tells them all to his silent psychoanalyst, Dr. Spielvogel. The novel's earliest, and funniest, chapters concern Portnoy's adolescence, and they include many graphic descriptions of masturbation that outraged rabbis and other self-appointed guardians of the culture. Despite (or perhaps because of) their admonitions, *Portnoy's Complaint* became the best-selling book in the country and propelled Jewish-American fiction into the mainstream of popular culture. Reviewers particularly praised Roth's authentic use of dialect and his wicked sense of humor.

> "Portnoy's Complaint... *is playfully and painfully moving...and perhaps more important, a deliciously funny book, absurd and exuberant, wild and uproarious.... Not since* Catcher in the Rye *have I read an American novel with such pleasure."* (*Josh Greenfield,* New York Times)

Our Gang (RANDOM HOUSE, 1971; REVISED, BANTAM, 1973) • Now that Roth had finally found an identity for himself as a "funny" satirical writer, he of course decided to write another satirical book. Now who could Roth, a liberal Jew, make fun of in the early 1970s? President Nixon, of course—or as he's caricatured here, Trick E. Dixon. At its best, the novel has a clever topicality that recalls Art Buchwald; its theme of political doubletalk, however, is strictly Orwellian. "A writer with Roth's comic gifts can't but produce some outrageously hilarious moments," Arthur Cooper wrote in the *Saturday Review*. "But Roth is only partly successful for, while his aim is true, his satire isn't Swift. Occasionally his anger gets the best of him, and his humor sours."

The Breast (HOLT, RINEHART & WINSTON, 1972; REVISED, FARRAR, STRAUS & GIROUX, 1980) • Kafka turned Gregor Samsa into a dung beetle, but Roth has other plans for thirty-eight-year-old comp lit professor David Kepesh. He wakes up one day to find that he's been transformed into a six-foot-long mammary gland. However, Kepesh's plight quickly loses its humor as Roth describes his spiritual agony. This brief novella (just seventy-eight pages long) was hotly debated by literary heavyweights, most of whom thought it was brilliant. In the *New York Times*, John Gardner called *The Breast* "terrific for a thing of its kind: inventive and sane and very funny, though filthy.... It's incredible, in fact, how smart [Roth] is for a man so hung up with his you-know-what." However, *Washington Post* reviewer L. J. Davis called the book an instance of "cashing in on an author's reputation."

The Great American Novel (HOLT, RINEHART & WINSTON, 1973) • This novel, as told by Communist sportswriter Word Smith, is the suppressed story of the Patriot League, the one-time stomping ground of Babylonian fireballer Gil Gamesh and the great slugger Luke Gofannon. Sadly, the league's final season was so embarrassing to the national pastime that its entire existence has been, like Stalin's commissars, airbrushed from history. As baseball burlesque, the novel is fabulous; as political allegory, it's less so. "Roth's talent for cruel and shameless comic extravagance gives us marvelously raunchy vignettes of the sporting life, and he gleefully exploits our readiness to let baseball stand for American itself," Thomas R. Edwards observed in the *New York Times*. "But bad taste alone doesn't make successful art, though of course it helps, and the book is too long for its own energies to sustain."

My Life as a Man (HOLT, RINEHART & WINSTON, 1974) • This is one of those books that the critics loved—in *Newsweek*, Peter S. Prescott called it Roth's best book—yet it never caught on with the reading public. Part of the problem was that it's difficult to read, full of time and persona shifts. The first two sections are short stories featuring a writer named Nathan Zuckerman. Then, in the long section entitled "My True Story," we learn that these stories within the story have been written by narrator Peter Tarnopol, another of Roth's outwardly successful yet romantically troubled Jewish intellectual heroes. A tireless self-justifier, Tarnopol is hounded by a loathsome wife, and his shrink doesn't seem able to help. According to *The New Yorker*, "The only problem with this hilarious, amazing book is that the earnest elements—the pleading, the melodrama, the horror—are often upended by all the fooling around."

The Professor of Desire (FARRAR, STRAUS & GIROUX, 1977) • Roth's ninth novel tells the story of David Kepesh prior to his transformation in *The Breast:* from his boyhood in the Catskills, where his parents run a kosher hotel, to the summer in his midthirties when he returns to the mountains with his adoring mistress. However, as narrated by Professor Kepesh, the novel reads more like an extended lecture, relieved occasionally by Kepesh's dialogues with his analyst (in which Roth satisfies his need to explain his intentions to the reader). Even so, Roth remains a formidable stylist, and *The Professor of Desire* features a far more developed, reflective narrative voice than his earlier sexually anguished works. "He may be going in circles," Robert Towers wrote in the *New York Review of Books*, "but at least he's sailing in the mainstream of his talent and not stranded in those swampy backwaters from which *The Great American Novel* and *The Breast* emerged."

* The Ghost Writer (FARRAR, STRAUS & GIROUX, 1979) • In this American Book Award finalist, twenty-three-year-old Nathan Zuckerman makes a literary pilgrimage to the Berkshire home of E. I. Lonoff, a reclusive writer of austere brilliance. Zuckerman is apparently in the market for a surrogate father because a story he has written about a family scandal has alienated his father. Zuckerman is thus torn between his art and his origins.

"I had only to read the two openings sentences of The Ghost Writer *to realize—with a long sigh of anticipated pleasure—that I was once again in the hands of a superbly endowed storyteller."* (*Robert Towers,* New York Times)

Zuckerman Unbound (FARRAR, STRAUS & GIROUX, 1981) • If you hadn't already begun to suspect that Nathan Zuckerman's life bears a close resemblance to that of his creator, this novel makes the comparison obvious. It takes place in the aftermath of Zuckerman's wildly successful 1969 novel *Carnovsky*, a blasphemous satire of sexual obsession. The only other major character is Alvin Pepler, a former TV quiz show star who hounds Zuckerman, first flattering him and then accusing Nathan of stealing his life story. Meanwhile, Roth makes jokes about the nature of fame and the relationship between authors and readers. "Not that the novel is at all straightforward autobiography," Richard Gilman wrote in the *National Review*. "Roth is too much the artist for that. But there is something disingenuous about his attempt wholly to disassociate himself from his protagonist." About the plot, Anatole Broyard noted in the *New York Times*, "Except for Pepler, Zuckerman contends only with himself much of the time, and while Mr. Roth manages this with wit and grace, it is generally true that we are most appealing ourselves when we are with someone else."

The Anatomy Lesson (FARRAR, STRAUS & GIROUX, 1983) • Roth's third Zuckerman novel was nominated for both an American Book Award and a National Book Critics Circle Award. Now forty, Zuckerman has mysterious—presumably psychosomatic—neck and back pains that keep him from writing. Intellectually exhausted, he spends most of the day lying on a rubber mat on the floor of his apartment. Although he's comforted by four women, Zuckerman is essentially the only character in the novel. "For most of *The Anatomy Lesson*, Roth's narrative hand is wonderfully sure, his comic timing worthy of the Ritz brothers," Gary Giddins wrote in the *Village Voice*. "Not since Henry Miller has anyone learned to be as funny and compassionate and brutal and plaintive in the space of a paragraph."

Zuckerman Bound: A Trilogy and Epilogue (FARRAR, STRAUS & GIROUX, 1985) • This anthology collects the first three Zuckerman novels—*The Ghost Writer, Zuckerman Unbound,* and *The Anatomy Lesson*—and adds, as an "epilogue," a new novella called "The Prague Orgy," in which Nathan meets a Czech writer and travels to Prague in search of a rare Yiddish manuscript. The story comically contrasts Nathan's self-conscious concerns with the truly frightening problems faced by writers behind the Iron Curtain. "At once both the bleakest and the funniest writing Roth has done," Harold Bloom declared in the *New York Times*. "The totality is certainly the novelist's finest achievement to date."

The Counterlife (FARRAR, STRAUS & GIROUX, 1986) • In this National Book Critics Circle Award winner, Roth repeatedly draws the reader's attention to the fact that the characters are his creations, with no existence other than to serve his whims. Thus, in the first section, Zuckerman's brother Henry, a middle-class dentist with a family and a mistress, dies during a heart operation—and in the second section, he flees his family to become a militant Zionist in Israel. In the third section, Nathan himself has the operation and dies and then attends his own funeral service. *The Counterlife*, according to Martin Amis in the *Atlantic Monthly*, "is so formidably good, and so perversely surprising, that it prompts a question: How did [Roth] get here? How did he wind up with *this?*" Yet in the *New York Review of Books*, Josh Rubins wrote that the book's "structural miscalculations and floundering impulses make *The Counterlife* a much less absorbing novel than it might have been."

Deception (SIMON & SCHUSTER, 1990) • In this novel that again explores the line between fiction and reality, a writer named Philip lives in London with his dreary wife, Claire. One day, she finds a diary containing his record of various sexual performances in which she didn't take part. When she confronts him, he tells her the diary is a writing exercise, the product of his imagination. What is truth, and what is lie? What is genuine, and what is fiction? Writing in the *American Spectator*, Mark Steyn compared this novel to *Leaving a Doll's House*, the vitriolic 1996 memoir by Roth's former wife, Claire Bloom. "What's striking is how much more persuasive the...showbiz memoir is than the great novelist's work," Steyn wrote. "By comparison with his banal roman à Claire, her account has the sharper crises...and the more telling details."

Operation Shylock: A Confession (SIMON & SCHUSTER, 1993) • Roth won a PEN/Faulkner Award for this novel about a character named Philip Roth who travels to Israel to confront a man claiming to be Philip Roth, who's promoting a movement called Diasporism. The imposter wants Ashkenazi Jews to return to Europe and relinquish Palestine to the Arabs, thereby avoiding an otherwise inevitable nuclear war. Other major characters include a Palestinian friend of Roth's who wants to recruit him and a Mossad agent who wants Roth to participate in Operation Shylock, a scheme to uncover Jewish-American backers of the PLO. "This Dostoevskian phantasmagoria is an impressive reassertion of artistic energy," John Updike wrote in *The New Yorker*, "and a brave expansion of Roth's 'densely over-stocked little store of concerns' into the global marketplace."

Sabbath's Theater (HOUGHTON MIFFLIN, 1995) • This National Book Award winner features the disturbed, demonic, aging puppeteer Mickey Sabbath, whom one critic has called "a geriatric Alexander Portnoy." However, while Portnoy was young and exuberant, Sabbath is morose and considering suicide: His lover has recently died of cancer, and he can't even manipulate his puppets because of his crippling arthritis. In this confessional, Mickey looks back on his erotically obsessed life and prepares for death. In the *Los Angeles Times*, Richard Eder pointed out that, with Sabbath, "Roth has swollen his normally out-sized, brilliant, and intolerably self-immured protagonist into something monstrous and unhinged." And, according to James Wood in *The New Republic*, the author has done so brilliantly: "Roth's prose, moving on its thousand racing feet, is so mobile here, so absorptive."

American Pastoral (HOUGHTON MIFFLIN, 1997) • Through the prism of Nathan Zuckerman, his classmate at Newark's Weequahic High, we learn the story of Seymour "Swede" Levov, a golden-boy superathlete who married the blond (and Gentile) Miss New Jersey and inherited his father's multimillion-dollar glove business. Then, during the 1960s, Swede's life falls apart as his daughter, radicalized by the Vietnam War, joins the Weathermen and takes part in a bombing that kills a man. "*American Pastoral* is a little slow—as befits its crumbling subject, but unmistakably slow all the same—and I must say I miss Zuckerman's manic energies," Michael Wood observed in the *New York Times*. "But the mixture of rage and elegy in the book is remarkable, and you have only to pause over the prose to feel how beautifully it is elaborated."

BIOGRAPHY

THE SON OF AN INSURANCE SALESMAN, Philip Roth grew up in a predominantly Jewish lower-middle-class neighborhood in Newark, New Jersey. He attended Weequahic High and then the Newark branch of Rutgers University before transferring after his freshman year to Bucknell, where he edited the literary magazine. He earned his B.A. in 1954 and his master's in English a year later at Chicago. He entered the army in 1955 but was discharged after he injured himself during basic training. Back at Chicago, he pursued a Ph.D. for a year before dropping out of the program in 1957 and taking a job as a film and TV critic for *The New Republic*.

His first book, *Goodbye, Columbus*, published when he was twenty-six, won him a great deal of critical praise, a National Book Award, and the enmity of most rabbis, but it didn't earn him a lot of money. A decade later, he published *Portnoy's Complaint*, which earned him no awards but even more rabbinical acrimony and a great deal of money. That same year, 1969, the popular feature film *Goodbye, Columbus*, starring Richard Benjamin and Ali MacGraw, was released, and Philip Roth became a household name.

In addition to his novels, Roth has written a number of well-received memoirs. (In fact, more than most writers, Roth has always granted interviews and written articles explaining and defending his work.) In 1988, he published *The Facts: A Novelist's Autobiography*, an account of his life that begins with his early childhood and ends in the late 1960s. Three years later, he wrote *Patrimony: A True Story* about the last months of his father's life. It won a National Book Critics Circle Award.

NEXT ON THE READING LIST: Jorge Amado, Martin Amis, E. L. Doctorow, Milan Kundera, Steven Millhauser, Amos Oz, John Updike

Salman Rushdie

(b. June 19, 1947)

"In life [Rushdie] is a migrant and exile, in fiction a fantasist and historian.... [He] is always testing the tenets of history, politics, and art; for him, composition is inseparable from intellectual improvisation."
—*Margo Jefferson,* Voice Literary Supplement

Grimus (GOLLANCZ, 1975; OVERLOOK, 1979) • Rushdie's first published novel is part political satire, part science fiction. It tells the story of Flapping Eagle, an outcast American Indian blessed—or cursed—with immortality who, in his search for ultimate truth, must solve a series of intricate conundrums. David Wilson in the *Times Literary Supplement* called *Grimus* a "strikingly confident first novel [that] is a convoluted fable about the human condition."

✳ Midnight's Children (KNOPF, 1981) • Winner of Britain's celebrated Booker Prize, *Midnight's Children* presents an epic account of modern India from the perspective of the men and women of the title, those born during the first hour of Indian independence in August 1947. The narrator of this boisterous tale is Saleem Sinai, born on the exact stroke of midnight and master of telepathic powers that enable him to see into men's hearts and minds (as well as communicate with all the other midnight's children). In Rushdie's hands, Saleem's story is also India's story: As Clark Blaise pointed out in the *New York Times,* Rushdie manages to "smuggle Saleem into every major event in the subcontinent's past thirty years."

> "Midnight's Children *will surely be recognized as a great tour de force—a dazzling exhibition of the gifts of a new writer of courage, impressive strength, the power of both imagination and control, and sheer stylistic brilliance." (Anita Desai,* Washington Post)

Shame (KNOPF, 1983) • Rushdie's third novel is a political allegory set in an unnamed country that can only be Pakistan. Using a complex cast of characters and an even more complicated plot, Rushdie analyzes the theme of shame, showing its profound psychological and cultural consequences and the terrible violence that it promotes. In this story, he focuses on the rivalry between Islander Harappa and Raza Hyder, two pitiless enemies who bear more than a passing resemblance to Pakistani strongmen Zulfikar Ali Bhutto and Mohammad Zia ul-Haq. According to Christopher Lehmann-Haupt in the *New York Times*, "*Shame* does for Pakistan what Mr. Rushdie's equally remarkable...*Midnight's Children* did for India."

* The Satanic Verses (VIKING, 1988) • Rushdie's most acclaimed (and, to Muslims, most infamous) work shows off his characteristic wit and irreverence. The story begins, quite literally, with a bang, as a bomb explodes aboard an Air India flight over England. Two Indian men fall twenty-nine thousand feet to earth: Matinee idol Gibreel Farishta acquires a halo after his plunge, while Saladin Chamcha, who does voice-overs for radio and television, becomes a satyrlike creature with horns and a tail. After the elaboration of numerous subplots, the novel concludes with a confrontation between Gibreel and Saladin. As often happens with Rushdie's work, some critics found the book confusing: Michael Wood in *The New Republic* called *The Satanic Verses* "Rushdie's most bewildered book, but...also his most thoughtful." Much harsher were the Muslim clerics who denounced the novel for its insultingly lewd portrayal of the prophet Mohammad.

> *"Rushdie's furious, organizing energy seems to mark him as an angel of coherence. He has obviously read his García Márquez, his Joyce, his Thomas Pynchon. He shares with those authors the desire to assemble everything he has known and seen and make it all fit together, beautifully. In his fourth novel, Rushdie has done just that." (Paul Gray, Time)*

East, West (PANTHEON, 1994) • These short stories further develop many themes already familiar to readers of Rushdie's novels: the claims of religion on people not otherwise disposed to piety, the persistence of history and culture in the modern world, and especially the conflicts faced by people caught between the spheres of East and West. Rushdie divides this collection into three parts—"East," "West," and "East, West"—to emphasize the geographical implications of each tale. According to Richard Eder in the *Los Angeles Times*, "Two or three of these stories...gleam as exuberantly as anything [Rushdie] has done."

The Moor's Last Sigh (PANTHEON, 1995) • Rushdie's first novel since he went into hiding in 1989 appeared with great fanfare and much anticipation, and it didn't disappoint. *The Moor's Last Sigh* chronicles the rise, decline, and fall of a Portuguese merchant family living in India. The narrator, Moraes Zogoiby, is a half-Christian, half-Jewish native of Bombay and the last of his clan. Rushdie injects a great deal of modern Indian history into the story, which even touches on such recent events as the BCCI scandal and the rise of Hindu fundamentalism. The geography is equally broad, ranging from the Zogoiby spice business in Cochin to Malabar Hill, the wealthy Bombay suburb where Moraes's mother is a local celebrity. "So, another brave and dazzling fable from Salman Rushdie, one that meets the test of civic usefulness—broadly conceived—as certainly as it fulfills the requirements of true art. No retort to tyranny could be more eloquent," Norman Rush wrote in the *New York Times*.

BIOGRAPHY

SALMAN RUSHDIE WAS BORN IN Bombay in June 1947, just two months before India achieved its independence. He grew up in a Muslim family, speaking both English and Urdu. His love of literature came from likely sources: His mother frequently told him stories drawn from the history of their family, while his father—a businessman well read in Arabic, Persian, and Western literature—amused Rushdie and his three sisters with fairy tales. By the time Rushdie was five, he has said, he knew that he wanted to become a writer.

In 1961, Rushdie's parents sent him to Rugby, an elite secondary school in Britain, but that experience wasn't entirely beneficial: He was lonely and had to suffer the "minor persecutions and racist attacks" of his classmates, he has said. On the other hand, Rushdie remembers his college years at Cambridge much more fondly: He found kindred intellectual spirits, majored in history, and joined the Footlights, a student theater club. After receiving his master's degree with honors in 1968, Rushdie worked briefly for a theater group in London and then as an advertising copywriter while he wrote his first novel. (It was never published.) *Grimus* appeared in 1975, and though it wasn't a commercial success, it did pique the interest of some science-fiction buffs. Rushdie's breakthrough came six years later with the publication of *Midnight's Children*. He has said that he thought the book's dark themes and fantastic subject matter would alienate readers; instead, it sold more than 250,000 copies in Great Britain alone.

The 1983 publication of *Shame* solidified Rushdie's reputation, but it was *The Satanic Verses*, published in 1988, that changed his life. Because portions of the book offended Muslims, it was banned in India and throughout the Middle East. Moreover, on February 14, 1989, the Ayatollah Ruhollah Khomeini of Iran pronounced a *fatwa*, or death sentence, on Rushdie and all those associated with the novel's publication. Immediately, Rushdie went into hiding. It was thought at the time that this situation would be only temporary, but Khomeini died without retracting the *fatwa*. Although Rushdie has publicly apologized (and made more and more public appearances), he remains in hiding, his life still threatened.

NEXT ON THE READING LIST: Louis de Bernières, Carlos Fuentes, Gabriel García Márquez, Milan Kundera, Naguib Mahfouz, V. S. Naipaul

Carol Shields

(b. June 2, 1935)

*"It is this author's habit of paying humorous and loving
attention to her characters that her readers value most of all
in her work. Carol Shields demonstrates that there are no
small lives, no lives out of which significance does not shine.
She makes us aware that banality, ultimately, is in the eye
of the beholder."*
—Merna Summers, Canadian Forum

Small Ceremonies (McGraw-Hill Ryerson, 1976; Penguin, 1996) • Popular
with readers but ignored by most critics until its republication, Shields's
debut novel chronicles a year in the life of biographer Judith Gill (née
McNinn), a middle-class suburbanite with "an unhealthy lust for the lives of
other people." Fascinated by what the people around her conceal, she
muses on the relationships of fact to fiction and real life to biography.
"Learning to know herself provides the key to understanding others in this
engaging short novel," Charles Solomon wrote in the *Los Angeles Times.*

The Box Garden (McGraw-Hill Ryerson, 1977; Penguin, 1996) • This book,
a dark companion to *Small Ceremonies,* concerns Judith's sister, poet
Charleen Forrest (also née McNinn). Charleen travels to Toronto with
her fifteen-year-old son to attend her venomous mother's second wedding. Dreading the reunion, she also brings along her orthodontist
boyfriend, Eugene, to provide comfort that she'll badly need. According
to Carol Anshaw in *Newsday,* "Anyone who enjoyed *The Stone Diaries*
should be a little happier for the reappearance of this work from
Shields's apprenticeship."

Happenstance (McGraw-Hill Ryerson, 1980; Macmillan of Canada, 1982;
Penguin, 1994) • This is a two-for-one, his-and-hers story of a happy marriage
in midlife crisis. The two novellas that make up this volume were originally
published separately: Jack Bowman's side of the story appeared as
Happenstance in 1980; his wife Brenda's riposte was published as *A Fairly
Conventional Woman* in 1982. For the first time in twenty years, the couple is
separated when Brenda travels to a crafts convention in Chicago. During
their long weekend apart, both spouses encounter situations that cause
them to reconsider the course of their lives together. Reviews were mixed:
In the *Los Angeles Times,* Elizabeth Benedict wrote that Jack and Brenda's
"ordinary lives are hugely engrossing and sharply, satirically fixed at the
edges of the social and intellectual trends of the 1970s." However, according to *Books in Canada* reviewer Julie Beddoes, "One longs for less portrait
painting and more event."

Various Miracles (STODDART, 1985; PENGUIN, 1989) • With this first collection of short stories, Shields begins to experiment. Her characters remain largely ordinary people, yet their lives seem much more subject to the vagaries of coincidence and fantasy. "Avoiding cuteness on the one hand and pomposity on the other, Ms. Shields frequently succeeds in twirling fragmentary daydreams and peculiar anecdotes into tiny fictions of sizable impact," Josh Rubins observed in the *New York Times*.

Swann: A Mystery (STODDART, 1987; VIKING, 1989) • This gently satirical novel, another experiment, won Canada's Arthur Ellis Award for crime writing. Shields uses four separate voices to tell the story of the late Mary Swann, a Canadian farm wife who produced some extraordinary poetry. Those four voices belong to the feminist scholar who "discovered" Swann, Swann's biographer, her publisher, and the town clerk. (The clerk attributes the many water references in Swann's poetry not to a "yearning for baptism" but to the fact that there was no well on the Swann property.) In the *New York Times*, Christopher Lehmann-Haupt called the book "intriguing and often charming" but agreed with most reviewers that the final section was disappointing.

The Orange Fish (RANDOM HOUSE OF CANADA 1989; VIKING, 1990) • In this collection, Shields demonstrates her "extraordinary ability to find both mystery and meaning in the chaos of everyday life," Brent Ledger wrote in *Maclean's*. While the stories here are more traditional in form than those in *Various Miracles*, Shields remains interested in life's daily accidents and the emotional nuances of small events. "Sharp, funny, and compassionate, Shields's tales of order among the random have an elegance that is no accident," Ledger concluded.

A Celibate Season (COTEAU, 1991) • Shields teamed up with Blanche Howard, another respected Canadian writer, to pen this epistolary novel whose theme is marriage. Howard takes the role of Jock (short for Jocelyn), a lawyer serving on a public poverty commission that takes her away from her family. Shields plays Charles, her husband, an unemployed architect and at-home father to their teenage children. Writing in the *Ottawa Citizen*, Chetan Rajani called the book a "juicy, fun read," if somewhat frivolous.

The Republic of Love (VIKING, 1992) • A woman who can't commit and a man who commits too easily experience love at first sight in this novel that *New York Times* reviewer Elinor Lipman called a "touching, elegantly funny, luscious work of fiction." Switching between male and female viewpoints, Shields tells the love story of Fay McLeod, a folklorist studying mermaids, and Tom Avery, a late-night DJ. Both are lonely, jaded people who long for more meaning in their lives.

* The Stone Diaries (RANDOM HOUSE OF CANADA, 1993; VIKING, 1994) • Shields's breakout book won her a Pulitzer Prize, a National Book Critics Circle

Award, and Canada's Governor General's Award, and it was short-listed in Britain for a Booker. Using a blend of first-person and third-person narration, letters, newspaper clippings, recipes, and short poems, Shields describes the life of Daisy Goodwill Flett from her dramatic birth in Manitoba to her less-than-dramatic death in a Florida nursing home.

> *"Ignore what you have read elsewhere about* The Stone Diaries *being the story of an ordinary woman. No one in a Shields novel is ordinary. Her people, touched by some outside awareness, transcend the everyday."* (*Allyson F. McGill,* Belles Lettres)

Larry's Party (VIKING, 1997) • Shields again chronicles a life, this time a man's, in order to explore, as she says, "what it's like to be an ordinary, middle-aged guy at the end of the century." Each of the book's fifteen chapters takes on one aspect of good-natured, laid-back Larry Weller's life. We have "Larry's Work," "Larry's Friends," and even "Larry's Penis." The essay format, however, caused some reviewers to complain that the book lacked drama. Writing in *Newsday*, Dan Cryer noted that *Larry's Party* "doesn't quite measure up" to *The Stone Diaries* but called it "a novel of substance and deep feeling."

BIOGRAPHY

CAROL SHIELDS WAS BORN IN Oak Park, Illinois, where, she has said, "wanting to be a writer was like wanting to be a movie star." Like many women of her generation, she didn't wait long before getting hitched. Shortly after her graduation from college, she married Don Shields, a Canadian engineer from Manitoba whom she had met during a college semester in England. After their 1957 wedding, Shields concerned herself primarily with raising the couple's five children. "I drifted into writing fiction," she remembered. "I certainly never set out with a plan for a career path. With five children, I was just too busy."

Shields began to write during the 1960s, but with only an hour of free time each day, "my first novels were very short." Although she was already past forty when *Small Ceremonies* was published, she has never expressed regret over her late start, saying that she began writing when she was ready to begin.

A naturalized Canadian with dual citizenship and "a foot on either side of the border," Shields is currently chancellor of the University of Manitoba, where she formerly taught English (and where her husband serves as dean of the engineering department). Of her writing, Shields has said, "I'm not interested in intricate plots. I'm interested in the way people bump up against each other and against events. And I do love making sentences."

NEXT ON THE READING LIST: Margaret Atwood, Andrea Barrett, Pat Conroy, Ellen Gilchrist, Alice Munro, Iris Murdoch, Muriel Spark

Leslie Marmon Silko

(b. March 5, 1948)

"At her best, Leslie Silko is very good indeed. She has a sharp sense of the way in which the profound and the mundane often run together in our daily lives. And her sense of humor is acute."

—N. Scott Momaday, New York Times

Ceremony (VIKING, 1977) • Tayo, a half-breed World War II veteran, returns to the Laguna Pueblo reservation shattered by his experience. Struggling to maintain his sanity and adjust to civilian life, he tries to purify himself through tribal ritual but fails. Eventually, he befriends another half-breed, Betonie, who teaches him the value of ceremony: that ceremony isn't merely ritual, not merely *form*, but a comprehensive means of conducting one's life. According to Frank MacShane in the *New York Times*, *Ceremony* "is one of the most realized works of fiction devoted to Indian life that has been written in this country, and it is a splendid achievement."

Storyteller (SEAVER, 1981) • In this mélange that's more than a volume of collected works, Silko weaves together poetry from her 1974 collection *Laguna Woman* and some previously published short stories with histori-cal anecdotes, folktales, autobiography, and photographs taken by her father and grandfather to create a "retelling" in the oral tradition of the Laguna Pueblo. Silko makes numerous connections between the past and the present as she celebrates the Indian cultural heritage that has given her "an entire history, an entire vision of the world which depended upon memory and retelling." In the *Saturday Review*, James Polk wrote, "Although many of her stories traverse familiar territory—the dislocation of a disinherited people—her perceptions are acute, and her style reflects the breadth, the texture, and the mortality of her subjects."

✱ Almanac of the Dead (SIMON & SCHUSTER, 1991) • In this novel, Silko's Native American characters wage war against an Anglo culture irre-deemably perverted by pornography, drug abuse, violent crime, degrada-tion of the environment, and many other varieties of evil. For example, one character, a former topless dancer with a cocaine habit, has a child with her bisexual lover, whose other lover becomes so jealous that he has the child kidnapped and dismembered—while capturing the murder on film. The leaders of the Indian resistance are twin sisters Zeta and Lecha, caretakers of the Almanac of the Dead, an ancient collection of tribal nar-ratives. When the decoded text instructs them that the time is right for a major offensive against European hegemony, they set in motion a secret scheme to reclaim the tribal land once taken by the conquistadors and later the cavalry.

> *"Appearing on the eve of the quincentennial of Columbus's arrival in the Americas,* Almanac of the Dead *burns at an apocalyptic pitch—passionate indictment, defiant augury, bravura storytelling." (Elizabeth Tallent,* New York Times)

BIOGRAPHY

In 1872, LESLIE MARMON SILKO'S great-grandfather, Robert G. Marmon, settled in the pueblo of Laguna, about forty miles west of Albuquerque. His second wife, Marie Anaya Marmon, was a Laguna woman, and when Silko was a child, her great-grandmother still lived next door. Marie Marmon and several of Silko's older aunts made sure that she understood and appreciated the ways and beliefs of the Laguna people.

At the same time, Silko attended reservation schools run by the Bureau of Indian Affairs and, after the fifth grade, Catholic schools in Albuquerque, where she also attended the University of New Mexico, graduating in 1969 with a B.A. in English. After college, Silko entered law school as part of a program to train Indian attorneys but she didn't stay long. Instead, deciding to pursue a career as a writer, she taught for two years at Navajo Community College in Arizona before moving to Alaska. During her two years in Ketchikan she wrote *Ceremony*, and then she moved back to the Southwest, where she taught at the University of New Mexico and then the University of Arizona as she prepared *Storyteller* for publication in 1981. That same year, Silko received from the MacArthur Foundation a five-year "genius" grant that enabled her to write *Almanac of the Dead*.

In addition to her works of fiction, which blend the Western form of the novel with the Laguna oral tradition, Silko has published a collection of essays entitled *Yellow Woman and a Beauty of the Spirit: Essays on Native American Life Today* (1996). She has been divorced twice and has two sons.

NEXT ON THE READING LIST: Louise Erdrich, Gabriel García Márquez, Cormac McCarthy, John Nichols, Michael Ondaatje

Mona Simpson

(b. June 14, 1957)

"[Simpson's] language can be breathtaking in the simple beauty of its imagery or in its combination of the lyrical and the astute. [Simpson] demonstrates…a spectacular talent for rendering tumultuous emotional states with eloquence and economy."
—*Jim Shepard*, New York Times

* Anywhere But Here (KNOPF, 1987) • In this novel's opening scene, Adele, cursed with a hunger for glamour and success, leaves her twelve-year-old daughter, Ann, by the side of an empty highway and drives away, returning a short time later. This sequence succinctly demonstrates their relationship as they travel across the country in a Lincoln Continental that's not paid off to fulfill Adele's dreams of launching Ann's career as a child actress in California.

> *"If* Anywhere But Here *carries echoes of the 'on the road' novel, the 'small town' novel, and the Western-pioneer novel, Ms. Simpson also succeeds in creating a wholly original work—a work stamped with the insignia of a distinctive voice and animated by two idiosyncratic and memorable heroines." (Michiko Kakutani, New York Times)*

The Lost Father (KNOPF, 1991) • Simpson picks up the story of Ann Stevenson where *Anywhere But Here* left off. Now twenty-eight, she lives in New York City, where she attends medical school. She has also resumed her birth name, Mayan, given her by the Egyptian academic father who abandoned her as a child. This novel recounts Mayan's obsessive efforts to find her "lost" father. Simpson admirer Michiko Kakutani described *The Lost Father* as "one of those books that takes over the reader's life for a couple of days, a book that should galvanize Mona Simpson's reputation as one of the most accomplished writers of her generation."

A Regular Guy (KNOPF, 1996) • Although critics had praised the quirky first-person narration of *Anywhere But Here* and *The Lost Father*, Simpson switched to a third-person voice for this story of Tom Owens, a character loosely based on Simpson's half brother Steve Jobs, a founder of Apple Computers. *A Regular Guy* presents one decade in the hectic life of Owens, a biotech whiz kid who runs the Fortune 500 Genesis Corporation. Owens's funky New Age solutions to his corporate and personal problems intrigued some reviewers, but most found him dull. According to *Time*'s Martha Duffy, "Simpson can be a strong, sinewy writer, and it may be that this novel…is simply a misstep."

BIOGRAPHY

ALTHOUGH MONA SIMPSON'S OWN father left her family when she was thirteen, she doesn't consider her experience unusual, just extreme. "Who really had a father?" she has asked. "Even people who did have fathers didn't. I grew up in the 1950s and 1960s. Men were working."

After her fatherless teenage years in Green Bay, Wisconsin, Simpson attended the University of California, Berkeley, graduating in 1979. Four years later, she received an M.F.A. from Columbia University. Her first novel, *Anywhere But Here*, published in 1986, received a great deal of critical praise, although Simpson herself later indicated that she wasn't satisfied with it. In interviews, she has told of drafting and redrafting the book several times but never quite managing to match it to the vision with which she began.

Simpson currently teaches creative writing at Bard College. When she writes, she has explained, she works without an outline, preferring to generate her stories one paragraph at a time. Like most novelists, she doesn't consider her books autobiographical in the traditional sense. "I'm not sure what autobiography is," she has said. "If you're talking about—strictly speaking—events, then no. It's definitely not a memoir; it's definitely not nonfiction. If autobiography includes our imagination, then, of course, everything that we write is autobiographical. I think, for people who write fiction or poetry, our wager is that what we imagine is truer or as true to us as the mess of life and the mess that happens."

NEXT ON THE READING LIST: Andrea Barrett, Kaye Gibbons, Ellen Gilchrist, David Guterson, Jane Hamilton, Ursula Hegi, Lorrie Moore

---

Jane Smiley
(b. September 26, 1949)

"Smiley subverts satire, making it sweeter and ultimately more pointed.... [She] has created what modern novel readers have until now been able only to dream about, that elusive, seemingly impossible thing: a fresh, literary, modern twentieth-century nineteenth-century novel."
—*Cathleen Schine*, New York Review of Books

Barn Blind (HARPER & ROW, 1980) • Smiley's first novel tells of a long hot summer on an Illinois horse farm. Kate Karlson's single-minded devotion to maintaining the farm and excelling at horse shows blinds her to the needs of her husband and four children. Her problem becomes particularly obvious when tragedy strikes the family. Critics praised Smiley's warm evocation of farm routine, as well as her deft manipulation of the psychological nuances of family life. According to *New York Times* reviewer Michael Malone, "Smiley handles with skill and understanding the mercurial molasses of adolescence and the inchoate, cumbersome love that family members feel for one another."

At Paradise Gate (SIMON & SCHUSTER, 1981) • Another family drama, *At Paradise Gate* observes the reactions of Anna Robinson and her three adult daughters to the imminent death of their father, Ike. The daughters' return home revives sibling rivalries, and they argue incessantly among themselves about the best way to care for their dying father. Meanwhile, Anna reexamines her years with Ike, reflecting on the mysteries and miseries of married life and the prospect of living alone. In the *Washington Post*, Susan Wood called the novel "a sensitive study of what it means to grow old and face death, and of the courage to see clearly what one's life has meant."

Duplicate Keys (KNOPF, 1984) • For her third novel, Smiley tried a mystery. The principal characters are a group of transplanted midwesterners living in Manhattan. Alice Ellis, the librarian heroine, is best friends with Susan, the roommate of rock musicians Denny and Craig, both of whom have been murdered. "A first-rate cliffhanger," Lois Gould called the book in the *New York Times*. However, while praising the novel's "bright and energetic" treatment, Malcolm Boyd of the *Los Angeles Times* found its plot "slack and predictable."

The Age of Grief (KNOPF, 1987) • This collection of a novella plus five short stories provides more of the sympathetic analyses of marriage, family, and friendship that filled Smiley's first three novels. In the title novella, the narrator realizes that his wife no longer loves him. In the story "Long Distance," the protagonist confronts the probability that his life has assumed its "final form." As Laura Furman wrote in the *Los Angeles Times*, "Smiley's people come alive not in the dilemmas that motor the stories along but in the luminous details and sensual observations that the writer gives them."

The Greenlanders (KNOPF, 1988) • Smiley sets this 558-page historical novel in fourteenth-century Greenland, where Icelandic colonists struggle to survive in a formidable land. Composed as overlapping tales with interspersed prayers and adages, *The Greenlanders* re-creates the storytelling style of Old Norse folklore. Its principal narrator is Gunnar Asgeirsson, born in 1352, whose voice describes the day-to-day hardships of the Greenlanders during a time when the colony is in decline. Reviewers generally praised Smiley's copious research and authentic portrayal of a remote subject, yet many found fault with the novel's rather weak plot. "It takes a certain disciplined curiosity to get through this tome, except by incremental readings, perhaps on a hundred winter nights," Howard Norman wrote in the *New York Times.*

Ordinary Love and Good Will (KNOPF, 1989) • With these two novellas, Smiley returned to more familiar themes of love and family. "Ordinary Love" tells the story of Rachel Kinsella, whose marriage broke up when she admitted to an affair with a neighbor and her husband left with their five children. Many years later at a family reunion, Rachel tells her children the never-revealed truth of what happened, and they respond with tales of their own harrowing experiences with their father. In "Good Will," the Millers, a Pennsylvania farm family, raise their own food, make their own furniture, and live without central heating, electricity, a telephone, or a car. Yet problems lurk beneath the surface of their bucolic self-sufficiency. "With this volume," Michiko Kakutani wrote in the *New York Times*, "Jane Smiley ratifies her claim as one of her generation's most eloquent chroniclers of ordinary familial love, its pleasures and its frightening hazards."

* A Thousand Acres (KNOPF, 1991) • This Pulitzer Prize winner transplants Shakespeare's *King Lear* to Zebulon County, Iowa, where Larry Cook abruptly decides to deed his thousand-acre farm to his three daughters— Ginny, Rose, and Caroline. When Caroline hesitates to accept, her imperious and intolerant father cuts her out of the deal. Then, once he gives away the farm, he becomes unhinged, drinking too much and behaving increasingly erratically. According to Christopher Lehmann-Haupt in the *New York Times*, "Lear's ghost in these pages serves the exalted purpose of lending what might have seemed a lurid prairie melodrama the dimensions of a classical tragedy."

> "A Thousand Acres *is the big book that will finally earn [Smiley] the wider audience she deserves."* (*Ron Carlson,* New York Times)

Moo (KNOPF, 1995) • Smiley's setting for this successful campus satire is a large midwestern university known as "Moo U." because of its nationally famous agriculture college. As one might expect, *Moo* has a large roster of zany characters, from the state's anti-intellectual governor, who thinks of the Moo U. faculty as "pinheads, eggheads, knuckleheads," to economics professor Lionel Gift, who conspires with a greedy chicken billionaire to mine gold in a Costa Rican rain forest. Fortunately, Chairman X, the Marxist head of the school's horticulture department, is out to foil Gift's plans. Smiley moves the plot along with a complicated series of romances that ultimately transform both their participants and the university. "*Moo* is not only a delectably entertaining comedy, but also a comedy in the truest Chekhovian sense: sad, resonant and wise," *New York Times* critic Michiko Kakutani wrote.

BIOGRAPHY

JANE SMILEY'S PARENTS DIVORCED when she was quite young. Her father was a career soldier in the army, her mother an editor at the *St. Louis Globe Democrat.* Smiley grew up in St. Louis with her mother, whom she has credited with encouraging her interest in literature. Smiley attended Vassar College, majoring in English, and married her first husband, John Whiston, while a student there in 1970. She graduated a year later, writing a novel for her senior thesis. Years later, she described the experience as one that persuaded her to become a fiction writer: "I knew this was for me, this creation of worlds."

Following her graduation, Smiley spent a year in Europe, taking part in a medieval archaeological dig in England. She and her husband then moved to Iowa City, where Whiston enrolled in a graduate program at the University of Iowa. Inspired by a professor there to pursue a graduate degree herself, Smiley subsequently earned three of them: an M.A. in 1975, an M.F.A. in 1976, and a Ph.D. in 1978. It was during a Fulbright-financed year in Iceland studying Old Norse literature (the subject of her doctoral dissertation) that Smiley first conceived of the story for *The Greenlanders.*

Smiley divorced Whiston in 1975 and in 1978 married her second husband, William Silag, then a history professor at Iowa State University. Two years later, just as she was beginning a teaching career, she published *Barn Blind,* her first novel. Since then, Smiley has maintained both careers, writing fiction as well as teaching it at Iowa State. Meanwhile, she has raised three children. Smiley currently lives in Ames, Iowa, with her third husband, screenwriter Stephen Mortensen, who likes to call his six-foot-two wife "the tallest woman in American fiction."

NEXT ON THE READING LIST: E. L. Doctorow, Jane Hamilton, Ursula Hegi, Peter Høeg, John Irving, Anne Tyler

Susan Sontag

(b. January 16, 1933)

"The typical Sontag character is intelligent, self-analytical, and suffering from a non-specific form of anxiety or discontent. He may be obsessed by thoughts of freedom, while continually fettering himself at every turn. He may long for change and space, but he's unwilling to give up the brittle shell he is accustomed to inhabiting.... Generally, he feels burdened by a body of fashionable knowledge that fails to solve any of his real problems."
—*Anne Tyler,* The New Republic

The Benefactor (FARRAR, STRAUS & GIROUX, 1963) • In her first novel, Sontag dissects the dual nature of Hippolyte, a withdrawn young man who seeks to enact in his waking life the apparently greater reality of his dream world. Critics praised Sontag's intellectual daring in writing a novel meant to approximate the sensibility of current European fiction, but some found the exercise overly literary—academic, they complained, rather than felt.

Death Kit (FARRAR, STRAUS & GIROUX, 1967) • In many respects a companion piece to *The Benefactor* and reviewed about as unfavorably, Sontag's second novel shows her still in the thrall of a modern Continental literature that she has read widely yet cannot quite transcend. Again we meet a passive male protagonist, Dalton (Diddy) Harron, who conducts a kind of experiment in consciousness and perception—although this time it's death and dreams that obsess the hero. Featuring a more absorbing story than its predecessor, *Death Kit* concentrates on Diddy's efforts (did he?) to determine whether or not he committed a murder. The centerpiece, however, remains Sontag's own complex cerebrations.

I, etcetera (FARRAR, STRAUS & GIROUX, 1978) • More than a decade elapsed before Sontag published her next work of fiction, this erudite collection of eight stories. According to *New Republic* critic Anne Tyler, however, the contents of this book should more accurately be called comments or notes, "self-addressed notes at that." "We turn past the last page," she continues, "looking for one more page that will make the story come together." But, of course, it isn't there. "Even the freest internal voice," Tyler concludes, must "be screened for readability." In some places, however, Sontag does offer concrete characters snared in realistic predicaments. The results, unexpectedly affecting, hint that the author's narrative abilities may yet catch up to her learning.

✳ The Volcano Lover: A Romance (FARRAR, STRAUS & GIROUX, 1992) • This densely detailed historical novel, pointedly subtitled "A Romance," caught the literary world by surprise and became a best-seller at home and abroad. Set in Naples in 1772, the story features such real-life figures as Admiral Nelson and his notorious mistress, Emma Hamilton, who are brought vividly to life in Sontag's sweeping, glittering narrative. As one might expect, the book is formidably erudite—for example, Mozart and Goethe are both given walk-on roles. *The Volcano Lover* also considers the serious topics that have preoccupied Sontag from the beginning: the tension between imagination and reality and the rival claims of art and fact.

> *"There is an operatic quality to the tale...and a grand, at times majestic, sweep to the telling.... For the most part, the narrative is irresistible in its forward thrust. Some of the set pieces are worthy of a Marguerite Yourcenar or a Simon Schama, and there are wonderful touches of grotesque comedy."* (*John Banville*, New York Times)

BIOGRAPHY

SUSAN SONTAG IS ONE OF THE most erudite and wide-ranging writers of our time. Born in New York City, she early exhibited all the earmarks of an intellectual prodigy, graduating from high school at the age of fifteen before attending Berkeley, the University of Chicago, Harvard (where she received master's degrees in both English and philosophy), and finally Oxford. She was only seventeen when she married Harvard sociologist Philip Rieff in 1950. The couple were divorced in 1958 but had a son, David Rieff, who's himself now a writer.

Sontag gained prominence during the 1960s with her varied, elegant, and daring criticism. In "Notes toward a Definition of Camp," she rejected conventional distinctions between "high" and "low" art. And in such works as *Against Interpretation* (1966) and *Styles of Radical Will* (1969), she challenged the prevailing search for moral meaning in works of art and instead advocated aesthetic experimentation. Devoted to European art and ideas, Sontag has introduced Americans to the work of such transatlantic figures as Antonin Artaud, Roland Barthes, Elias Canetti, and E. M. Cioran.

Her critical and aesthetic interests recur in her fiction, giving Sontag's novels their heft and depth but at the same time making them seem emotionally barren and narratively inert. On the other hand, some critics have found in Sontag's erudition a welcome change from the predominant tone of American fiction. According to John Breslin in the *Washington Post*, "Sontag illuminates our contemporary situation with the peculiar radiance that comes from the fusion of wide learning, precise thinking and deep feeling."

NEXT ON THE READING LIST: A. S. Byatt, Joan Didion, Umberto Eco, Milan Kundera, Joyce Carol Oates, Kenzaburo Oe, Grace Paley

Muriel Spark
(b. February 1, 1918)

"We are never out of touch, in a Spark novel, with the happiness of creation; the sudden willful largess of image and epigram, the cunning tautness of suspense, the beautifully firm modulations from passage to passage, the blunt yet dignified dialogues all remind us of the author, the superintending intelligent mind."
—*John Updike,* The New Yorker

The Comforters (LIPPINCOTT, 1957) • Spark's debut novel, published when she was in her late thirties and a recent convert to Roman Catholicism, showed her to be a mature artist and a master of elegant, lapidary prose. Partly autobiographical, partly fanciful, *The Comforters* centers on the travails of literary critic Caroline Rose, who's at work on a study of the modern novel but wishes to write her own fiction instead. One critic called the book "a satisfying first novel" that promised much for Muriel Spark.

Robinson (LIPPINCOTT, 1958) • The title character, a recluse, lives on a small island in the Atlantic Ocean he has named for himself. Like Robinson Crusoe, Spark's Robinson keeps sparse company: a native boy and a cat. When a plane crashes on the island, three survivors—a salesman, a kinsman of Robinson's, and a journalist—disrupt Robinson's solitary existence. A far weaker effort than Spark's first novel, this tale struck critics as tedious in design and rather mechanically told.

The Go-Away Bird and Other Stories (MACMILLAN, 1958; LIPPINCOTT, 1960) • Spark first won attention as a short-story writer, and the form suits her gift for deft plotting and taut narration. This first collection of her work explores the same themes as her early novels, including the confrontation between a Christian worldview and the chaotic, amoral world. This particular theme emerges hauntingly in "The Twins," a chilling account of two precocious children and their demonic powers. A number of the stories are set in Africa, where Spark lived for several years. One of these, "The Portobello Road," Spark considers her finest.

＊ Memento Mori (LIPPINCOTT, 1959) • This brilliant black comedy, written in sparkling prose, made Spark's reputation as a novelist who can uniquely combine comic effects with spiritual themes. A group of upper-crust octogenarian friends begin to receive anonymous phone calls, one by one, from a stranger who warns, "Remember you must die." The menacing words force the elderly characters to reflect on their lives, especially the errors, deceptions, and self-delusions in which they've indulged.

The Ballad of Peckham Rye (LIPPINCOTT, 1960) • In this dark fable, Spark surprised readers and reviewers alike by turning to the ups-and-downs of the working class. A manufacturing company hires Dougal Douglas "to bring vision into the lives of the workers." Dougal sees himself, however, as "one of the wicked spirits that wander through the world for the ruin of souls." Cleverly plotted, the novel traces Dougal's impact—good in some instances, ill in others, and never quite what we expect—on the employees he's supposed to uplift. The *New York Times* called the book an unsubtle but expert fantasy with "a fresh comic style."

The Bachelors (MACMILLAN, 1960; LIPPINCOTT, 1961) • Like *Memento Mori*, this black comedy describes a close-knit community of characters—in this case, a group of bachelors plus their friends and lovers. Spark also explores her usual religious themes, but in an unusual way: by exploring a cult called the Interior Spiral of the Wider Infinity. One of the cult members, Patrick Seton, a professional psychic, plans a young woman's murder. Critics praised Spark's expert handling of the material and her depiction of the novel's eccentric, egomaniacal characters.

Voices at Play (MACMILLAN, 1961; LIPPINCOTT, 1962) • Spark's second short-story collection includes four "ear-pieces," radio scripts written for the BBC. The radio-play form comes easily to Spark because of her precise ear for both dialogue and the telling absurdities of human speech. Again, Africa is a favored locale in such stories as "The Curtain Blown by the Breeze" and the much-anthologized "Bang-Bang You're Dead."

* The Prime of Miss Jean Brodie (MACMILLAN, 1961; LIPPINCOTT, 1962) • Spark's most famous novel (serialized in *The New Yorker* and later made into a popular movie) is set in the author's hometown of Edinburgh during the 1930s, although the story flashes forward to the present. The protagonist, a romantic egotist, teaches at the Marcia Blaine School for Girls, where she dominates a group of favored teenage pupils, her "crème de la crème," through the force of her own overwrought personality. The novel explores the malign influence that Miss Brodie has on these impressionable young lives.

> *"It is as good as anything Mrs. Spark has done and, as should be clear by now, that means to me that it is very good indeed.... Mrs. Spark's powers of invention are apparently inexhaustible, and these unique and impressive powers make her a novelist worth taking very seriously." (Samuel Hynes, Commonweal)*

The Girls of Slender Means (KNOPF, 1963) • Like its predecessor, this novel shuttles between the past and the present but is "much more predictable and much less effective," said one critic. Its story is set in 1945 in a London hostelry established "for the Pecuniary Convenience and Social Protection of Ladies of Slender Means below the age of Thirty Years." Spark captures the feel of wartime London with impressive accuracy, introducing the expected religious theme through the ordeal of a young male poet who suffers the throes of conversion.

✻ The Mandelbaum Gate (KNOPF, 1965) • This extended narrative—much longer than Spark's previous novels, more straightforwardly religious, and more conventionally plotted—features a protagonist, Barbara Vaughan, who resembles the author in that she's half Jewish by birth and a convert to Roman Catholicism. Barbara goes to Israel to tour the shrines and also be near her lover, an archaeologist working on a Dead Sea excavation. While in Israel she meets an Englishman, Freddy Hamilton, who accompanies her on a dangerous trip to Jordan, where she's mistaken for an Israeli spy.

> "The Mandelbaum Gate *is a fascinating performance, less obviously cute than some of [Spark's] earlier books. It crosses the tradition of the novel of female sensibility with modern exotic fiction.... It is not a book to miss.*" (*Malcolm Bradbury,* New York Times)

Collected Stories (MACMILLAN, 1967; KNOPF, 1968) • This book, intended to widen Spark's readership beyond her loyal admirers, shows her range as a writer at once comic and serious, stylistically inventive yet concerned with traditional themes. It includes all the stories published in her first two collections, plus four hitherto uncollected ones. "The Playhouse Called Remarkable," written expressly for this collection, comments on Spark's own experiences as a literary figure. It's also a parable about the mysterious origins of art, described here as a gift bestowed on humanity by the Moon people.

The Public Image (KNOPF, 1968) • Spark continues her exploration of ethical and spiritual issues in this economical and witty novel, a sly commentary on the excesses of the 1960s, especially among the well-to-do. The story is set in Rome, where Spark herself moved in 1967, and depicts the haphazard, hedonistic lives of some of those who choose to live in the Eternal City. The protagonist, Annabel Christopher, an actress who stars in low-budget films, is very much concerned with her "public image." And she has great cause to be when her husband, Frederick, a part-time actor and screenwriter, concocts a bizarre real-life scenario for the two of them to act out.

The Driver's Seat (KNOPF, 1970) • A partner, thematically, to *The Public Image*, this acerbic novel owes a great deal to contemporary Italian cinema, especially to the work of Fellini and Antonioni. Its locale is unspecified, and the present-tense narrative jumps occasionally into the future. But the story, about people's fascination with celebrity, clearly describes the psychotic determination of the protagonist, Lise, to attract the attention of

Interpol and "the journalists of Europe." One word that kept cropping up in reviews of *The Driver's Seat* was "strange."

Not to Disturb (MACMILLAN, 1971; VIKING, 1972) • Spark's mordant gift for capturing the absence of moral values in the modern world is demonstrated once again in this macabre study of evil that verges on, though doesn't embrace, the grotesque. Baron Klopstock becomes involved in a sordid triangle that includes his wife as well as Victor Passerat, the secretary they share. The servants at Klopstock's Swiss estate, led by the butler, Lister, choose "not to disturb" the trio as their jealous rages generate a violent, gruesome climax. But, said one critic, *Not to Disturb* is, ultimately, "too little about too little."

The Hothouse by the East River (VIKING, 1973) • Set in New York City, Spark's home for several years during the 1960s, this complex allegory is also *about* New York, "home of the vivisectors of the mind, and of the mentally vivisected still to be reassembled." The story centers on the Hazletts, who live in an overheated apartment near the East River. The book includes a sustained attack on psychiatry—which is, for Spark, emblematic of the illness that has infected modern society, a society in which "sick is real." Diane Johnson, writing in the *Washington Post*, admitted that the novel was no *Mandelbaum Gate*, but she thought it nevertheless showed Spark's "complete mastery of all the novelist's means."

The Abbess of Crewe (VIKING, 1974) • Subtitled "a modern morality tale," this slapstick thriller describes the title character's unscrupulous campaign to win an election at an English abbey. The chicanery includes a burglary and the use of bugging devices, and the cast features a collection of bumbling lackeys. Critics noted the all-too-obvious parallels with the Watergate scandal then dominating headlines. Both Michael Wood (in the *New York Review of Books*) and John Updike (in *The New Yorker*) disliked the book. (The story was later made into the 1976 film *Nasty Habits*.)

The Takeover (VIKING, 1976) • Spark returns to Italy for this tale of tenacious greed. Its protagonist is a man convinced that he's descended from both Caligula and "Diana of the Woods." Thus empowered, he "takes over" a house in Nemi owned by a rich American friend and surrounds himself with a trio of male secretaries. The story unfolds against the backdrop of political extremism and economic crisis that overtook Italy during the mid-1970s. In her *New York Times* review, Margaret Drabble remarked of *The Takeover* that Spark's theme was "too large" for so slender a book.

Territorial Rights (COWARD, McCANN & GEOGHEGAN, 1979) • Spark's fifteenth novel is an intricately plotted comedy of European manners. It satirizes a group of men and women, mainly Britons, who settle in or near the Pensione Sofia in Venice. The characters are in pursuit of something they regard as rightfully theirs—in most cases, a lover. Writing in *The New Statesman*, David Lodge said that *Territorial Rights* "tickles, it intrigues, it beguiles. If, in the end, it disappoints, that is because the author is one of our most gifted and original novelists."

Loitering with Intent (Coward, McCann & Geoghegan, 1981) • In this witty and accomplished autobiographical novel, narrator Fleur Talbot, a successful and celebrated writer, recalls her coming of age in 1949 London, a time and place that Spark is able to evoke with rare precision. "I see no reason to keep silent about my enjoyment of the sound of my own voice as I work. I am sparing no relevant facts," writes Fleur. But she may also be somewhat batty: The incidents she describes curiously parallel those she set down in her first novel, in progress during this remembered period in her life. The *New York Review of Books* called the *Loitering with Intent* "intelligent comedy of a sort that will give more pleasure than nine-tenths of what is acclaimed as good fiction today."

Bang-Bang You're Dead and Other Stories (Granada, 1982) • This volume includes ten previously collected stories, plus two first published in *The New Yorker:* "The Gentile Jewesses" and "The First Year of My Life," both of which have distinctly autobiographical elements. The second, a bravura performance, is narrated by an infant born, like Spark, "on the first day of the second month of the last years of the First World War." The story intercuts the narrator's perception of civilian absurdities with disturbing images of World War I carnage.

The Only Problem (Coward, McCann & Geoghegan, 1984) • Multimillionaire Harvey Gotham, a Canadian expatriate, has hidden himself away in rural France, where he's writing a study of the Book of Job. Harvey believes that Job is the Bible's "pivotal" book because it confronts "the only problem" of serious import, God's apparent willingness to allow suffering. However, Harvey's ruminations are interrupted and his calm is shattered when his wife (whom he had abandoned) shows up as a newborn terrorist wanted by the police. "A good and profound novel lies scattered among the inklings of *The Only Problem*, but the author seems distracted," John Updike wrote in *The New Yorker.*

* The Stories of Muriel Spark (Dutton, 1985) • This omnibus collection spans thirty-five years of writing and shows the dazzling range of a major contemporary author. There are stories set in Africa, England, and Scotland. The volume includes all of Spark's previously collected tales, plus four new ones—"The Executor," "Another Pair of Hands," "The Dragon," and "The Fortune Teller"—all of which appeared originally in *The New Yorker.*

"There are stories here of loneliness and the separateness of each individual in the world, and tales of thwarted love, jealousy, murder, lingering feuds, greed,

*ghosts both wise and wicked, demon-seed children with perfect manners, blush-
ing girls and twisted crones. Spark reports them all with cool and precise observation that is distant enough to be absolutely unsparing, yet close enough to be
both moved and moving.*" (*Alan Ryan,* Washington Post)

A Far Cry from Kensington (HOUGHTON MIFFLIN, 1988) • Spark's eighteenth
novel, set in a London rooming house in 1954, is a comedy of the drab,
straitened postwar England that she excels at re-creating. The genteel
renters—who include a medical student, a compulsively neat nurse, a
Polish émigré, and others—all make do with hot plates and a shared bathroom. Mrs. Hawkins, the story's narrator, is a young war widow whose work
at a publishing company brings her into contact with the villainous Hector
Bartlett, a grubby writer whose sole talent is for self-promotion. One
reviewer called this Spark's "most delightful novel in years."

Symposium (HOUGHTON MIFFLIN, 1990) • In this surprise best-seller, Spark
satirizes downward mobility in the conversational arts—specifically, from
Plato's *Symposium* to the current turgid academic sort. The participants in
Spark's titular symposium are the guests at a dinner party hosted by an
artist and his mistress. The claret flows and the champagne sparkles, but
the conversation, alas, does neither. Instead, the guests, a cross section of
trendy Londoners, reiterate the tiresome banalities that pass for enlightened conversation in this era of chitchat. Merle Rubin of the *Christian
Science Monitor* pointed out that Spark neglected to go beneath the surface
of her characters; even so, Rubin still considered *Symposium* "a polished,
very professional...divertissement."

Reality and Dreams (HOUGHTON MIFFLIN, 1997) • Spark explores the relationship between reality and imagination in this comedy about a British
filmmaker, Tom Richards, who awakens in a hospital room to find himself
nearly crippled by a fall from a crane on the set of his latest feature. The
movie had been based on the simple but memorable image he recently
glimpsed of a young girl grilling hamburgers at a campground in the south
of France. When Tom returns to the movie set, his real life, in all its messiness, becomes even further entwined with the invented one he dreamily
projects onto the screen. "The humor is unsophisticated, but skillfully
deployed, as by a brilliant stand-up comic," Gabriele Annan wrote in the
New York Review of Books.

Open to the Public (NEW DIRECTIONS, 1997) • Although mostly a greatest-hits
volume, this collection of thirty-seven tales from the 1950s through the
1990s does contain ten uncollected examples of Spark's recent work.
However, some of the new stories are as short as three or four pages, and
none compares with such old chestnuts as "The Go-Away Bird," "The
Portobello Road," "The Twins," or "Bang-Bang You're Dead"—all of which
are included here. Spark "has written some things that seem likely to go on

being read as long as fiction in English is read," Richard Jenkyns wrote in the *New York Times*, "so it is not very strong criticism to say that only a few of these stories show her at her best."

BIOGRAPHY

ONE OF THE MOST PROLIFIC of postwar British novelists, Muriel Spark was born in Edinburgh, Scotland, the daughter of a Jewish engineer named Camberg and his Protestant English wife. She was educated at James Gillespie's High School for Girls, where she studied under a teacher who later became the model for the title character in *The Prime of Miss Jean Brodie*. In 1937, she married Sydney O. Spark and went to live with him in Northern Rhodesia. Although the marriage ended after seven years, it did produce a son. During World War II, Spark worked in London as a propaganda writer for the British Foreign Office.

After the war, she became involved in London literary life as an editor and a critic. Her first books were studies of Mary Shelley, Emily Brontë, and John Masefield. Then in 1951, she entered one of her first short stories, "The Seraph and the Zambesi," in a writing contest on Christian themes sponsored by *The Observer*. She won first prize, and the story's unusual treatment of its subject attracted considerable attention. Thus encouraged, Spark wrote more stories and continued to set many of them in Africa.

When an editor suggested she try her hand at a novel, Spark went ahead, but skeptically. "I thought it was an inferior way of writing," she later explained. "So I wrote a novel to work out the technique first, to sort of make it all right with myself to write a novel at all." At the same time, she struggled with a more profound life change: her conversion to Roman Catholicism. For this, Spark credits her close study of Cardinal Newman, the great nineteenth-century Oxford cleric. Reading Newman "helped me find a definite location," Spark has said. Catholicism "provided my norm...something to measure from." The result of this twin rebirth—as a novelist and as a Catholic—was *The Comforters*.

Spark's debut novel featured what would soon emerge as signature traits in her work: clever plotting; cool, epigrammatic prose; unshakable mental poise; and serious religious themes. *The Comforters* was well received, as were (with rare exceptions) the many others that followed. Meanwhile, Spark emerged as the outstanding Catholic writer of her English generation—the true heir, many have said, to Evelyn Waugh and Graham Greene. (In fact, Greene had regularly subsidized Spark's work with cash gifts early in her career.)

NEXT ON THE READING LIST: Anita Brookner, Gail Godwin, Penelope Lively, Alison Lurie, Iris Murdoch, Carol Shields, Anne Tyler, Fay Weldon

Robert Stone

(b. August 21, 1937)

"Robert Stone has established a world and style and tone of voice of great originality and authority. It is a voice without grace or comfort, bleak, dangerous, and continually threatening.... Stone has a Hobbesian view of life—nasty, brutish and short—but it is also fiercely contemporary."
—A. Alvarez, New York Review of Books

✶ A Hall of Mirrors (HOUGHTON MIFFLIN, 1967) • Stone's debut won a William Faulkner Foundation Award as the most notable first novel published in 1967. Its surrealistic story, told in haunting prose, centers on the adventures of Reinhardt, a brilliant musician turned transient alcoholic who has drifted to New Orleans, a city "in which the American condition is driven to extremity." There he meets up with a cast of marginal cast-offs, each of whom seems to embody hidden truths about the dark side of modern American culture.

> *"Stone throws away brilliant stories which would provide full-length books for lesser writers; yet nothing is ever wasted, every item in every shop window helps drive the narrative on.... [He shows] how the individual meets and fuses with the social body, and where pathology infects the process, in a way I have not seen done before."* (*Ivan Gold*, New York Times)

✶ Dog Soldiers (HOUGHTON MIFFLIN, 1974) • Winner of a National Book Award, this novel describes the last days of the Vietnam War, a time of despair and moral confusion. The protagonist, John Converse, a journalist working in Saigon, meets an American woman who lures him into a plot to smuggle three kilograms of heroin into Southern California. Part thriller, part political allegory, this book, in effect, brings the war home to America.

> *"Most of* Dog Soldiers *is as precise as the cross hairs on a rifle sight. With fearful accuracy it describes a journey to hell and pronounces an epitaph on a time that has not ended."* (*Paul Gray*, Time)

A Flag for Sunrise (KNOPF, 1981) • Anthropologist and ex–CIA agent Frank Holliwell travels to an impoverished Central American country, where he becomes entangled in the machinations of spies, gunrunners, revolutionaries, and various burned-out cases, including drunks and drug users. The book also pursues a religious theme: Holliwell is a Catholic, as are the novel's two other main characters. The book's sweep and seriousness won praise and a PEN/Faulkner Award, but some reviewers found its political message grating and overstated.

Children of Light (KNOPF, 1986) • A dark, brooding picture of contemporary Hollywood, Stone's fourth novel is based on his own unhappy experiences writing film scripts for his first two novels. *Children of Light* features an array of repellent Hollywood types, including a vicious writer who fell from grace (into alcoholism) after writing a single good novel and now grinds out "nonfiction writing for quality magazines." Stone's sympathy is reserved for only two characters: Walker, an aging actor cum screenwriter hooked on cocaine, and Lu Anne, a schizophrenic actress. Critics praised Stone's prose and dialogue but found the book heavy handed.

✻ Outerbridge Reach (TICKNOR & FIELDS, 1992) • Stone's debt to nautical classics by Melville, Conrad, and Hemingway is apparent in this tale of a man pitted against nature. Unlike the typical Stone protagonist, Owen Browne is the ideal northeastern WASP: Vietnam veteran, husband, and father, with a copywriter's job at a Connecticut yacht brokerage. His life changes when he pilots a sailboat in a solo race around the world. Stone counterpoints Owen's story with those of his unhappy wife and a third character, a hedonistic filmmaker who's making a documentary about Owen's family.

> *"Robert Stone's blend of heroic aspiration and mordantly deflationary irony results in something like tragicomedy—maybe even something like Shakespeare, our best tragic comedian. But whatever you call it,* Outerbridge Reach *seems to me a triumph—a beautifully and painstakingly composed piece of literary art." (William Pritchard, New York Times)*

Bear and His Daughter (HOUGHTON MIFFLIN, 1997) • In his first short-fiction collection, selected from stories published over a thirty-year period, Stone vividly etches the inner landscapes of a copious variety of misfits, outcasts, and down-at-the-heels characters. The protagonists of "Miserere" and "Absence of Mercy" seem ready to explode with tension and rage as they're subjected to the cruelties and corruptions of post-Vietnam America. The title work, a novella published here for the first time, describes the reunion of an alcoholic poet and his emotionally troubled daughter. Most critics, though impressed, suggested that Stone's talents were better suited to the novel.

BIOGRAPHY

ONE OF THE MOST ACCLAIMED novelists of his generation, Robert Stone followed a tortuous path to literary eminence. Born in Brooklyn, he never knew his father, a former railroad detective who deserted Stone's mother before their son was born. Shortly after Robert turned six, his schoolteacher mother was hospitalized with schizophrenia. For a time, he was boarded at a Catholic school, where he was beaten by students and teachers alike. On his mother's release, Stone went to live with her again, but she was unable to resume her career as a teacher, and the two lived in seedy hotel rooms on Manhattan's West Side.

A gifted pupil and writer, Stone won a short-story contest in high school but dropped out a few months before graduation to join the navy. He became a journalist in the service and developed a lifelong fascination with the sea. After his discharge in 1958, he enrolled in New York University and worked as a copyboy for the *Daily News*. Around this time, he met Janice Burr, his future wife. Although she held a master's degree in counseling, she eventually became his editorial assistant and all-purpose helpmate—"secretary, proofreader, cook, chauffeur," as Stone has said. They have two children, both fully grown.

In 1960, the couple moved for eight months to New Orleans, where Stone gathered the material that eventually became his first novel, *A Hall of Mirrors*. The book was five years in the writing, most of it done while Stone was on fellowship in the writing program at Stanford. Through the Stanford program, Stone met Ken Kesey and the Merry Pranksters, who introduced him to LSD. As a result, drug use recurs in Stone's fiction, and his prose has, at times, a vivid, almost hallucinatory realism.

Stone later traveled to London and Vietnam. This second experience, though it lasted only six weeks, profoundly affected him. Vietnam, he has said, was an "enormous, endless, boundless, topless, bottomless mistake, something I was not used to seeing the United States do. It gave everybody a sense of vertigo." It also provided the impetus for his second novel, *Dog Soldiers*, and echoes of Vietnam sound throughout his later work, which is intensely preoccupied with the decay of values in post-Vietnam America.

The recipient of many honors and prizes, Stone has been a writer in residence at Princeton, Amherst, and elsewhere. He and his wife live in Westport, Connecticut, and have second homes on Block Island (off the Rhode Island coast) and Key West. Not a prolific writer, Stone struggles with each book and is prone to fits of depression. "I see this enormous empty space from which God has absented himself," Stone once told an interviewer. "I see this enormous mystery that I can't penetrate."

NEXT ON THE READING LIST: Madison Smartt Bell, Robert Olen Butler, Richard Ford, Jim Harrison, Tim O'Brien

Graham Swift

(b. May 4, 1949)

"He is pyrotechnic, convoluted, and highly literary; he has his roots planted firmly in English literature.... If his families are dysfunctional, it is in the way that the families of Hamlet and Oedipus are."
—MacDonald Harris, New York Times

The Sweet-Shop Owner (ALLAN LANE, 1980; WASHINGTON SQUARE, 1985) • Swift's first novel tells the perfectly English story of a stolid, unhappy middle-class family. Willy married Irene in order to set himself up in business with her family's money. Now, decades later, he sits in his sweet shop and reflects on a life of bitterness and small indignities. Frank Rudman, writing in *The Spectator*, said that Swift's "impressive" first novel had captured "the essence of the small, modest but obliging variety of family establishments that made up High Street business before the remorseless blight of supermarkets."

Shuttlecock (ALLAN LANE, 1981; WASHINGTON SQUARE, 1985) • A man working in the local historical archives comes across disturbing information about his father, hailed as a hero after enduring Nazi torture during World War II. The information suggests that the old man was actually a traitor. One file will settle the matter for sure; but our hero, unable to face what he might find, destroys the file before reading it. *London Magazine* called *Shuttlecock* "a novel of ideas" and "an entertaining psychological mystery-thriller."

Learning to Swim and Other Stories (LONDON MAGAZINE EDITIONS, 1982; POSEIDON, 1985) • Critics have generally found Swift's command of the short story several steps beneath his mastery of the novel, principally because the tautness of the form seems to limit him. The best of these stories is the title effort, in which a father gives his son a swimming lesson during which the entire history of an angry, loveless marriage is told. Otherwise, the tales come off, as Jonathan Penner wrote in the *Washington Post*, like "studies in the economics of emotion: arid Anyman versus angry Anywoman."

* Waterland (HEINEMANN, 1983; POSEIDON, 1984) • As a child, Tom Crick discovered a corpse amid the marshland of England known as the Fens. As an adult, now married and a history teacher, Crick reflects on the horrific events that followed his discovery and the disasters that loom in his present life. This is Swift's masterpiece to date, a book that unfolds elegantly, shifting from detective story to historical treatise to psychological study.

"[Swift] tells a family saga of incest, madness, murder, and suicide that in its raw state would make the average thriller reader's toes curl. He does not offer it in the raw state, of course, but transformed by memory and desire." (*Hugh Hebert*, The Guardian)

Out of This World (POSEIDON, 1988) • Harry is a retired photojournalist who experienced the hells of both World War II and Vietnam. His wife is dead, and he's currently estranged from his daughter, Sophie. Composed of dueling narratives offered by Harry and Sophie, *Out of This World* uses photography as its controlling conceit, especially the degree to which images can capture reality. However, the conceit doesn't work: The novel is flat and its characters are forced and uninteresting. "The plot comes at us bittily, and the voices sound thin," Hermione Lee wrote in *The Observer*.

Ever After (KNOPF, 1992) • This is a bleak novel about a professor who, as it opens, has recently endured the deaths of his closest loved ones and his own suicide attempt. We learn that his university post is unearned, having been created by his stepfather during a fit of nepotism, and that his research is all a sham. There's a sort of glumly comedic undercurrent, but as Stephen Wall wrote in the *London Review of Books*, "In the end...the different areas of narrative interest in *Ever After* disperse rather than concentrate attention."

Last Orders (KNOPF, 1996) • A butcher has died, and his last request was to have his ashes scattered into the sea at Margate. Four of his pals undertake to satisfy this wish, and during their *Canterbury Tales*–like journey, we learn their stories. It turns out that most of them fought together in the same regiment during World War II. According to Melissa Bennetts in the *Christian Science Monitor*, the book "reads as a poignant set of variations on John Donne's theme 'No man is an island.'"

BIOGRAPHY

ONE MIGHT EXPECT THAT AN author whose most evocative work centers on the English Fens would hail from there. In fact, Graham Swift was born and raised in South London, and before writing *Waterland*, he had scarcely been to this wild, marshy region of East Anglia. One of the refrains that Swift tends to repeat during interviews is that autobiography is an overused element in fiction. He says that he prefers to rely on a combination of research and imagination, with the emphasis on imagination.

That isn't to say he doesn't have preoccupations that manage to enmesh themselves in his work. One certainly is history—World War II in particular, which he features in nearly all his novels. Some critics have ascribed this war's ubiquity to the impact that it had on Swift's parents. His father, Allen, flew missions for the Royal Navy, while his mother, Sheila, lived in London during the Blitz.

After graduating from Cambridge University, Swift held a succession of English department posts until *Waterland* was published in 1983, when he quit teaching and devoted himself full time to writing. His greatest passion, other than his craft, is fishing, and he has coedited *The Magic Wheel: An Anthology of Fishing in Literature.*

NEXT ON THE READING LIST: Beryl Bainbridge, Francisco Goldman, Ursula Hegi, Kazuo Ishiguro, David Lodge, Iris Murdoch

---

Amy Tan
(b. February 19, 1952)

"Tan's characters, regardless of their cultural orientation or age, speak with authority and authenticity. The details of their lives, unfamiliar to most American readers, are rendered with such conviction that almost immediately their rules seem to become the adages and admonitions with which we ourselves grew up."
—*Michael Dorris,* Chicago Tribune

* The Joy Luck Club (PUTNAM, 1989) • Made up of sixteen interconnected stories told by four Chinese immigrant women and their four American-born daughters, *The Joy Luck Club* explores both the impact of past generations on the present and the nature of mother-daughter relationships. The first two sections recount the mothers' lives in China and their daughters' childhoods in the United States. The third section, "American Translation," relates the daughters' struggles to be simultaneously modern and traditional. In the final section, the mothers and daughters achieve a sort of reconciliation. A huge critical and commercial success, *The Joy Luck Club* was nominated for a National Book Award, and it remained on the *New York Times* best-seller list for nine months.

> *"The only negative thing I could ever say about this book is that I'll never again be able to read it for the first time.* The Joy Luck Club *is so powerful, so full of magic, that by the end of the second paragraph, your heart catches; by the end of the first page, tears blur your vision; and one-third of the way down on Page 26, you know you won't be doing anything of importance until you have finished this novel."* (*Carolyn See,* Los Angeles Times)

The Kitchen God's Wife (PUTNAM, 1991) • Tan's second novel not only fictionalized her mother's life but also took literary revenge against the patriarchal myths under which Chinese women have labored for thousands of years. Pearl may be at home in the American world of fast food, loose family ties, and egalitarian marriages, but her widowed mother, Winnie Louie, has never quite adapted. When Pearl reluctantly visits her mother in Chinatown, Winnie Louie unexpectedly reveals the harrowing events that preceded her escape from mainland China. After listening to her mother's confession, Pearl reveals her own painful secret. Once again, reviewers applauded Tan's gift: In the *Washington Post*, Wendy Law-Yone called *The Kitchen God's Wife* "bigger, bolder, and, I have to say, better" than *The Joy Luck Club; Time* critic Pico Iyer wrote that "Tan has transcended herself again."

The Hundred Secret Senses (PUTNAM, 1995) • Rather than probe yet another mother-daughter relationship, this time Tan tackles sisterhood. Olivia is the daughter of a Chinese-American father and a Caucasian mother. When she's three years old, her father dies. A few years later, she's reunited with her eighteen-year-old Chinese half sister, Kwan. Because Kwan is clumsy, can barely speak English, and believes that she can communicate with spirits, Olivia treats her dismissively. However, Kwan remains devoted to her younger sister and continues through the years to encourage her to awaken to the reality of the spirit world. Although a few critics suggested that Tan was becoming a bit formulaic and others felt that she didn't handle the supernatural very well, most liked the book. According to Michael Harris in the *Los Angeles Times*, "*The Hundred Secret Senses* shows that Tan's storytelling skills are as intact as ever. It's surely the feel-good ghost story of the year."

BIOGRAPHY

IN 1947, JOHN TAN EMIGRATED from China to California, where he worked as an engineer and served as a Baptist minister. His wife, Daisy, fled China two years later, leaving behind three daughters from a previous marriage. When Amy Tan was born in Oakland, her parents gave her the Chinese name En-Mai, which means "blessing of America." According to Tan, her ambitious parents fully expected her to become both a neurosurgeon and a concert pianist.

In 1967, Tan's older brother, Peter, died of brain cancer, and her father succumbed to the same disease a few months later. A devastated Daisy Tan consulted a Chinese geomancer and, following the advice that she was given, moved with her remaining children to Europe to escape the evil influence of their "diseased" house. Fifteen-year-old Amy finished high school at the Collège Monte Rosa Internationale in Montreaux—where, she has said, she felt like an alienated outsider among the children of ambassadors, princes, and tycoons. According to Tan, because "being good" hadn't saved either her father or her brother, she rebelled, falling in with drug dealers and nearly eloping to Australia with a mental patient who claimed to be a German army deserter.

After returning to the United States, Tan enrolled as a premed student at Linfield College in Oregon, later earning her bachelor's and master's degrees from San Jose State. In her midthirties—by then a happily married yet overworked technical writer—Tan joined a weekly fiction group, hoping to resolve her abiding sense of anger and cultural confusion. Although her first novel, *The Joy Luck Club*, paid homage to her grandmother (before her suicide at thirty-nine, she was the number three concubine to a wealthy man), Tan wrote the book mainly for her mother. In her dedication, she wrote, "You asked me once what I would remember. This, and much more." Tan has also written two children's books, *The Moon Lady* (1992) and *The Chinese Siamese Cat* (1994).

NEXT ON THE READING LIST: Edwidge Danticat, Cristina Garcia, Penelope Lively, Toni Morrison, Gloria Naylor

Melanie Rae Thon
(b. August 23, 1957)

"The reader is swept along not only by Ms. Thon's remarkable characterizations but also by the taut, magic current of her prose, which carries an exhilarating rhythmic punch."
—*Constance Decker Thompson,* New York Times

Meteors in August (RANDOM HOUSE, 1990) • Lizzie Macon, the narrator of this coming-of-age story, grows up during the 1960s in a Montana mill town beset by racial tensions between the Anglo and Indian populations—not to mention rampant alcoholism and adultery. Lizzie goes through a series of identity crises as she becomes aware of the shortcomings of her parents and her own emerging sexuality. Complicating matters is the memory of Lizzie's older sister, Nina, who ran away after becoming pregnant by her Indian boyfriend. "[Thon] is adept at evoking the kind of rugged place where American Gothic citizens, fresh from running a man out of town, change from their bloodstained clothing to attend Sunday services," Ralph Sassone wrote in the *New York Times.* "On the whole, though, Lizzie's internal journey is obscured by the many melodramatic episodes that crowd the novel."

Girls in the Grass (RANDOM HOUSE, 1991) • In this well-received collection of eleven short stories, Thon continues to explore the deep yearnings of adolescence. In the title story, for example, three teenagers probe their sexuality by playing Truth or Dare. "These stories are mute, not subtle; they're good, but not passionate," Susan Osborn observed in the *Philadelphia Inquirer.* "Instead of imparting a sense of urgency, they reveal something of the strange and often callow ways some people flounder through their lives." According to Lisa Failer's review in the *Detroit Free Press,* "The real brilliance of *Girls in the Grass*...is reflected in the depth of character Thon reaches."

Iona Moon (POSEIDON, 1993) • Thon based this novel, her second, on characters who appeared in two short stories in *Girls in the Grass.* The narrator of the title is a poor farm girl with bad teeth, an aroma of cows about her, and a reputation for being easy. At the beginning of the novel, she has a fling with golden-boy Jay Tyler. Class differences immediately pull them apart, Iona's mother dies, and she subsequently leaves town. Meanwhile, Jay suffers a tragedy of the sort that brings down class barriers so that by the time Iona returns to White Falls, Idaho, there's hope for both of them. "In luminous, stately prose, Melanie Rae Thon gives us a powerful account of those who long to love while they walk on reality's pained limbs," Shelby Hearon wrote in the *Chicago Tribune.*

* First, Body (HOUGHTON MIFFLIN, 1997) • These seven stories are relentless in their depiction of misery. Thon's characters—a pack of runaways, unwed mothers, drug addicts, and alcoholics—are people with nothing more to lose. They make choices and regret them immediately. They accept defeat as inevitable and then wallow in their own self-pity.

> "*Throughout* First, Body *I found myself longing for a little distance, a little room to breathe. Refusal to grant it constitutes not merely a basic aspect of Ms. Thon's style, but perhaps an act of solidarity with her walking wounded in the tight places they inhabit. If they don't get any respite, why should we?*" (*Rand Richards Cooper*, New York Times)

BIOGRAPHY

MELANIE RAE THON WAS BORN IN Kalispell, Montana, to an architect and a housewife. She spent her undergraduate years at the University of Michigan, where she received a bachelor's degree in 1980. Two years later, she earned a master's degree from Boston University. Remaining in the Boston area for the next decade or so, she taught writing and literature at a number of local colleges, including Emerson and Harvard. In 1996, *Granta* named her one of the twenty Best Young American Novelists. That same year, she accepted a teaching job at Ohio State.

"I write about people and situations that trouble me," Thon told one interviewer. "Every story is a mystery until you write it: If you knew where you were going, there would be no reason to write. My first short story took eight years; it was that long before I found the truth. Facts can be misleading; the emotional truth is what matters."

NEXT ON THE READING LIST: Dorothy Allison, Amy Bloom, Ivan Doig, Mary Gaitskill, Jane Hamilton, Cormac McCarthy

---

William Trevor

(b. May 24, 1928)

"William Trevor is an Irishman who lives in England and writes often about the English. He is a moral realist who possesses a deliciously dry wit, a nice sense of the macabre, and a warm sympathy for the flawed and suffering characters he creates with such fine psychological precision."
—*Patrick McGrath*, New York Times

A Standard of Behavior (HUTCHINSON, 1958) • Trevor wrote this novel while working as an advertising copywriter—and it shows. The book's artificial storyline—about a pretentious young man beset by love problems—introduces, poorly, Trevor's lifelong preoccupation with lonely, confused characters. The book received only a few reviews, the best of which called it "not a distinguished piece of work," and Trevor later disowned it.

The Old Boys (BODLEY HEAD, 1964; VIKING, 1964) • When old school chums, now in their eighties, come together again, the slowness and wisdom of age eventually give way to the jealousies and pettiness of youth. In the background looms the ghost of their dead housemaster, a drunkard and deviant whom these octogenarians have nevertheless spent their lifetimes admiring. Writing in the *New York Times*, Robert Towers called *The Old Boys* "a harshly comic novel of willful and perverse old age."

The Boarding House (BODLEY HEAD, 1965; VIKING, 1965) • In this satisfying little novel about the meanness of the bourgeoisie, the owner of a boarding house dies and bequeaths the establishment to two tenants, who set about terrorizing and evicting the other lodgers. *The New Republic* praised the book for its "wayward humor."

The Love Department (BODLEY HEAD, 1966; VIKING, 1967) • Edward, a hapless hero plucked from the pages of a medieval romance, leaves a monastery to work for the "love department" of a major popular magazine. There, he's assigned the task of tailing a renowned womanizer and reprobate. "The vulgarity of contemporary conceptions of love and marriage is a time-honored theme," commented *The New Republic*, "but Trevor fails to get very far with it."

The Day We Got Drunk on Cake (BODLEY HEAD, 1967; VIKING, 1968) • This collection of Trevor's early short stories embraces a fairly narrow range of characters and sentiments. Although Trevor is Irish, his years in England show through clearly here: There's little of the pubby loquaciousness that one expects to find in Irish yarns. Instead, we meet lots of stiff, lonely Brits who, in middle age, seem emotionally lobotomized. Peter Buitenhuis, writing in the *New York Times*, described these stories as "clever, meticulously written, brittle tales."

Mrs. Eckdorf in O'Neill's Hotel (BODLEY HEAD, 1969; VIKING, 1970) • A legendary Dublin hotel has fallen on hard times. The hard-nosed Mrs. Eckdorf arrives from Germany to create a photo essay that will capture on film the place, its people, and their secrets. Soon enough, the hotel and its occupants exact their revenge. *Time* called the novel a "disturbing sketch of human weaknesses" as well as "Trevor's sardonic back-of-the-hand to the non-Celtic Mrs. Eckdorfs of this world."

Miss Gomez and the Brethren (BODLEY HEAD, 1971; PENGUIN, 1997) • Miss Gomez, a Jamaican transplanted to London, heads a cast of misfits living on the same shabby street. Initiating them into a church called the Brethren of the Way, she feeds them absurd dreams that come to replace reality. "Triumphantly, Mr. Trevor has made his novel into a warm celebration of Miss Gomez," Jonathan Raban wrote in *The New Statesman*.

* The Ballroom of Romance (BODLEY HEAD, 1972; VIKING, 1972) • Even more intently than in his previous collections, Trevor focuses here on the lonely and the hopeless, describing in depth the walls that hem them in so that we can feel anguish and pity at their fate. The title story presents a rural Irishwoman who has lost her chance to marry. Now she tends to the needs of her ailing father, her only escape from drudgery being the weekly shows at the local music hall.

> *"At least three of the short stories in this collection are as excellent as it is possible for a short story to be…deserving to be treated as classics of the form." (Auberon Waugh, The Spectator)*

Elizabeth Alone (BODLEY HEAD, 1973; VIKING, 1974) • The climax of this quiet but very deep character study comes when its middle-aged heroine enters a hospital for a hysterectomy and comes to terms with the meaning of the procedure. The *Times Literary Supplement* called *Elizabeth Alone* "a more substantial and a more disturbing novel than Mr. Trevor's other panoramas of tragicomedy."

* Angels at the Ritz (BODLEY HEAD, 1975; VIKING, 1976) • Trevor reaches his peak as a short-story writer with this collection that Graham Greene called possibly the best in English since Joyce's *Dubliners*. In "Mrs. Acland's Ghosts," we watch in quickly alternating amusement and horror as a woman engages the collection of spirits that haunt her house. Another story, "In Isfahan," Anne Tyler wrote, "shimmers like a yard of changeable taffeta."

> *"Nothing seems alien to him; he captures the moral atmosphere of a sleek advertising agency, of a shabby West End dance hall, of a minor public school, of a shotgun wedding in an Irish pub."* (*Ted Solotaroff*, New York Times)

The Children of Dynmouth (BODLEY HEAD, 1976; VIKING, 1977) • This portrait of an amoral teenager running amok in a seaside village, destroying other people's lives for his own amusement, got mixed reviews. In the *New York Times*, Joyce Carol Oates called this Whitbread Prize winner "Trevor's finest novel so far" and "a small masterpiece of understatement." On the other hand, *The New Statesman* thought that Trevor deserved "the old accusation of blowing up a short-story idea to novel length."

Lovers of Their Time (BODLEY HEAD, 1978; VIKING, 1979) • Employing a wider-than-usual focus in these stories, Trevor consistently allows the outside world to impinge on the small pains of his characters. Thus, world war and the Irish "troubles" figure prominently. Similarly, when a prim spinster is propositioned by a lesbian, we know that Trevor is upsetting his character's lives in stranger ways than ever. In the *Atlantic Monthly*, Benjamin DeMott called *Lovers of Their Time* a "bold, original, energetically ambitious work."

Other People's Worlds (BODLEY HEAD, 1980; VIKING, 1981) • A wealthy widow marries a younger, poorer man. Sadly, as the novel progresses, his sanity dissolves, and we're forced to watch as the woman suffers the consequences of the single love-inspired decision of her life. John Updike called *Other People's Worlds* "a dense and constantly surprising work, grimly humorous, total in its empathy, and pungent with the scent of evil and corruption."

Beyond the Pale (BODLEY HEAD, 1981; VIKING, 1982) • What unites these twelve stories is Trevor's detailed exploration of the cracks he has found in the facade of bourgeois propriety. All these tales, as Peter Kemp observed in the *Times Literary Supplement*, "automatically discharge little piles of dirty linen" in the form of sexual perversion, or blackmail, or both. Kemp concluded that this "small-scale world—two dimensional and programmed to familiar routines—functions as a peep show rather than a microcosm."

* Fools of Fortune (VIKING, 1983) • In this political novel, a rarity for Trevor, the forces of history matter more than the quirks of personality. An Irishman loves an Englishwoman, but they're separated for many years after English soldiers destroy his home in the aftermath of the 1916 Easter Rebellion. The *Washington Post* called Trevor's Whitbread Prize winner a "benchmark novel against which other contemporary novels will have to be measured."

> *"The ultimate reunion of [the two lovers and their daughter] is exquisitely rendered in a brief final chapter that will seal the book in your memory."* (*James Idema,* Chicago Tribune)

The News from Ireland (VIKING, 1986) • This typically strong short-story collection ranges broadly from the sex-fearing woman who marries a homosexual to the proper English tourists who decide to visit Italy. The best is the title story, set during the mid-nineteenth-century Irish potato famine, when a family of English property owners attempts in small and poignantly pointless ways to ease the suffering around them. "A canny master of the short-story form, Mr. Trevor writes with a thoroughly assured, old-fashioned kind of omniscience, conjuring up whole characters in a couple of lines," Michiko Kakutani wrote in the *New York Times.*

The Silence in the Garden (VIKING, 1988) • Trevor uses another well-to-do Anglo-Irish family as the focus of what John Naughton called in *The Listener* a "beautifully crafted book." With its squires and scullery maids, the story, set in the early twentieth century, reads like a rural *Upstairs, Downstairs,* but this soap opera has a philosophical backbone.

Family Sins (VIKING, 1990) • The twelve stories in this collection describe family ties as well as family turmoil. Most involve contorted or strangled love. In the most effective and chilling of these tales, a poor peasant girl is forced into the service of a loathsome old man, who masturbates as he watches her going about her chores. Dean Flower, writing in the *Hudson Review,* called *Family Sins* "powerful material."

Two Lives (VIKING, 1991) • Or two novellas. The first, "Reading Turgenev," features an Irish peasant girl's star-crossed match with a sour, impotent farmer. Her only joy comes from listening to a male cousin read Turgenev to her. The second novella, "My House in Umbria," is less typical of Trevor—and less successful. A woman narrates the improbable story of her life: Sold by her parents, she becomes a prostitute but later finds romance. "The first [novella] is a grim threnody," Julia O'Faolain wrote in the *Times Literary Supplement,* "the second is lacking in particularity."

* Felicia's Journey (VIKING, 1994) • In this classic morality tale, which won the Sunday Express Book of the Year Award, Felicia travels from Ireland to the English Midlands in search of the man who made her pregnant. She arrives armed with a small amount of money and the naive belief that, when he learns of her condition, he will do the right thing. In her weakened state, however, she falls prey to a sociopathic male and a religion-mad female.

> *"[Eventually] the drama begins to take on the classic outline of a battle for a soul, waged between the forces of good and evil.... The resolution the novel arrives at...is deeply right and satisfying."* (*Patrick McGrath,* New York Times)

After Rain (VIKING, 1996) • This collection of short stories, published as the author neared age seventy, is as full of the tiny, mad, perfect details of ordinary life as any of his previous work: the little boys who pour wet cement into their father's golf bag, the woman who wakes up on the first morning of her widowhood. According to Richard Eder in the *Los Angeles Times*, Trevor tills "a small patch," but this patch Eder likens to "the few acres of French vineyard that produce Le Montrachet."

BIOGRAPHY

WILLIAM TREVOR COX, THOUGH an Irishman by heredity, has been called English by temperament. After his birth in County Cork, his family moved often—thirteen times before William reached college age. As a result, the young man often felt, he has said, like "a bit of an outsider and a loner." Because his first love was art (he's a gifted sculptor and has had several one-man exhibitions), he took a job after college as an art teacher in England. There he found that the wry, restrained English perspective suited him, and he has lived in England more or less ever since.

Trevor eventually gave up sculpting because, he later said, it lacked humanity. When he switched to writing, he dropped his last name to differentiate his two artistic careers. Several critics have ascribed sculptural qualities to Trevor's fiction, particularly the manner in which he chips away at the surfaces of his characters to reveal their inner textures. Trevor has also been astonishingly prolific. In addition to his many novels and story collections, he has written ten plays and numerous television and radio scripts, as well as a highly regarded memoir, *Old School Ties* (1976), and two books of essays.

Trevor's focus has nearly always been on poor people—not necessarily the financially poor, but people who lack something basic: money, love, common sense, luck. "I'm very interested in the sadness of fate," he once said, "the things that just happen to people." His short stories, considered among the finest in the language, are regularly compared with those of Joyce and Chekhov to show the degree to which Trevor has honed the form.

NEXT ON THE READING LIST: Roddy Doyle, Naguib Mahfouz, Alice Munro, Iris Murdoch, Edna O'Brien, Grace Paley

Anne Tyler

(b. October 25, 1941)

"It's hard to classify Anne Tyler's novels. They are Southern in their sure sense of family and place. They are modern in their fictional techniques, yet utterly unconcerned with the contemporary moment.... Tyler occupies a somewhat lonely place, polishing brighter and brighter a craft many novelists no longer deem essential to their purpose: the unfolding of character through brilliantly imagined and absolutely accurate detail."
—*Katha Pollitt*, New York Times

If Morning Ever Comes (KNOPF, 1964) • Tyler's subtle and evocative (yet slow-moving) first novel tells the story of Ben Joe Hawkes, a law student at Columbia University. Unhappy and out of place in New York City, Ben Joe drops out of school and hurries home to North Carolina, where he takes charge of his family, a sea of eccentric women who include Joe's widowed mother, his grandmother, and his six sisters. Reviewers praised the twenty-two-year-old author's depth of human understanding, her keen eye for domestic detail, and her remarkably mature prose.

The Tin Can Tree (KNOPF, 1965) • The accidental death of a six-year-old girl, Janie Rose Pike, profoundly affects the lives of those closest to her: her mother, Lou, who begins to neglect her other child, Simon; and Lou's relatives and neighbors, all inhabitants of the same three-family house on the edge of a North Carolina tobacco field. Like so many of Tyler's novels, this one untangles the complex relations among family members and features a large cast of oddballs united in their confusion regarding the demands of day-to-day life. Christopher Lehmann-Haupt of the *New York Times* called the subject matter "slight" but admitted that Tyler had "squeezed more emotional power from it than one would have thought it contained."

A Slipping-Down Life (KNOPF, 1970) • This unusual coming-of-age tale, mistaken for a young-adult novel, wasn't widely reviewed on publication, but at least one revisionist critic has since called it a "minor classic." Based on a real story, it describes how teenager Evie Decker—fat, unattractive, unhappy, and passive—surprises herself when she impulsively carves the name of a local rock idol, Drum Casey, onto her forehead. This act of self-mutilation attracts the attention of Drum and his manager, but soon Evie develops a new sense of identity and drifts away from Drum.

The Clock Winder (KNOPF, 1972) • Tyler has dismissed her fourth novel, another growing-up story, as boring, but many critics considered it livelier and better paced than its predecessors. Elizabeth Abbott, the daughter of a Baptist preacher, drops out of college and becomes a live-in helper to a wealthy widow, Mrs. Emerson, two of whose sons fall in love with Elizabeth. Even more interesting to Tyler, however, are the contrasts and similarities between the Abbotts and the Emersons.

✷ Celestial Navigation (KNOPF, 1974) • More intricate than her previous books, Tyler's breakthrough novel is a deep meditation on human perception and the conflicts arising between art and life. Told from the viewpoints of six people, the book displays Tyler's deepening sense of character and place. The protagonist, Jeremy Paulding, is an artist who specializes in sculpture and collage. He's also an agoraphobe who suffers anxiety attacks if he strays too far from the Baltimore house that he shares with several boarders.

> *"Tyler is especially gifted at the art of freeing her characters and then keeping track of them as they move in their unique and often solitary orbits. Her fiction is filled with displaced persons who persist stubbornly in their own destinies."* (*Gail Godwin*, New York Times)

✷ Searching for Caleb (KNOPF, 1976) • This novel charts the history of the Pecks, a Baltimore family known for its longevity and closeness. First cousins Justine and Duncan have married and live in the home of their grandfather, ninety-three-year-old Daniel Peck, who's still searching for his half brother, Caleb, missing since 1912. Daniel enlists the help of detective Eli Everjohn, a dead ringer for Abraham Lincoln, "even to the narrow border of beard along his jawline." But the book's charm resides in Tyler's exploration of the subtle traces of lineage that reach across generations and make the members of one family distinguishable from all others.

> *"Out of her fascination with families—with brotherly men and auntly women, with weak sisters and mama's boys, with stay-at-homes and runaways—Anne Tyler has fashioned...a lovely novel, funny and lyric and true-seeming, exquisite in its details and ambitious in its design. She here construes the family as a vessel of Time."* (*John Updike*, The New Yorker)

Earthly Possessions (KNOPF, 1977) • Narrator Charlotte Emory, a thirty-five-year-old housewife and sometime photographer, relates two stories. One is a meticulous hour-by-hour account of the harrowing few days she spent in the company of an amateurish bank robber, Jake Simms Jr., who abducted her at the scene of a bungled crime. This story alternates with Charlotte's reminiscences of her dreary upbringing in a "big brown turreted house" in Baltimore. The two narratives, so different on the surface, overlap in subtle, arresting ways. Even so, *New York Times* reviewer Anatole Broyard called the novel "just another one of those slightly stale, wry books that so many women writers seem to be turning out."

Morgan's Passing (KNOPF, 1980) • Morgan Gower leads an outwardly conventional life: He works in a hardware store, is sensibly married to a practical and good-natured woman, has six daughters, and is comfortably settled in a roomy old house. However, Morgan has a secret life—rather, many secret lives. An incurable imposter, he variously poses as a prospector, an explorer, a shoemaker, a priest, a postman, and more. Reviewers wanted to like *Morgan's Passing* very much, but most found something in the book that irked them. For instance, James Wolcott wrote in the *New York Review of Books* that "never has one eccentric [in a Tyler novel] so noisily nudged the other characters into the wings."

* Dinner at the Homesick Restaurant (KNOPF, 1982) • Tyler's ninth novel brought her both fame and her first commercial success. It describes the Tull family, Pearl and her three children, who live in a seedy frame house in Baltimore. The novel opens with Pearl, on her deathbed at age eighty-five, recalling all that has happened to her family. Succeeding chapters tell the stories, one by one, of Pearl's three children, each of whom has been scarred by the absence of their father, a traveling salesman who abandoned the family when the children were small.

> *"Funny, heart-hammering, wise, it edges deep into truth that's simultaneously (and interdependently) psychological, moral and formal—deeper than many living novelists of serious reputation have penetrated, deeper than Miss Tyler has gone before. It is a border crossing."* (*Benjamin DeMott,* New York Times)

* The Accidental Tourist (KNOPF, 1985) • This National Book Critics Circle Award winner enhanced Tyler's reputation as perhaps the most outstanding contemporary novelist of domestic life. Forty-three-year-old Macon Leary abhors all change. A writer of guidebooks for reluctant travelers, he visits the world's major business destinations, always searching for familiar and convenient comforts—a McDonald's in Amsterdam, a Taco Bell in Mexico City. Back home in Baltimore, however, Macon becomes a helpless witness to his own unraveling world, which includes the departure of his wife and the gruesome death of his son.

> *"It is a beautiful, incandescent, heartbreaking, exhilarating book. A strong undercurrent of sorrow runs through it, yet it contains comic scenes…that explode with joy…. There's magic in it, and some of its characters have winning eccentricities, yet more than any of Tyler's previous books it is rooted firmly, securely, insistently in the real world."* (*Jonathan Yardley,* Washington Post)

* Breathing Lessons (KNOPF, 1988) • Tyler won a Pulitzer Prize for this tender, funny, penetrating portrait of marriage. The story begins and ends on a single day. Ira and Maggie Moran, married twenty-eight years, drive ninety miles from their Baltimore home to Pennsylvania for the funeral of the husband of one of Maggie's school friends. As the day unfolds, Tyler creates lovingly detailed portraits of Ira and Maggie, two very different people who have somehow managed to build a meaningful life together. Ira is modest, reserved, methodical, and competent. Maggie is impulsive, emotional, and a meddler. The quiet drama of the book revolves around the midlife crisis in which both Ira and Maggie become ensnared.

> *"The characters are finely drawn and are appealing because of their Everyman qualities, and their daring to attempt to change what is unsatisfactory in their lives. Tyler tackles contemporary issues such as divorce, single parenthood, and extramarital affairs, but she does it in such a way that they take a back seat to what she sees as ultimately most important: family loyalty and love."* (*Suzanne L. MacLachlan*, Christian Science Monitor)

Saint Maybe (KNOPF, 1991) • Tyler's long-standing interest in religion supplies the theme for this best-seller about Ian Bedloe, a character who bears a heavy burden of guilt. He believes himself responsible for the death of his older brother, Danny, who has left behind a wife and three small children. Ian, the possible saint, subsequently serves out a near-lifetime of expiation—the book takes place over two decades—during which he faces a sequence of difficult choices, each a test of his growing sainthood. "Tyler's alchemy is wonderfully at work in her latest novel," wrote Judith Timson in *Maclean's*.

Ladder of Years (KNOPF, 1995) • A modern-day fairy tale with a feminist slant, Tyler's thirteenth novel tells how Delia Grinstead, mildly piqued by her family, walks out on them during a seashore holiday. Determined, like so many other Tyler characters, to change her life, Delia begins a new existence in a nearby town, where she meets up with—you guessed it!—a large cast of colorful eccentrics. Although not one of her most probing works, *Ladder of Years* "contains bright, sparkling dialogue and luminous, stray observations," according to Gene H. Bell-Villada in *Commonweal.*

BIOGRAPHY

ANNE TYLER—"OUR FOREMOST POET OF FAMILY LIFE," one critic called her—was born in Minneapolis to a chemist and his wife. Devout Quakers, the Tylers lived in a succession of religious communities in the Midwest and South, at last settling in North Carolina, where Anne attended high school. A precocious child, she was just sixteen when she entered Duke University, where she majored in Russian, studied writing with Reynolds Price, and was elected to Phi Beta Kappa. Tyler subsequently studied Russian on the graduate level at Columbia and worked briefly as a Russian bibliographer.

Tyler's first novels, published during the 1960s when the author was in her twenties, were cherished by a small group of readers and critics. John Updike, an early champion of her work, time and again reviewed her novels in *The New Yorker*, and eventually his consistent praise attracted some attention. Reviewing *Earthly Possessions*, Updike wrote that Tyler "continues to demonstrate a remarkable talent and, for a writer of her acuity, an unusual temperament. She is soft, if not bullish, on America," finding even in its banalities "a moonlit scenery where poetry and adventure form as easily as dew."

Intensely private, Tyler keeps a low profile in Baltimore, where she has lived since 1967. Although she has amassed a considerable following, she ducks interviews, avoids television, and doesn't lecture or teach. The closest she has come to having a public presence was a brief period during the late 1970s and early 1980s when she wrote fiction reviews for *The New Republic.* Tyler has instead devoted herself to her fiction and her family— her husband, Taghi Modarressi, a psychiatrist and writer whom she married in 1963, and their two children.

In one of her rare interviews, Tyler cited Eudora Welty as a major influence: "Reading her taught me there were stories to be written about the mundane life around me." Welty showed her, she said, "that very small things are often larger than the large things."

NEXT ON THE READING LIST: Pat Conroy, Ellen Gilchrist, Barbara Kingsolver, David Lodge, Cathie Pelletier, Carol Shields

John Updike
(b. March 18, 1932)

"Updike achieves a sense of the mind in its mysterious landscape. It is not an eccentric mind, but one called up through confident allusion to common experience. It occupies a landscape not of dream and the subconscious, nor of social realism, but of the worn paths and familiar places of vernacular experience, come directly out of childhood."
—Marilynne Robinson, New York Times

The Poorhouse Fair (KNOPF, 1959; REVISED, KNOPF, 1977) • This novel looks ahead to the 1970s, when Updike imagines that a welfare bureaucracy will have evolved to meet the needs of every citizen (except, of course, his spiritual ones). The focus of the novel is the annual fair staged by the Olinger Poorhouse, a charity home for eccentric senior citizens who rebel against their overly managed care. The *New York Times* called the novel "a work of art," and the *Chicago Tribune* praised its "brilliant use of words...and subtle observations." However, in his 1963 essay on Updike, Norman Podhoretz dismissed *The Poorhouse Fair* as "overly lyrical, bloated like a child who has eaten too much candy."

The Same Door (KNOPF, 1959) • Updike wrote many of these short stories for *The New Yorker* while he was a staff writer there during the mid-1950s. Based largely on his Pennsylvania childhood and the early years of his first marriage, they're filled with horse chestnut trees, telephone poles, porches, and green hedges, yet already an important theme is present: the loss of youth, particularly the glory of one's high school years. In the *Sewanee Review,* Richard H. Rupp called the collection "technically flawless."

* Rabbit, Run (KNOPF, 1960) • This novel, beloved by college English professors, probes the psyche of Harry "Rabbit" Angstrom. Once celebrated as a high school basketball star, Rabbit now finds it difficult to surrender his adolescence and accept his lack of adult success. He runs away from the suffocating creep of responsibility and middle age into an affair with a woman not his wife—ultimately finding, in his own words, "achievement in defeat." Rabbit's erotic adventures, which shocked many readers in 1960, prompted one reviewer to call him "spiritually desolate."

> *"What distinguishes* Rabbit, Run *from all of Updike's other work...is its dynamic balance between description and narrative energy; as Rabbit escapes from one enclosing situation to another, the pace never flags, and yet the physical and psychological details have never been more sharply in focus." (Richard Locke,* New York Times)

Pigeon Feathers (KNOPF, 1962) • In such stories as "A Sense of Shelter" and "Flight," Updike describes high school students who feel the urge to leave home yet fear the act of leaving. Other tales, such as "Wife-wooing," move Updike beyond adolescence into more lyrical, meditative subjects. However, according to one reviewer, "When the time comes to touch the essential, the writer's grip slips, almost from embarrassment, into rhetoric, and feelings become aesthetic sensations." These and the Pennsylvania stories in *The Same Door* were later collected in *Olinger Stories* (1964).

The Centaur (KNOPF, 1963) • This National Book Award winner is often compared with *Rabbit, Run:* Although George Caldwell is older and less adventurous than Rabbit Angstrom, he's similarly a former high school athletic star trapped in a middle-class life that he'd like to escape. However, whereas Rabbit runs, George stays put, as his son appreciatively recounts. Updike has said that this novel, his favorite, was created as an homage to his own father, who sacrificed much to sustain the Updikes during the Great Depression. One critic called *The Centaur* "a pyrotechnical display of unique originality and power.... The final chapter, culminating in the father's virtuoso mad lecture on the history of the universe, is superb. I can think of nothing in fiction to surpass it since the Nighttown scene in *Ulysses*."

Of the Farm (KNOPF, 1965) • In this companion piece to *The Centaur,* the characters' names have changed (from the Caldwells to the Robinsons), but the story remains loosely that of the Updikes: A middle-aged son (the Updike character) must unravel the myths of his family's history in order to meet the needs and demands of an aging parent. Joey works for a New York advertising agency despite his domineering mother's desire that he become a poet and care for the family farm. According to one critic, "This short but highly charged novel is a psychological thriller that takes place during one weekend when Joey brings his second wife, Peggy, and his stepson to the farm for Mrs. Robinson's blessing." Unlike *The Centaur*'s Peter Caldwell, however, Joey Robinson doesn't find resolution nearly so easily.

The Music School (KNOPF, 1966) • These short stories excavate the foundations, both physical and spiritual, of marriage. Their sarcastic, cynically comic tone matches Updike's view of the new "post-Pill paradise": As the narrator of one story reflects, "We are all pilgrims, faltering toward divorce." The men of these stories, in particular, having failed to find spiritual comfort in religion, look for it in haphazard sexual encounters.

Couples (KNOPF, 1968) • Set during the Kennedy-filled year of 1963, *Couples* examines the sexual habits of Tarbox, Massachusetts, a middle-class suburb of Boston. Called "the thinking man's *Peyton Place*," the novel displays Updike's continuing interest not only in sex but also in the ways that carnality undermines lofty intentions. Carpenter Piet Hanema appreciates fine craftsmanship in his work, yet he can't achieve that same quality in his personal life. When religion fails to quell his doubts, he leaves his wife, Angela, for his mistress, Foxy. "Yet after pages and pages of [Updike's] minutely detailed impressions," Elizabeth Dalton wrote in the *Partisan Review*, "the accumulated effect is one of waste.... It's all so immensely *written*."

Bech: A Book (KNOPF, 1970) • This comic portrait made up of seven interlocking episodes opens with a letter to Updike from Henry Bech, his cranky, self-centered author-hero. In the letter, Bech tells Updike, "If you must commit the artistic indecency of writing about a writer, better I suppose about me than about you." Although Bech seems to be a conglomeration of Saul Bellow, Norman Mailer, and other well-known Jewish writers, most reviewers shrewdly noted that Updike himself is present as well. According to *The New Republic*, "What Updike has to say about literature, when he's not trumping up modest love affairs for Bech, is that the literary life has become a depressing racket."

Rabbit Redux (KNOPF, 1971) • Updike returns a decade later to Rabbit Angstrom, bringing him face to face with the Vietnam War, black power, hippies, drug addiction, Middle American anger, and the moon shot. Once threatened by suburban domesticity, Rabbit now worries about social upheaval and the fact that there's nowhere left to run. His wife, Janice, has left him; his surviving son is a needy teenager; and now he's shacked up with a hippie girl. "The book is cleverer than a barrel full of monkeys, and about as odd," Christopher Ricks wrote in the *New York Review of Books*. "It never decides just what the artistic reasons...were for bringing back Rabbit instead of starting anew." In general, *Rabbit Redux* is considered the least of the four Rabbit books.

Museums and Women (KNOPF, 1972) • In this collection, which one reviewer called "every inch an Updike," little things make life meaningful: A father happens to notice that his daughter is graceful; another man decides over a game of solitaire not to get a divorce. A special section in *Museums and Women* contains stories about Richard and Joan Maple, a Boston suburban couple featured in Updike's later work. "The stories in this collection are the work of perhaps the finest literary craftsman in America today," Joseph Kanon wrote in the *Saturday Review*. "The prose is as beautiful—and surprisingly fresh—as ever, and the tone is, again, that of reason, with a wry sense of humor and a head-shaking sense of wonder."

A Month of Sundays (KNOPF, 1975) • Returning to the religion theme featured earlier in *Couples*, Updike selects as his hero a disgraced minister, Thomas Marshfield, who has seduced the church organist and subsequently been exiled to a desert retreat. Assigned the task of writing a journal about his spiritual recovery, Marshfield instead seduces the retreat's housekeeper. Peter S. Prescott in *Newsweek* called *A Month of Sundays* "Updike's most playful, most cerebral, most self-regarding novel.... There is also much of Updike's best writing here—a high incidence of the right image or metaphor for any given scene—and, in a sermon justifying adultery and divorce, a set piece that is perhaps the best that Updike has ever done."

Marry Me: A Romance (KNOPF, 1976) • The place is suburbia during the early 1960s. Jerry Conant is a hopeless romantic with three kids. Sally Mathias is a beautiful blond who reads Camus and also has three kids. They're married, but not to each other, so they have an affair. Then they decide to divorce their spouses and build a new life together—but Jerry hesitates. He has both personal and religious reasons: the classic Updike formula for dramatic tension. For the most part, reviewers didn't much like the characterizations in this novel, though many singled out Jerry's wife, Ruth, as Updike's best-drawn female character yet. "Updike is always at his best handling the social matter: cars, children, parties, the drinks," Alfred Kazin wrote in *The New Republic*. "There is all that American role playing [here], very real indeed.... But the *people* in this book are just not interesting."

The Coup (KNOPF, 1978) • Updike set this comic novel in the imaginary African country of Kush, which he called "the emptiest part of the world I could think of." Its sardonic narrator is Col. Hakim Félix Elleloû, the recently ousted president of Kush, who recounts the events of his ill-fated regime. Among the most amusing passages are those describing American efforts to woo this military dictator, including the delivery of an enormous shipment of Trix cereal and potato chips to feed the starving citizens of drought-stricken Kush. "Call *The Coup* a caper, an indulgence, a tract, a chronicle, a fable—and it is all these things at different times," Alastair Reid wrote in *The New Yorker*. "The fact is that Updike's sentences can be read with the pleasure that poetry can."

Too Far to Go: The Maple Stories (FAWCETT, 1979) • With this collection of seventeen stories, most previously published in *The New Yorker*, Updike returns to suburbia and the lives of Joan and Richard Maple, the couple last seen in *Museums and Women*. These stories explore their two-decade-long good-bye: In "Here Comes the Maples," for example, Richard recalls that he failed to kiss Joan during their wedding ceremony. "It strains one's credibility to read divorce stories in which none of the partners say 'I could kill you!' or 'You'll be sorry!'" Paul Theroux observed in the *New York Times*. "But perhaps this is the very feature that distinguished them from the common run of howling, wound-licking, look-what-you-did-to-me fictions of recent years. They are the most civilized stories imaginable, and because of this the most tender."

Problems and Other Stories (KNOPF, 1979) • Like *Too Far to Go*, this batch of stories was collected from Updike's work in *The New Yorker*. Although it isn't organized around a particular set of characters or a specific theme, most of the tales concern domestic trauma. The most noteworthy is "The Gun Shop," in which Updike contrasts a country-bred father with his city-bred son during a Thanksgiving weekend visit to the old family farm. "*Problems and Other Stories* won't be surpassed by any collection of short fiction in the next year, and perhaps not in the next ten," John Romano declared in the *New York Times*. "Its satisfactions are profound, and the proper emotion is one of gratitude that such a splendid artistic intelligence has been brought to bear on some of the important afflictions of our times."

* Rabbit Is Rich (KNOPF, 1981) • This novel, the third of the Rabbit books, won Updike an American Book Award, a National Book Critics Circle Award, and a Pulitzer Prize. Reviewers unanimously praised the novel's wisdom and concluded that Updike had entered a new "mature" phase in his writing career. In fact, the book's subject is maturity: It's the 1970s, and Rabbit Angstrom is now forty-six years old. He's back with his wife, Janice, and has inherited her father's Toyota dealership. Their college-dropout son has married his pregnant girlfriend. However, life is still unfair: On a Caribbean wife-swapping vacation, Rabbit loses out on his dream girl and gets stuck with his second choice.

> "Updike's own proud voice rings out with a new steeliness—and lamentation—about rich, wasteful, wholly selfish, and hard-talking America.... [Rabbit Is Rich] is wittier about the Middle America layer than anything since 1922 and Babbitt." (*Alfred Kazin*, New York Review of Books)

Bech Is Back (KNOPF, 1982) • As in *Bech: A Book*, Updike presents the action here in seven interlocking episodes. This time around, Bech has a new wife and a new novel whose potent scenes of sex and violence make him a celebrity and give Updike the opportunity to satirize the cult of fame in modern America. According to Christopher Lehmann-Haupt in the *New York Times*, the best piece is "Bech Wed." Yet "even here," Lehmann-Haupt wrote, "so violent is the contrast between Bech's intricate interior musings and a nearly silly parody of the contemporary publishing scene that we wonder for a moment if Mr. Updike hasn't lost control."

The Witches of Eastwick (KNOPF, 1984) • Divorcées Jane, Sukie, and Alexandra have discovered magical powers in their manless lives, yet they would have remained the anonymous witch-queens of Eastwick, Rhode Island, had Darryl Van Horne—a wealthy unmarried musician—not come to town. Although at first they succumb to his (literally) devilish charms, the three witches eventually find a way to rid themselves of the wicked Van Horne, but not before they learn the limits of their sexual liberation. According to Margaret Atwood, writing in the *New York Times*, "Much of *The Witches of Eastwick* is satire, some of it literary playfulness and some plain bitchery.... Any attempt to analyze further [might] be like taking an elephant gun to a puff pastry."

Roger's Version (KNOPF, 1986) • This novel reinvents Hawthorne's *The Scarlet Letter* from a modern point of view. Rev. Roger Lambert is a divinity school professor experiencing a crisis of faith. Graduate student Dale Kohler wants Roger's help with a grant that would fund Dale's project to prove God's existence using computers. Meanwhile, this being an Updike novel, Roger's neglected wife, Esther, seduces Dale, and Roger himself finds distraction with his teenage niece. "This is a tremendously expert novel," Martin Amis wrote in *The Observer*. "As with Roger, this book's cargo of disgust (disgust for the corporeal, disgust for the contemporary) is perfectly offset by the radiance of the humor, the perceptions, the epiphanies."

Trust Me (KNOPF, 1987) • As Marilynne Robinson remarked in her *New York Times* review, some of these stories are "wonderful" and "some...seem to me less than wonderful." In "The City," one of the better ones, a traveling computer salesman learns from a novel discomfort in his bowels that he's ill. His condition lands him in a municipal hospital, where strangers heal him. "Convention would have this a cold and anomic experience," Robinson observed, "but in this story it is beautiful."

S. (KNOPF, 1988) • Rewriting *The Scarlet Letter* once again, Updike focuses this time on the Hester Prynne character. Perhaps in response to complaints that he never properly sympathized with feminism, Updike has his forty-two-year-old heroine, Sarah, leave her domineering, unfaithful husband so that she can undertake a search for truth and meaning. Arriving at a Hindu ashram in Arizona, she writes to her husband, her mother, her daughter, her dentist, her analyst, and her hairdresser a series of letters that forms the basis of this satirical epistolary novel. "Sarah says that men 'always come on too strong or not strong enough,' and both of these seem to be true of Mr. Updike," Anatole Broyard wrote in the *New York Times*. "In entering the mind, body, and feelings of Sarah Worth, Mr. Updike may be trying to make not only sex, but the opposite sex, finite. If this is so, he has succeeded too well."

* Rabbit at Rest (KNOPF, 1990) • The fourth and final Rabbit novel, which won both a Pulitzer Prize and a National Book Critics Circle Award, finds Harry's marriage to Janice once again on the rocks. His relationship with his cocaine-addicted son, Nelson, is also strained. And even worse, the fifty-six-year-old Rabbit has learned, after a heart attack, that his days are numbered.

> *"From now on it is going to be hard to read John Updike without seeing all his earlier work as a long rehearsal for the writing of this book. Rabbit at Rest is that good.... It is a book that works by a steady accumulation of a mass of brilliant details, of shades and nuances, of the byplay between one sentence and the next, and no short review can properly honor its intricacy and richness. It must be read." (Jonathan Raban, Washington Post)*

Memories of the Ford Administration (KNOPF, 1992) • For some reason, an association of historians asks Alf Clayton, a jaded and philandering professor at an obscure junior college, to recount his impressions of the Ford administration. For an equally murky reason, Alf's analysis of the sexually liberated 1970s becomes inextricably entangled with his never-completed biography of James Buchanan. It seems that the breakup of the family unit during the sex-mad 1970s has brought to Alf's mind the disintegration of the Union just before the Civil War. "Juxtaposing scenes from Alf Clayton's life with scenes from Buchanan's, Updike unveils a series of comical, poignant, and unexpected contrasts and similarities between the two eras," Merle Rubin wrote in the *Christian Science Monitor*.

Brazil (KNOPF, 1994) • Star-crossed lovers Tristao, a poor black thief from the slums of Rio, and Isabel, a rich white member of the Brazilian ruling class, meet on the egalitarian Copacabana beach, where Tristao disavows his life of crime and pledges unwavering fidelity to Isabel. However, this promise—sealed with a stolen ring—proves difficult to keep. A turning point comes when Isabel consults an Indian shaman, who casts a spell reversing their skins: As a rich white thief and his black socialite wife, the couple become much more socially acceptable. "Readers may well wonder whether they are watching a virtuoso Anglo craftsman in a dazzling display of Latin fireworks or whether they have inadvertently stumbled into an X-rated version of *Flying Down to Rio*," *Christian Science Monitor* critic Merle Rubin remarked. "What seems certain is that a great deal of beautiful writing...has been used to dress up a story that is little more than a collection of clichés about women, men, blacks, whites, Indians, settlers, love, sex, class, and money."

The Afterlife and Other Stories (KNOPF, 1994) • In these stories, most of which were previously published in *The New Yorker*, Updike explores the lives of aging male characters who have finally become more preoccupied with death than with sex. In fact, much of the sex in these stories is represented by its debris—ex-wives, ex-lovers, children. Some familiar faces appear, such as those of Richard and Joan Maple; others are new. According to Ian Sanson of *New Statesman & Society*, "Updike is as impressively bright and enthusiastic as ever: all the more so because *The Afterlife* is about growing old and getting slow."

In the Beauty of the Lilies (KNOPF, 1996) • In this novel, which opens in 1910 New Jersey, the Rev. Clarence Wilmot, having lost his faith, leaves his church and becomes a traveling encyclopedia salesman. Thus begins the saga of the Wilmot clan, which Updike follows through four generations, ending with the modern recruitment of Clarence's dimwit great-grandson Clark by a Waco-style cult. "*Lilies* is a departure for Updike, a roman fleuve that takes up its characters, holds them in their segment of time, and relinquishes them to make way for a new segment of time and a succeeding generation of characters," Richard Eder explained in the *Los Angeles Times*. "Clarence loses faith, Clark finds it, and their opposite motions are both disastrous." Writing in the *New York Times*, Julian Barnes called the book "a deeply disenchanted...novel of accumulated wisdom."

Toward the End of Time (KNOPF, 1997) • Updike sets this novel in the year 2020, after an unspecified war between China and the United States has toppled the government, turned the Great Plains into a radioactive dust bowl, and left local affairs in the hands of thugs who demand protection money. Otherwise, daily life doesn't seem to have changed very much. The book's narrator, a sixty-six-year-old retired stockbroker named Ben Turnbull, still uses FedEx to get his bond slips and still cares little for anyone else. (If you count backward from 2020, the 1980s were Ben's heyday, and Updike seems to be implying that the intervening nuclear exchange may have been history's revenge on Ben—and America—for that decade.) More than most Updike works, *Toward the End of Time* received very mixed reviews: Writing in the *New York Times*, Margaret Atwood called it "deplorably good." However, according to *New Republic* reviewer Robert Boyers, "for all its technical beauties, its proficiencies of diction and syntax, Updike's new novel is especially disheartening in its specious and half-hearted attempts to situate its private malaise in the aftermath of a terrible historical catastrophe."

BIOGRAPHY

JOHN UPDIKE WAS BORN IN rural Shillington, Pennsylvania, which he later transformed into the fictional town of Olinger. Early in his writing career, when his work—*The Same Door, The Centaur, Of the Farm*—was much more explicitly autobiographical, he returned often to Olinger's familiar streets (though not as often, it seems, to Shillington).

In 1953, while he was a student at Harvard, he married his first wife, Mary, with whom he subsequently had four children. At Harvard, he studied English literature and edited the *Harvard Lampoon,* but his ambitions lay elsewhere: He wanted to be a cartoonist, specifically an illustrator for Walt Disney.

After graduating summa cum laude in 1954, he won a yearlong fellowship to the Ruskin School of Drawing and Fine Art in Oxford. Yet on his return, when Disney wouldn't hire him, he joined the staff of *The New Yorker,* which had earlier published one of his short stories. Updike spent the next two years contributing his wit to the "Talk of the Town" column before moving to Massachusetts and concentrating his full-time efforts on fiction. Of course, he maintained his relationship with the magazine, which has continued to publish most of his short fiction, essays, and criticism.

Famous for his stories of white males and their sexual misadventures, Updike has explored in great detail these men's physical, sexual, intellectual, political, financial, and spiritual lives. His greatest creation has unquestionably been Harry Angstrom, the eponymous hero of the four Rabbit novels, the last two of which won Pulitzer Prizes. Each of these novels defined a decade during which Updike produced, more likely than not, some of the best fiction.

Updike and his first wife separated in 1974, the marriage soon ending in divorce. Three years later, he married his second wife, Martha. Making no secret of his fictional use of these relationships, Updike has told a number of interviewers that the Maples stories, in particular, have drawn on his personal experiences. It's a process that Updike describes as "loving": "In the author's mind, it's always loving to try to get some qualities of the person into print—even if it doesn't seem flattering to the person." His first wife, Mary, has said, "I've gotten used to being written about."

NEXT ON THE READING LIST: Margaret Atwood, Ann Beattie, Amy Bloom, Richard Ford, Iris Murdoch, Grace Paley, Philip Roth

Mario Vargas Llosa

(b. March 28, 1936)

"Mario Vargas Llosa has begun a complete inventory of the political, social, economic, and cultural reality of Peru. This inventory is necessarily controversial. Very deliberately, Vargas Llosa has chosen to be his country's conscience."
—*Suzanne Jill Levine*, New York Times

The Time of the Hero (EDITORIAL SEIX BARRAL, 1963; GROVE, 1966) • Vargas Llosa's first novel grew out of his unpleasant experience as a student at a Peruvian military academy. It tells the story of a cadet who steals an exam to help out his mates. The theft is witnessed by another cadet, who ultimately reports it. The authorities investigate, but the informer is killed and military leaders cover up the death to protect the "honor" of the institution. The Peruvian army organized a public burning of the book, which R. Z. Sheppard of *Time* called "a brutal slab of naturalism about life and violent death."

The Green House (EDITORIAL SEIX BARRAL, 1966; HARPER & ROW, 1968) • Vargas Llosa's second novel also draws on autobiographical material: the author's memories of the small Peruvian jungle town in which he lived as a boy. The novel's two main characters are Sergeant Lituma and Bonifacia, a girl raised by Spanish nuns. The green house of the title, a brothel in the coastal city of Piura, is the central location at which the entire cast eventually congregates. Critics praised the novel's use of multiple storylines, flashbacks, and fragmentary dialogue and its blending of omniscient and first-person narratives, but some readers—because the book is indeed complex—may find it difficult to read.

* Conversation in the Cathedral (EDITORIAL SEIX BARRAL, 1969; HARPER & ROW, 1975) • By the time Vargas Llosa published his third novel, also not an easy read, he was firmly established as one of the stars of the Latin American "fiction boom" of the early 1970s. *Conversation in the Cathedral* recounts a four-hour discussion in a Lima bar between Santiago Zavala, the ne'er-do-well scion of a wealthy family, and Ambrosio, his family's former chauffeur. The setting is 1950s Peru during the last days in power of dictator Manuel Odría. Santiago expresses his disgust at his father's corrupt dealings with the government, his own arrest by Odría's secret police, and his current job as a crime reporter. Ambrosio replies by providing some of the more sordid details of the sexual escapades of Santiago's father.

"Conversation in the Cathedral, *the latest and most brilliant novel of Peru's Mario Vargas Llosa, [is] one of the most scathing denunciations ever written on the corruption and immorality of Latin America's ruling classes.* " (*Penny Lernoux,* The Nation)

Captain Pantoja and the Special Service (EDITORIAL SEIX BARRAL, 1973; HARPER & ROW, 1978) • This satire of the Peruvian military's obsession with discipline and efficiency tells the story of Capt. Pantaleón Pantoja, a model officer entrusted with the task of running a secret prostitution service for sex-deprived soldiers in the jungle. The captain dedicates himself to his mission, calculating not only the exact number of prostitutes necessary but also the number of orgasms each soldier requires. Critics welcomed the book's broad humor, which marked a departure from the serious tone of Vargas Llosa's earlier fiction.

The Cubs and Other Stories (HARPER & ROW, 1979) • This collection of stories gathers together many of Vargas Llosa's youthful writings. The novella of the title tells the tragic story of a young boy, Cuéllar, who's emasculated by a dog bite. Because of this accidental castration, Cuéllar becomes a demoralized outsider in Peru's macho patriarchal society. Critics noted the sophistication apparent in the young Vargas Llosa's writing but lamented the weak characterizations. "There is a certain shallowness in the work, a failure to find the depths the subject seemed to promise," Michael Wood wrote in the *New York Review of Books.*

Aunt Julia and the Scriptwriter (EDITORIAL SEIX BARRAL, 1977; FARRAR, STRAUS & GIROUX, 1982) • Vargas Llosa returned to a comic mode for this melodramatic (and somewhat autobiographical) account of Mario, an eighteen-year-old radio journalist who marries Julia, his thirty-two-year-old aunt (but not his blood relative). Mario's attempts to write serious fiction, all failures, contrast to the successes of his radio colleague, Pedro Camacho, a Bolivian writer of soap operas who churns out story after story of incest, prostitution, and religious fanaticism. Writing in the *New York Times,* William Kennedy called the book a "screwball fantasy" whose "principal achievement is the rendering of a vast comic landscape...that never ceases to entertain."

✻ The War of the End of the World (EDITORIAL SEIX BARRAL, 1981; FARRAR, STRAUS & GIROUX, 1984) • This book, generally regarded as Vargas Llosa's masterpiece, is a historical novel reminiscent of nineteenth-century adventure narratives. Based on a Brazilian writer's famous account of an actual rebellion, *The War of the End of the World* tells the apocalyptic story of a fanatical preacher, Antonio Conselheiro, who gathers about him poor peasants inspired by his prophecies of an imminent end to the world. Because both the state and the church believe that Conselheiro's activities are subversive, the army is deployed to pacify the group.

"The greatest qualities of this excellent novel are...its refusal ever to abandon the human dimension in a story that could so easily have become grandiose; also a sense of ambiguity, which enables Vargas Llosa to keep his characters three-dimensional...; and finally, a profound awareness of the tragic irony that makes tens of thousands of ordinary women and men die fighting against the republic that was created, in theory, precisely to serve them." (Salman Rushdie, The New Republic)

The Real Life of Alejandro Mayta (EDITORIAL SEIX BARRAL, 1984; FARRAR, STRAUS & GIROUX, 1986) • This novel tells two stories simultaneously—one of the life of Alejandro Mayta, a Marxist revolutionary, and another of the author's own attempts to fictionalize Mayta's failed Andean revolution. It was not a favorite of the critics, many of whom found it repetitive, pointing out that it covered much the same ground as Vargas Llosa's earlier, better works.

Who Killed Palomino Molero? (EDITORIAL SEIX BARRAL, 1986; FARRAR, STRAUS & GIROUX, 1987) • This novella, written in the style of detective fiction, recounts the attempt of Lieutenant Silva and Sergeant Lituma to solve the titular crime. The two policemen encounter great resistance in their search for the truth, and it soon becomes apparent that the murder is inextricably related to Peru's corrupt social mores, which sanction both racial and economic discrimination. "The crime is solved," Richard Lourie wrote in the *New York Times*. "Or is it? Every clean line that Mr. Vargas Llosa draws he then immediately smudges into ambiguities. Not murky, but all too vivid, these are the ambiguities of reality itself."

The Storyteller (EDITORIAL SEIX BARRAL, 1987; FARRAR, STRAUS & GIROUX, 1989) • This novel opens in Florence, where the narrator—a cynical Peruvian—is attending an exhibition of photographs. In one of these photographs, a man tells a story to a group of remote Amazon Indians encircling him. The narrator recognizes the man: It's his old college friend Saul Zuratas, a half-Jewish anthropologist who has since "gone native"—that is, lost his scientific detachment. One story quickly introduces another in this "science fiction" (fiction about science) that Ursula K. Le Guin, writing in the *New York Times*, called Vargas Llosa's "most engaging and accessible book."

In Praise of the Stepmother (TUSQUETS, 1988; FARRAR, STRAUS & GIROUX, 1990) • In this short novel, Vargas Llosa returns to the humorous tone and erotic themes that he used to such great effect in *Aunt Julia and the Scriptwriter*. The titular stepmother is Lucrecia, the warmly carnal second wife of Don Rigoberto, whose prepubescent son worships her in every manner that he's quickly becoming able to imagine. While noting its rather slight intellectual content, many critics enjoyed the book's humor. But *New York Times* reviewer Anthony Burgess—who called *In Praise of the Stepmother* "an erotic novel, not a pornographic one"—ultimately decided that he was "not greatly impressed."

Death in the Andes (Planeta, 1993; Farrar, Straus & Giroux, 1996) • Vargas Llosa tells this ambitious story, set in Peru's formidable Andes Mountains, mostly from the point of view of Corporal Lituma, a police officer sent there to protect construction workers from Shining Path guerrillas. Lituma's attempts to find three men who've disappeared from the construction camp constitute the main narrative action, but there are numerous subplots— some erotic, some mystical, and others brutally violent. Madison Smartt Bell wrote in the *New York Times* that this sprawling, at times almost incoherent book was "fascinating without being fully satisfying," while Paul Gray of *Time* praised "Vargas Llosa's meticulously realistic description of this high, unforgiving landscape and the haunted people who perch there."

BIOGRAPHY

Mario Vargas Llosa was born in Arequipa in southern Peru. Because his parents separated at the time of his birth, he was raised in the home of his maternal grandfather, who held a succession of government jobs. As a result, the family moved frequently. Vargas Llosa's childhood was spent first in Cochabambo, Bolivia, and later in Piura in northern Peru. When Vargas Llosa was fourteen, his parents reconciled, and he moved with them to Lima. His authoritarian father, who didn't share Vargas Llosa's literary interests, forced him to attend a military academy for two years, an experience that marked the author for life. He hated the school's brutality, which he saw as emblematic of Peruvian society at large. In fact, this brutality became the subject of his first novel, *The Time of the Hero*.

At Lima's University of San Marcos, Vargas Llosa studied literature and law, but his political opposition to the military dictatorship then in power had a greater influence on his intellectual development. He joined a student cell of the Peruvian Communist party though later left it to join the Christian Democrats. Meanwhile, he wrote short stories and read William Faulkner with intense admiration.

When Vargas Llosa was nineteen, he married his thirty-two-year-old aunt, Julia Urquidi Illanes. Although she was an aunt only by marriage, the union scandalized his family (and ended in divorce a short time later). Like many Latin American writers of his generation, Vargas Llosa subsequently moved to Paris to pursue a literary career. He taught Spanish at a Berlitz school and worked as a journalist for a French broadcasting company before the success of his first two novels demonstrated that he could make a living as a writer.

During the late 1980s, Vargas Llosa became active again in Peruvian politics as the leader of a movement protesting governmental plans to nationalize the banks. The movement led to the establishment of Fredemo, a liberal political party that supported democracy, a free-market economy, and individual liberty. In 1989, a coalition led by Fredemo chose Vargas Llosa as its candidate for president. Although he eventually withdrew from the race, Vargas Llosa played an important role in legitimizing his party, both within

Peru and internationally. Now in his sixties and still writing, Vargas Llosa is often mentioned as a leading candidate for a Nobel Prize in literature.

NEXT ON THE READING LIST: Isabel Allende, Jorge Amado, Louis de Bernières, Carlos Fuentes, Francisco Goldman, V. S. Naipaul

---

Alice Walker
(b. February 9, 1944)

"Virginia Woolf said that 'the words ride on the back of the rhythm.' The rhythms of Alice Walker's prose are beautiful and characteristic, flexible, vigorous, easy, the gait of a hunting lion. Even when the pace of the story crowds and races and the words are choked with meaning and intent, the rhythms never falter. The lion goes her way."
—*Ursula K. Le Guin,* San Francisco Review of Books

The Third Life of Grange Copeland (HARCOURT BRACE JOVANOVICH, 1970) • Walker's first novel introduces one of her most prevalent themes: the oppression of the black family by its disenfranchised males. By 1920, when the book opens, thirty-five-year-old Grange Copeland has already been defeated by his hard life of sharecropping in rural Georgia. After driving his wife to suicide, he abandons his children to seek a more successful life in the North. Even so, he passes on his legacy of hate and violence to his son, Brownfield, who grows up to murder his own wife. Thereafter, Grange returns to raise Brownfield's youngest child, Ruth. The redemptive relationship that he forges with his granddaughter saves Grange, who in turn saves Ruth. According to Jay L. Halio, writing in the *Southern Review,* "The honest treatment of both past and present, the worst aspects of which Miss Walker does not flinch at, help make *The Third Life* a convincing and stirring novel. So do its firm, tight control and its eloquence."

In Love and Trouble: Stories of Black Women (HARCOURT BRACE JOVANOVICH, 1973) • Most of the women in these stories are southern blacks who, often despite their reluctance, challenge the social conventions of sex, race, and age that bind them. Among the pieces is "Everyday Use," perhaps Walker's most anthologized story, in which Maggie, a woman who doesn't know much about the new "blackness," nonetheless celebrates her heritage through quilting. Of particular interest to Walker is what happens when black women discover that their loyalty to black men has been misplaced. Several black male reviewers complained that Walker's men were too one dimensional, yet feminist critics, such as Barbara Smith in *Ms.*, applauded Walker's efforts: "These stories are not pretty," Smith observed. "When the reality is prettier, as a result of the implementation of black *and* feminist goals and values, the stories will be prettier, too."

Meridian (HARCOURT BRACE JOVANOVICH, 1976) • Although Meridian Hill begins college in Atlanta at the height of the civil rights movement, she fails to become the sort of revolutionary that her new peer group expects. Instead, she becomes gravely ill and fails to recover until she admits to herself that her vital work lies not in revolution but in the preservation of older black values. Discarding her possessions, she becomes an ascetic living among and serving the people of the rural South. Although *The New Yorker* questioned Walker's heavy use of symbolism, Marge Piercy of the *New York Times* deemed *Meridian* "a fine, taut novel that accomplishes a remarkable amount."

You Can't Keep a Good Woman Down (HARCOURT BRACE JOVANOVICH, 1981) • Even more so than *In Love and Trouble*, Walker's second collection of short stories demonstrates the possibilities open to black women, even in a society permeated by sexism and racism. Such stylistically innovative stories as "Advancing Luna—and Ida B. Wells" and "Coming Apart" address issues raised by many feminists during the 1970s—such as abortion, pornography, and interracial rape—analyzing them from a political as well as a personal perspective. "Walker's work should be admired," Carol Rumens declared in the *Times Literary Supplement*, "not because it represents a flowering of black or female consciousness, but because at best it brings to life the varied scents and colors of human experience."

* The Color Purple (HARCOURT BRACE JOVANOVICH, 1982) • Having been criticized in the past for making her narrator's voice too strongly her own, Walker here avoids her usual polemics and instead allows the heroine, Celie, to describe her life in an engaging and subtly humorous manner despite its many horrors. After being repeatedly raped by her stepfather, teenage Celie enters into a loveless marriage with Albert, a widower who also beats and torments her. Thereafter, she writes a series of letters that form the basis of this epistolary novel. Eventually, Celie comes to reject the patriarchal God of Western tradition because, if He existed, He certainly wouldn't have allowed the degradation that she has endured. At that moment, Albert's mistress, the flamboyant Shug Avery, appears to offer Celie both love and a genderless god that she can accept. Most reviewers agreed with *New York Times* critic Mel Watkins that this Pulitzer Prize and American Book Award winner "brings into sharper focus many of the diverse themes that threaded their way through [Walker's] past work."

"The storytelling style of The Color Purple *makes it irresistible to read.... By the end of the novel, we believe that this poor, nameless patch of land in the*

American South is really the world—and vice versa. Conversations between Celie and Shug have brought us theories of philosophy, ethics, and metaphysics—all with a world vision that seems more complete for proceeding from the bottom up." (*Gloria Steinem, Ms.*)

The Temple of My Familiar (HARCOURT BRACE JOVANOVICH, 1989) • This perhaps overly ambitious novel has neither a conventional linear plot nor fully realized characters. Instead, using multiple narrative voices and abrupt shifts in time and place, Walker offers a profusion of observations on such diverse issues as ecology, spirituality, and animal rights as she exhumes African and South American goddesses dethroned long ago because of male jealousy. Miss Lissie—"a sort of black Shirley MacLaine," according to Rhoda Koenig in *New York*—recalls the days of mother worship in Africa and proclaims herself to be one such goddess. Pointing out that the novel demanded a tremendous suspension of disbelief, most reviewers concluded that few readers would be quite so willing. "Pantheistic plea, lesbian propaganda, past-lives chronicle, black-pride panorama, *The Temple of My Familiar* doesn't really gel at any junction," James Wolcott observed in *The New Republic.*

Possessing the Secret of Joy (HARCOURT BRACE JOVANOVICH, 1992) • In this novel, Walker addresses female genital mutilation as it is practiced in certain African, Asian, and Middle Eastern cultures. Although she again makes use of multiple viewpoints, Walker concentrates on that of Tashi, a character who appeared earlier in *The Color Purple*. Tashi has since returned to Africa, where she willingly undergoes a ritual clitoridectomy. However, when the procedure nearly kills her, she experiences a severe emotional crisis, which leads to a confrontation with M'Lissa, the fearsome tribal circumciser. "*Possessing the Secret of Joy* is not [Walker's] best fictional effort," Mel Watkins wrote in the *New York Times*, "but its focus on one of the most debated and disturbing feminist issues puts it among her most powerful works."

BIOGRAPHY

ALICE WALKER WAS THE YOUNGEST of eight children raised by sharecroppers in Eatonton, Georgia. When she was eight, she was accidentally blinded in her right eye. When she was fourteen, her favorite brother paid to have the scar tissue removed. During the intervening six years, however, Walker's unsightly appearance made her feel like an outcast, and in her isolation she turned to reading. She also began to write poems. Regarding her poetry, Walker has said, "I have climbed back into life over and over on a ladder made of words."

Walker recalls, in particular, three gifts that her mother bought for her out of her meager income: a sewing machine so that she could make her own clothes, a suitcase so that she could travel, and a typewriter so that she could write. After two years as a scholarship student at Spelman, a prestigious black women's college in Atlanta, Walker transferred to Sarah Lawrence, an even more elitist women's college in Bronxville, New York, where she was one of only six black students. During the summer of 1964, between her junior and senior years at Sarah Lawrence, she traveled to Kenya. After that trip, she became pregnant and considered suicide until a friend located a doctor willing to perform an abortion. This traumatic senior-year experience led directly to the completion of her first volume of poetry, *Once*, published in 1968.

In 1966, while working in Mississippi on a voter registration drive, Walker met law student Melvyn Leventhal. A year later, she married him, and they moved to Mississippi, where Leventhal helped prosecute a number of school-desegregation cases. For several years, they were the only married interracial homeowners living in the state (miscegenation was still illegal in Mississippi). By 1974, however, their marriage was ending and Walker returned to New York City, where she became an editor at *Ms.* Four years later, she relocated to San Francisco, and four years after that the publication of *The Color Purple* made her a literary celebrity.

In addition to *Once*, Walker's poetry collections have included *Revolutionary Petunias* (1973), *Goodnight, Willie Lee, I'll See You in the Morning* (1979), *Horses Make a Landscape Look More Beautiful* (1984), and the anthology *Her Blue Body Everything We Know* (1991). She's also the author of many works of nonfiction, including the collections *In Search of Our Mothers' Gardens* (1983) and *Living by the Word* (1988), which *Los Angeles Times* reviewer Derrick Bell called "vintage Alice Walker: passionate, political, personal, and poetic." Walker followed her first volume of memoirs, *The Same River Twice* (1996), with *Anything We Love Can Be Saved* (1997).

NEXT ON THE READING LIST: Isabel Allende, Bebe Moore Campbell, Terry McMillan, Toni Morrison, Gloria Naylor

Fay Weldon

(b. September 22, 1933)

"Like so many of her fellow ironists—Evelyn Waugh and Muriel Spark come to mind—Ms. Weldon can lay waste the pretensions of a decade in the sketch of a single dinner party. And, like her greatest predecessor, Jane Austen, she specializes in that particularly risible comedy of errors that exists between those incompatible creatures, men and women."
—Michael Malone, New York Times

The Fat Woman's Joke (MACGIBBON & KEE, 1967; PUBLISHED IN THE U.S. AS *...AND THE WIFE RAN AWAY*, MCKAY, 1968) • Alan and Esther Sussman embark on a crash diet to forestall middle age. Soon Alan has an affair with his comely secretary, and an outraged Esther flees to a dingy basement apartment, where she proceeds to gorge herself. Although various characters, including Alan's mistress, urge Esther to reconcile with her husband, she stubbornly clings to the dubious satisfactions of the single life. "Everything that is to concern Fay Weldon in her later work," *New York Times* critic Mary Cantwell observed when the book was republished in 1981, "is already sprung full-blown" in this novel, a skillful minor work originally written as a play for British television.

Down among the Women (ST. MARTIN'S, 1971) • This loosely autobiographical novel, more elaborately structured than Weldon's first, spans twenty years in the lives of five women whose identities keep getting submerged in their relationships with men. The stories of Scarlet (the Weldon character) and her four girlfriends reflect changes in British society between 1950 and 1970. The entire narrative takes the form of a rumination that Scarlet's friend Jocelyn has while sitting on a park bench. As one reviewer noted of this comic saga, Weldon's ability to blend "the terrible and the ridiculous is one of the major reasons why a novel filled with the pain endured by women...is neither painfully depressing nor cheerfully sentimental."

Female Friends (ST. MARTIN'S, 1974) • The title characters in Weldon's third novel are emotionally needy girls from very different backgrounds. They become friends when all three are evacuated from London during the Blitz. The narrative hops back and forth in time as Chloe, Marjorie, and Grace grow up, meet disagreeable men, and cling to one another for comfort. According to the *Times Literary Supplement*, "The main idea—an exhortation to women to pull together—is put over very well." Arthur Cooper of *Newsweek* concurred, adding that "Weldon shares Mary McCarthy's rare talent for dissecting complex relationships as well as McCarthy's misanthropic bitchiness."

Remember Me (RANDOM HOUSE, 1976) • This ghost story examines the persistence of the mother-child bond. Madeleine haunts her former husband's current spouse, the mean-spirited Lily, until Lily begins to take more seriously her obligation as stepmother to Madeleine's daughter, Hilary, an overweight and graceless teenager. Most reviewers agreed with John Braine's assessment in *Books and Bookmen* that *Remember Me* exhibited to good effect Weldon's "sardonic, earthy, disenchanted, slightly bitter but never cruel sense of humor." However, a few critics did make the point that, despite her undeniable ability to create characters and sustain a narrative, Weldon hadn't yet hit her stride as a novelist. "*Remember Me* has the breathlessness of an Iris Murdoch novel, and some of its inventiveness," Joyce Carol Oates wrote in the *New York Times*. "But it lacks depth and resonance, and it resolves itself as glibly as any situation comedy."

Words of Advice (RANDOM HOUSE, 1977) • Victor is a middle-aged antiques dealer. Elsa is his nineteen-year-old social-climbing mistress. Hamish is an elderly millionaire. Gemma is Hamish's beautiful but hysterical (and paralyzed) wife. Gemma instructs Victor to bring Elsa to Hamish's castle because she wants Elsa to bear a child for her. In fact, Gemma is prepared to keep Elsa locked up until she complies. Originally a play, *Words of Advice* is clearly intended as a satiric modern fairy tale, though its thinly developed characters and improbably exaggerated situations made it a little too "stylish" for most critics. Writing in the *New York Times*, Martin Amis called the book a "raffish, open-ended novel, in which all kinds of cockeyed notions, crooked parallels, and unassimilated themes can be harmlessly let out to play." (This novel was published in Britain as *Little Sisters*.)

Praxis (SUMMIT, 1978) • In this Booker Prize nominee, Praxis Duveen, an extravagant failure as both a wife and a mother, commits a celebrated murder from which she emerges as both a victim and an apostle of the women's movement. While confined to her room by injuries sustained after her release from prison, she writes her life story, hoping to uncover "the root of my pain and yours." According to Kelly Cherry in the *Chicago Tribune*, "The writing throughout is brisk and ever so slightly off the wall—sufficiently askew to convey the oddness of events, sufficiently no-nonsense to make that oddness credible."

Puffball (SUMMIT, 1980) • Concentrating here on the physical aspects of being a woman, Weldon goes so far as to include a great deal of technical information on fertility, conception, and fetal development. The novel opens as Liffey Lee-Fox persuades her pompous husband, Richard, to give up city life in exchange for her promise to become pregnant. However, as soon as Liffey settles into her new country home, a jealous neighbor well versed in the dark ways of the countryside threatens her as-yet-unborn child. Writing in the *Times Literary Supplement*, Anita Brookner called the novel "a fantasy for the tired businesswoman.... *Puffball* is also more awkward in tone than [Weldon's] earlier novels, though it perhaps marks a transitional phase in the author's career."

Watching Me, Watching You (SUMMIT, 1981) • This volume contains eleven short stories in addition to Weldon's 1967 debut novel, *The Fat Woman's Joke*. As *New York Times* reviewer Mary Cantwell pointed out, the men and women of these darkly comic tales "have lots of proximity but no relating." In "Holy Stones," for example, a recently married middle-aged journalist takes his pious young wife to Israel so that she can learn the dangers of "irrational" religious belief. When she remains more devoted to her God than to her husband, he retaliates by having an affair. As James Lasdun conceded in *The Spectator*, "Fay Weldon damns her men with efficiency, and these stories remain extremely compelling."

The President's Child (HODDER & STOUGHTON, 1982; DOUBLEDAY, 1983) • In this novel, Weldon combines her customary feminist concerns with a parody of the technothriller genre. Raised in the Australian outback, Isabel moves to England, where she attaches herself to a series of rich men and becomes a successful journalist. Along the way, she becomes pregnant by Dandy Ivel, a handsome American politician recently chosen by a group of enormously powerful men as their future candidate for president. Isabel bears Dandy's son without any fuss, but six years later she discovers that these men want to "eliminate" her rather than risk exposure of the affair. Although in the *Village Voice* Carol Sternhell cheered Weldon for taking her "refreshingly unromantic portrait of men several steps further into a nightmare vision of male conspiracy," a number of male reviewers continued to lambaste Weldon for sketching her male characters so thinly and harshly, and even Harriet Waugh in *The Spectator* called *The President's Child* "tiresome and contrived reading."

* The Life and Loves of a She-Devil (HODDER & STOUGHTON, 1983; PANTHEON, 1984) • Unlike some Weldon heroines, Ruth doesn't merely endure—she gets even. One night when she spills the soup while serving dinner, the dog and cat go wild and her in-laws start quarreling. This racket interrupts her accountant husband, Bobbo, in midreverie as he contemplates his glamorous romance-novelist mistress, Mary. Running upstairs to the bathroom, Ruth locks herself inside. Following her, an equally distressed Bobbo utters these fateful words: "I don't think you are a woman at all. I think that what you are is a she-devil!" Thus enlightened, Ruth accepts her true nature. "I want revenge," she declares. "I want power. I want money. I want to be loved and not love in return."

> *"In an age where much fiction is cut-rate minimalist or cocaine chic, Ms. Weldon shows us another path. She is complex, smart, and political without cheating us on esthetics. And she is profoundly funny. Her* Life and Loves of a She-Devil *is a small masterpiece of invective, the ultimate feminist revenge*

novel, but one so truly amusing and consistently intelligent that even a guilt-ridden male chauvinist can't resist it." (*Robert Ward,* New York Times)

Letters to Alice on First Reading Jane Austen (RAINBIRD, 1984; HARCOURT BRACE JOVANOVICH, 1986) • For this cross between an epistolary novel and a paean to Literature, Weldon invents for herself a imaginary niece, Alice, who has just begun studying English literature at college. As the book opens, Alice writes to her famous aunt, complaining that the novels of Jane Austen seem to her "boring, petty, and irrelevant." Aunt Fay responds with a series of letters that discuss what's important in life and literature. (Most important in life, Weldon tells us, *is* literature.) The result, according to Ian Hislop in *Books and Bookmen,* "is a witty, convincing, and spirited defense of the practice of reading and writing fiction."

Polaris and Other Stories (HODDER & STOUGHTON, 1985; PENGUIN, 1989) • These twelve stories, which range in style from natural realism to nearly Gothic horror, explore all of Weldon's familiar concerns: sexual politics, family life, adultery, and even gynecology. According to *New York Times* reviewer Robert Ward, "Most of the stories have a dead-on surety of tone." However, Ward added, "If Ms. Weldon's writing has one serious flaw, it is her lack of confidence in her readers; too often she steps in and adds these little messages [when] no moralizing is needed."

The Shrapnel Academy (HODDER & STOUGHTON, 1986; VIKING, 1987) • Refugees from an Agatha Christie novel gather in a remote grand English country house named after the man who invented the exploding cannonball. The occasion is the Shrapnel Academy's annual Eve of Waterloo Dinner. A "shrine to the ethos of military excellence," the academy is run by Joan Lumb, a bossy sergeant major in skirts and her large staff of oppressed third worlders. Chief among these is the mad butler Acorn, who has been secretly plotting the overthrow of Upstairs. Clancy Sigal, writing in the *New York Times,* called *The Shrapnel Academy* a "mildly funny romp [though] shooting fish in a barrel is not normally Ms. Weldon's sport."

The Hearts and Lives of Men (HEINEMANN, 1987; VIKING, 1988) • In this fairy tale for adults, which opens in London during the Swinging Sixties, Clifford and Helen meet at a party and fall in love. However, when their daughter, Nell, is born, a bad fairy—actually, Clifford's former lover Angie—hovers over her cradle, determined to ruin her parents' marriage and win Clifford back. Angie sets in motion a chain of events resulting in a series of storybook adventures for "little" Nell that recall those of her Dickensian predecessor. "If *The Hearts and Lives of Men* were set to music," Cyra McFadden wrote in the *Chicago Tribune,* "we'd have an opera, complete with passions on a grand scale, a plot with no logic but its own, and a rousing final curtain. As it is, we have a bravura novel from Fay Weldon, or to be more accurate, another bravura novel."

The Rules of Life (HARPER & ROW, 1987) • It's the year 2004, and the British Museum has become a temple devoted to the Great New Fictional Religion, which has replaced Christianity. Sitting at his console, Weldon's narrator, a priest, listens to the recorded recollections of ghosts, hoping to gain some wisdom from the dead. One ghost in particular, a recently deceased professional mistress named Gabriella, has dictated from beyond the grave her self-serving "rules of life." Listening to Gabriella's seductive voice, the priest falls in love. Although Weldon's "glimpse into the future allows her to comment ironically on the present," Emily Leider pointed out in the *New York Times*, she "teases us with heady themes but fails to develop them. She soon wearies of her heroine—a woman as flimsy as the white silk shift she dies in—and so do we."

✻ The Heart of the Country (HUTCHINSON, 1987; VIKING, 1988) • Real estate broker Harry Harris abandons his wife, Natalie, for a local carnival queen, but not before he empties out their bank accounts and Natalie's jewelry box. With two children and a hungry Alsatian to feed, not to mention a mountain of debt to pay off, the seemingly helpless, doll-like Natalie has no choice but to confront her new circumstances. In the process, she discovers a resilience and a will to survive that she never knew she had. The novel's shrewd, bitchy, unsentimental narration comes courtesy of Sonia, another abandoned wife, who shelters Natalie and her children after Natalie loses her house.

> *"With sure, succinct craft, Weldon melds highly comic fiction with acerbic social outrage. Even Sonia's occasionally over-shrill polemics are rescued by a manic, marvelous wit. With hell-bent, head-on energetic style and skill,* The Heart of the Country *lifts effortlessly above its considerable weight of rightful indignation. It is a provocative, brilliantly controlled performance."* (Melissa Pritchard, Chicago Tribune)

Leader of the Band (HODDER & STOUGHTON, 1988; VIKING, 1989) • This picaresque romp features Starlady Sandra, a brilliant astronomer who also happens to be a television star. Swept off her feet by Mad Jack, a trumpet player in a Dixieland band, she leaves her boring barrister husband and joins Jack on tour. "Fay Weldon's wit, her intellect, her love of play—usually so effective—get in the way in *Leader of the Band*," Robert Ward wrote in his *New York Times* review. "There is ice where there should be warmth, opinions where there should be flesh and blood."

The Cloning of Joanna May (COLLINS, 1989; VIKING, 1990) • Childless, sixtyish Joanna May is the spurned former wife of Carl May, a giant of the nuclear power industry who sadly spent much of his childhood chained in a dog kennel. As she recuperates from her divorce, Joanna discovers that, three decades earlier, Carl had secretly cloned her. In other words, there are now four other Joannas out there! "If the targets...are a bit easy and shopworn by now—television, nuclear energy, soulless science, big business, male power, clinging or frivolous women—the joy of watching Ms. Weldon's quirky talent at work on them isn't at all diminished," Robert Houston wrote in the *New York Times*.

Darcy's Utopia (HARPERCOLLINS/UK, 1990; VIKING, 1991) • When Eleanor Darcy's husband, an important government adviser, is jailed for misappropriation of public funds, Eleanor becomes an instant media celebrity. Using her newfound access to the media, she presents, during a series of interviews, her utopian vision of a future without sexual hostility. According to Eleanor's plan, first wives will get along with second wives and children will stop resenting their parents. Writing in the *San Jose Mercury News*, Francine Prose called *Darcy's Utopia* "immensely entertaining" and added that Weldon "has given us a barbed, provocative book infused with admiration for the will to bring about political change, a belief in its necessity, and a prudent suspicion of those who would offer a Master Plan."

The Moon Over Minneapolis (HARPERCOLLINS/UK, 1991; PENGUIN, 1992) • These short stories continue Weldon's exploration of man's inhumanity to woman. Although many of the female protagonists eventually succumb to either economic or sexual oppression (or both), they nevertheless manage in some way to subvert the phallocratic order of things. In "The Search for Mother Christmas," for example, a poor, dispossessed single mother reinvents Santa Claus in her own image. "*Moon Over Minneapolis* is witty and acerbic but ultimately disappointing," Helen Kay concluded in the *Times Literary Supplement*. "Although she continues to develop her scenes skillfully, Weldon has not extended her range to new social or psychological territory."

Growing Rich (HARPERCOLLINS/UK, 1992) • Based on a serial that she wrote for British television, Weldon sets this soap opera in Fenedge, a bit of East Anglia at the end of nowhere. Her story has three heroines: Laura, Annie, and Carmen. As the book opens, they're virginal sixteen-year-olds plotting to escape their small-town lives. More rebellious than her friends, Carmen aspires to art school but soon finds herself being wooed by the Devil himself on behalf of Sir Bernard Bellamy, the local Faust. "Like life," Diana Souhami observed in *The New Statesman*, "*Growing Rich* is fecund, capricious, surprising, and odd—and like life, elusive of meaning in the end." Yet, as *The Observer* pointed out, "given Weldon's reputation as a pessimist and moralist, *Growing Rich* is a very jolly book."

Life Force (VIKING, 1992) • This ribald novel untangles twenty years in the lives of several upper-middle-class Londoners. The life force of the title is symbolized by Leslie Beck, a politically and morally incorrect businessman with a rather large penis. (Actually, his penis is the real life force.) To Leslie's four lovers, there's no greater raison d'être: One look at Leslie's organ and they're hooked. Aside from his sexual virility, however, Leslie is a louse. "Leslie's life force is male," Michael Malone pointed out in the *New York Times*, "but it is females who in the marvelous art of Fay Weldon's novel take that life force and with it create life."

Trouble (VIKING, 1993) • Annette and Spicer have been married for a decade now—the second marriage for both of them—and Annette believes that they're happy. When she becomes pregnant, however, Spicer begins seeing a crackpot New Age/Jungian psychotherapist, who persuades him that he's really unhappy, largely because his wife doesn't appreciate him. Most reviewers considered this stinging attack on therapy, based largely on Weldon's personal life, her best book in years. "The writing is as highly polished as ever," Judy Cooke noted in *The New Statesman*. "It hits an authentic, anguished note and holds it. Word is out that this is the big one." (This novel was published in Britain as *Affliction*.)

Splitting (ATLANTIC MONTHLY, 1995) • Still reeling from the shock of catching her mother in a miniskirt—with a live-in lover, no less—seventeen-year-old rock star Kinky Virgin (née Angelica White) removes the rings from her nose and becomes the docile bride of fat and lazy Sir Edwin Rice. Years later, when Angelica is falsely accused of adultery, Edwin sues for divorce but keeps the nearly one million pounds that Angelica has contributed to the Rice family accounts. What happens next? This being a Fay Weldon novel, Angelica and her multiple personalities get even, of course. In *Newsday*, Dan Cryer called *Splitting* "high-spirited fun," and Ellen Akins in the *Los Angeles Times* liked the book's "shrewd insights" and "witty asides."

Worst Fears (ATLANTIC MONTHLY, 1996) • Minor actress Alexandra Ludd lives happily in a historic English cottage with her husband, Ned, a forty-nine-year-old drama critic. Yet early on in this tale, Ned dies suddenly, apparently from a heart attack, while Alexandra is away in London. Later, we learn that naughty Ned wasn't alone when he died and that his marriage to Alexandra was something of a sham. "Ms. Weldon's earlier books are hysterical, fierce, and gleefully mean in a way that only British novelists seem to be able to get away with," Karen Karbo wrote in the *New York Times*. "Yet *Worst Fears* also possesses a few uncharacteristically quiet moments, the sort that betray an unvarnished kindness that's part of genuine understanding."

Wicked Women (ATLANTIC MONTHLY, 1997) • Writing about wicked women is nothing new for Fay Weldon, yet the twenty short stories in this collection feature women who are wicked in a very 1990s sort of way. For example, in "Heat Haze," a wicked daughter scuttles her father's gay fling. The *Atlanta Journal and Constitution* called these stories "better than a martini, twice as sharp, and always served with a twist."

BIOGRAPHY

FAY WELDON'S LITERARY TALENT presumably came from her mother's side of the family. Her father was a Worcestershire physician, but her maternal grandfather, Edgar Jepson, wrote best-selling romantic adventures; her uncle Selwyn Jepson wrote mysteries and thrillers, as well as scripts for film, television, and radio; and even her mother, Margaret Jepson Birkinshaw, published two light novels during the 1930s under her maiden name.

When Weldon was still very young, her parents emigrated to New Zealand; when she was six, they divorced; and when she was fourteen, she returned to England with her mother and sister. Her adolescence was, by Weldon's own account, a time of hardship and deprivation. It was also a time in which she lived in a household made up exclusively of women: herself, her mother, her sister, and her maternal grandmother. Weldon has since suggested that this experience freed her of the need for male approbation and thus has allowed her to write more openly and honestly.

In 1949, Weldon enrolled as a scholarship student at St. Andrew's University in Scotland, graduating just three years later with a master's degree in economics and psychology. By 1955, however, she had become an unwed mother struggling on her own to support her infant child. In 1960, she married antiques dealer Ronald Weldon, with whom she later had three more sons. (The couple divorced in 1994.)

Slowly Weldon built a career for herself as an advertising copywriter. Her success in that field encouraged her to write theatrical plays as well as scripts for radio and television. The success of these ventures, in turn, prompted her to write novels. She began in 1966 by adapting and expanding "The Fat Woman's Tale," a script that she had written for Granada Television. Her first novel, *The Fat Woman's Joke*, appeared a year later.

Although Weldon is often faulted for sketching her characters too thinly, especially the men, her outrageous wit and caustic intelligence have always more than compensated for this deficiency. Anita Brookner has called Weldon "one of the most astute and distinctive women writing fiction today," and few critics have challenged that assessment.

NEXT ON THE READING LIST: Beryl Bainbridge, David Lodge, Alison Lurie, Terry McMillan, Lorrie Moore, Iris Murdoch, Cathie Pelletier

John Edgar Wideman
(b. June 14, 1941)

"As is the case with fellow Modernist dream masters like Faulkner, Toni Morrison, Ornette Coleman, and any Abstract Expressionist you can name, Wideman demands that his readers work with him in making connections, drawing conclusions, following the map of his characters' souls."
—*Gene Seymour*, The Nation

A Glance Away (HARCOURT, BRACE & WORLD, 1967) • Wideman's first novel, which takes place in a single day, has two foci: Eddie Lawson, a black man just released from a drug treatment center, and Robert Thurley, a white college professor who considers his own homosexuality a disease. The bridge between these two men is an albino who's both Eddie's friend and the professor's occasional lover. Wideman's highly literary language is at times lyrical, at times too packed with style, but Harry Roskolenko in the *New York Times* thought enough of *A Glance Away* to call it "a powerfully inventive novel."

Hurry Home (HARCOURT, BRACE & WORLD, 1970) • This enormously complex novel is nearly sunk by its many devices—flashbacks, rapid shifts of tense and person, chunks of dreams—yet it stays afloat because of the beauty with which it renders pain. In its pages, an unemployed black lawyer and a white writer wander through Europe—one realizing that he has unfinished business at home, the other searching for a lost son. David Littlejohn, writing in the *Saturday Review*, suggested that *Hurry Home* was "primarily an experience, not a plot: an experience of words, dense, private, exploratory, and nonprogressive."

The Lynchers (HARCOURT BRACE JOVANOVICH, 1973) • As with Wideman's first two novels, reviewers found an elegant vision here—but also an overabundance of literary tricks. A black intellectual named Littleman concocts a plan to lynch a white policeman in order to make up for decades of black lynchings. A teacher named Orin stands in his way. Many critics, including Joseph Flora in the *Michigan Quarterly Review*, compared this novel with the works of James Joyce, although not in entirely positive ways: "Time is jumbled; Wideman relies heavily on interior monologue. Joycean also is the dash at the beginning of the speech to indicate dialogue."

Damballah (AVON, 1981) • This interconnected collection of short stories was published simultaneously with the novel *Hiding Place*, and both are set in the Homewood neighborhood of Pittsburgh, where Wideman grew up.

All the stories feature mythic characters from a single family, including an African ancestor who's brought to America as a slave and then tortured because he won't give up his tribal customs. "In freeing his voice from the confines of the novel form," Mel Watkins wrote in the *New York Times*, "[Wideman] has written what is possibly his most impressive work."

Hiding Place (AVON, 1981) • Tommy commits a robbery, during the course of which he apparently kills his partner. He runs away but finally returns, bored and lonely, to Homewood, where he's killed. An ancient relative, Mother Bess, tells his story, weaving it into folklore. "By going home to Homewood," Wilfred Samuels wrote in the *American Book Review*, "Wideman has found a voice for his work and consequently a means of celebrating Afro-American culture."

* Sent for You Yesterday (AVON, 1983) • Wideman's third book-length fiction set in Homewood won a PEN/Faulkner Award and inspired Don Strachan in the *Los Angeles Times* to champion Wideman as "the black Faulkner, the softcover Shakespeare." This novel's actions begins when fugitive Albert Wilkes returns to Homewood several years after killing a policeman.

> *"The book is written in what once we called substandard English; then dialect; now, more respectably, Black American English. It is kin to the language of* The Color Purple—*and as accessible—but tells a truer, less sentimental tale." (Adrianne Blue, The New Statesman)*

Reuben (HOLT, 1987) • Reuben is a bent, wizened black lawyer who tells the story of his life to one of his clients. Its central event occurred when Reuben was much younger, pimping for white fraternity boys. They lured him into a sexual interlude with a black whore, the result of which was a racially motivated beating that ended in death and disfigurement. But, as Noel Perrin pointed out in the *Washington Post, Reuben* is much more myth than novel: "Mostly you have the voice of John Edgar Wideman, narrating as a tribal storyteller might, mesmerizing his audience."

Fever (HOLT, 1989) • Because the stories in *Damballah* were so closely interconnected, Wideman considered this his first true short-fiction collection. Most of the tales are set in Philadelphia, and many involve storytelling itself, especially the difficulty one encounters in attempting to remove a story from its natural terrain. Thus, in one instance, a Jewish man finds himself unable to recount his concentration camp experience to a black maid. Unfortunately, according to Herbert Mitgang in the *New York Times*, the stories are "fragmentary in their plots" and "strained in [their] writing."

Philadelphia Fire (HOLT, 1990) • Wideman based this novel on the 1985 bombing of the MOVE house in Philadelphia. He was apparently fascinated

by the irony that the assault, which killed eleven members of the black militant group, was ordered by a black mayor, Wilson Goode. Charles Johnson,
writing in the *Washington Post,* called *Philadelphia Fire* "a book brimming over
with brutal, emotional honesty and moments of beautiful prose
lyricism...but by no means a page-turner."

The Stories of John Edgar Wideman (PANTHEON, 1992) • This volume gathers
together the stories previously published in *Damballah* and *Fever* and adds
ten new ones, collectively entitled "All Stories Are True." These new stories,
set in Homewood, present a broken, imagistic picture of characters and
events there. They reinforce one another, Michael Gorra observed in the
New York Times, "slowly building up an image of a place, of a world—street
corners, playground basketball, churches, bars and stores and street ven-
dors and ever-branching family trees."

The Cattle Killing (HOUGHTON MIFFLIN, 1996) • After a six-year hiatus, Wideman
published this lush intellectual novel that takes on no less a subject than
the black experience in America. Its principal narrator is an unnamed
black preacher who wanders about in eighteenth-century America, trying
to spread the gospel but more often than not being spurned by whites. An
outbreak of the plague in Philadelphia becomes both the pivotal event in
this story and a roundabout metaphor for racism. As Paul West noted in
the *Washington Post,* Wideman "writes from a vulnerable heart with an educated, worldly compassion that is bound to leave a scar."

BIOGRAPHY

JOHN EDGAR WIDEMAN GREW UP IN the black ghetto of Pittsburgh known as
Homewood. When he was twelve, his family moved to the well-to-do white
neighborhood of Shadyside. These two very different environments shaped
both the man and his fiction. From an early age Wideman experienced success: as a star basketball player, as president and valedictorian of his high
school class, as a Phi Beta Kappa graduate of the University of Pennsylvania, and as only the second black Rhodes Scholar.

In most of these areas, the standards of success were set by whites. In
his fiction, however, Wideman has concerned himself with the black experience, especially the life of Homewood. His unusual blend of subject and
style—Wideman typically writes about the lowest inner-city life in the highest, most literary prose—has annoyed some critics but won praise from
many more. It has often been suggested, though, that Wideman's heavily
stylized writing has prevented his novels from reaching a popular audience.

Wideman, who has taught at many universities, has won a
PEN/Faulkner Award (for *Sent for You Yesterday*) and been nominated for
a National Book Award (for his 1984 memoir *Brothers and Keepers*). He was
named a MacArthur fellow in 1993. In a recent interview, he remarked
on his own success in comparison to the failure experienced by many of

his loved ones (his brother and his son are both in prison for murder): "I wasn't smarter than all my friends. You can look at me as a vindication of the system, or you can say, 'Jesus, why is there only one? What happened to all those other kids?'"

NEXT ON THE READING LIST: Robert Olen Butler, David Guterson, Charles Johnson, Cormac McCarthy, Toni Morrison, Gloria Naylor

❧

PHOTO CREDITS

ALLISON: Jill Posener; ALVAREZ: Daniel Cima; AMIS: Gary Isaacs; ATWOOD: Andrew MacNaughton; AUSTER: Lutfi Ozkok; BAINBRIDGE: Brendan King; BANKS: Marion Ettlinger; BARKER: Paddy Cooke; BARRETT: University of Rochester Medical Center Photography; BEATTIE: Rollie McKenna; BELL: Marion Ettlinger; BLOOM: Matthew Hranek; BOYLE: Pablo Campos; BROOKNER: Jerry Bauer; BROWN: Bruce Newman; BUTLER: Gray Little; BYATT: Peter Peitsch; CAMPBELL: Barbara DuMetz; CISNEROS: Rubén Guzmán; CONROY: Joyce Ravid; CREWS: Maggie Powell; DANTICAT: Nancy Crampton; DE BERNIÈRES: Secker & Warburg; DELILLO: Joyce Ravid; DEXTER: Marion Ettlinger; DIDION: Quintana Roo Dunne; DIXON: Mariah Hughs; DOCTOROW: Barbara Walz; DOIG: Carol M. Doig; DOYLE: Amelia Stein; ECO: Nancy Crampton; ERDRICH: Jerry Bauer; ESQUIVEL: Jerry Bauer; FORD: K. Beatty/Toronto Star; GAITSKILL: Marion Ettlinger; GARCIA: Norma I. Quintana; GARCÍA MÁRQUEZ: Palomares; GIBBONS: Doug Van de Zande; GILCHRIST: Pierre G. Walker III; GOLDMAN: Marion Ettlinger; GORDIMER: Isolde Ohlbaum; GUTERSON: Jill Sabella; HAMILTON: Robert Willard; HARRISON: Terry W. Phipps; HEGI: Gordon Gagliano; HIJUELOS: Roberto Koch; HOFFMAN: Debi Milligan; HØEG: Jo Selsing; IRVING: Cook Nielsen; ISHIGURO: Nigel Parry; KENNEDY: Mariana Cook; KINCAID: Mariana Cook; KINGSOLVER: Seth Kantner; KUNDERA: Aaron Manheimer; LEAVITT: Jerry Bauer; LESSING: Ingrid Von Kruse; LODGE: Isolde Ohlbaum; LURIE: Jimm Roberts/Orlando; MCCARTHY: Marion Ettlinger; MCGUANE: Marion Ettlinger; MCMILLAN: Jonathan Exley; MCMURTRY: Diana Ossana; MILLHAUSER: Emma Hanson; MOORE: Ron Kinmonth; MUNRO: Jerry Bauer; NAIPAUL: Jerry Bauer; NAYLOR: Donna DeCesare; NICHOLS: John Nichols; OATES: Mary Cross; ONDAATJE: Dominic Sansoni; OZ: Eric Feinblatt; EDNA O'BRIEN: Nigel Case; TIM O'BRIEN: Miriam Berkley; PALEY: Gentl & Hyers/Arts Counsel; PRICE: Caroline Vaughan; PROULX: Jon Gilbert Fox; ROTH: Nancy Crampton; RUSHDIE: Jonathan Cape; SHIELDS: Neil Graham; SILKO: Robyn Stoutenburg; SIMPSON: Gasper Tringale; SMILEY: Stephen Mortensen; SONTAG: Annie Leibovitz; SPARK: Jerry Bauer; STONE: Rollie McKenna; SWIFT: Mark Douet; TAN: Robert Foothorap; THON: Marion Ettlinger; TREVOR: Jerry Bauer; TYLER: Diana Walker; UPDIKE: Martha Updike; VARGAS LLOSA: Jerry Bauer; WALKER: Jean Weisinger; WELDON: Isolde Ohlbaum; WIDEMAN: Jerry Bauer.